Books That Invite Talk, Wonder, and Play

Books That Invite Talk, Wonder, and Play

Edited by

Amy A. McClure
Ohio Wesleyan University

Janice V. Kristo
University of Maine

National Council of Teachers of English
1111 W. Kenyon Road, Urbana, IL 61801-1096

Permissions acknowledgments appear on pages 333–35.

Manuscript Editor: Jane M. Curran
Production Editor: Rona S. Smith
Cover Design: Victoria Martin Pohlmann
Interior Design: Doug Burnett

NCTE Stock Number: 03707-3050

Library of Congress Cataloging-in-Publication Data
Books that invite talk, wonder, and play / edited by Amy A. McClure, Janice V. Kristo.
     p. cm.
     Includes bibliographical references.
     ISBN 0-8141-0370-7 (pbk.)
     1. Children's literature, American—History and criticism—Theory, etc. 2. Children's literature—Authorship. 3. Children—Books and reading. 4. Language arts. I. McClure, Amy A. II. Kristo, Janice V.
PS490.B66 1996
810.9'9287—dc20   95-52945
                                                CIP

Contents

A Note to the Reader

Books, books, and more books are found in abundance in many of today's classrooms all over the country. Children are learning how to select books for their own reading enjoyment and are responding to books in a multitude of memorable and exciting ways. Children are also reading to extend their understanding of themselves as writers and to find answers to their questions about the world around them.

Professional growth and development never cease for teachers who love literature and who wish to sharpen their ability to select the best titles and to challenge children to respond to literature in thoughtful and creative ways. Teachers who select books that are rich in language find that these authors provide students with insights into the use of imaginative language through their word choice, their use of dialect and interesting metaphors, and their ability to describe the strange as familiar and the familiar as strange. As we encourage children to sample from the rich literary buffet of picture books, poetry, fantasy, historical fiction, nonfiction, folklore, multicultural literature, and contemporary realistic fiction, we need to explore how to select titles that are of the highest quality in their use of language. We also need to examine how to bring reader and text together in thought-provoking and enriching ways. We want to encourage in-depth responses to books that challenge children to think and to respond in ways that go beyond a literal level of appreciation. We want to encourage children to interact with authors and poets as "wordcrafters" and to be able to expand upon their own writing and thinking because of the language they have encountered during reading. Yes, books, books, and more books are finding their way into classrooms. But let's bring the best books into the reading and writing worlds of our children.

The publication of *Books That Invite Talk, Wonder, and Play* celebrates over a decade of work by the Notable Children's Trade Books in the Language Arts Committee of the Children's Literature Assembly, a special interest group of the National Council of Teachers of English. Each year the committee selects between twenty and thirty of the most illustrative examples of the beauty and wonder of language found in books for children in kindergarten through grade eight. Books considered for the Notables listing must meet the following three criteria:

- focus specifically on language, such as plays on words, word origins, or the history of language

- demonstrate uniqueness in the use of language or style
- invite active response or participation from a K–8 audience, have an appealing format, have an enduring quality, or meet generally accepted criteria for the genres in which they are written

The committee members also strive to include a balance of genres, including poetry, historical fiction, picture books, realistic fiction, fantasy, folktales, biographies, and nonfiction.

The introduction by Susan Lehr, which provides a foundation for the chapters that follow, invites readers to examine the kinds of books we deem exemplary or unusual in language and style and to consider how we have used the criteria for book selection. Subsequent chapters focus on unique aspects of language use in a variety of genres, as well as an exploration of books that promote cultural diversity. Response suggestions are liberally sprinkled throughout each chapter as springboards for readers to create their own ways of encouraging children to linger over the rich language of each book. Chapter 11 by Barbara Chatton and Susan Hepler invites readers to consider ways to integrate responses to books throughout the curriculum. The book concludes with essays written by thirty-eight authors of Notable books. These authors reflect on their own process of writing and the decisions they make about such matters as wording, style, and the use of dialect.

Readers will see throughout the chapters in this collection that some book titles are followed by the letter N. These are Notable books and are not listed in the reference list at the end of each chapter. Instead, there is a complete list of Notable books at the end of the book.

Readers of this book may be interested in its companion volume, *Inviting Children's Responses to Literature: Guides to 57 Notable Books*, also published by the National Council of Teachers of English. This resource consists of book summaries of some of the most enduring Notable titles and suggestions for challenging readers to extend their appreciation of the books.

We hope readers enjoy our discussions of some of the most outstanding Notable books and plan their own engaging responses that will bring these books and children together.

Janice V. Kristo and Amy A. McClure

Wordcrafting: What Makes a Book Notable in the Language Arts?

Susan Lehr
Skidmore College

Authors are wordcrafters. What pulls a reader into a text? What makes that encounter a worthwhile experience? Think of familiar lines in children's literature where you sense passion and vibrancy of language within a special rhythm or structure: ". . . they roared their terrible roars and gnashed their terrible teeth. . . ." "Brown Bear, Brown Bear, what do you see?" "King Bidgood's in the bath tub and he won't get out. . . ." When an author shapes a story about a girl who lives alone on an island for eighteen years, as in Scott O'Dell's *Island of the Blue Dolphins* (1960), or builds a concise comparison between a wild turkey and a tame turkey, as in Dorothy Hinshaw Patent's *Wild Turkey, Tame Turkey* (1989), the author does so with attention to language, thus inviting a response from readers. Mem Fox (1992) writes in her autobiography that the books for children that are her own favorites use language in passionate ways. "By passion I mean a constant undercurrent of tension combined with compassion, which makes readers care desperately about the fate of the main characters . . . writing without passion is writing for oblivion" (p. 148). The tension and passion of which Fox writes come through in *Koala Lou* (1988, N), a story about a koala who places second in the Bush Olympics. "If the sentences have no special rhythm or structure, if the words are carelessly chosen and sloppily placed, the writing won't satisfy the reader's psyche" (Fox 1992, 147).

This chapter explores the concept of what makes a book notable in the language arts so that readers are able to develop a sense of what sets a book apart in its use of language or its capacity to evoke language from children. The following categories are

Special thanks to Eileen Hovey and her students at Willow Springs Elementary School, Fairfax, VA.

examined: 1) books that deal explicitly with the sensory experiences evoked by skilled wordcrafting and those in which characters are portrayed as writers; 2) books that demonstrate uniqueness in the use of language, style, original perspectives, or themes; and 3) books that invite children's response or participation. Subsequent chapters provide more in-depth analysis of the ideas described here.

Wordcrafting: Language That Tickles the Mind and Trickles off the Tongue

Children love the sounds that language makes. Authors create sound palettes which make the speaking of the words a delight. An author who has achieved this sense of wordplay, rhythm, and rhyme for emergent readers is Bill Martin Jr., with favorites like *Brown Bear, Brown Bear, What Do You See?* (1983, N), *Chicka Chicka Boom Boom* with John Archambault (1989, N), and *Polar Bear, Polar Bear, What Do You Hear?* (1991, N). Children like the familiar language play and patterning which these books share, especially the sounds the animals make—*growling, roaring, snorting, fluting, braying, hissing, trumpeting, snarling, yelping,* and *bellowing.* The language patterns in these books make for a natural entry into reading. Choral reading and creating new versions are natural extensions with books such as these. They build upon each other and yet introduce enough new vocabulary to make the experience one which encourages language growth and development.

"Yellow Butter, Purple Jelly, Red Jam, Black Bread" from the poetry collection by that name by Mary Ann Hoberman (1981) provides an opportunity for rich choral chanting in the classroom. As the poem is recited, the rhythm spins out of control. Hoberman deftly pulls the reader back with her final line: "Don't talk with your mouth full." Poems like these give children the opportunity to play with rhythmic sounds and strong visual imagery. Hoberman's collection of bug poetry (*Bugs,* 1976) is equally engaging, with its informative language, humor, and rhyme.

Denise Fleming's *In the Tall, Tall Grass* (1991, N) re-creates a familiar everyday experience through simple, vivid word images. "In the tall, tall grass . . . crunch, munch, caterpillars lunch . . . dart, dip, hummingbirds sip . . . ritch, ratch, moles scratch . . . lunge, loop, bats swoop" (unpaged, pp. 5–9, 18–19, 28–29). Feel the rhythm. Hear the sound of chewing in "crunch, munch" and digging in "ritch, ratch." Sixty-one carefully chosen words and sounds accompanied by bold grassy paintings on handmade paper create a pastiche of eating, digging, and darting. When a presentation of words is so tightly woven, each word is essential; one word out of place is jarring. Mundane phrasing is too familiar. Wordcrafters like Fleming agonize over each sound and image.

Picture books that juxtapose odd visual and written images can be satisfying and stimulating for readers, particularly those in the upper grades. In *The Mysteries of Harris Burdick* by Chris Van Allsburg (1984, N), full-page illustrations with intriguing captions naturally invite children to create stories and to think of explaining the mysteries. *Pish, Posh, Said Hieronymus Bosch* by Nancy Willard (1991, N) is an effective blend of bizarre language and illustration. Willard's poem is based on her studies of Hieronymus Bosch's fifteenth-century paintings of odd creatures and machines. Small wonder that the poem begins with the resignation of the good woman who looks after Hieronymus Bosch's house.

> "I'm quitting your service, I've had quite enough
> of your three-legged thistles asleep in my wash,
> of scrubbing the millstone you use for a dish,
> and riding to shops on a pickle-winged fish."
>
> "Pish, posh,"
> said Hieronymus Bosch. (Unpaged, p. 6)

Willard paints with words. Images of a "beehive in boots," a "pear-headed priest," or cats chasing cucumbers, "slickity-slink," suggest a raucous hilarity, a world beyond nonsense, especially when Hiernoymus Bosch corrects, "They go slippity-slosh!" The language captivates and pulls readers into the act of visualizing Willard's outrageous creatures. Older readers are challenged to imagine and perhaps invent their own odd creatures and machines in pictures and words.

The Writer's Perspective: Characters as Writers

Books written by authors about the craft of writing and narratives written as diaries show children how wordcrafting evolves. The origin of text and ideas can be studied and savored in these books. *The True Confessions of Charlotte Doyle* by Avi (1990, N) pulls the reader in dramatically with a first-person diary narrative of a young girl's adventures aboard the ship *Seahawk* in 1832. Her opening confession and warning to readers ensures that the book will not be abandoned. Because Charlotte tells everything to her diary, readers form an intimate relationship with her, seeing what she sees, becoming curious about what she does not know, and trying to solve problems with her as each new diary entry takes one deeper into Charlotte's high seas adventure. Her process of using writing to think through the dilemmas she faces provides a powerful model to young readers and writers.

Joan Blos's classic *A Gathering of Days: A New England Girl's Journal, 1830–32* (1979) is quite different from Charlotte Doyle's diary, but equally compelling. Catherine's experiences in the same time frame as Charlotte's make the books natural companions. The language and descriptions of daily life in both books are authentic to the historical period and teach children about the tastes, smells, and sights of the 1830s through compelling first-person narrative. Whereas Charlotte leaves England for New England, Catherine writes from the perspective of living in New Hampshire. She faces the social and moral issues of her day, including abolition and abetting a fugitive slave, the death of a friend, a new stepmother, and gaining her own independence. Readers are able to compare the choices that both young women make, as well as to explore the social milieu of the times because of the intimate knowledge they gain from the journal entries.

In order to help children focus on thinking like a writer, potential journal entries might include a comparison of their reactions to and feelings about Charlotte and Catherine and their situations. Children could be invited to discuss today's social dilemmas, possibilities, and constraints with regard to gender or race.

Zilpha Keatly Snyder's *Libby on Wednesday* (1990, N) is also realistic fiction with the added twist of having the main character enrolled in a writer's workshop at school. Within the framework of the story, readers learn about Libby from two rich perspectives: the author's narrative and Libby's journal. In Libby's eighth-grade class the children read their stories to each other. At one point a boy reads a piece that is so gripping that

> Libby caught her breath. It was as if she'd been listening so hard she'd almost forgotten to breathe. She felt drained and blank with listening. The others were blank-faced, too—no smiles or grins or frowns. Libby tried to think why. The story was short and nothing much happened, unlike G. G.'s other stories, where everything happened in horrible detail. (P. 119)

G. G. had written a piece about the agony of waiting for something which is never identified. The reader learns that he is waiting for the sound of his father coming home drunk. The book also illustrates and encourages children to be risk takers by showing the importance of sharing their written texts with other readers and writers. G. G. was willing to read his piece to his classmates because he trusted them—he knew that they would listen, and that their responses would be valuable and legitimate.

All three books have strong narrative frameworks and fully developed characters which pull children effectively into the story. The characters' journals give teachers the opportunity to discuss personal writing, word and topic choices, voice, and stance toward audience. Through their own journal entries, children can easily take on the perspectives of characters and can discuss motivation and choices that Charlotte, Catherine, and Libby make both as characters and as writers.

Where do authors get their ideas? Snyder implies we can write effectively when we write about what is known to us. G. G.'s most gripping piece springs from his own internal tension. In *The Spying Heart* (1989), Katherine Paterson writes personally about "the story of her lives," giving readers a glimpse at the origin of the fuel for her stories. She claims "incredibly" that her life is based on a true story, her story:

> Thus, in a real sense, I am constantly writing autobiography, but I have to turn it into fiction in order to give it credibility. "She lived to tell the tale," we say. Because what we applaud is not simply survival but the ability to step back, or beyond survival, to organizing the experience—to imagining—to telling the tale. (P. 8)

Analyzing writing from this vantage can be a freeing experience for young writers. Journals written in narrative fashion by characters such as Libby, Charlotte, and Catherine encourage children to write about their own experiences as they develop as young authors.

Books with Unique Language and Cultural Perspectives

Books are where we learn much about the world in which we live. This information seeking is critical on many levels, dealing with personal growth and understanding as well as the ability to function in the world as informed literate people. Well-written books which give readers insight into a variety of experiences, and which do so in a way that uses language in an exemplary fashion, are valuable for classroom use. Universal themes are apparent in many of these books, which celebrate differences as well as similarities.

Exemplary nonfiction books are especially useful for helping children expand their knowledge of and understandings about the world. The strong narrative style of some of these books, coupled with the rich information about other cultures or experiences, has given rise to a genre which I term *narrative nonfiction. The Day of Ahmed's Secret* by Florence Parry Heide and Judith Heide Gilliland (1990, N) is about a typical day for Ahmed in which he delivers fuel to his father's clients in Cairo, all the while yearning to share a secret with his family. The language used by Heide and Gilliland is as vivid as Ted Lewin's illustrations. Cairo throbs with life, colors, tastes, smells, sounds.

> Now as I lean against the old building, I think of the sea of sand that lies along our city. I have seen it, stretching as far as the old wind.
>
> My father says the wind carries sand all through the city to remind us that the desert is there, is there beside us, and is a part of us. (Unpaged, p. 18)

Later in the day Ahmed watches as a girl lowers a basket on a rope to a boy selling bread and watches as the boy puts some bread in the basket.

> Like me, he has many stops to make each day, but he is not strong enough to do what I do. No one lowers a rope to me for my heavy loads! No rope could carry what I carry.
>
> I hear the rosewater man before I see him. He clicks two cups together as he walks along the street so people will hear him and come to him for a drink. . . .
>
> I do not buy his rosewater, but seeing him has reminded me how hot and thirsty I am. (Unpaged, pp. 22–25)

Ahmed burns with his secret throughout the day as he delivers *butagaz*, or butane gas canisters, in his donkey cart.

> Finally I am home. It is sundown, it is the time of day when you cannot tell a white thread from a black one. My mother has already lighted the lanterns. Everyone is waiting for me. . . .
>
> It is time to tell my secret. I take a deep breath. (Unpaged, p. 29)

The story is captivating, as is the setting. Through Ahmed's use of words, the reader feels the sand of the desert in Ahmed's shoes, reads about delivering bread in a way that might be unfamiliar, and wonders what rosewater might taste like.

Books about real children going about their everyday tasks can also help children learn about the language of another culture. *Galimoto* by Karen Lynn Williams (1990, N), set in a small village in Malawi, is another vivid story about a young boy. Seven-year-old Kondi gathers pieces of wires throughout his village in order to construct a toy for the evening *galimoto* parade.

> Kondi took his wires back to the shade of the red flame trees in his village. Nearby his mother and sisters pounded their maize. They sang of the hard work they were doing.
>
> Kondi sorted his wires. There were thick pieces and thin pieces. Some wires were long and some were short. Kondi banged the bent and twisted ones with a stone to straighten them.
>
> Then he began. The thick wires made the frame. He wrapped the very thinnest wires at the joints to hold the galimoto together.
>
> "My galimoto will be a pickup," Kondi planned. "It will carry maize to the city."
>
> Kondi worked all afternoon. (Unpaged, p. 25)

Kondi's world is familiar because he likes to play, but the trees, the food, and his toys are different. The reader wants to know what a *galimoto* is and how Kondi will march with it in a parade. As he gathers wires for his toy, we read about his village and learn about his culture.

> *Chi, chi, chi, chi.* Kondi could hear the grinder at the flour mill. Many women with babies tied on their backs waited in the hot sun. Others arrived carrying heavy baskets of maize on their heads. (Unpaged, p. 14)

Again, what sets this book apart from many is the richness of the language used to describe Kondi's culture.

Urban America is richly explored by Patricia Polacco in *Chicken Sunday* (1992) by her narrative blending of two distinct American cultures. Appreciation and understanding are inherent in her story about misunderstanding. Polacco's gift is her ability to weave intergenerational characters in a loving tapestry. She fleshes out real people in the space of thirty-two pages. The children adore Miss Eula; they are fearful of Mr. Kodinski. Books like these use narrative to build strong themes beyond bridging racial prejudice and tension. Polacco's stories are frequently about people and harmony, but she does not state the obvious. Mr. Kodinski is an elderly Jewish man who falsely accuses the neighborhood children of breaking his shop window. Miss Eula is an elderly black woman who challenges the children to communicate, reach out, and understand. Rich language. Rich themes. Not so subtle lessons.

Realistic fiction with distinct cultural perspectives set in the twentieth century is becoming more prevalent in novels for older children. Books that can take children into other lands and experiences can make news headlines less remote. For example, a child's experiences of growing up in a war-torn country like Cambodia are compellingly described in *The Clay Marble* by Minfong Ho (1991, N). Dara, a young Cambodian child, remembers the village she has just left:

> I thought of our village. Sarun was right, I admitted silently. It was just an expanse of dried-up rice fields now, with a crumbling temple and flimsy huts. In the latest spate of fighting, the Khmer Rouge soldiers had even set fire to our houses and rice barns, so that the invading Vietnamese soldiers wouldn't be able to claim them. But that had left us with nothing to eat, no rice seed with which to plant our next crop of rice, not even a house to live in.

In this short paragraph, readers experience the numbing effect when soldiers destroy crops, homes, and temples. Ho offers vivid perspectives of Cambodian history and culture. Consider the language in this brief description of the Cambodian jungle: "Dappled shadows stirred under a thick canopy of wild tamarind and rain trees, but there was no sign of life on the narrow trail stretching out ahead of us." Ho eventually takes readers into a Thai refugee camp where two girls meet and form a fragile friendship. The author creates authentic pictures of life in the camp, the confusion, the dirt, the sense of a temporary safe haven, while at the same time presenting a compelling story about two girls who learn to play and be children in the middle of chaos. Dara and her new friend Jantu build a miniature village from mud, stones, and sticks:

> The toy village became the center of our world, and Jantu and I played with it every day. Each time we would add a few more things—a rice barn, rain barrels, a pigsty—and as Jantu shaped them, we would make up more stories about our new lives after we left the Border.

Many books are beginning to appear in this category of narrative nonfiction; many are written with passion and a longing for freedom, but not all are written with the depth and craft of the books mentioned above. Timely choice of topic will often give a book exposure, but the enduring qualities of the language in the books mentioned demonstrate the care with which the authors develop their characters and sensitively explore themes and topics that may not be familiar to American children. As Naledi is exposed to the system of apartheid when she travels to Johannesburg in Beverley Naidoo's *Journey to Jo'burg* (1985), set in the mid 1970s, so are readers exposed to that harsh system. Naidoo's craft has to do with the gradual awareness of the relationship between people that she builds for her readers; we care desperately about Naledi and her brother and sister.

Other unique perspectives that can add insight into human nature are seen in the many folktales that are being retold and authentically illustrated. For example, Paul Goble's scrupulously researched series of tales about the Plains Indian trickster Iktomi (which means *spider* in Sioux) offers humor amidst strong themes about human shortcomings. Goble's style invites oral participation from readers and listeners. When Iktomi speaks, albeit foolishly, gray italic lines of text indicate narrator asides, which invite speculation about Iktomi's foolishness and reinforce the oral tradition.

Every culture has numbskull and noodle-head tales celebrating the foolish attributes that people exhibit, such as false pride and vanity. Goble helps us to poke gentle fun at our own Iktomi-like behavior in *Iktomi and the Buffalo Skull* (1991, N). There are times when we all fall into the trap of getting a buffalo skull stuck on our heads, and since the skull is sacred in this tradition, the act suggests an irreverence as well as an act of putting one's nose where it does not belong. Retribution is swift. Folktales can provide a format for studying other cultures, customs, and unique language, and for exploring universal themes.

Unique Presentation: Information Books

Many notable books are noteworthy for their unique style and presentation. However, nonfiction titles are especially exemplary examples of this quality. As teachers continue to integrate children's literature into the curriculum, well-written nonfiction books are being published at amazing rates. Nonfiction books, an obvious asset to social studies, math, and science content, are often the center of thematic studies and are excellent resources for expanding language growth in content areas. Successful expository text should be clear in its use of terminology, providing clearly labeled illustrations, photographs, diagrams, maps, glossaries, and indexes when needed. A good use of these devices can be found in Raymond Bial's *Corn Belt Harvest* (1991, N), which takes readers through the entire corn cycle from growing to harvesting. Extensive information is provided in a straightforward text. Words are defined in context, so readers need not turn to a glossary or dictionary for information. The language is fresh and interesting: stalks of corn are "snatched by the teeth of combines." This use of language is what engages us as readers—making us care about what could be a relatively mundane topic.

Aliki does extensive research for both text and illustrations in her biographies and historical books, creating a rich and authentic palette of words about historical figures. She spends years researching her books and visiting primary sites, resulting in rich language tapestries describing memorable times and people. For example, in *The King's Day: Louis XIV of France* (1989, N), Aliki describes a typical day in the life of the king, providing facts and details that give a full word picture of the king's lengthy *Lever,* his daily getting-up ritual. The king was kissed every morning by his nurse, attended by dozens of courtiers, and dressed by other adults in a ritual that lasted two hours every day! It is this attention to historical authenticity through detailed language which makes for exciting and notable nonfiction biographies for young readers.

Expository writing is frequently linked with narrative in order to tell a story while presenting factual information. Again, borrowing from Mem Fox, the passion and tension in the writing of nonfiction makes the difference between a boring odyssey and an adventure. Author Christina Björk and illustrator Lena Anderson have created an adventure in Monet's garden with Linnea as the guide in *Linnea in Monet's Garden* (1987). The book works on several levels. Linnea and her friend, Mr. Bloom, travel from Sweden to Paris to research Monet's life and paintings. Linnea's interest in Monet is first sparked because she is an avid gardener and flower lover. With wit the author and illustrator walk readers through Monet's life, work, family, and times. It is a singular adventure showcasing this complex man's art and providing a solid example of how good authors of nonfiction bring passion to their work (Carr l982). Björk writes in Linnea's voice:

> We were standing in front of a painting with two white water lilies. I stepped a little closer to the picture and looked at it. It was then I noticed that the lilies were nothing but blobs and blotches of paint. But when I stepped away again, they turned into real water lilies floating in a pond—magic! (Pp. 14–15)

A child can easily understand and appreciate this effective description of impressionistic techniques. Björk does not tell and report; she pulls readers into a unique and appealing way of looking at Monet's world.

Informational books can also introduce new topics as well as provide different perspectives on familiar fare. Pappas (1991) worries that teachers of young children avoid nonfiction because of the primacy of narrative. Furthermore, narrative is perceived as being a more meaningful and accessible avenue of drawing young learners into literacy. Pappas's work with kindergarten children contradicts this romantic notion. Young children were able to retell nonfiction books with beginnings, middles, and endings in a cohesive fashion, improving with subsequent exposure to the book and opportunities for a second and third retelling. These children actually preferred nonfiction over fiction.

Unique Language Styles

One could argue that all notable books are unique in their style or use of language. Certainly all the books mentioned so far use language in an exemplary fashion. Sometimes, however, an author or poet makes a distinct impact in terms of presenting mood, sequencing words and ideas in such a unique and splendid way that one must take note. This is particularly true for poetry. Poet Karla Kuskin does so effectively with *Dogs and Dragons, Trees and Dreams* (1980), a selection of clever poems and one-liners about radishes and bugs, narratives about super glue and obnoxious trumpets, and snippets about her choices of topics. Consider the language in "Thistles," a compact tongue twister:

> Thirty thirsty thistles
> Thicketed and green
> Growing in a grassy swamp
> Purple-topped and lean
> Prickly and thistly
> Topped by tufts of thorns
> Green mean little leaves on them
> And tiny purple horns
> Briary and brambly

A spiky, spiney bunch of them.
A troop of bright-red birds came by
And had a lovely lunch of them. (P. 4)

The tongue trips lovingly over words crafted in this poem. Readers
will delight in the rhythms and blends.

Arnold Adoff achieves distinctive styling in *In for Winter, Out
for Spring* (1991, N), with illustrations by Jerry Pinkney. The perspective is that of a young girl whom we immediately meet as

> . . . Rebecca At Breakfast
>   Time
>   Becky By Lunch
>   But
>   Becka
>   Beck
>   Beck Come
>   Wash   Your
>   Neck
> Is Daddy's Supper
>   Song . . .
> I Am The Youngest And I Belong. (P. 7)

This is a poetic journal about a family who takes readers through the
seasons, complemented by Pinkney's glorious illustrations of leaves
floating all over the page in fall and mud splattering everywhere in
the spring. Each poem is a story, each page a sharing. Adoff lays the
words out carefully, precisely, and in a visually appealing manner.
What really draws readers in is the family whom we have the opportunity to meet, to hug, to dig with in the garden. Adoff's words
suggest belonging and being a part of a family. He creates vivid
images that linger, strings of words that keep coming back, and
sounds that will not let go.

Inviting Response to Literature

The last category for exploring notable books must of necessity
include all well-written books. How does one tap into response
effectively or choose the right book for the right situation? It is
acceptable just to read a book and shut it with a contented sigh; this
is a legitimate response. All books need not be analyzed to be fully
developed in the classroom.

Conversely, children grow as thinkers and readers if time is
well spent in talking about themes in books (Lehr 1991). Children
need time to mull over problems presented, to grieve when a character dies, and to make connections to their own lives. In studies with
elementary school children, I found that youngsters can become
involved with books in a total sense. They touch them lovingly; they
make connections to other titles they have enjoyed; they make

comparisons to their own lives; and they treat the characters as real people, analyzing their shortcomings, strengths, and motivation.

Some genres are less accessible to children because of the style and content of writing. Fantasy is a genre which children enjoy, but frequently they need adults to introduce them to it. Picture books of fantasy are highly visible in classrooms, but fantasy novels for older readers are less apparent. Although all well-written books have the capacity to evoke responses from readers, the focus here is on response within the context of titles of fantasy.

Fantasy has the capacity to pull readers into new ways of looking at the world, creating intense enjoyment during the act of reading or reading aloud. Fantasy can ignite the imagination and stimulate children to envision worlds uncharted. Younger children enjoy fantasy worlds in which animals or creatures talk, humor is evident, and characters take on childlike characteristics, such as in Pat Hutchins's *The Very Worst Monster* (1985), in which the concept of sibling rivalry is explored. Hutchins uses creatures as her characters, which creates a safer way of taking a look at the intense feelings children experience when a new sibling arrives. Her themes are relevant and deal typically with family issues. Kindergarten children listening to the sequel, *Where's the Baby?* (1988), created their own chaotic rooms where they had left gigantic messes behind. They identified with the messy, disappearing baby rather than the searching adults and Hazel. Through the use of collage, the children delighted in being Hazel's baby brother rather than Hazel, just for a while. They talked about their own experiences and made links to the themes and characters of the book. Only one child chose to clean up the mess that the baby had created. This young girl compared her picture to the chaotic picture in the book as she went along tidying things up.

A well-crafted fantasy challenges and evokes reaction from readers on several levels. David Wiesner's *Tuesday* (1991, N), works remarkably well as a wordless picture book inviting children to explore and imagine. One child responded: "The story begins before the title page. There's a clue. That frog is waking up, floating away." Readers are pulled in before the story begins. Children focus on details. "Look! The frog is turning off the TV." They make predictions and offer critiques. "Pigs are coming next. He shouldn't have put in that last picture. It's too easy to guess." Wordless picture books invite responses from all ages, both verbal and written. *Tuesday* typifies fantasy which is playful and humorous, prods the imagination, invites delicious meanderings, and awakens curiosities. Not since Molly Bang's *The Grey Lady and the Strawberry Snatcher* (1980) have I found one which invites such strong reactions from readers.

Older children clamor for secondary worlds into which they can escape. The worlds must be believable and consistent in their use of magic, according to Huck, Hepler, and Hickman (1993). There is a price to pay for using magic, for being wicked, or for traveling in time. Justice exists in some ultimate form. Conventional values are underscored in epic battles, quests, or worlds filled with miniature people who live between the cracks in our floors.

Redwall (1986) is such a book; Brian Jacques has created a world in Mossflower Wood in which themes are distinct and thoughtfully developed. Conflict is real. Fourth and fifth graders in a Washington suburb listened to their teacher, Eileen Hovey, read aloud *Redwall* each day after lunch. In this animal fantasy, good clashes with evil in the form of a peaceful wood and abbey inhabited by small creatures and a vile rodent named Cluny the Scourge. Jacques paints word pictures of characters and feasts, battles and bullies, tortuous climbs and hair-raising escapes. Mossflower Wood comes alive with vivid detail; it becomes a believable place like Narnia, Earthsea, or Prydain.

Redwall offers contrasts between characters. First there is a description of Matthias, a young mouse at the abbey:

> Matthias cut a comical little figure as he wobbled his way along the cloisters, with his large sandals flip-flopping and his tail peeping from beneath the baggy folds of an over-sized novice's habit. He paused to gaze upwards at the cloudless blue sky and tripped over the enormous sandals. Hazelnuts scattered out upon the grass from the rush basket he was carrying. Unable to stop, he went tumbling cowl over tail. (P. 13)

Compare this account of Redwall's hero to a description of the approaching villain:

> Cluny was coming!
> He was big, and tough; an evil rat with ragged fur and curved, jagged teeth. He wore a black eyepatch; his eye had been torn out in battle with a pike.
> Cluny had lost an eye.
> The pike had lost its life. (P. 17)

Chapters alternate back and forth between the peaceful world of Redwall Abbey and Cluny's inevitable attack.

Children in this elementary school exchanged letters and art with my college students in upstate New York, who were reading *Redwall* for a children's literature class. One young student, Tony, wrote a lengthy letter in which he talked about his personal interests, the salient features of the book, and a group project in which he was involved:

Dear Skidmore College Students,

My name is Tony. I like pizza, reading, playing Nintendo, & sports. I am 10 years old & in 5th grade. My class is a 4–5 combination class. I have 1 brother. His name is Jeff.

The book *Redwall* (did I get that right? Ah, yes, I did) is about a conquering rat who wants to take over Redwall Abbey. What a jerk! Anyway, Matthias, a warrior mouse, and all of Redwall fight back. Between wars, Matthias goes on a perilous journey to find the sword of Martin the Warrior.* Boring. Not!!! Hey, getting almost eaten by a cat, meeting an owl, killing a snake, and walking about 2,000 miles is not boring (Okay, so maybe the walking part is).

At the top of his letter he included the following additions in boxes:

* Read "MossFlower" for more on Martin the Warrior.
X Hey, who likes walking 2,000 miles? Not me!

He also included twelve detailed pencil drawings of scenes from *Redwall* with captions, labels, and chapter summaries interspersed.

Hillary, a college senior majoring in English, responded in a lengthy letter with personal information about her home and her interests, as well as her reactions to Tony's art and writing. In part, she wrote:

I really liked Redwall and it seems like you did too. I saw the cartoons you did of the book. They were great. I especially like the one where Cluny gets belled (smushed, really) by the Joseph bell—that evil scourge! . . .
P.S. Remember Martin! *RATDEATH*

Tony replied:

Dear Hillary,

Thank you for the letter & nice compliments. I liked them a lot. Well, enough sentiments. Let me get into my letter.

For one thing, I'm also planning on going to New York City. It seems nice from what I've heard about. I also have read Brian Jacques other books, *Mossflower* and *Mattimeo* and I am currently reading *Mariel of Redwall* (notice a pattern?). They all are good. And yes, I do like *Redwall* a lot! And the picture I drew was inspired by the dramatic ending to *Redwall*.

Some of the college students included artwork about the characters or scenes from the book. An art major drew a giant poster of Matthias with Martin's sword, which was received with excitement by the children and proudly hung in their classroom, prompting Tony to conclude:

P.S. If you're good at drawing, can you please send me a picture from *Redwall*. If not, no hard feelings!

The spellings and punctuation are Tony's; the letters were not corrected, but are first drafts, as letters typically are. This book engaged him completely as a reader and led him to all of the other books by the same author. His response was typical of other boys and girls at both grade levels in this classroom: highly personal and focused on the book, the language, and the actions of the characters. Using the language of the letter allowed Tony to respond in a different fashion than in a group project or a more formal piece of writing. Having a person to correspond with encouraged this personal stance. Tony was invested, and in his second letter the tone became even more conversational. He concluded:

> I liked reading your letter a lot. Thanks, once again. I very truly hope you'll write back! See ya!
>
> Sincerely, Tony

Many of the students wrote about favorite sections of the book, traits of characters they liked, and the fact that Jacques uses unique accents and dialects for the various creatures. They liked the battle against evil, the humor, the danger, the noble nature of Matthias, the appetite of Basil Stag Hare, and the fact that Silent Sam finally talked. A well-written book invites response on many levels.

Children engaged with worthwhile books may want to reflect, share, chatter, argue points of view, or discuss alternatives. Like the children listening to *Redwall*, they may want to read similar books by the same author. They may decide to write about characters, to stage plays about favorite scenes, to research related information, or to reread dramatic scenes aloud. Choice is central to response, as is ownership. Children responding to *Redwall* were personally invested. They were allowed to immerse themselves in the book experience, an aesthetic experience encouraging them to "savor the images, the sounds, the smells, the actions, the associations and the feelings that the words point to" (Rosenblatt 1991, 447). A combination of good literature and the time to reflect and extend the experience can effectively invite child participation and response.

Conclusion

Notable books in the language arts share an exemplary use of language or the ability to stimulate thought and language use, wordplay, or imaginative response from children. Good books are catalysts; they evoke a response. They invite us to think; they agitate; they cause us to grow. We applaud; we disagree. We know we could do better when characters make poor choices. A well-written book does not leave us alone; we are left with perplexing questions rather than neatly packaged answers.

This book takes a look at those words and sentences, the ones in well-written books that invite children to read, to write, to speak, and to listen to language. Readers of this book probably already use or expect to use children's literature with children at home and in the elementary classroom. There are over 80,000 titles already in print and thousands published annually, so choosing and using quality literature with children can be a challenging as well as a delightful task. This book is based on enduring titles that have been selected by people who work with children and literature. Response suggestions are not exhaustive but promote excellence in terms of quality of language. They have been used effectively with children in elementary and middle school classrooms. The focus of the following chapters, then, is on the language quality in selected children's literature and how to facilitate the language arts through the use of wonderful books.

References
Professional Resources

Brett, B. 1989. "Selecting Children's Books: 'The Rarest Kind of Best.'" In *Children's Literature in the Classroom: Weaving Charlotte's Web,* edited by J. Hickman and B. Cullinan. Boston: Christopher Gordon.

Carr, J. 1982. *The Literature of Fact.* Chicago: American Library Association.

Fox, M. 1992. *Dear Mem Fox, I Have Read All Your Books Even the Pathetic Ones, and Other Incidents in the Life of a Children's Book Author.* San Diego: Harcourt Brace Jovanovich.

Huck, C., S. Hepler, and J. Hickman. 1993. *Children's Literature in the Elementary School,* 5th ed. San Diego: Harcourt Brace Jovanovich.

Lehr, S. 1991. *The Child's Developing Sense of Theme: Responses to Literature.* New York: Teachers College Press.

Pappas, C. 1991. "Fostering Full Access to Literacy by Including Information Books." *Language Arts* 68 (6): 449–62.

Paterson, K. 1989. *The Spying Heart: More Thoughts on Reading and Writing Books for Children.* New York: E. P. Dutton.

Rosenblatt, L. 1991. "Literature—S.O.S.!" *Language Arts* 68 (6): 444–48.

Children's Books Cited

Bang, Molly. 1980. *The Grey Lady and the Strawberry Snatcher.* New York: Four Winds Press.

Björk, Christina. 1987. *Linnea in Monet's Garden.* Illustrated by Lena Anderson. New York: Farrar, Straus and Giroux.

Blos, Joan. 1979. *A Gathering of Days: A New England Girl's Journal, 1830–32.* New York: Charles Scribner's Sons.

See the Bibliography of Notable Books at the end of the book for bibliographic information about cited Notable Books. The Notable titles do not appear in this reference list.

Ehlert, Lois. 1990. *Growing Vegetable Soup*. San Diego: Harcourt Brace Jovanovich.

Hoberman, Mary Ann. 1976. *Bugs*. New York: Viking.

———. 1981. *Yellow Butter, Purple Jelly, Red Jam, Black Bread: Collected Poems*. New York: Viking.

Hutchins, Pat. 1985. *The Very Worst Monster*. New York: Greenwillow Books.

———. 1988. *Where's the Baby?* New York: Greenwillow Books.

Jacques, Brian. 1986. *Redwall*. New York: Philomel Books.

Kuskin, Karla. 1980. *Dogs and Dragons, Trees and Dreams*. New York: Harper and Row.

Naidoo, Beverley. 1985. *Journey to Jo'burg: A South African Story*. Illustrated by Eric Velasquez. New York: J. B. Lippincott.

Polacco, Patricia. 1992. *Chicken Sunday*. New York: Philomel Books.

I Literary Genres and Literary Language

How can teachers help children become attuned to the language of well-written books from various genres? As children read and respond to many kinds of text within a genre, they become aware of and appreciate the many ways in which authors work with language. Thus, children can become aware that nonfiction writing, for example, has particular characteristics that delineate it from poetry. Conversely, children need to see that the use of language often transcends genres and that authors deliberately use techniques from one genre to subtly craft a fresh approach in another. For example, nonfiction writers sometimes use metaphors and alliterative phrases to make their texts more musical—more like poetry.

When children become aware of the author's craft and how it varies across genres, they can use this knowledge to enlarge and deepen their own responses. It is through these new understandings about how writers use language to shape and mold their texts that readers develop more informed and sophisticated responses. The chapters in this section show teachers how to help such understandings evolve.

Janice Kristo and Linda Lamme describe how teachers can "spark the mind and fuel the imagination" when sharing picture books which present language that "is woven into the tapestry of extraordinary artwork." They show how teachers can develop an atmosphere that invites children into picture books, as they wonder about the language and use it to gather data about their own responses. Amy McClure demonstrates how to help children become more sensitive to the musical language of poetry. She then suggests how teachers can help children try out their tentative understandings about poetic language by creating their own poetry. Next, Sylvia Vardell explains how children can learn to appreciate the "language of facts" as they discover how authors use language to present information. She examines many examples of well-written nonfiction and then suggests classroom activities which stimulate language growth and critical thinking. To conclude this section, Christine

Francis describes teaching practices that encourage students to examine the language and structure of novels so they are able to think more critically about those elements.

Picture Books: Language That Sparks the Mind and Fuels the Imagination

Janice V. Kristo
University of Maine

Linda Leonard Lamme
University of Florida

Dear Tawanda:

Our teacher read us a book called *Cactus Hotel*. We liked the title Brenda Guiberson gave to her book. It's about a cactus that starts from a seedling and grows to fifty feet. A gila woodpecker started to make a cactus hotel. A bunch of animals came to live in the cactus. Then one day the cactus hotel fell down. It was too old to stand. You'll have to read the book to find out what happened to all the animals that lived in the book. Let me know what you think about it.

With love from Guess Who?

Picture books that spark the mind and fuel the imagination lead to responses such as this informative book recommendation from a third grader to a first grader. Blending the ingredients of high-quality picture books with teachers who marvel at their language and artistic wizardry can produce electrifying experiences in the

The authors wish to acknowledge the contributions of Jeanne Hodesh, Castine, ME, and the following teachers: Adele Ames, Capri Street School, Brewer, ME; Judy Arey, Appleton Village School, Appleton, ME; Pat Dickinson, Fayette Central School, Kents Hill, ME; Debbie Gallagher, Talbot Elementary School, Gainesville, FL; Mary Giard, Abraham Lincoln School, Bangor, ME; Debbie King, Asa Adams School, Orono, ME; Ellen Lopez, Braden River Elementary School, Manatee County, FL; Linda McKinley, Challenger 7 School, Broward County, FL; Alice Motycka, Adams School, Castine, ME; and Priscilla Sawyer, Pendleton Street School, Brewer, ME.

classroom. Picture books are a perfect medium to help children become powerful word watchers and users.

Picture books have an impact upon children's language development, but some are more powerful language enhancers than others. Some books are so outstanding that they elicit wonderful conversations about books. They inspire children to wonder and to think creatively and imaginatively about what they are reading. Other books invite analysis and thoughtful interpretation of stories. Through the clever interplay of illustration and text, these books foster language by encouraging its use. When children are so excited about a book that they are compelled to talk and write about it, there is a language explosion in the classroom that has a powerful impact upon children's literacy development.

In this chapter we invite readers to explore the world of pictures and words in order to help students of all ages expand and enrich their use of oral and written language. We share information about both kinds of language-enhancing books—those that promote discussion and enthusiastic responses to literature in general, and those that encourage specific attention to language elements within the book. The perfect blending of words and pictures provides opportunities to play with language structures. As Burke (1990) notes, "young children are nudged to talk" as they interact with particular picture books.

Invitations to Enjoy Books

A special kind of atmosphere can develop in a classroom when the teacher shares a picture book aloud. It is an exciting invitation for all to enter other worlds and to become mesmerized by words and pictures. A teacher's dramatic reading, with just the right touch of animation, can relay the powerful message that there are wonderful discoveries to be made that lead to literary talk about books. Kiefer (1989) states:

> I found that many children like to take time with picture books and that picture books that are artistically demanding or puzzling, like *The Grey Lady and the Strawberry Snatcher*, *Outside Over There*, and *Song of the Horse* are books that engender the most long-lasting and deepest responses on the part of the children. It would seem that when artists are intensely involved in the creation of meaning through the medium of the picture book, they have the potential to destroy complacency, to uncover needs, to pique curiosity, to evoke enthusiasm, and to arouse passion. (Pp. 86–87)

The sophistication of many picture books, such as *Anno's U.S.A.* by Mitsumasa Anno (1983, N), Christophe Gallaz's *Rose Blanche* (1985, N), Chris Van Allsburg's *The Stranger* (1986, N), Nancy Willard's *Pish, Posh, Said Hieronymus Bosch* (1991, N), and David

Wiesner's *Tuesday* (1991, N), encourages opportunities to "linger over pictures" and, as Bader (1976) suggests, provides time to consider the language and pictures together to create new meanings or interpretations. Picture books even give children the means to become, in Chamber's (1985) term, "intergalactic readers," to reach beyond what is comfortable in terms of genre, and to weave their own wonders with words and pictures.

In addition to sharing splendid books, teachers offer invitations to book responses by encouraging children to talk about the books that they read independently in literature discussion groups and informal conversations. Children enjoy sharing their own book discoveries. Teachers can invite rich conversational opportunities about picture books by beginning with the children's own "agenda." Instead of asking the more typical kinds of comprehension questions, teachers might start by sharing their wonderments or puzzlements, such as, "I wonder what kind of house hermit crab will finally find to his liking," while reading Megan McDonald's *Is This a House for Hermit Crab?* (1990, N). Invite children to predict an ideal home for a hermit crab. Upon completion of the reading of this book, begin with such invitations for conversations as, "I wonder if hermit crab will adapt well to his new home."

The more engaged readers become in books, the more they will want to talk about their reading experiences. Invite children to examine such aspects of picture books as the overall design, endpapers, dedication page, style of illustration, and print format. Explore the endpapers to learn something about the author and illustrator. Notice if there are acknowledgments or informational writings that give clues about why the author wrote the book or about resources the author used to make the writing accurate and authentic. Move toward engaging students to discuss what they think, discover, and notice about the book.

Encourage children to wonder specifically about the language in a particular book, with a statement like, "I wonder why Brenda Guiberson called the saguaro a 'cactus hotel'" (*Cactus Hotel,* 1991, N). Students can also collect interesting words from stories. One second grade collected the word *hoisting* from Faith Ringgold's *Tar Beach* (1991, N), *owling* from Jane Yolen's *Owl Moon* (1987, N), *petticoats* and *blab school* from Gloria Houston's *My Great-Aunt Arizona* (1992, N), and *hurdy gurdy* from Megan McDonald's *The Potato Man* (1991). Invite children to find wonderful uses of imagery like "a stony necklace," used to describe a stone wall in Francis Ward Weller's *Matthew Wheelock's Wall* (1992), and snow "whiter than the milk in a cereal bowl" from *Owl Moon*.

Sometimes children can be invited to gather data about their own responses to books as a way of examining the books more closely. For example, ask the children to remember where they laughed the most while reading Nancy Van Laan's *Possum Come a-Knockin'* (1990, N). As they note the funny parts, they can examine the author's language and the illustrations to determine elements in each that foster humor.

Children can conduct language inquiry projects through the literature that they share. They might explore the names of characters in the books they read. Are the names symbolic? Does that mean anything? How do the names match the story characters' temperaments? Children might inquire into the dialects used by story characters. They might compare the terminology used in fiction and nonfiction books on the same topics. Invitations to explore the content and language of books in greater depth provide opportunities for children to talk about books in fresh and different ways.

Other conversational opportunities can arise with open-ended questions such as those adapted from Aidan Chambers's "Tell Me Framework" (1985). Chambers recommends that teachers avoid asking *Why?* after every response, as this often tends to box in the reader and even limits responses. Instead, he suggests using a more invitational approach: "Tell me more about what you're thinking."

In *Grand Conversations: Literature Groups in Action,* Peterson and Eeds (1990) also recommend that teachers adopt a more open-ended questioning and comment style. To initiate "grand conversations" over books, they suggest helping students dialogue about their personal responses to books as an entrée into discussing a more in-depth interpretation of plot, character, setting, point of view, and so on.

Borders and Naylor, in *Children Talking about Books* (1993), also enthusiastically recommend that teachers listen more and do less talking. They suggest three discussion prompts for this purpose:

What did you notice about the story?

How did the story make you feel?

What does the story remind you of in your own life?

There are many exciting ways to respond to literature: shared wondering, asking open-ended questions, exploring all aspects of picture books, conducting inquires, and gathering data about the language in books. What is common to all of these strategies is that they empower children to make their own judgments about books and encourage them to construct knowledge about literature and the role that language plays in picture books. The teacher takes on the role of a reader, posing questions and sharing comments that are puzzling and that accurately reflect reactions to books.

Picture Books That Evoke Enthusiasm

Graeme Base's book *The Eleventh Hour: A Curious Mystery* (1989, N) offers the reader a mystery to solve by examining extraordinary full-page illustrations and a rhyming text that quickly draws the attention of even the most reluctant reader. Invite students to talk about what they notice in this intriguing book. Illustrations and text offer clues as to which animal invited to Horace the elephant's eleventh birthday party ate the bountiful celebration feast. Base's clever book will shift the reader from a comfortable sitting position to one where eyes and mind are actively engaged in search of "Who done it?" Some children may also want to take a closer look at *The Eleventh Hour* in terms of the craft of the "literary artist" (Cianciolo 1990), speculating on the ways in which Base went about creating a mystery through pictures and text. In pairs, students may try creating their own mystery using a similarly alliterative language style.

Another title that generates many revisits is Chris Van Allsburg's *The Mysteries of Harris Burdick* (1984, N). This book delights the eye and challenges the mind. At the beginning of the book, Van Allsburg sets the stage for readers to speculate on the origin of these seemingly unrelated drawings with only captions for text. Chamber's (1985) questions ("Is there anything that puzzles you about the book?") would be a great place to begin discussion. Again, the ingenious work of this author/illustrator may stimulate readers to use language in many exciting ways. For example, students might experiment with form and content to produce a similar kind of book. They might use one of the drawings as a springboard to create a different caption, a newspaper story, or an editorial, or to experiment with another form of writing. Students might also enjoy taking on the role of detective to piece together a story line about the origin of the drawings and to speculate about the character of Harris Burdick.

Pish, Posh, Said Hieronymus Bosch by Nancy Willard (1991, N) and illustrated by the Dillons is a special book. Both the text and the illustrations transport the reader to a world of medieval beasts via exquisite paintings capturing the life, artistic style, and times of Bosch, a fifteenth-century artist. Initially, some students may find the text of this picture book somewhat intimidating, so teachers may want to model their fascination with Willard's flair with language, both in style and choice of words, by reading the book aloud. Willard is, indeed, a master at weaving her words in a rich tapestry paralleling the extraordinary artwork of the Dillons. At the beginning, the housekeeper for artist Hieronymus Bosch laments her job because of all the weird creatures she needs to care for in his home:

> "How can I cook for you? How can I bake
> when the oven keeps turning itself to a rake,
> and a beehive in boots and a pear-headed priest
> call monkeys to order and lizards to feast?" (Unpaged, p. 8)

Help children linger over the language and savor every tasty morsel. Try such questions as the following (adapted from Chambers 1985):

When you first saw the book, what kind of book did you think it was going to be?

What caught your attention about the language in this book?

Was there anything that puzzled you about the words?

How did the language sound when you read this book aloud?

Was it different from reading it to yourself?

Some books are soft, quiet, and almost understated. *Home Place* by Crescent Dragonwagon (1990, N) is a memorable story of several hikers who discover a house foundation in the woods and speculate on past residents. Jerry Pinkney's haunting and dreamy watercolors transport the reader to another time. Similarly, the language of this book evokes a sense of wonder and impending discovery:

And if there was a house, there was
a family.
Dig in the dirt, scratch deep, and what
do you find?
A round blue glass marble, a nail.
A horseshoe and a piece
of plate. A small yellow bottle. A china doll's arm.
(Unpaged, p. 10)

What an adventure it would be to investigate an area around school in the same sort of way by first speculating and then researching what used to exist there fifty years ago, one hundred years ago, or even earlier. In *Appalachia: The Voices of Sleeping Birds* (1991, N), author Cynthia Rylant and illustrator Barry Moser build a sense of life in Appalachia through words and expressive watercolors. A companion title would be Rylant's earlier work *When I Was Young in the Mountains* (1982). A sense of place, peacefulness, and valuing nature is also offered to the reader in Peter Parnall's beautiful book *Quiet* (1989, N). Ask students what these stories made them wonder about. Did the stories make them think in new ways? How did the words make them feel? What emotions were evoked as they listened to the beauty and rhythm of the language? Did the words make them feel as though they were "inside the story"?

The perfect blending of words and illustrations may also result in stories that help children step outside of themselves and vicariously explore how book characters solve problems. Faith Ringgold's *Tar Beach* (1991, N) is the story of how Cassie Louise Lightfoot dreams of stepping outside of herself and going wherever she wants from the rooftop of her Harlem apartment building. The borders of each page of this glorious book were reproduced from the original story quilt. Children might read of characters who conquer fears and overcome life's obstacles in such excellent titles as *Amazing Grace* by Mary Hoffman (1991, N) *Galimoto* by Karen Lynn Williams (1990, N), *Thunder Cake* by Patricia Polacco (1990, N), *Brave Irene* by William Steig (1986, N), and *The Ghost-Eye Tree* by Bill Martin Jr. and John Archambault (1985, N). *Rose Blanche* by Christophe Gallaz (1985, N), a book to share with older students, is the story of a young girl during the Nazi occupation, told through haunting illustrations and economical use of language. The story of *Rose Blanche* is a powerful one. After reading the book aloud, ask students what they wondered about as they listened to the story. How did the author use words to evoke emotions? Was there anything puzzling about this story?

Several titles are perfect for children's experimentations with various forms of dramatic activity to further extend their appreciation of the language of these books. What better way for children to feel the confidence of Grace in *Amazing Grace* than to dramatize some of the same storybook characters she has read about, or to feel the scared feelings of the characters in *Thunder Cake, Brave Irene*, and *The Ghost-Eye Tree* by designing a skit, role-playing some of the powerful scenes, and discussing the ways in which the characters grew and changed throughout the stories. Children can describe the language in their skits that signified scared feelings, as well as words and actions that made them feel more in charge. Revisiting the stories leads to discussions about how the authors and illustrators used language and artwork to describe these feelings.

Wordless picture books also stimulate the imagination and invite opportunities for experimentation with language. A wonderful example is *Anno's U.S.A.* (1983, N). Mitsumasa Anno is a master storyteller, using pictures as his medium. His story is that of the traveler who sails to the west coast of the United States and journeys to the east coast, going backward through history. Again, this is another example of a picture book that older audiences will appreciate. They can "test" their observational skills by locating and talking about famous personages and historic sights in Anno's illustrations. Another enticing almost wordless picture book is David Wiesner's Caldecott winner, *Tuesday*. Readers can speculate about Wiesner's active imagination as they tell their own stories, either in written or oral form, of the evening frogs floating through the air on their lily pads to explore the doings of the local inhabitants. Children can create their own wordless picture books depicting what happens when ordinary creatures do extraordinary things. Students might also enjoy designing a script for *Tuesday*. Oh, what those frogs might say if only they could talk! It might also be interesting to discuss connections with Van Allsburg's works, such as *The Mysteries of*

Harris Burdick. Readers may notice some similarities in the faces of the people depicted in both books; there seems to be a certain sense of surprise, wonderment, and disbelief. Again, there is lots to wonder about, think about, and talk about.

Picture Books That Invite Readers into Language Play

One of the easiest and most pleasant ways to socially construct learning is by playing (Gentile and Hoot 1983; Schrader 1990). Language is best learned by actually experiencing it and using it, not by studying it. Experiences with high-quality literature provide young readers with powerful language models. These kinds of books encourage children to play with language, and by so doing, they become more proficient readers, writers, and speakers (Blatt 1978). Language play is one of the best ways for children to gain a heightened sensitivity to the sounds and rhythms of language and to become aware of the function and power of words.

Teachers at all grade levels need to see the rich opportunities for conversation that can come about by sharing books in which language ripples off the tongue and meanders through the mind. Wray and Medwell (1991) state, "In the view of the learner as an active constructor of knowledge (rather than a passive receiver), talk has the place of a medium, probably the most powerful medium, for pushing forward new interpretations, debating their implications, trying out possibilities and linking new ideas with those previously held" (p. 9). The books described in this section contain language that is so melodious and rich that the books really must be shared aloud and interactions encouraged before, during, and after the reading. In other words, teachers need not wait until after they finish reading a book aloud for book talk. Instead, engage children in conversation all the way through the book. As Chambers (1985) suggests, we really do not know a book until we have talked about it. Children need exposure to conversational opportunities in order to communicate ideas and reactions to books, to learn the power of book talk as a way to express what they know and feel about the language of books. A child's anecdote or response may, in fact, link with another's reaction and lead to new insights and understandings. One open-ended question at the outset (such as those mentioned previously in this chapter) can lead to a ripple effect between and among children—like a pebble thrown into a pool of water. Where it will land and how many splashes it will make is difficult to predict. So teachers need to refrain from talking too much; let children dominate the conversation and express ideas and reactions through exploratory talk.

Allen, Giard, and Kristo (1991) discovered that first-grade children's responses to literature in Mary Giard's classroom fell into four categories: nonword responses, literal word responses, evaluative responses, and extension responses.

Nonword Responses

Intent upon a story, children will often listen with eyes closed and their bodies moving in rhythm with the actions from the text.

Literal Word Responses

Children enjoy playing with the sounds of language, often repeating refrains and interesting combinations of words. Other literal responses include asking about unknown words: "What does *bold* mean? That's a funny word" (p. 5).

Evaluative Responses

Children are quick to pose questions about the format and illustrations of a book:

Why isn't there a dedication?

I didn't picture him looking like that. (P. 6)

Going beyond the physical characteristics of a book, children also demonstrate understanding of characters and their motivations. For example, when reading Hoffman's *Amazing Grace*, children wondered whether Grace would succeed in what she wanted to do and were concerned about why she was not more accepted, since she was such a good actress. At this level of response, the teacher guided students in discussing how character actions and intentions relate to their own lives.

Extension Responses

Children in this classroom experience literature in many ways, from hearing books from many genres read aloud to books read in small groups, as well as self-selected titles read by individual students. Children explore varied responses to the literature they experience and, by so doing, sometimes offer critical analysis or quite a different slant to the story.

For example, as a reaction to Susan Jeffers's *Snow White* (1980), one child remarked, "This woman isn't like the women we've seen in other fairy tales." After hearing Cynthia Rylant's *When I Was Young in the Mountains*, children suggested that they write and illustrate their own version of "When I Was Young in Bangor, Maine."

Language Play Using Alphabet Books

Alphabet books were once written primarily to teach young children the alphabet. Lately the motives for writing alphabet books appear to be more creative—to explore a topic such as plants or flowers in depth; artistic—to visually explore a specific theme; or language oriented—to play with the rich sounds of language. Each of these motives provides books that stretch thought and encourage language play, thus making them appropriate for children of any age level. *Old Black Fly* by Jim Aylesworth (1992, N) is representative of a fascinating and multidimensional kind of alphabet book, featuring that pesky fly we all remember as having bugged us until we finally swatted it. "He lapped up the *Milk* in poor kitty's bowl. He nibbled on the *Noodles* in the casserole." It is clearly the rhythm of the language in these books that makes them enjoyable stimuli for oral chanting and language play. Musical accompaniments can add to the merriment. While the alphabet is used to organize the theme, the real delight in the language stems from the use of alliteration and rhyme, which makes these alphabet books so memorable.

In one first-grade classroom, seven-year-old Ary picked up *Old Black Fly,* which had been read aloud to him three months earlier, and eagerly turned the pages. Soon he started chanting:

> Old black fly's been
> buzzin' around,
> buzzin' around,
> buzzin' around,
> Old black fly's been
> buzzin' around,
> and he's had a very
> busy bad day.
>
> He ate on the crust
> of the Apple pie.
>
> He bothered the Baby
> and made her cry.
>   Shoo fly!
>   Shoo fly!
>   Shooo. (Unpaged, pp. 3–5)

How had Ary, who listened to this book just once or twice several months earlier, been able to remember this chant word for word? Elements such as alliteration, repetition, predictable rhythm and rhyme, and familiar phrases helped fix the text in his mind. The lines "Shoo fly! / Shooo" reminded him of the line "Fly's in the buttermilk, shoo fly shoo" from a favorite song, "Skip to My Lou My Darling." After an initial reading of the text, children giggled at the pictures, especially the one of the parrot with a belly button. They laughed at the places the fly traveled, especially on the pile of underwear for the letter U. Ary's teachers had invited children to compare Aylesworth's *Old Black Fly* to Steven Kellogg's *There Was an Old Woman Who Swallowed a Fly* (1974), creating connections that further solidified elements of the story for these young readers. Reading *Old Black Fly* over and over and savoring the rich sounds of the language enabled Ary and his classmates to more easily reconstruct the text during subsequent readings.

Brightly colored collage illustrations adorn Lois Ehlert's *Eating the Alphabet: Fruits and Vegetables from A to Z* (1989, N). This illustrator places a diverse collection of fruits and vegetables on each page to form a delectable array that looks good enough to eat. *Eating the Alphabet* is more like traditional alphabet books in that it pictures particular items upon the page designated for each alphabet letter. Yet, because the book is themed, it encourages students to think about all the vegetables and fruits that begin with each letter of the alphabet. Books like *Eating the Alphabet* encourage children to play verbal language games, such as an alphabetic "Twenty Questions" on any topic, from fruits and vegetables to insects and mammals.

Some alphabet books are particularly effective in using alliteration to personalize the information in a way that naturally invites children to play with language. *Alison's Zinnia* by Anita Lobel (1990, N) focuses upon the theme of flowers. On each page, a girl does something to a flower en route to presenting it to the girl on the next page:

> Florence found a Forget-me-not for Gloria.
> Gloria grew a Gaillardia for Heather.
> Heather hosed a Hyacinth for Irene. (Unpaged, pp. 11–13)

Full-colored illustrations of the flowers are on the top of the page, while a smaller horizontal illustration of the child doing the action described in the text is on the bottom. Many language-related activities can arise from this book. First, the language is enjoyable to read aloud; the alliterative words flow wonderfully and gracefully. Children can also study different types of flowers, seeking out the derivations of their names. In addition, the book invites text innovations. Using the same pattern, children can write and design their own books on such topics as fruits, vegetables, toys, cars, sports, and so on. Because Lobel's book arose from street names, students could also explore the origins of the street names in their neighborhoods, or perhaps the origins of town, city, and state names as well. Students may also expand on Lobel's format with another topic from a thematic study, such as trees, birds, or outer space. Using the alphabet format is a creative way to report on information from any unit of study.

Other authors of alphabet books play with alliterative language. "Ben brought bagels" and "Dan did dumplings" are examples of multiethnic foods that children bring to a feast in Anne Shelby's *Potluck* (1991). *Alligator Arrived with Apples: A Potluck Alphabet Feast* by Crescent Dragonwagon (1987, N) has a similar content and format. In this book, it is animals that bring the foods to a potluck vegetarian feast for Thanksgiving, with a particular food selected for each letter of the alphabet. "Acton appeared with asparagus soup," and "Graham had gone to Garbanzo's bakery to get good garlic bread"; these examples are indicative of Dragonwagon's use of lively alliterative language and also raise the topic of nutrition. One class invited parents and children to bring food for an international potluck breakfast one Saturday morning. Each child and parent prepared a dish related to the family's ethnic origins and created an alliterative line to accompany the food. The literary contributions were then combined into a class alliterative alphabet book.

Some alphabet books integrate language play with artistic challenges, such as Graeme Base's *Animalia* (1986, N). On each page of this intriguing book, the illustrator has subtly painted numerous objects that begin with a particular letter of the alphabet. The text mentions some of them in alliterative format, such as "Crafty Crimson Cats carefully catching Crusty Crayfish" and "Jovial Jackals Juggling Jugs of Jelly in the Jungle." More items than cats and jackals appear in the full-page colorful illustrations, which leads to wonderful opportunities to discover and name the objects: a natural language play activity. One class made decorative collages of items beginning with each letter of the alphabet and labeled them with alliterative poems.

The Handmade Alphabet by Laura Rankin (1991, N) acquaints children with another way of making meaning and seeing words by introducing the manual alphabet of American Sign Language. This book also offers a host of different words to consider, such as *asparagus, erasers, ornament, palette,* and *thimbles.* One first-grade class was so fascinated by this book that the students' conversation seemed to go on forever. They enjoyed talking about how different this book is from other alphabet books, and they were eager to tell their friends about how the book made them think about the alphabet in a totally different way.

It is the rhythm, the rhyme, and the bouncy, playful language in *Chicka Chicka Boom Boom* by Bill Martin Jr. and John Archambault (1989, N) and Aylesworth's *Old Black Fly* that make these alphabet books so memorable and easy to chant. In *Chicka Chicka Boom Boom,* little lowercase alphabet letters challenge each other to climb to the top of the coconut tree, which bends with their weight. Finally, "Chicka chicka . . . BOOM! BOOM!" All the letters end up in a heap at the bottom of the tree, to be rescued by adults, posing as uppercase letters. Children chuckle at "skinned-knee d" and "black-eyed p" as they chant the refrain.

The children in Debbie King's first-grade class eagerly made puppets and performed *Chicka Chicka Boom Boom* as a play, with a large painted coconut tree for a backdrop. This same class worked with the physical education teacher to form the letters of the alphabet with their bodies, demonstrating a great way to integrate classroom activities with specialists. Another enthusiastic group of first graders in Adele Ames's classroom designed and wrote "The Chicka Chicka Boom Boom Christmas Alphabet Book," which begins:

> A holiday
> Blitzen
> Christmas tree
> Dasher
> Elves
>
> Friends
> Guests
> Happy
> Icicles
> Jolly
>
> Kris Kringle
> Lights
> Mary
> Noel
> On Comet!

Chris Van Allsburg offers a visual challenge and stimulation with language in *The Z Was Zapped: A Play in Twenty-Six Acts* (1987, N). In this surreal book, a simple sentence explains what happens to each alphabet letter. Examples include "The R was Rolled off-stage," "The S was simply Soaked," and "The U was abruptly Uprooted" (unpaged, pp. 40, 42, 46). The fun comes in guessing what each sentence will be after studying the illustration on the preceding page, an activity that encourages children to play with the alphabet using both language and visual play. In one class, two second graders made up their own version using Van Allsburg's pattern. They created a black light show and musical accompaniment with the assistance of their music teacher.

Another alphabet book begging for revisits is Ann Jonas's *Aardvarks, Disembark!* (1990). This is the alphabetic story of Noah and the Ark. Noah calls the animals from the ark from Z to A—a real twist on the usual alphabet book. The format of the book is out of the ordinary as well; the book is to be read sideways. Readers will note that many of the animals are unusual and have names that are odd and challenging to say, such as *rasses, rheas, ratels,* and *sisakas*. A distinctive feature of this book is a glossary identifying the animals as endangered or extinct. Pairs of students would have fun finding more endangered and extinct animals and creating their own illustrated alphabet books.

Alphabet books, then, use a variety of linguistic formats to engage children in reading and remembering texts. They provide opportunities for children to play with alliteration, rhythm, and rhyme as well as invitations to explore thematic studies across the curriculum. Books like these are particularly ideal for giving shy or developmentally delayed children confidence in their oral language.

Chants and Song Picture Books

Music provides an added dimension to our enjoyment of language. Lyrics are often more easily remembered when they are accompanied by a melody than when they are words of a poem. The language benefits of singing are many. Terms used in lyrics typically have specific ethnic, cultural, or scientific meanings. Syntax is manipulated to sound rhythmic and musical. Words are used to create moods, to persuade, to inform, to describe, and to entertain, making singing and language inextricably linked. Helping children become aware of these language dimensions as they read or learn a chant or song heightens their enjoyment and empowers them as language users.

One type of song is a monotonous chant that is sung to alleviate boredom while completing routine or mundane repetitive tasks. *Busy Monday Morning* by Janina Domanska (1985, N) presents a chant sung by farmers in the fields of Poland as they planted and harvested their hay. In this version, a boy and his father mow on Monday, rake on Tuesday, dry on Wednesday, pitch on Thursday, stack on Friday, haul on Saturday, and rest on Sunday. The music to the song is included at the end, although the words in the book are an abbreviated version of the entire song. One fifth-grade class used this book to help them understand the work chants sung by workers as they built the transcontinental railroad. The students found work chants, analyzed the language, and created their own chants from the perspective of Irish, Chinese, and African American workers. Children could also create songbooks celebrating activities they do in school and at home.

Folk songs are happy celebrations of life, often with an underlying message or moral that accompanies the frivolity. The theme in *All God's Critters Got a Place in the Choir* by Bill Staines (1989, N)—that everyone is accepted and needed—is played through an analogy: our voices may all be different, yet we all fit in. As Staines puts it:

> Some sing low, some sing higher,
> some sing out loud on the telephone wire,
> and some just clap their hands,
>   or paws,
>   or anything they got. (Unpaged, pp. 6–8)

The rollicking, exuberant phrases invite children to clap and sing along and to really feel the rhythm and liveliness of the language. The humor of the animals singing together makes a joyful song to which children can improvise accompaniments. Older students might create other images to express the same theme honoring diversity.

Nursery rhymes and play rhymes have lasted through the centuries because of their rhythmic, alliterative, and repetitive melodies and lyrics. To capitalize on children's natural interest in nursery rhymes, many book illustrators select a rhyme and illustrate it in picture book format. *This Old Man: The Counting Song* by Robin Michal Koontz (1988, N) and Carol Jones's version of *This Old Man* (1990) are excellent examples to compare and contrast. The Jones version has holes on the page of each stanza that help children predict the rhyme in the song. Because many young children are already familiar with the words of such songs, they can enjoy singing them on their own, matching verses with the pictures. Children just beginning to read learn to match the language they know with the words which represent the message. Try other songs in picture book format, such as Paul Zelinsky's *The Wheels on the Bus* (1991) and Nadine Bernard Wescott's *The Lady with the Alligator Purse* (1990). The rhythmic language of Margaret Mahy's *Seventeen Kings and Forty-Two Elephants* (1987, N) invites drum improvisation for accompaniment. Children react joyously to the "music that the marchers made" and to such verses as

> Seventeen kings on forty-two elephants
> Going on a journey through a wild wet night
> Baggy ears like big umbrellaphants,
> Little eyes a-gleaming in the jungle light. (Unpaged, pp. 4–5)

Similarly, it is hard to read Van Laan's *Possum Come a-Knockin'* without clapping and joining in the chant:

> Possum come a-knockin'
> at the door, at the door.
> Possum come a-knockin'
> at the door. (Unpaged, p. 5)

> Granny was a-sittin'
> and a-rockin' and a-knittin'
> when a possum come a-knockin'
> at the door. (P. 6)

> Brother was untanglin'
> all the twiny line for fishin'
> while Sis was tossin' Baby
> and Pappy was a-whittlin'
> and Pa was busy fixin'
> and Ma was busy cookin'
> and Granny was a-knittin'
> when a possum come a-knockin'
> at the door. (Pp. 11–12)

One class of second graders rounded up very simple props (a scarf for granny, a doll as a baby) and acted out the chant, using a narrator, eight parts, and the audience for the refrain.

Who Is the Beast? by Keith Baker (1990, N) is a chant with a repetitive beginning to each stanza: "The beast, the beast! I buzz along. I see his legs, sure and strong" (pp. 8–9). The clues build until the "beast" looks into a pond and realizes that he has the same characteristics as this mythical beast. As he gives another look, the cumulative pattern reverses itself, and the conclusion is reached that we are all beasts, an ecological and humanitarian message.

We're Going on a Bear Hunt by Michael Rosen (1989, N) is a game in book format, following the same kind of cumulative language pattern. Through pictures, this version of the traditional clapping game and chant involves a family with four children and a dog, who go through different settings to hunt for a bear. When the bear is found, they rapidly return, repeating the motions backwards to the beginning of the adventure. The traditional sounds of moving through the various obstacles, which have made this book such a great resource for language play, are enlivened in this version by new sounds, such as "squerch, squerch" (to describe walking through mud) and "stumble-trip, stumble-trip."

After Alice Motycka's second-grade class heard her read *We're Going on a Bear Hunt,* students talked about going on different kinds of hunts. Next, Motycka webbed their topics on the board along with challenges to the hunt. One second grader, Jeanne, prepared a topic web for a bird hunt, including all the obstacles along the way, and then wrote her story (see figure 1.1).

These participatory books celebrate language through motion, action, and drama. They encourage children to use language in creative patterns, enhancing flexibility and mastery in choral speaking. Children can easily read and perform or create innovations from these books, providing further meaningful opportunities for language play.

Predictable Books: Playing with Natural Language Patterns

Most good predictable books use the natural language of talk and literature and thus differ from the traditional easy readers written with limited vocabulary. Because they have repetitive refrains and logical sequences of cumulative texts, these predictable books are easy to read and provide natural opportunities for language play and early success with reading. Often they have surprising, humorous, yet predictable, endings. In *The Doorbell Rang* by Pat Hutchins (1986, N), Tom and Victoria have to share their cookies with friends who keep arriving at the door until there is just one cookie left for each child. Then the doorbell rings. Throughout the story the children have claimed that "No one makes cookies like Grandma." Who

Figure 1.1.
Student's web of bird hunt
and story based on web.

We're Going on a Bird Hunt

We're going on a bird hunt. We're going to catch a big one. What a beautiful day! We're not scared. A jungle. We can't go over it. We can't go under it. Oh no! We have to go through it! Shweeeeee Shweeeeee Shweeeeee!

We're going on a bird hunt. We're going to catch a big one. What a beautiful day. We're not scared. A desert. We can't go over it. We can't go under it. Oh no! We have to go through it! Haaath Haaath Haaath Haaath!

We're going on a bird hunt. We're going to catch a big one. What a beautiful day. We're not scared. Ooze. We can't go under it. Oh no! We have to go through it! Sloooosh Sloooosh Sloooosh Sloooosh!

We're going on a bird hunt. We're going to catch a big one. What a beautiful day. We're not scared. Oh, rattlesnakes. We can't go under them. Oh no! We have to go through them! Sweees Sweees Sweees Sweees!

We're going on a bird hunt. We're going to catch a big one. What a beautiful day. We're not scared. A spaghetti cave. We can't go over it. We can't go under it. Oh no! We have to go through it! Swaththths Swaththths Swaththths!

We come to a meadow. We see a tree with a bird in it. We take the bird home, and we keep it as a pet. Tweet Tweet Tweet!

is at the door? Why, it's Grandma, with a whole tray of cookies, of course. Children enjoy repeating the refrain and acting out the sequence of visitors.

In a similar fashion, McDonald's *Is This a House for Hermit Crab?* is the account of a hermit crab's search for a suitable home. The crab searches in a number of unsuitable places, including a fish net, an empty bucket, and a tin can. The repetitive sounds make this a great choice for a read-aloud. Each time hermit crab rejects the lodging possibility, he steps "along the shore, by the sea, in the sand . . . *scritch-scratch, scritch-scratch*" until he eventually is washed out to sea. Children can key into the sounds of the language as well as the content of the story. But what does the crab find when he reaches the bottom of the ocean? As he races along the ocean floor to avoid his enemy, the pricklepine fish, he scurries under an empty shell, of course. This is the ideal book to compare from a language perspective with Mary Ann Hoberman's *A House Is a House for Me* (1982) and Eric Carle's *A House for Hermit Crab* (1987), as well as a good choice for a thematic unit on habitats or the seashore.

Polar Bear, Polar Bear, What Do You Hear? (1991, N), written by Bill Martin Jr. and illustrated by Eric Carle, is another popular choice with lots of possibilities for reading and writing. The accurate, specific verbs that Martin uses make the animals in this book come alive. Martin's precise writing can encourage children to analyze the verbs they use in their own writing, replacing general verbs with specific ones. Many children will be familiar with Martin's earlier work *Brown Bear, Brown Bear, What Do You See?* (1983) and can be invited to discuss the similarities in the texts. Because both books follow an easily discernible pattern, young writers can use the patterns to create their own new versions.

Other Interesting Opportunities for Literary Language Play

A trend in children's literature is to publish books which play with the content and language of traditional folktales and fairy tales. These books tend to twist the original story in some way to make it humorous. Typically they share the same story from a different character's perspective or extend the story in predictable but humorous ways. In a review of such books, Martinez and Nash (1992) call these spin-offs, extensions, and modern-day variants of tales and rhymes "extended language play." The effect, they claim, is "upbeat and downright zany."

Four authors who specialize in such tales are Jon Scieszka, Janet and Allan Ahlberg, and William Steig. *The Jolly Postman; or, Other People's Letters* (1986, N) and *The Jolly Christmas Postman* (1991) by the Ahlbergs use a rhyming text to relate the postman's travels as he delivers letters, postcards, invitations, greeting cards, and get-well cards to nursery rhyme and fairy tale characters. Much of the wording in the letters, on the envelopes, and in the rhymed text is humorous and a play on the language of the original tales. The book contains envelopes that hold the actual pieces of mail. Children love making similar flap books and folded manipulative books with letters to storybook characters. They also enjoy writing letters and delivering or mailing them.

Scieszka has written several picture books which play with classical stories. His most popular, *The True Story of the Three Little Pigs!* (1989, N), tells the wolf's version of the tale about the three little pigs. His hilarious version portrays the wolf as totally innocent, except for devouring the pigs, much as a human might eat a hamburger. In *The Frog Prince, Continued* (1991), the original story is extended to a humorous and unexpected ending. When children write their own continuations to fantasy stories, they can capture the language of the original versions and put it to new uses.

Steig's *Shrek* (1990, N) reverses the classical fairy tale characters, making them the ugliest that the reader can imagine. Periodically in the story, Steig uses verse, alliteration, and imagery to create a hilarious tale that ends as all fairy tales do, with Shrek finding his princess. She, of course, is the ugliest princess imaginable. Children enjoy the contrasts of good and bad, pretty and ugly, and smart and dull as well as the absurd humor and language.

James Stevenson is another author who plays with language. In *Yuck!* (1984, N) he employs alliteration in the ingredients of Emma's recipe (gnat knuckles and spider spit, for example). His other stories, such as those featuring a grandfather telling his grandchildren about his youth, are written in cartoon format and use exaggeration as a technique for humorously stretching a story.

Most children have their own stories about how they lost their teeth. In Tom Birdseye's *Airmail to the Moon* (1988, N), Ora Mae Cotton of Crabapple Orchard has the humiliating experience of loosing her tooth and being unable to leave it for the tooth fairy. Only after accusing every family member of theft does she discover the missing tooth at the bottom of her pants pocket, right where she put it. The language in this story is full of figures of speech from the Appalachian Mountain region. The book is a linguistic delight that encourages children to tell their own lost-tooth stories and to explore the figures of speech used by their own family members and friends.

Many picture books naturally invite play and experimentation through conversation, writing, and drama. Language play "knits" a group together and contributes to building a literate and language-rich classroom. The sharing of literature aloud "anchors the sounds of the language of literature in the minds of the students. Children of all ages absorb the language they hear" (Peterson and Eeds 1990).

It is interesting that language play is rarely mentioned in books that discuss literature-based curricula. Instead, teachers are encouraged to help children transcend the text of the stories they read by focusing upon literary elements such as characterization, plot, setting, mood, and theme, but rarely do these books mention focusing upon language. In many cases it is how the author uses and even plays with language that provides the emotional impact of a story, poem, or nonfiction book. It is important, then, to treat language play and manipulation seriously and to help children become aware of and interested in playing with language as they interact with books. Playing with language helps readers transcend the text and find their own interpretations of literature.

Language and Cultural Identity

When Jonda was asked why she liked *Green Lion of Zion Street* by Julia Fields (1988, N), she replied, "I don't know. I just like it. I like the way it sounds." As a class, we read the book together and noticed that in some places the book is written in dialect and in other places it is written in formal English. We wondered why the language varied that way. Jonda likes Patricia McKissack's books, too.

"Maybe it's because of the dialect," she says. "It sounds so real." Dialect in children's books makes stories authentic. Yet very few books—even those that tell stories about people who speak dialects other than formal English—share those dialects in the text.

Dialect adds interest to a story beyond that of the content and illustrations. *Airmail to the Moon* by Birdseye and *A Regular Rolling Noah* by George Ella Lyons (1982) tell stories of children who live in Appalachia. Both stories are told in the first person, and the narrator speaks in dialect. As a result, each book brings readers into the intimacy of an Appalachian community and presents an entertaining story that is made even more enjoyable by the language used.

The children in an Alaskan classroom divided a bulletin board in two, with one side for their writings in the heritage dialect that they spoke at home and the other side for their writings in formal English. Sometimes they translated their stories told in heritage language into formal English so that they could share them with children in another community. These children noticed how some authors write in heritage dialects, but most use formal English. Their fascination with dialect and the power with which they can use different dialects will serve them well as they bridge the gap between their home culture and the world outside their community.

Creative Book Titles

One of the most challenging tasks in writing a piece is to give it a title. Examining book titles is one way to get some ideas for titles that are descriptive and attractive. The title of a book is like a commercial for the story inside. It is an invitation to read the book. The titles help unlock the messages inside and arouse curiosity about language. Because *Amazing Grace* by Hoffman is the title of a popular hymn, people remember the title of the book. *Anna Banana and Me* by Lenore Blegvad (1985) is a clever title because the name rhymes. *Bringing the Rain to Kapiti Plain* by Verna Aardema (1981) has rhyme and rhythm. Some titles are questions, like *May I Bring a Friend?* by Beatrice Schenk de Regniers (1964) and *Where Does the Trail Lead?* by Burton Albert (1991). Paul Coltman makes up words for *Tog the Ribber* (1985). Names of characters can be titles of books, like *Max* by Rachel Isadora (1976), *Frederick* by Leo Lionni (1967), and *Chrysanthemum* by Kevin Henkes (1991), who endures teasing because of her name. Story titles incorporate alliteration, like *Night Noises* by Mem Fox (1992), *Noisy Nora* by Rosemary Wells (1973), *Whistle for Willie* by Ezra Jack Keats (1964), *Englebert the Elephant* by Tom Paxton (1990), and *Rosie and the Rustlers* by Roy Gerrard (1989). Some titles give evidence of regional or ethnic dialects, like *Come a Tide* by George Ella Lyon (1990) and *She Come Bringing Me That Little Baby Girl* by Eloise Greenfield (1974).

Some book titles just make you curious. What is a *Thunder Cake* (Patricia Polacco, 1990, N) or a *Chalk Doll* (Charlotte Pomerantz, 1989)? What might make the noises in *When the Woods Hum* by Joanne Ryder (1990)? Opposites invite curiosity, as in *Just Plain Fancy* by Patricia Polacco (1990). Some book titles contain words from other languages, like *Galimoto* by Karen Lynn Williams (1990, N), the name of a pull toy made out of wire in Malawai, *El Chino* by Allen Say (1990), and *Abuela* by Arthur Dorros (1991). Merely focusing children's attention on the importance of book titles can generate a lot of language learning.

Not a Conclusion but a Beginning

Encourage children of all ages to read and enjoy picture books. The words should be luxuriant, rich examples of language woven into the tapestry of extraordinary artwork; the words should spark the mind, fuel the imagination, and invite many opportunities for a host of responses. The authors and illustrators of the Notable picture books are our national treasures. Invite students to the banquet table filled with some of the best books and encourage them to savor and appreciate the remarkable and powerful ways in which words and pictures work with each other in harmony and beauty.

References

Professional Resources

Allen, J., M. Giard, and J. Kristo. 1991. "Read Aloud: Prime Time Instruction." *New England Reading Association Journal* 27:2–13.

Bader, B. 1976. *American Picturebooks from Noah's Ark to the Beast Within.* New York: Macmillan.

Blatt, G. T. 1978. "Playing with Language." *The Reading Teacher* 31:487–92.

Borders, S. G., and A. P. Naylor. 1993. *Children Talking about Books.* Phoenix: Oryx Press.

Burke, E. M. 1990. *Literature for the Young Child,* 2d ed. Needham Heights, MA: Allyn and Bacon.

Chambers, A. 1985. *Booktalk: Occasional Writing on Literature and Children.* New York: Harper and Row.

Cianciolo, P. 1990. *Picture Books for Children,* 3d ed. Chicago: American Library Association.

Gentile, L. M., and J. L. Hoot. 1983. "Kindergarten Play: The Foundation of Reading." *The Reading Teacher* 36:436–39.

See the Bibliography of Notable Books at the end of the book for bibliographic information about cited Notable Books. The Notable titles do not appear in this reference list.

Kiefer, B. 1989. "Picture Books for All the Ages." In *Children's Literature in the Classroom: Weaving Charlotte's Web,* edited by J. Hickman and B. Cullinan. Norwood, MA: Christopher Gordon.

Martinez, M., and M. F. Nash. 1992. "Bookalogues: Talking about Children's Literature." *Language Arts* 69 (January): 62–68.

Peterson, R., and M. Eeds. 1990. *Grand Conversations: Literature Groups in Action.* New York: Scholastic.

Schrader, C. T. 1990. "Teaching Children While They Play: Encouraging Emergent Writing and Reading." *Day Care and Early Education* 17:22–25.

Wray, D., and J. Medwell. 1991. *Literacy and Language in the Primary Years.* New York: Routledge.

Children's Literature

Aardema, Verna. 1981. *Bringing the Rain to Kapiti Plain: A Nandi Tale.* Illus. by Beatriz Vidal. New York: Dial Books.

Ahlberg, Janet, and Allan Ahlberg. 1991. *The Jolly Christmas Postman.* Boston: Little, Brown.

Albert, Burton. 1991. *Where Does the Trail Lead?* Illus. by Brian Pinkney. New York: Simon and Schuster.

Blegvad, Lenore. 1985. *Anna Banana and Me.* Illus. by Erik Blegvad. New York: Atheneum.

Carle, Eric. 1987. *A House for Hermit Crab.* Saxonville, MA: Picture Book Studio.

Coltman, Paul. 1985. *Tog the Ribber.* Illus. by Gillian McClure. New York: Farrar, Straus and Giroux.

de Regniers, Beatriz Schenk. 1964. *May I Bring a Friend?* Illus. by Beni Montresor. New York: Macmillan.

Dorros, Arthur. 1991. *Abuela.* Illus. by Elisa Kleven. New York: E. P. Dutton.

Fox, Mem. 1992. *Night Noises.* Illustrated by Terry Denton. San Diego: Harcout Brace Jovanovich.

Gerard, Roy. 1989. *Rosie and the Rustlers.* New York: Farrar, Straus and Giroux.

Greenfield, Eloise. 1974. *She Come Bringing Me That Little Baby Girl.* Illus. by John Steptoe. New York: Harper and Row.

Henkes, Kevin. 1991. *Chrysanthemum.* New York: Greenwillow Books.

Hoberman, Mary Ann. 1982. *A House Is a House for Me.* Illus. by Betty Fraser. New York: Penguin.

Isadora, Rachel. 1976. *Max.* New York: Macmillan.

Jeffers, Susan. 1980. *Snow White.* New York: Scholastic.

Jonas, Ann. 1990. *Aardvarks, Disembark!* New York: Greenwillow Books.

Jones, Carol. 1990. *This Old Man.* Boston: Houghton Mifflin.

Keats, Ezra Jack. 1964. *Whistle for Willie*. New York: Viking.

———. 1971. *Over in the Meadow*. New York: Four Winds Press.

Kellogg, Steven. 1974. *There Was an Old Woman Who Swallowed a Fly*. New York: Four Winds Press.

Langstaff, John. 1957. *Over in the Meadow*. New York: Harcourt Brace Jovanovich.

Lionni, Leo. 1967. *Frederick*. New York: Alfred A. Knopf.

Lyon, George Ella. 1982. *A Regular Rolling Noah*. Illus. by Stephen Gammell. New York: Macmillan.

———. 1990. *Come a Tide*. Illus. by Stephen Gammell. New York: Orchard Books.

Martin, Bill, Jr. 1983. *Brown Bear, Brown Bear, What Do You See?* Illus. by Eric Carle. New York: Henry Holt.

McDonald, Megan. 1991. *The Potato Man*. Illus. by Ted Lewin. New York: Orchard Books.

Paxton, Tom. 1990. *Englebert the Elephant*. New York: William Morrow.

Polacco, Patricia. 1990. *Just Plain Fancy*. New York: Bantam Books.

Pomerantz, Charlotte. 1989. *Chalk Doll*. Illus. by Frané Lessac. New York: Harper and Row.

Ryder, Joanne. 1990. *When the Woods Hum*. New York: William Morrow.

Rylant, Cynthia. 1982. *When I Was Young in the Mountains*. Illus. by Diane Goode. New York: E. P. Dutton.

Say, Allen. 1990. *El Chino*. Boston: Houghton Mifflin.

Scieszka, Jon. 1991. *The Frog Prince, Continued*. Illus. by Steve Johnson. New York: Viking.

Shelby, Anne. 1991. *Potluck*. Illus. by Irene Trivas. New York: Orchard Books.

Weller, Francis Ward. 1992. *Matthew Wheelock's Wall*. New York: Macmillan.

Wells, Rosemary. 1973. *Noisy Nora*. New York: Dial Books.

Wescott, Nadine Bernard. 1990. *The Lady with the Alligator Purse*. Boston: Little, Brown.

Zelinsky, Paul. 1991. *The Wheels on the Bus*. New York: E. P. Dutton.

2 Poetic Texts and Poetic Language

Amy A. McClure
Ohio Wesleyan University

It doesn't always have to rhyme,
but there's the repeat of a beat, somewhere
an inner chime that makes you want to
tap your feet or swerve in a curve;
a lilt, a leap, a lightning-split:—
thunderstruck the consonants jut,
while the vowels open wide as waves in the noon-
    blue sea.

You hear with your heels, your eyes feel
what they have never touched before:
fins on a bird, feathers on a deer;
taste all colors, inhale
memory and tomorrow and always the tang is
    today.

Eve Merriam, "Inside a Poem," *It Doesn't Always Have to Rhyme*,
1964

Poetry is musical language. It skips, it sings, it tugs at you with an insistent voice that rings through your head, tapping out a rhythm that will not let you go. Poets love the harmony of sound and rhythm that words can create. To a poet, a word is a wonderful phenomenon, full of complexity and possibility. Poets try to get inside and around words, going beyond surface meanings to examine sounds, textures, rhythms, and connotative qualities. They hope this exploration will help them capture the precise feelings and images they want their readers to experience. Good poems make us sigh and say, "Yes, that's just the way it is. . . . I never thought of it

The author wishes to acknowledge the following Ohio teachers and librarians who contributed their time and ideas to this chapter: Joan Smith, Emerson School, Westerville; Karen Hildebrand, Willis Middle School, Delaware; Frank Hatcher, Greensview School, Upper Arlington; Janet Carlson, Emerson School, Westerville; Judy Markham, Columbus School for Girls, Columbus; Sarah Richards, Griffin Thomas Elementary, Dublin.

quite that way." That is the power of poetry—to use words to move us, to make us see ordinary everyday images in new ways, and to help us appreciate the ways in which ordinary words can be made to sparkle. This close attention to words gives poetry a unique voice that differs from other genres.

However, it takes an enthusiastic teacher who is sensitive to where children are in their appreciation of poetry to help them value the language of poetry. The purpose of this chapter is to provide readers with an understanding of how they can help children, in the words of poet Joanne Ryder, "look at [their] own world through a new window, [their] poem, and see the marvels all around" (quoted in *The Place My Words Are Looking For,* edited by Paul B. Janeczcko [1990, N], p. 105) and to speak the language of poetry.

Connecting Poetry with Other Literature

Every writer of poetry is first a reader of poetry. Poetry is an oral art; it must be read aloud to be truly appreciated. If children are to develop thoughtful, informed responses to the language of poetry, they must become familiar with a wide range of poems written by professionals as well as their peers. They need to hear poetry read aloud and have opportunities to savor their favorites on their own or with friends. They must begin to see how writers of prose also use the language of poetry to add subtle rhythm and imagery to their writing. These activities provide children with models of how poetry looks, how poets use language to describe phenomena, and how various poetic elements can complement and extend the meaning of both poetry and prose. Most importantly, continued exposure to quality poems can lead to a more informed appreciation of poetry as a form of expression as well as an awareness of how it permeates life.

Some teachers begin helping children appreciate poetic language by connecting it with prose. Third-grade teacher Sarah Richards had almost finished reading Frances Hodgson Burnett's *The Secret Garden* (1962) with her children when she brought in a selection of poems chosen to go along with the feelings and characters in the book. Some were her personal favorites, whereas others were poems she had discovered while browsing through books gathered from the library. Included were Aileen Fisher's "I'd Not Be a Robin" and "I Wonder How a Robin Hears," in *Feathered Ones and Furry* (1971), and Rachel Field's "Some People," in *Favorite Poems Old and New,* compiled by Helen Ferris (1957). As Richards read each poem, she asked the group to think about how that poem might be connected to an event in the novel or to a particular character. Then the children were encouraged to find poems on their own to fit the book. Similarly, after reading the same book, a fifth grader in Judy

Markham's classroom wrote a series of poems that reminded her of Mary Lennox, the main character. The following poem is one from the collection:

> A secret garden.
> You find the key,
> And fit it into a lock, hidden in a wall.
> Covered by a dark veil of ivy.
> You take a deep breath,
> And slowly turn the key.
> The door noiselessly opens,
> And you step inside,
> Quickly close the door,
> And look around.
> Everything looks dead,
> But you hope that everything is wick;
> And as wick as wick can be.
> You hear someone calling your name,
> And you sneak out,
> As silently as you came in.
> And close the hidden door behind you,
> And hide the key behind a loose brick.
> You run away smiling,
> Because you know you have a secret to keep,
> And you know that you will come back
> To your secret garden.

Librarian Karen Hildebrand did a similar activity with middle school students using Gary Paulsen's *Hatchet* (1987, N). She selected the poems "In the Middle" and "Long Ago Days" from Myra Cohn Livingston's *There Was a Place, and Other Poems* (1988, N) to reflect Brian's feelings about his parents' divorce; "I Am Young" from Jo Carson's *Stories I Ain't Told Nobody Yet* (1989), Sarett's "The Loon" from Burton E. Stevenson's *Home Book of Modern Verse* (1950), and "Stars" from Livingston's *Sky Songs* (1984, N) to describe Brian's feelings of loneliness after the crash; and Arnold Adoff's *Tornado!* (1976) to give students a heightened perspective of Brian's experience with a tornado. She then encouraged them to find other poems or write their own to reflect their responses to Paulsen's book. Their choices ranged from Carl Sandburg's "Lost," in *Rainbows Are Made,* compiled by Lee Bennett Hopkins (1982), to Shel Silverstein's "Forgotten Language," in *Where the Sidewalk Ends* (1974), chosen because a student felt it captured Brian's feelings of increased powers of observation after spending fifty-four days alone in the wilderness. Some of the students felt compelled to write their own poems, like the following:

Hatchet

The hatchet is everything
The food, the shelter, the protector.
It is life.

Only the hatchet can cut the fine wood
Only the hatchet may help me from
    death to life.

The woods are lonely, cold and hungry
Only the hatchet to keep me
    alive within.

(quoted in Zitlow 1992)

Thus poetry added a rich dimension to the children's responses to the literature they were reading. They, in turn, were able to develop their own poetic language because of their exposure to so much of it.

Discovering Poetic Language in Other Genres

The language of picture books is often poetic. In such books the illustrations create an image, but the carefully chosen, spare, rhythmic, poetic-like language gives definition and feeling to the visual image. Thus, teachers can ask children to listen for alliteration and assonance in lines like "the hurly-burly, topsy-turvy, lashing gnashing teeth of rain" in Bill Martin Jr. and John Archambault's *Listen to the Rain* (1988, N), or "ritch, ratch, moles scratch" in Denise Fleming's *In the Tall, Tall Grass* (1991, N). Teachers can help children appreciate the melodious poetic prose of Nancy White Carlstrom in *Goodbye Geese* (1991, N) as she personifies winter with such phrases as "she has an icy stare that freezes the rivers and ponds. . . . she'll shade this place with darkness" (unpaged, p. 14). Or children can be encouraged to move to the gentle rhythm of well-placed words in Julia Fields's *The Green Lion of Zion Street* (1988, N) as she describes an overpowering fog-shrouded statue of a green lion:

'Cause when they cross that bridge,
When they cross that bridge,
on that ridge,
they are going to see something crouched
up there, lolled up there
to give anybody a scare.

Crescent Dragonwagon uses similarly rhythmic free verse, with poetic-like language in *Home Place* (1987, N) to describe an approaching summer storm:

the swing begins to sway
as the wind comes up

as the rain comes down . . .
the dry dusty earth soaks up the water
the roots of the plants, like the daffodil bulbs
the mama planted, hidden under the earth, but alive
and growing . . . (Unpaged, p. 19)

Beautifully written novels can also provide opportunities for experiencing poetic language. In *Tuck Everlasting* (1975), Natalie Babbitt uses vivid, descriptive language to describe the first week of August as "curiously silent . . . with blank white dawns and glaring noons, and sunsets smeared with too much color" (p. 1). Patricia MacLachlan uses active verbs, onomatopoeia, subtle alliteration, and metaphoric images in the opening page of *Journey* (1991, N):

Mama named me Journey. Journey, as if somehow she wished her restlessness on me. But it was Mama who would be gone the year that I was eleven—before spring crashed onto our hillside with explosions of mountain laurel, before summer came with the soft slap of the screen door, breathless nights, and mildew on the books. (P. ix)

Even well-written nonfiction often has a poetic quality. Drew Nelson uses detailed, vivid descriptive language to portray the life and death struggles of wild animals in *Wild Voices* (1991, N). Cynthia Rylant eloquently and poetically describes life in the Appalachian Mountains in *Appalachia: The Voices of Singing Birds* (1991, N). Joanne Ryder, in *Mockingbird Morning* (1989), combines vivid illustrations with poetic descriptions of nature, as in the following description of the morning light on the pond:

Several tiny suns
flicker on the water
brightening
your tree room.

Look up
and watch
the pond light
dance along
the tall dark
branches.

Look down
and watch
pond patterns
ripple across

your smooth brown
arms and legs.

Strategies for Sharing Poetry

Many teachers begin using poetry with children by reading light, humorous poems on a topic and by encouraging laughter as well as comments from the group about their own similar experiences. They then read a more complex work on that same topic, generating more thoughtful, informed responses once the simpler pieces have been shared. For example, several teachers start with poems about cats since their students have many personal experiences with cats to bring to a sharing session. Shel Silverstein's "The Lost Cat," in *A Light in the Attic* (1981), is a light, humorous piece that can be used to begin a discussion. Then teachers could read Rosalie Moore's "Catalogue," found in *Reflections on a Gift of Watermelon Pickle, and Other Modern Verse,* edited by Dunning, Lueders, and Smith (1966), to show how a poet creates vivid images through carefully selected and artfully arranged words. Moore uses wonderfully alliterative and powerfully descriptive phrases in her poem, such as "they spread out comfort underneath them" (to describe sleeping cats) and "sleek as a grape slipping its skin" (describing how cats jump). Children respond excitedly to these images, invariably drawing from their own experience to make comparisons to their own cats. Yet they also expand their experience, looking at cats in a new light after encountering the poem's imagery. Valerie Worth's "Cat," from *Small Poems* (1986), elicits similar reactions, such as the following response written by a second grader:

> I like this poem because it makes me feel like I am a cat that is bathing myself. When I watch my cat take her bath, her leg is locked high at her back [referring to Worth's description]. When my cat is done, her tongue is still out between lip and lip [again she paraphrases Worth's language]. It has a lot of feeling because it makes me think I am a cat [who] likes to bathe myself.

Reading other cat poems like those in Arnold Lobel's *Whiskers and Rhymes* (1985, N) and Nancy Larrick's *Cats Are Cats* (1988) can further expand children's ideas and perceptions. But any topic in which children have an interest can serve as a focus for such sessions.

Teachers should be careful not to leave children with the notion that there is one "correct" interpretation of a poem. Research probing children's attitudes toward poetry reveals that the most frequent explanation for negative attitudes is teacher insistence on analysis and interpretation (Painter 1970; Verble 1973). Yet we should not go too far in eliminating all thoughtful probing of poetry. Sometimes in our well-intended desire to let children just enjoy poetry, we fail to help them discover why a poem appeals to them. We have all had poetry just read aloud to us, and although we may have enjoyed the lilt and flow of the words, we probably rarely experienced the joy of discovering the reason for our delight. Understanding can deepen enjoyment. Teachers are depriving children if they do not show them how to uncover the subtle nuances of meaning and the ways in which poets shape language to convey those meanings. Teachers need to take a middle road—encouraging children to explore, question, play with words, and repeat phrases they find particularly pleasing. Heard (1989) calls this "making joy," a perfect term to describe how teachers and children should view the reading of poetry.

Enjoyment will not come instantly, however. Children used to the instant gratification of cartoons and half-hour situation comedies are more attuned to light, humorous Silverstein verses than thoughtful pieces. A teacher does not usually get immediate positive feedback when reading more complex poetry like that written by Eve Merriam, Langston Hughes, or Myra Cohn Livingston. However, children who are continually exposed to good poetry and who are encouraged to explore how words are organized into pleasing alliterative phrases or how one thing is compared to something unexpected eventually tire of Silverstein and other poets like him.

Most importantly, class discussions about poetry show children how to think about poetry. Many children are unfamiliar with what can be said in these discussions and usually fall back on phrases like "It's funny" or "It's good" or "It's kind of boring" because they lack a repertoire of words to use. They need experience with the kinds of comments people make about poetry (and literature in general) and how discussions evolve. When teachers lead these conversations, they model the questioning and discussion behaviors they hope children will acquire. Eventually, as children gain competence and confidence, they can be expected to take an increasingly active role in these discussions.

Helping Children Appreciate the Language of Poetry

Teachers are often unsure of the specific focus of these sessions. Initially, it is helpful to students to point out interesting or well-selected words. Fifth-grade teacher Judy Markham did this when she read aloud Myra Cohn Livingston's "Remembering," in *Remembering, and Other Poems* (1989), and Harry Behn's "The Seashell," in *Crickets and Bullfrogs and Whispers of Thunder*, compiled by Lee Bennett Hopkins (1984), as part of a literature unit on selkies, mermaids, and other literary sea creatures.

"How many of you have been to the beach where there were seashells?" she asked the group. "Do you remember what it felt like? What words does Livingston use to describe the experience?"

"I like how she calls them 'the ocean's bones.' That's a different way to say it," observed one child.

Markham held up a shell from her own collection. "When I saw this this summer, it looked like a bone to me," referring to Livingston's comparison of a shell to a bone. She then probed for further response. "How is this poem descriptive? How else does she describe the shells?"

"I liked the part where she talks about tiny black rocks caught in snails . . . hundreds of snails," said another child.

"When you think of the beach, what do you experience with your senses? . . . What are some words that describe what you feel?"

The group eagerly offered ideas: "hot," "crunching under my feet," "tangy air," "seagulls swooping and chasing each other." They then went on to compare their responses to the words Livingston used in her poem, marveling at how appropriately she described the beach.

These students had a similar discussion after reading Eve Merriam's "Autumn Leaves" (1984) and were amazed at all the ways she described leaves: "tumbledown leaves," "butterfly leaves," "sailboat leaves," and "windstorm leaves." When sharing Carl Sandburg's "Bubbles" (in Hopkins 1982), they talked about how "flickered out" was such an unusual way to describe a bubble bursting and how his reference to bubbles having "rainbows on their curves" was a unique comparison. Afterward a child commented, "I liked this poem . . . the words show you that something special can happen in only thirty seconds."

Sometimes it is helpful to encourage children to focus on a specific technique a poet uses to heighten the impact of the words. Judy Markham did this when she read aloud Langston Hughes's "April Rain Song," in *Piping down the Valleys Wild: Poetry for the Young of All Ages*, compiled by Nancy Larrick (1968). As the discussion evolved, one child commented that the poem repeated. Markham seized that opportunity to follow up on this commonly used poetic technique.

"What repeats?" she asked.

"He repeats the same word in the first three lines and the same word in the last three lines," responded Katie.

"Why do you think he did that?" Markham asked, probing for more depth of response. After much discussion, the group decided this gave more of a feel of the rain and how the sound of raindrops repeats over and over.

It is also helpful to explain the meanings of words that are not part of the children's vocabulary. When third/fourth-grade teacher Frank Hatcher read "Kaleidoscope" from Myra Cohn Livingston's *Space Songs* (1988, N), he asked his class to define the word *kaleidoscope*, realizing they would miss the sense of the poem if they had no concept of this word. Similarly, when reading aloud "Water Striders" from Paul Fleischman's *Joyful Noise: Poems for Two Voices* (1988, N), the group discussed what kind of bugs these were and their personal experiences with bugs in watery locales.

Additionally, teachers can point out how poets use words in unusual ways. Instead of saying, "Anna walked through the grass" in *Wild Wild Sunflower Child Anna* (1987, N), Nancy White Carlstrom writes:

> Skipping through
> the snaggle bush,
> slipping in her tangle rush.
> Burr babies riding
> on her shoulders,
> burr babies sleeping
> in her hair. (Unpaged, p. 14)

And instead of saying, "Anna rolls down the hill," she describes the experience as

> Flying in the field
> in the greening
> of the morning.
> Anna drifts,
> Anna glides,
> Anna's arms open wide
> for the sun rolling
> sky falling. (Unpaged, p. 8)

Deborah Chandra gives a unique voice to leaves as she describes how they are

> Grieving for summer
> With gasps and sighs,
> Crackling
> And crunching,
> They call their
> Goodbyes! (P. 25)

in the poem "Autumn" in her eloquent collection, *Balloons, and Other Poems* (1990, N). Poets work hard choosing the right words for a poem—original words that evoke a vivid image, precise words that describe exactly how something is, words that sound just right. This is what we want children to begin to understand and appreciate.

Making word banks or charts when reading poetry is another good way to get children focused on the words and how poets use words uniquely. Children can collect and categorize words that are unusual or that sparkle, phrases that compare one thing with another, or interesting metaphorical images. Becoming a collector of words makes children more appreciative of the monumental work poets go through to discover just the right words for a poem. One teacher made a "Sounds Like Poetry" sign for a section of her chalkboard to record the imagery she heard in her students' everyday talk. Soon they began contributing to the board themselves, bringing in bits of conversation that linked their language to the language of poetry (Lenz 1992).

Soon children become attuned not only to the language of poetry but also to the voice of individual poets, particularly their favorites. "I can tell this one's by Valerie Worth" or "That sounds like Adoff" are comments teachers begin hearing as children gain experience with poetry and are able to make connections between poems on the basis of voice and style.

Making Poetic Language Come Alive

Reading poetry aloud followed by discussion or other language activities is not the only way to help children appreciate the language of poetry. Choral reading is an activity which also fosters more thoughtful, informed responses. As the group reads and rereads a poem, students make decisions about how to perform it based on the words and meaning. Does it call for a question/answer format? a solo voice followed by the group in unison? Where are the loud and soft parts? What actions should be added? As students make these decisions, they pay close attention to the poem's language—how the words communicate certain ideas, images, and feelings and how pitch and pacing can add to a poem's effect. Sometimes a teacher will give the same poem to different groups and have each group create a choral reading to present to the others. Later, students can compare the differing interpretations, discussing how each group reacted differently to the poem's words and images.

Second-grade teacher Joan Smith often turns choral reading into a Readers Theatre performance. She reads many poems aloud and encourages her students to act them out. Students pick their favorites, and Smith combines these with poems the children write themselves in a choreographed program which the children present to their parents. Some of the poems are done in unison, sometimes one child recites a repeating line while the others join in on verses, or partners take turns on alternating lines. The children decide on the program format, based on their reaction to each poem and its language. Making these decisions clarifies and deepens their appreciation of how poets use language. Smith's colleague Janet Carlson, who teaches a third/fourth-grade class for gifted children, asks her students to work on a poem in pairs, listening to the language and then deciding how to act it out, what props to use, and how it should be presented.

Students in the class of second-grade teacher Lisa Lenz (1992) use highlighter pens to mark their own copies of poems—what they notice about the wording, what they feel should be emphasized, how the lines should be broken up so as to best convey the meaning. They then help each other prepare their "poetry performances," working on different ways to emphasize the words or break up the lines to convey the ideas. These activities help children return to the heart of a poem, rediscovering what initially attracted them to it. Peers act as sounding boards, providing helpful feedback on how to change one's voice or where to add gestures for emphasis. Videotaping the final performances can be a powerful way to help children under-stand how others react to the meaning of a poem.

Another way to help students examine the language of poetry more closely is to have them do author studies. Judy Markham helps her students create a Poet Fair as a way to focus and intensify their work with poetry. Children each select a poet to study in depth. They read all that poet's works, write publishers for biographical data, and scour reference books for information about their chosen person. They then create a fair booth (out of a washing machine box) "advertising" each poet's work. Some students display favorite quotes or poems on posterboard. Others wear T-shirts hand-printed with poems and information about the poets, bring in props (such as a cake with a rose on it for Karla Kuskin's *A Rose on My Cake* (1964), display books, and create bookmarks containing quotes from their favorite poems. Some become the poet and answer questions as they think that person would, while others come as a character from a particular work by that poet. Everyone who visits the fair must pay the price of admission: one poem which they have either collected or written.

Children can also be encouraged to keep observation note-books in which they record what they notice in the world around them. They can then go back and underline words and phrases that seem to speak poetically. This encourages children to connect poetry to their lives, using its language to help them examine their lives from a new perspective. They can also use their journals to collect their favorite poems and to respond to poetry they read or hear: what grabs them, remembered phrases or lines that stay in their minds, favorite images, and the like. Or they can record their own ideas for writing—snippets of phrases, interesting words, compari-sons that come to mind in the course of a day. This helps them get into the voice of a poet, discovering poetic language for themselves.

As teachers do more and more of these activities, they discover that children begin sharing poetry spontaneously with each other. They trade poems they like, seek out new poems by poets whose work they have come to enjoy, find poems on special topics or areas of interest, or just have a good time with a friend—with poetry as the focus.

Helping Children Make Poetic Language Their Own

Once children have been exposed to many examples of good poetry, they can experiment with their growing awareness of poetic language by trying it out for themselves. This experimentation with writing, in turn, usually makes them more appreciative of the crafting involved in the poetry they read (McClure, Harrison, and Reed 1990).

Teachers can help by urging children to experiment with the words they want to use in their own poems. Heard (1989) compares words to geodes: "rough and ordinary on the outside, hiding a whole world of sparkling beauty inside." Poets work diligently to find that beauty, experimenting with many combinations of words to describe the gentle tapping of the rain on the window or how a train whistle sounds in the middle of the night. They try to convey experience through language that is concrete and visual. Children need to focus just as intently on the language of their own poems.

One way teachers can help is to ask children to circle the common words in their poems that have grown stale from overuse, words like *pretty, nice, beautiful,* and *fun.* Teachers can encourage children to brainstorm alternatives and then experiment with the different combinations of words generated. Older children can use a thesaurus to help them find different, more descriptive words. Younger children can ask friends to help, or they can try to envision an idea or experience in their minds and then describe this picture as precisely as possible.

Fifth/sixth-grade teacher Peg Reed is particularly skilled at helping children experiment with words in their poetry. In the following incident she helped Johnny work on his poem about time:

> "What's the main thing you're trying to get across to people, Johnny, when they read your poem?"
>
> "To tell what happens with time?" he responded.
>
> "What about using some figurative language here . . . a metaphor, or simile . . . . What might you do with something like that? What else changes with time?" Peg's voice trailed off as she waited for Johnny to think.
>
> "Days change with time," he tentatively ventured.
>
> "Okay . . . days change to what?" Peg asked again.
>
> "Weeks," answered Johnny.
>
> "All right," said Peg, "Days do *what* into weeks? People change with time and days do *what* into weeks?" She seemed to be trying to get Johnny to think divergently and consider unusual ways to describe change.
>
> "They *grow* into weeks?" he offered.
>
> "They *form* into weeks?" suggested Stacie.
>
> "That's a good idea, Stacie," said Peg. "Listen, though, he had an interesting one."
>
> Johnny read aloud:

People change with time.
Like days grow into weeks.

"What do you think?" Peg asked him. "That's a good comparison because humans grow and days grow and change too. I like what you have so far."

Peg moved on to other children. Johnny, in contrast to his previous tentativeness, seemed confident and motivated as he vigorously scribbled ideas, experimenting with various words and meanings. Several days later Johnny once again brought his poem to Peg. She was amazed by what he had created but sensed he wasn't done yet.

"What else do you want to talk about?" she prodded. "Where are *you* in all this?"

"I am now," answered Johnny. "Hey, that sounds good. I'm gonna write it." The revised poem read as follows:

Time

People change with time
Like days grow into weeks
The past is grandfather to the future
And I am now.

(McClure, Harrison, and Reed 1990)

Conclusion

James Britton (1982) states that poetry must be read and reread before it becomes understandable and "owned" by the reader. This is our goal when sharing poetry with children. Reading, rereading, savoring the feel of the words in your mouth and on your tongue, and then sharing these delights with each other will surely create lovers of poetry who see poetic language as a distinct way to view the beauty and uniqueness of our world.

References
Professional Resources

Britton, J. 1982. "Reading and Writing Poetry." In *Prospect and Retrospect: Selected Essays of James Britton,* edited by Gordon Pradl. Montclair, NJ: Boynton/Cook.

Heard, G. 1989. *For the Good of the Earth and Sun: Teaching Poetry.* Portsmouth, NH: Heinemann.

Lenz, L. 1992. "Crossroads of Literacy and Orality: Reading Poetry Aloud." *Language Arts* 69:597–603.

McClure, A., P. Harrison, and S. Reed. 1990. *Sunrises and Songs: Reading and Writing Poetry in an Elementary Classroom.* Portsmouth, NH: Heinemann.

Painter, H. 1970. *Poetry and Children.* Newark, DE: International Reading Association.

Verble, D. 1973. *A Road Not Taken: An Approach to Teaching Poetry.* Nashville: Tennessee Arts Commission, sponsored by the National Endowment for the Arts.

Zitlow, C. 1992. "Getting inside a Story with Poetry Links." Paper presented at the Spring Conference of the National Council of Teachers of English, Washington, DC.

Children's Literature

Adoff, Arnold. 1976. *Tornado!* Illustrated by Ronald Himler. New York: Delacorte Press.

Babbitt, Natalie. 1975. *Tuck Everlasting.* New York: Farrar, Straus and Giroux.

Burnett, Frances Hodgson. 1962. *The Secret Garden.* Illustrated by Tasha Tudor. New York: J. B. Lippincott.

Carson, Jo. 1989. *Stories I Ain't Told Nobody Yet.* New York: Orchard Books, 1989.

Dunning, Stephen, Edward Lueders, and Hugh Smith, eds. 1966. *Reflections on a Gift of Watermelon Pickle, and Other Modern Verse.* Glenview, IL: Scott, Foresman.

Ferris, Helen, comp. 1957. *Favorite Poems Old and New.* New York: Doubleday.

Fisher, Aileen. 1971. *Feathered Ones and Furry.* New York: Thomas Y. Crowell.

Hopkins, Lee Bennett, comp. 1982. *Rainbows Are Made: Poems by Carl Sandburg.* San Diego: Harcourt Brace Jovanovich.

———. 1984. *Crickets and Bullfrogs and Whispers of Thunder.* San Diego: Harcourt Brace Jovanovich.

Kuskin, Karla. 1964. *A Rose on My Cake.* New York: Harper and Row.

Larrick, Nancy. 1988. *Cats Are Cats.* Illustrated by Ed Young. New York: Philomel Books.

Larrick, Nancy, comp. 1968. *Piping down the Valleys Wild: Poetry for the Young of All Ages.* New York: Dell.

Livingston, Myra Cohn. 1984. *Sky Songs.* Illustrated by Leonard Everett Fisher. New York: Holiday House.

———. 1989. *Remembering, and Other Poems.* New York: Macmillan.

Merriam, Eve. 1964. *It Doesn't Always Have to Rhyme.* New York: Atheneum.

———. 1984. *Jamboree: Rhymes for All Times.* Illustrated by Walter Gaffney-Kessell. New York: Dell.

See the Bibliography of Notable Books at the end of the book for bibliographic information about cited Notable Books. The Notable titles do not appear in this reference list.

Ryder, Joanne. 1989. *Mockingbird Morning*. Illustrated by Dennis Nolan. New York: Macmillan.

Silverstein, Shel. 1974. *Where the Sidewalk Ends*. New York: Harper and Row.

———. 1981. *A Light in the Attic*. New York: Harper and Row.

Stevenson, Burton E., comp. 1950. *Home Book of Modern Verse*. New York: Henry Holt.

Worth, Valerie. 1972. *Small Poems*. Illustrated by Natalie Babbitt. New York: Farrar, Straus and Giroux.

3 | The Language of Facts: Using Nonfiction Books to Support Language Growth

Sylvia M. Vardell
University of Texas at Arlington

Good stories cause us to ponder and reflect, sharing our responses, turning them over in our minds. Good nonfiction books can have that same power. Take a look at the 1992 winner of the NCTE Orbis Pictus Award for Outstanding Nonfiction for Children, *Flight: The Journey of Charles Lindbergh* by Robert Burleigh. It is based on Lindbergh's own journal account of his amazing 33½-hour solo airplane trip from New York to Paris, and it is riveting reading:

> To sleep is to die!
> These are some of the things he does to stay awake:
> He leans his face near the open window to feel the cold air.
> He holds his eyelids up with his fingers to keep them from closing.
> He remembers growing up on a farm in Minnesota.
> He remembers being a trick pilot, and walking out on a plane's wings.
> He remembers the people in St. Louis who paid for this plane.
> Sometimes he takes a sip of water from his canteen.
> He also has five chicken sandwiches with him. That is all the food he has brought.
> But he eats nothing. It is easier to stay awake on an empty stomach.
> (P. 16–17)

Thanks to Meena Khorana, University of Indiana, and to the following Texas teachers who shared their insights: Sue Abar, grade three, Grand Prairie ISD; Ann Fiala, Chapter I, Victoria ISD; Julie Fulps, grade six, Arlington ISD; Hank Hoaldridge, grade five, Fort Worth ISD; Debra Selby Long, kindergarten, Victoria ISD; Gloria Nordeen, grade five, El Campo ISD; Jennifer Smithers, grade five, Irving ISD; Stephannie Waller, grade one, Arlington ISD.

Flight is illustrated with expansive, expressive paintings by Mike Wimmer which perfectly capture the scenery and the emotions of this *true* story. The best nonfiction for children is interesting, lively, relevant, and appealing. What's more, the factual content of such nonfiction books is a perfect springboard for supporting language growth.

Through reading, reading aloud, listening to, and talking about nonfiction books, children can raise questions and share impressions in an active processing of new information. As many researchers have noted, such talk is an essential way of learning for children (Cazden 1988; Golub 1988). As children verbalize their thinking, they realize *what* they are thinking. For nonfiction, this oral dynamic is particularly important since children are often encountering brand-new information in the text of an informational book. As they try to assimilate this knowledge, talking about it helps them sort out their thoughts. Hearing the responses and questions of their peers assists them in confirming or expanding their own interpretations. Nonfiction offers the additional advantage of making subject-matter learning more accessible through talking about current books. If students are studying volcanoes, for example, a reading and discussion of the Notable book *Pompeii: Exploring a Roman Ghost Town* by Ron and Nancy Goor (1986, N) will add a human dimension to the usual textbook treatment. Students will surely be drawn to talk about the daily life of Pompeii as it was immortalized by the eruption of Vesuvius. Then teachers can share Patricia Lauber's Newbery Honor Book *Volcano: The Eruption and Healing of Mount St. Helens* (1986) and can help students make connections with contemporary times, comparing Pompeii and the Washington site. Kathryn Lasky's *Surtsey: The Newest Place on Earth* (1992, N) adds yet another perspective on the creative force of volcanoes. Such discussions are excellent opportunities for critical thinking and the language associated with it.

Heath (1983) advocates talk as an essential part of the language arts curriculum in all content areas. Klein (1979) argues that "talk opportunities" should be consciously built into all aspects of the curriculum so that children gain experience using talk for many different purposes and in many different contexts. The nonfiction books from the Notables list provide just such entry points. They offer an excellent sampling of the newest and best that the genre has to offer. From wordless books to alphabet books, concept books to factual resource books, and biographies to books about language itself, the nonfiction Notables can be used across the curriculum to stimulate children's talk and exploration about words, people, and the world around them.

Nonfiction Notables

The nonfiction books which have been selected for the Notable Children's Trade Books lists over the years reflect both the outstanding quality and amazing variety now available within this genre. They meet the highest standards for literary quality: accuracy, organization, design, and style. They cover a wide range of topics from natural history (birds, ecology, dinosaurs) to language itself (words, symbols, writing tips for kids). Nonfiction especially lends itself to application across the grades because its content is valuable whenever the particular topic arises. The simple language of a nonfiction picture book is helpful when new and unfamiliar information is presented to older readers. When the topic is relevant and interesting, younger children can enjoy the excellent illustrations and selected excerpts from informational books which are longer and more difficult than these children might be able to read independently. The following examples show just how this can happen—how nonfiction books both enrich the curriculum content and stimulate language growth.

Criteria for Selecting Nonfiction Read-Alouds

One of the easiest places to incorporate good nonfiction books, but also one of the most overlooked, is reading aloud. Many teachers read good books aloud to their students as a way to expose their students to more literature. Yet, fiction tends to dominate most read-aloud selection lists. Indeed, not all informational books lend themselves to being read aloud. (But neither do all fiction books!) Many nonfiction books, however, captivate listeners and offer interesting information to learn about as well. Such books can supplement subject-matter study in the content areas, providing an introduction to new vocabulary in a relevant context. Reading aloud nonfiction also provides exposure to another mode of writing, as well as an opportunity to teach about the craft of writing.

An interesting and lively style of writing is the first criterion when selecting quality nonfiction books to read aloud. Consider, for example, the first sentences of *Is This a House for Hermit Crab?* by Megan McDonald (1990, N):

> Hermit Crab was forever growing too big for the house on his back.
> It was time to find a new house. He crawled up out of the water looking for something to hide in, where he would be safe from the pricklepine fish.
> He stepped along the shore, by the sea, in the sand . . . *scritch-scratch, scritch-scratch. . . .* (Pp. 7–9)

Downs Matthews's *Polar Bear Cubs* (1989) also shares factual information in prose full of imagery. Note the book's conclusion:

By the time they are two years old, polar bear cubs can live alone in the Arctic. Their mother has taught them how to walk over snow and ice and swim in the cold water. They know how to make a bed in the snow and keep warm during the winter storms, and they have learned the ways of seals and how to hunt for them. They know how to wash after eating and keep themselves clean. It is time for them to leave their mother and go their separate ways. (Unpaged, p. 22)

Also of critical importance is the accuracy and currency of information in a nonfiction book. Patricia Lauber's *The News about Dinosaurs* (1989, N) is an excellent model of this. In fact, as she contrasts new discoveries about dinosaurs with previous erroneous suppositions, she concludes:

THE NEWS IS:

Scientists will be finding new dinosaurs and learning about dinosaur lives for years to come. And when they do, their discoveries will be reported in the news. (P. 47)

Another example, Sally Ride and Susan Okie's *To Space and Back* (1986), relates firsthand experiences of Ride's space shuttle travels and reproduces NASA photographs to offer the most up-to-date information possible:

I start each day on the space shuttle just as I do on Earth: I wash my face, brush my teeth, comb my hair, and use the toilet. In space my usual way of doing all these things is different because water, toothpaste, hair, and body wastes are weightless. (P. 48)

If a nonfiction book is well organized, it also enables readers to quickly grasp the overall focus of the book as well as what specific information is shared about the topic. A clear organizational scheme also allows a teacher to choose only the most relevant portions to read aloud at appropriate times. For example, one might share only the lunch-time rituals of Louis XIV's routine in Aliki's *The King's Day* (1989, N):

The King had dinner—his *Petit Couvert*—at one o'clock.
When he dined in private, he ate alone—
    but he was never really alone.
Servants, and perhaps a guest or two,
    stood around and waited and watched. (Unpaged, p. 20)

The menu might be four soups, a stuffed pheasant,
    a partridge, a duck, some mutton, sliced ham, three salads,
    boiled eggs, a dish of pastry, fruit, and compotes. (P. 23)

Many works by Russell Freedman also have a clear organizational layout. Chapter headings offer subtopics for reading aloud, such as "Buffalo Magic," "The Hunt," and "From the Brains to the Tail" in Freedman's *Buffalo Hunt* (1988); "Frontier Schools" and

"Games, Parties, and Celebrations" in his *Children of the Wild West* (1983); and "At Home," "At School," "At Work," and "At Play" in his *Immigrant Kids* (1980). Teachers could easily select a particular section to share, based on the interests of the class.

For reading aloud to a large group or the whole class, it is another plus if a nonfiction book is visually stimulating and well designed. The colorful renderings of birds (to actual scale) in Lois Ehlert's *Feathers for Lunch* (1990, N) is one outstanding example. Francine Patterson's *Koko's Kitten* (1985) is another, with its many full-page color photographs featuring close-up scenes of Koko the gorilla and her pet cat. The paintings of Kenneth Lily add visual excitement to Joanna Cole's *Large as Life* (1985) books about animals—*Large as Life: Daytime Animals Life Size* (1985), *Large as Life: Nighttime Animals Life Size* (1985), and *Large as Life: Animals in Beautiful Life-Size Paintings* (1990). Colorful illustrations or powerful photographs quickly capture students' attention, and in a nonfiction book they offer information as well as aesthetic appeal.

At the intermediate grades, some nonfiction books, like novels, can even be read aloud in increments over an extended period. Bill Peet's autobiography, *Bill Peet* (1989), is one excellent example of a book that could be used for this purpose. In fact, biographies and autobiographies often work particularly well since they are human stories which are given a real voice through reading aloud.

Students can also offer their favorite books on subjects of particular interest to them. With minimal preparation, they can even be the readers themselves. It is perfectly acceptable to share only *parts* of a book, choosing select excerpts to read aloud.

Nonfiction books offer a literary experience during read-aloud time equal to any good work of fiction. In addition, as students hear good examples of nonfiction read aloud, they become more comfortable reading these books silently on their own, and it is easier for them to create their own expository texts because they have models upon which to build. As students listen to quality nonfiction, they can also be exposed to topics, vocabulary, and ideas that challenge them, going well beyond what they might choose to read on their own. Many students will pick up one of these nonfiction books, even if it is supposedly "too difficult," because the topic interests them. Some children are even drawn into reading for pleasure through nonfiction, despite previous reluctance to pursue fiction reading.

Examples of Nonfiction Read-Alouds

There are many different ways to share nonfiction orally in the classroom, from choosing books that supplement the curriculum to investigating world records and true-to-life trivia (Vardell and Copeland 1992). One kindergarten teacher read aloud Seymour Simon's *Whales* (1989) to share some of the author's vivid descriptions of the different kinds of whales while displaying the excellent photographs Simon has gleaned from scientific sources. One particular passage generated intense interest:

> The humpback whale is longer than a big bus and heavier than a trailer truck. Some great whales are even larger. Just the tongue of a blue whale weighs as much as an elephant. (Unpaged, p. 6)

The teacher built on student interest by leading a focused discussion on the topic; she used the K-W-L strategy (Ogle 1986) to talk about and list collaboratively with the students what they already *k*new about whales and what they *w*anted to know; then they added additional information about what they *l*earned as they went along.

For shared reading in other primary classrooms, some teachers created their own "big book" versions or giant-sized extensions of nonfiction books to supplement their assortment of fiction titles (e.g., *Fish Eyes* (1990), *Red Leaf, Yellow Leaf* (1991, N), and others by Lois Ehlert). Using Bruce McMillan's *Eating Fractions* (1991), for example, students paired up to produce poster-sized pages featuring giant drawings of their favorite foods, subdivided into fractional parts. They even wrote the recipes, cooked the dishes, and ate the foods as the children do in the McMillan text. Though this is primarily a drawing, writing, and reasoning activity, the children read these books aloud independently after responding to the text.

Other teachers encourage students to create their own "innovations" or extensions of favorite informational picture books, either individually or as a class collaboration. One third-grade teacher asked her students to try their own variations of favorite titles, with each student creating a page following the book's pattern; then they combined all their pages into a class book. One of the most popular books they produced in this manner was modeled after Margaret Wise Brown's *The Important Book* (1949):

> The important thing
> about a spoon is
> that you eat with it.
> It's like a little shovel,
> You hold it in your hand,
> You can put it in your mouth,
> It isn't flat,
> It's hollow,
> And it spoons things up.
> But the important thing
> about a spoon is
> that you eat with it. (Unpaged, p. 3)

Here Are My Hands (1987) and other books by Bill Martin Jr., as well as Eric Carle's *The Very Hungry Caterpillar* (1969), *The Very Busy Spider* (1984), and *The Very Quiet Cricket* (1990), are other favorite texts which weave factual information into a story frame and which could be used as the basis for text innovations.

At the intermediate grades, even more experimentation in oral reading is possible. Students might enjoy connecting information from a variety of sources. For example, Robert Burleigh's true story *Flight* (1991) is an excellent cover-to-cover read-aloud which can lead students to further reading and research on aviation history and to a longer book, *The Wright Brothers* by Russell Freedman (1991), from which they can share excerpts orally.

In another example, students could first read aloud the description of Inuit beliefs of the Nativity in Normee Ekoomiak's *Arctic Memories* (1990, N). They could also consider the historical information about the evolution of Christmas in James Cross Giblin's *The Truth about Santa Claus* (1985):

> Life in New Amsterdam changed drastically when the British, who were at war with the Dutch, seized the city in 1664 and renamed it New York. The new British residents celebrated Christmas instead of St. Nicholas Day, and told their children that Father Christmas, not St. Nicholas, brought them gifts on Christmas Eve. Descendants of the original Dutch settlers preserved many of their traditions, however, and Dutch children continued to believe in St. Nicholas— or *Sinter Claes,* as they called him for short.
>
> As the years passed, and the British and Dutch colonists intermarried, Sinter Claes and Father Christmas gradually became blended into a single gift-bringer. By the end of the Revolutionary War in 1783, he had acquired a new, American name: Santa Claus. (P. 41)

A discussion could evolve in which students compared these contrasting beliefs and customs.

A sixth-grade teacher even connected reading aloud with using media. She shared Jean Craighead George's *One Day in the Tropical Rain Forest* (1990) while she played an audiocassette of jungle sound effects in the background. The following passage describes a three-toed sloth hanging on the underside of a branch of a cashew tree, with a fuzzy baby clinging to her chest and other "residents" as well:

> The mother was an apartment house. In her long fur lived not only plants but some ninety little creatures. Among the tenants were pretty sloth moths, glossy beetles, and numerous pink or white mites. None could survive anywhere but on a sloth in a tropical rain

forest. They were stirring. This was a big day for the tenants. The sloth was going to make her weekly trip to the floor of the forest, and they, of course, were going with her. (P. 7)

The combination of intriguing information, highly descriptive language, and realistic sound effects made the experience of hearing this book something the students would not forget.

Through listening to quality nonfiction being read aloud, students can learn new information that will enrich not only their literary background but their content-area knowledge base as well. From Ehlert's *Feathers for Lunch* (1990, N), students can quite naturally learn bird names, such as the American robin, blue jay, northern cardinal, house wren, red-headed woodpecker, northern oriole, and the mourning dove. They may even absorb a few French terms, such as *lever* (the getting-up ceremony), *grand couvert* (supper), or *coucher* (the going-to-bed ceremony), in addition to historical information about the "Sun King," by listening to Aliki's *The King's Day* (1989, N). Teachers can encourage students to experience books and information they might not tackle on their own while they supplement the textbook treatment of a topic. A follow-up discussion of new ideas and vocabulary encountered in the context of a well-written book makes the information even more real and relevant to students, rather than merely rote.

Readers Theatre

One intriguing way to involve students in the process of reading literature aloud is through using nonfiction books as the text for Readers Theatre adaptations (Young and Vardell 1993). Once the students are somewhat familiar with a book or topic, they can take the text of a good nonfiction book and turn it into a kind of script. They then read the parts from their usual seats without memorizing their lines or using costumes or props to perform. For their first experience or for younger readers, the teacher can develop the script, but the scripting process itself is also an excellent language-learning activity for students. With abundant dialogue in speech balloons, Joanna Cole's Magic School Bus books work especially well for initial experiences with Readers Theatre. In *The Magic School Bus Lost in the Solar System* (1990, N), the following "script" is a typical one that can quickly emerge:

> *Narrator:* As usual, it took a while to get the old bus started. But finally we were on our way. As we were driving, Ms. Frizzle told us all about how the Earth spins like a top as it moves in its orbit. It was just a short drive to the planetarium, but Ms. Frizzle talked fast.
>
> *Boy 1:* This bus is a wreck.

Girl 1: At least it started this time.

Janet, Arnold's cousin: We have *new* school buses at our school.

Ms. Frizzle: When the earth spins we say it *rotates.* The earth makes one complete rotation—turn—every 24 hours. (Unpaged, p. 7)

Joan Anderson's photo-essay books—*Christmas on the Prairie* (1985, N), *The First Thanksgiving Feast* (1984), and others—also offer nearly "ready-made" scripts filled with language of the people of the times. In *Christmas on the Prairie,* a living history museum near Noblesville, Indiana, is the setting for a Christmas celebration set in 1836:

> "We brought you some special cookies," Mother said, placing them on the table.
> "Well, thank you," the Widow exclaimed, pleased by the thought-ful gesture. She looked at Edward and Jenny. "It don't seem long since my young'ns were your age. My late husband Jacob used to play Belznickel on Christmas Eve. Have you ever heard of Belz?"
> "No," Jenny said, her eyes all round and curious.
> "Well," the widow began, "he was an old man, dressed in odd clothes, who came banging at the door. My young'ns were always frightened so they hid behind my skirts. Once inside, Belznickel would ask: 'Have the children been good this year?'"
> "Before I could answer, he would pull out a big stick in order to spank them," the widow continued. "I would quickly answer yes and he would promptly drop the stick, reach into his pockets, and throw love cookies and nuts about. As the young'ns scampered to collect the goodies, Belz would disappear." (Unpaged, p. 29)

Many other nonfiction books—such as Gail Gibbons's *Fire! Fire!* (1984, N), Kathryn Lasky's *Sugaring Time* (1983, N), Jean Craighead George's *One Day in the Alpine Tundra* (1984, N), and Joan Lowery Nixon's *If You Were a Writer* (1988, N)—also easily lend themselves to Readers Theatre adaptation. Take the book *If You Were a Writer,* for example. Students can use the dialogue already present and assign it to Melia, Mother, Uncle John, and other characters described in the book. Other expository passages can be assigned to a narrator, even several narrators. These portions can also be short-ened or omitted to maintain the pace.

Melia: She's under a spell.

Mother: It's not a bad kind of spell. It's just called "thinking of what to write next."

Melia: When do you get out of the spell?

Mother: When the right words come.

Melia: How do you know what they are?

Mother: If you were a writer, you'd know. You'd feel them inside you, and you'd know they were right.

Narrator: Melia went outside. She climbed into the branches of the oak tree, and watched afternoon melt into evening, and tried the feel of words. She saw a flash of gold streak through an orange sunset . . .

Melia: . . . glittering and glowing. (Based on the text on pp. 9–11, unpaged)

In this participatory reading activity, the text comes alive. The content is more lively and personal, the oral reading active and expressive. It's also a motivating way for students to absorb new information from a work of nonfiction.

Critical Thinking and Language Use: Linking Nonfiction and Fiction

To initiate a lesson involving critical thinking, a sixth-grade teacher attached two hula hoops to the chalkboard. She then led the students in a discussion of the unique aspects of Gary Paulsen's fiction which they had been reading, including *The Island* (1988, N), *The Winter Room* (1991, N), *Hatchet* (1987, N) and *Dogsong* (1985). She listed attributes of these novels in one portion of the Venn diagram created by the hula hoops: nature settings, survival themes, often a lone protagonist, suspenseful, and distinctively short and sometimes incomplete sentences. The class then focused on the unique qualities of Paulsen's autobiographical *Woodsong* (1990, N), putting these traits on the other side of the diagram: conflict with nature, author as character, survival, distinctively short and sometimes incomplete sentences. This exercise helped the students visualize the overlapping information and think critically about how much of Paulsen's fiction is based on his own life experiences and personal point of view. As they linked his fiction with his autobiography, students saw how the nonfiction work also reflects the author's distinctive voice and style of writing.

Linking fiction and nonfiction is an excellent way to involve students in critical thinking, as they consider questions such as the following:

How do fiction and nonfiction authors use facts?

What kinds of research do fiction authors conduct?

Do nonfiction authors have a distinctive style of writing?

How do they hook the reader?

Students involved in learning more about their favorite writers through author studies or a featured "author of the week" can particularly benefit from this activity. Many prominent authors have written both factual and fictional books. Can students recognize what makes these authors' particular style distinctive across genres? Students may want to research their favorite nonfiction authors, using professional reference sources such as the *Junior Book of Authors* or by writing the publishers or even the authors themselves.

Through listening to several works by one author read aloud over time, students often come to notice particular attributes which mark the author's style. Students who gather regularly in response groups can also focus on multiple works by one author. Each group member might read a different Gary Paulsen book, for example, and then the students could gather to discuss commonalities and differences. In contrasting the books by authors who write both fiction and nonfiction works, students can begin to see both genres more clearly and to recognize how writers bring their own personalities to whatever they write. Students may well find that Paulsen's use of language and sentence patterning is particularly distinctive.

Other authors who have written both fiction and nonfiction works also demonstrate distinctive qualities which children can recognize and discuss. Joanna Cole's humor is one of her trademarks both in her nonfiction Magic School Bus series and in many of her fiction titles, such as *The Missing Tooth* (1989), *Mixed-Up Magic* (1987), and *Norma Jean, Jumping Bean* (1987). As both author and illustrator, Aliki often experiments with book design and format in her works, using hand lettering, cartoon panels, and even captions in *How a Book Is Made* (1986, N), *The King's Day* (1989, N), and *Feelings* (1984), among others. And author Jean Craighead George is known for her particular passion for nature and wildlife, demonstrated beautifully in such nonfiction titles as *One Day in the Alpine Tundra* (1984, N), *One Day in the Tropical Rain Forest* (1990), and other "One Day" books, and fiction titles for the intermediate grades such as *Julie of the Wolves* (1972) and *My Side of the Mountain* (1959).

Students who are led to think critically about literature through listening, reading, and responding orally to multiple works of one author can bring a deeper understanding to their own writing efforts. Linking the nonfiction and fiction works of individual authors is an excellent way to begin.

Biographies: Resources for Stimulating Critical Thinking

Several of the nonfiction titles on the Notables list are biographies or biographical books: collective biographies, "a day in the life of" stories, autobiographies, and personal memoirs. Typical titles include Piero Ventura's *Great Painters* (1984, N), Pat Cummings's *Talking with Artists* (1992, N), Lyle W. Dorsett and Marjorie Lamp Mead's *C. S. Lewis Letters to Children* (1985, N), Milton Meltzer's *Dorothea Lange: Life through the Camera* (1985, N), Beverly Gherman's *Georgia O'Keeffe: The Wideness and Wonder of Her World* (1986, N) and

E. B. White: Some Writer (1992, N), Diane Stanley and Peter Vennema's *Bard of Avon* (1992, N), Aliki's *The King's Day* (1989, N), Gary Paulsen's *Woodsong* (1990, N), and Normee Ekoomiak's *Arctic Memories* (1990, N). These biographies can also be useful for developing children's language through reading aloud, modeling different formats for writing, and stimulating critical thinking. For example, one fifth-grade teacher had his students choose a famous person to study. Rather than simply write a biographical report, students each researched biographical information from several sources, developed and sequenced notes for an oral presentation, and, finally, dressed up as the character to tell about themselves. The teacher videotaped each of these presentations as a "This Is Your Life" kind of show. Motivation was high, and the students developed a very personal connection with their subjects; in addition, they practiced oral reporting in front of a group. For a study of Georgia O'Keeffe, for example, students might study both the Gherman biography and the briefer narrative found in Leslie Sills's *Inspirations* (1989), a collective biography featuring several women artists. The final presentation might include dressing up in an artist's smock and standing near an easel with a giant splash of red color on poster board and a cow's skull displayed nearby.

Myra Zarnowski (1990) describes in detail several other excellent alternatives for biographical study across the grades which promote reading and responding as well as reading and writing. These include a "snapshot" approach to help students actually draw and visualize scenes in the life of their particular subject and a nonchronological approach to arranging information using flashbacks, flash-forwards, or retrospectives to help them discover underlying patterns or connections in the life of their subjects. These options offer a fresh alternative to the traditional reading and writing of biography and autobiography and lend themselves to interesting oral presentation and dramatization.

Biographies are also useful for modeling the process of critical thinking. Many subjects have been written about by several different authors. Thus, students can read two different biographies written about the same person (more than two for older students) and can compare each author's treatment of the subject. For example, consider this excerpt from *Columbus* (1955) by Ingri and Edgar D'Aulaire:

> The natives had never seen white men or sails before. They thought that gods had descended from the heavens on white-winged birds. They led the white gods to their homes in the shady, green jungle and eagerly set before them a feast. Hungrily Columbus and his men seized the tropical fruits and strange foods offered to them. The

Spaniards did not mind being treated like gods by these gentle heathens to whom they had come to bring the Christian faith. (P. 34)

Contrast this with Jean Fritz's *Where Do You Think You're Going, Christopher Columbus?* (1980):

> But if the Spaniards were surprised to see naked natives, the natives were even more surprised to see dressed Spaniards. All that cloth over their bodies! What were they trying to hide? Tails, perhaps? The natives pinched the Spaniards to see if they were real and agreed that, pale as they were, they were flesh and bone. But where had they come from? There were no such people in the world they knew; they must have dropped from the sky. So they gave the sky-people what gifts they had: cotton thread, darts, and parrots. (Pp. 31–32)

By examining two biographies on the same subject, students can contrast the authors' points of view as well as their inclusion or omission of information. Through engaging in this critical process, they may come to a clearer understanding of the subjectivity and voice that are present to some degree in all writing—even in the writing of nonfiction.

Generating Discussion: Using Nonfiction "Core Books"

There is a growing trend to use sets of books in classroom reading in order to provide common ground for discussion among students. Multiple copies of titles are used so that everyone (or groups of students rotating through sets) can read E. B. White's *Charlotte's Web* (1952), for example, and share their reactions. Unfortunately, this activity rarely includes class sets of nonfiction, although some nonfiction books which bear repeated reading and close analysis would work very well here. Peter Spier's *People* (1980), for example, is an excellent book which could be used in this way. Through an abundance of highly detailed illustrations, some of the unique qualities of many countries and cultures are presented, as well as those attributes which are universal. In this "core book" approach, students can take the time to pore over the many examples of clothes, games, homes, pets, holidays, foods, religions, jobs, and even alphabets from around the globe. They can then share their own particular traditions and explore new experiences. Further reading and discussion can delve into specific cultures in more depth, or students can pursue a clearer understanding of the modern-day aspects of various cultures. In another instance, one children's literature class read Patricia Lauber's *Tales Mummies Tell* (1985, N) and then talked about it in class as a group. Next, students made connections with other books they knew about mummies and ancient life or other books written by Lauber; they brainstormed possible response activities that would extend and reinforce their learning.

Many of the other nonfiction Notables (and other nonfiction titles) are excellent choices for small-group reading and responding. These are books which have received both critical praise and popular acclaim and which offer a depth of information and detail warranting extended scrutiny and examination. They also provide children with examples of language used effectively to convey information. A short list of exemplary titles might include Aliki's *The King's Day* (1989, N), Bruce McMillan's *The Baby Zoo* (1992, N), Mary D. Lankford's *Hopscotch around the World* (1992, N), and Lois Ehlert's *Feathers for Lunch* (1990, N), *Planting a Rainbow* (1988), *Growing Vegetable Soup* (1987), and *Red Leaf, Yellow Leaf* (1991, N) for the primary grades. For the intermediate grades, many of the following titles would stimulate several response possibilities: Patricia Lauber's *The News about Dinosaurs* (1989, N), any of Joanna Cole's Magic School Bus books, Jim Arnosky's *Otters under Water* (1992, N), Bruce Brooks's *Nature by Design* (1991, N), Raymond Bial's *Corn Belt Harvest* (1991, N), Russell Freedman's collective biography *Indian Chiefs* (1987), Jerry Stanley's fascinating *Children of the Dust Bowl: The True Story of the School at Weedpatch Camp* (1992), and even Mitsumasa Anno's sophisticated wordless books *Anno's U.S.A.* (1983, N) and *Anno's Counting Book* (1977).

As with whole-group reading of fiction, the emphasis with nonfiction books is on sharing responses and knowledge. Through this "sample book," the teacher can guide students in learning how to read closely, encouraging them to ask questions and compare opinions. This investment of time also allows students more opportunity to digest all the new information a good nonfiction book has to offer.

Children as Experts

Most children have many interests outside the walls of the classroom. They play on soccer or baseball teams, have collections, and enjoy hobbies. One Chapter I reading teacher used the notion of children's specialized expertise (Graves 1983) to encourage her students to share their knowledge about hobbies, interests, trips, or other topics on a regular basis. Students also individually selected and shared nonfiction books they discovered in their particular interest area. (The Eyewitness series offers students a good place to start, with topics as diverse as skeletons, money, ancient Egypt, birds, cars, butterflies, trees, flags, fossils, insects, music, sports, shells, and spiders.) As children volunteered their own experiences, books, and information, other students began to know whom to consult for information on certain topics. This also provided a more comfortable context for practicing speaking in front of an audience.

Sometimes the teacher scheduled somewhat formal sessions when particular students had "hot" topics to share. More often, interests were expressed spontaneously as students read and responded to literature. She invited the "experts" to share their background information and then to present any additional information obtained from books or any related artifacts. Gradually, over the course of the year, the teacher even brought in students from other classes and adults from the community to serve as resource people with expertise in certain areas as the need arose—just like doctors, lawyers, and business people consult specialists in the real world.

Some students acquired a repertoire of specialized vocabulary for certain subjects (such as football terms or computer jargon), which they shared with the group. Like Frank and Ernest, literary characters who offer their services as temporary help in Alexandra Day's *Frank and Ernest* (1988, N), many students know many different kinds of slang. When Frank and Ernest manage a minor league baseball team in Day's *Frank and Ernest Play Ball* (1990, N), they learn several new terms, such as *rubber arm, foot in the bucket,* and *meal ticket.* Students who feel comfortable sharing their specialized knowledge not only help their peers (and teacher) understand their particular world of words; they also receive affirmation of their value to the class and their status as an "expert."

In a fifth-grade class, this idea of "children as experts" took hold in a unique way when various students demonstrated specific expertise in editing, using an index, and spelling challenging words. Gradually, over the course of the year, it became apparent that one young girl had a real gift for editing papers for mechanics—errors just jumped out at her. Without any teacher prompting, students began to ask this student to look over their papers. What may be surprising is how many Notable nonfiction books offer assistance for this very area of language study: Susan and Stephen Tchudi's *The Young Writer's Handbook* (1984, N), Cathryn Berger Kaye's *Word Works: Why the Alphabet Is a Kid's Best Friend* (1985, N), Carol Lea Benjamin's *Writing for Kids* (1985, N), Aliki's *How a Book Is Made* (1986, N), Carol Korty's *Writing Your Own Plays: Creating, Adapting, Improvising* (1986, N), Leonard Everett Fisher's *Symbol Art: Thirteen Squares, Circles, Triangles from Around the World* (1985, N), and Joan Detz's *You Mean I Have to Stand Up and Say Something?* (1986, N). Even the biographies *Bard of Avon: The Story of William Shakespeare* by Diane Stanley and Peter Vennema (1992, N) and *E. B. White: Some Writer!* by Beverly Gherman (1992, N) offer insight into the writing process and the power of language. A library of reference tools for language study and children's writing has gradually evolved throughout the Notables. These are excellent nonfiction books which offer students objective advice to support their language growth.

Using the model of students as "experts" helped them make several connections. It showed them that their world outside of school had relevance to what they were learning about in school, that they could learn a great deal from each other, and that books help supplement this process. Nonfiction books are particularly useful here in that their purpose is to inform. As students discover books that fit their interest areas, they also gain a great deal of working knowledge on how to use a library. They begin to read on their own, choosing their own books. Many can even go on, of course, to write about their interest areas for reports and original books.

Conclusion

These are a few of the ways that nonfiction Notable Children's Trade Books can be incorporated into the classroom to stimulate talk, thought, and response. Reading aloud and talking about good nonfiction books on relevant topics can also serve to prepare students for field trips, guest speakers, and special events; to supply information about holidays and seasonal celebrations around the world; to tie in with current events; and to better prepare students for reading, understanding, and writing nonfiction. To assist the teacher in finding quality nonfiction literature for classroom use, *Eyeopeners: How to Choose and Use Children's Books about Real People, Places, and Things* (Kobrin 1986), *Best Books for Children* (Gillespie and Naden 1990), and *Adventuring with Books: A Booklist for Pre-K–Grade 6* (Jensen and Roser 1993) are excellent selection tools which feature extensive nonfiction titles for children categorized by a vast array of subjects.

We should not underestimate children's fascination with facts. They love make-believe stories, but *true* stories are especially captivating. Nonfiction is informative, and it can also provide a literary experience. And for some students who have not previously been "turned on" to books, nonfiction may be the key, often luring the reluctant reader to books that explore a personal interest. Through listening to and talking about some of these nonfiction Notables, children can learn new words, new facts, and about new authors. But even more importantly, they will be invited to wonder—to wonder why, how, and how come—and to read more and talk about it.

References
Professional Resources

Cazden, C. B. 1988. *Classroom Discourse: The Language of Teaching and Learning*. Portsmouth, NH: Heinemann.

Gillespie, J., and C. Naden. 1990. *Best Books for Children*, 4th ed. New York: R. R. Bowker.

Golub, J., ed. 1988. *Focus on Collaborative Learning: Classroom Practices in Teaching English, 1988.* Urbana, IL: National Council of Teachers of English.

Graves, D. 1983. *Writing: Teachers and Children at Work.* Portsmouth, NH: Heinemann.

Heath, S. B. 1983. "Research Currents: A Lot of Talk about Nothing." *Language Arts* 60:999–1007.

Jenson, J. M., and N. L. Roser, eds. 1993. *Adventuring with Books: A Booklist for Pre-K–Grade 6,* 9th ed. Urbana, IL: National Council of Teachers of English.

Klein, M. L. 1979. "Designing a Talk Environment for the Classroom." *Language Arts* 56:647–56.

Kobrin, B. 1988. *Eyeopeners: How to Choose and Use Children's Books about Real People, Places, and Things.* New York: Viking.

Ogle, D. M. 1986. "K-W-L: A Teaching Model That Develops Active Reading of Expository Text." *The Reading Teacher* 39 (6): 564–70.

Vardell, S. M., and K. Copeland. 1992. "Reading Aloud and Responding to Nonfiction: Let's Talk about It." In *Using Nonfiction Trade Books in the Elementary Classroom: From Ants to Zeppelins,* edited by E. B. Freeman and D. G. Person. Urbana, IL: National Council of Teachers of English.

Young, T., and S. M. Vardell. 1993. "Weaving Readers Theater and Nonfiction into the Curriculum." *The Reading Teacher* 46 (5): 396–409.

Zarnowski, M. 1990. *Learning about Biographies.* Urbana, IL: National Council of Teachers of English.

Children's Literature

Aliki. 1984. *Feelings.* New York: Greenwillow Books.

Anderson, Joan. 1984. *The First Thanksgiving Feast.* Boston: Houghton Mifflin.

Anno, Mitsumasa. 1977. *Anno's Counting Book.* New York: Thomas Y. Crowell.

Brown, Margaret Wise. 1949. *The Important Book.* Illustrated by Leonard Weisgard. New York: Harper and Row.

Burleigh, Robert. 1991. *Flight: The Journey of Charles Lindbergh.* New York: G. P. Putnam's Sons.

Carle, Eric. 1969. *The Very Hungry Caterpillar.* New York: G. P. Putnam's Sons.

See the Bibliography of Notable Books at the end of the book for bibliographic information about cited Notable Books. The Notable titles do not appear in this reference list.

———.1984. *The Very Busy Spider.* New York: G. P. Putnam's Sons.

———. 1990. *The Very Quiet Cricket.* New York: Philomel Books.

Cole, Joanna. 1985. *Large as Life: Daytime Animals Life Size.* Illustrated by Kenneth Lily. New York: Alfred A. Knopf.

———. 1985. *Large as Life: Nighttime Animals Life Size.* Illustrated by Kenneth Lily. New York: Alfred A. Knopf.

———. 1987. *Mixed-Up Magic.* New York: Hastings House.

———. 1987. *Norma Jean, Jumping Bean.* New York: Random House.

———. 1989. *The Missing Tooth.* Illustrated by Marylin Hafner. New York: Random House.

———. 1990. *Large as Life: Animals in Beautiful Life-Size Paintings.* Illustrated by Kenneth Lily. New York: Alfred A. Knopf.

D'Aulaire, Ingri, and Edgar Parin D'Aulaire. 1955. *Columbus.* New York: Dell.

Ehlert, L. 1987. *Growing Vegetable Soup.* San Diego: Harcourt Brace Jovanovich.

———. 1988. *Planting a Rainbow.* San Diego: Harcourt Brace Jovanovich.

———. 1990. *Fish Eyes.* San Diego: Harcourt Brace Jovanovich.

Freedman, Russell. 1980. *Immigrant Kids.* New York: E. P. Dutton.

———. 1983. *Children of the Wild West.* New York: Ticknor and Fields.

———. 1987. *Indian Chiefs.* New York: Holiday House.

———. 1988. *Buffalo Hunt.* New York: Holiday House.

———. 1991. *The Wright Brothers.* New York: Holiday House.

Fritz, Jean. 1980. *Where Do You Think You're Going, Christopher Columbus?* New York: G. P. Putnam's Sons.

George, Jean Craighead. 1959. *My Side of the Mountain.* New York: E. P. Dutton.

———. 1972. *Julie of the Wolves.* New York: Harper and Row.

———. 1990. *One Day in the Tropical Rain Forest.* New York: Thomas Y. Crowell.

Giblin, James Cross. 1985. *The Truth about Santa Claus.* New York: Thomas Y. Crowell.

Lauber, Patricia. 1986. *Volcano: The Eruption and Healing of Mount St. Helens.* New York: Bradbury Press.

Martin, Bill, Jr. 1987. *Here Are My Hands.* New York: Henry Holt.

Matthews, Downs. 1989. *Polar Bear Cubs.* New York: Simon and Schuster.

McMillan, Bruce. 1991. *Eating Fractions.* New York: Scholastic.

Patterson, Francine. 1985. *Koko's Kitten.* New York: Scholastic.

Paulsen, Gary. 1985. *Dogsong.* New York: Bradbury Press.

Peet, Bill. 1989. *Bill Peet: An Autobiography.* Boston: Houghton Mifflin.

Ride, Sally, and Susan Okie. 1986. *To Space and Back.* New York: Lothrop, Lee and Shepard Books.

Sills, Leslie. 1989. *Inspirations: Stories about Women Artists.* Niles, IL: Albert Whitman.

Simon, Seymour. 1989. *Whales.* New York: Thomas Y. Crowell.

Spier, Peter. 1980. *People.* New York: Doubleday.

Stanley, Jerry. 1992. *Children of the Dust Bowl: The True Story of the School at Weedpatch Camp.* New York: Crown.

White, E. B. 1952. *Charlotte's Web.* New York: Harper.

4 Notable Novels in the Classroom: Helping Students to Increase Their Knowledge of Language and Literature

Christine Doyle Francis
Central Connecticut State University

> *Hannah:* I like reading novels because I get involved with other people in other places. Sometimes I'm surprised to find that I totally identify with people in a completely different situation than me. I've had to read books for school that I hate and wouldn't even finish if I didn't have to, but they'll get better and I end up really liking them.
>
> *Jen:* You understand books better when you hear how other people feel about them. You can end up looking at them in a completely different way.
>
> *Steph:* But it changes how you look at it. I hate to stop and analyze every little thing all the time, and answer all those boring questions. I like reading because it takes me away into someone else's world. I don't care what I'm *supposed* to think about it.

As these excerpts from a conversation among eighth-grade students demonstrate, introducing novels in the classroom can be an unpredictable experience. But as Louise Rosenblatt (1983) states,

> Our business is to contribute to a continuing process of growth in ability to handle responses—linguistic, emotional, intellectual—to

---

Thanks to Hannah Doran, Jen Francis, and Stephanie Schur, who were eighth-grade students in 1992–93 at Sedgwick Middle School, West Hartford, CT, for their comments on novel reading.

literary texts . . . to improve the quality of our students' actual
literary experience . . . to bring to our students at each stage of their
development sound literary works in which they can indeed become
personally involved. (Pp. 282–83)

The purpose in using novels in the language arts classroom, then, is
not to negate or invalidate the students' initial, emotional response—
on the contrary, members of the NCTE Notable Children's Trade
Books in the Language Arts Committee specifically seek novels
which they believe will evoke response from the intended age group,
but which will also "give [students] the means for moving from
naive emotional responses to mature and complex responses which
incorporate emotional, cognitive, and aesthetic dimensions" (Stott
and Moss 1986; emphasis added). This chapter explores some specific ways in which language arts teachers can move beyond posing
typical kinds of comprehension questions, thus enhancing students'
growth toward more complex responses to language and literature.

Providing Guidance at the Prereading Stage

Davis and McPherson (1989) assert that it is in the prereading stage
that "teachers have the greatest opportunity to influence students'
reading." At this stage, teachers have the opportunity to invite
students to consider pertinent background information to help build
a common foundation for meaning making.

   Novels removed from present times may pose special challenges for readers. For instance, third or fourth graders beginning
Patricia MacLachlan's *Sarah, Plain and Tall* (1985, N) could benefit
from a brief discussion of the concept of a mail-order bride. One
might preface an explanation of Paul Fleischman's *Saturnalia* (1990,
N) with some historical background on conflicts between Native
Americans and colonists in late seventeenth-century New England,
including King Philip's War. Students about to read Katherine
Paterson's *Lyddie* (1991, N) should first be familiar with some basic
aspects of life in nineteenth-century New England textile mills. In an
appendix to *Lyddie*, Paterson herself lists background material she
used to write the novel; in addition, teachers might wish to consult
Bernice Selden's *Mill Girls: Lucy Larcom, Harriet Hanson Robinson,
Sarah G. Bagley* (1983, N), a book that will introduce students to some
of Lyddie's real-life counterparts. Also, since Lyddie frequently
compares her position to that of a slave after she hesitantly harbors
and helps a fugitive slave, some information about the abolitionist
movement of the 1840s and the Fugitive Slave Laws might also be
pertinent. Referring students to Virginia Hamilton's *Anthony Burns:
The Defeat and Triumph of a Fugitive Slave* (1988, N) could help provide
further information about these historical eras.

   Literary allusions may also confuse students whose literary
backgrounds have not included experience with famous authors or

characters mentioned in some of these novels. A teacher might want to share basic information on Charles Dickens (particularly including his popularity in the mid-nineteenth century and the general plot of *Oliver Twist*) prior to reading *Lyddie*. Or teachers might share information about Edgar Allan Poe before reading Avi's *The Man Who Was Poe* (1989, N), or on the major gods in Norse mythology before tackling Doris Buchanan Smith's *Voyages* (1989, N). Of course, any of these topics could provide a class with ample follow-up activities as well, so the prereading information need not be exhaustive. Further, teachers need not assume a total absence of historical background on students' part nor shoulder the entire responsibility for providing it. A preliminary classroom discussion designed to draw upon the students' existing knowledge on a subject will help the teacher determine how much more background might be needed. Further information might be provided by reports from groups of students, or the teacher may wish to make use of this opportunity to team up with a social studies or history teacher to provide some cross-curricular benefits. The general idea is to build on students' background knowledge prior to reading in order to decrease confusion and to increase both enjoyment and comprehension.

Mapping to Facilitate Understanding: Plot

Even if a novel poses no special problems arising from the reader's inexperience with its setting or characters, its length can still impede the accurate, orderly recollection of plot development that is the essential basis for more complex interpretive skills. Research indicates that graphic representations of plot structures aid students' comprehension (Fitzgerald, 1989); indeed, many teachers have found discussion webs or other kinds of mappings (see, for example, Alvermann 1991 and Flender 1985) to be useful in enhancing postreading discussions. However, as Davis and McPherson (1989) have observed in regard to story maps, and as Sonia Landes (1989) comments in regard to chapter titles, these tools can also be useful before and during the reading process. A variety of graphic depictions of a novel—charts, time lines (see figure 4.1), graphs of a character's physical or emotional rise and fall from chapter to chapter (see figure 4.2)—might be suggested to students, depending on the structure of the work and the types of post-reading discussions the teacher wishes to encourage. The purpose, at this stage, is to assist students in remembering the plot details in the order in which they occur—to make sure they notice the details that they will later spend more time reconsidering and interpreting.

Books in which the characters undertake a physical journey especially lend themselves to this approach because they suggest the use of "mapping" in a literal sense. For instance, students can more easily follow Ged's many travels in *A Wizard of Earthsea* by Ursula Le

Figure 4.1.
Time line for *The Borning Room.*

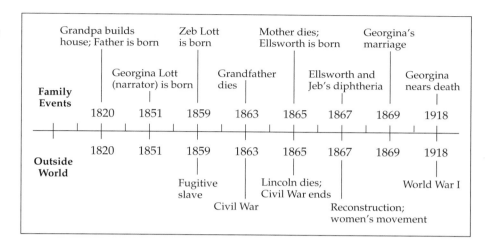

Figure 4.2.
Graph of main character's emotional ups and downs in *Journey.*

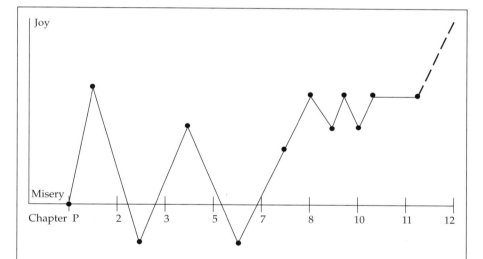

Chapter Event

Prologue: Grandfather says Journey's mother will not be coming back; Journey hits him.

Chapter 2:   Letter from mother arrives; money, no message.

Chapter 3:   Journey takes pictures of Grandfather and baby Emmett.

Chapter 5:   Journey finds out that his mother tore up his baby pictures.

Chapter 7:   Journey gets a cat—Bloom.

Chapter 8:   Bloom finds the box of torn pictures.

Chapter 10: Bloom has kittens in the picture box; Journey takes a family picture; mother calls.

Chapter 11: Journey talks to Grandfather about his mother; he has told her that "nothing is perfect. Some things are good enough."

Chapter 12: Journey and Grandfather develop pictures together in the barn.

Figure 4.3.
Map of Ged's travels
in *A Wizard of
Earthsea.*

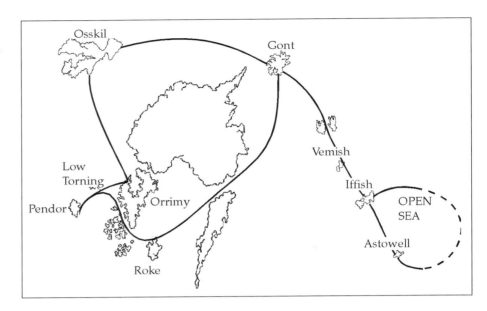

Figure 4.3.
Map of Ged's travels
in *A Wizard of
Earthsea.*

Guin (1968) if they pinpoint his movements on maps similar to those provided in the book (see figure 4.3), while also noting on a chart the major plot developments at each stop (see table 4.1). The completed map/chart combination gives students an aid to remembering complex plot details and provides a visual depiction of the novel's double-spiral structure. In studying E. L. Konigsburg's *From the Mixed-Up Files of Mrs. Basil E. Frankweiler* (1967), students can add maps of Connecticut and Manhattan to the map of the Metropolitan Museum of Art included in the text. Again, physically tracing the journey and charting what happens in each place gives students easy references for later discussion. Furthermore, mapping Claudia and Jamie's circular journey represents graphically how their quest narrows and then expands in scope. The heroine's journey in *Lyddie* and Gary Paulsen's journey across Alaska in the autobiographical *Woodsong* (1990, N) may also be mapped in this way since the actual places the characters traverse are mentioned in the text.

Even if no recognizable terrain is involved in a novel, quest stories of any kind may suggest mappings that can be used as organizational tools. Students could "map" E. L. Konigsburg's *Up from Jericho Tel* (1986, N) by keeping an account of each of Jeanmarie and Malcolm's visits to Tallulah and the results. Following the same principle, students could chronicle Wil Neuton's visits to the island he discovers in *The Island* by Gary Paulsen (1988, N) and note what he discovers or observes each time. This type of nongeographic mapping can be an effective way to get students to notice the language of a text and how changes in language relate to character development. In *The Island,* for example, students might note that upon Wil's first visit to the island in chapter 3, his language indicates that he perceives it as his personal refuge: "See what I have found—an island all for myself" (p. 22). When he spends a day on the island observing the heron in chapter 7, his developing ability to enter into the lives of other creatures provides him with insight into his own life:

> But it was not enough to see [the heron] as he is and then I decided that the way to look at him . . . might be to see where they aren't; to look for the shadow of them instead of the body of them. . . .
>
> I could see the heron in all the things the heron was, without seeing the heron at all, and it . . . made me see in a new way and, finally, made me look at myself in that new way.
>
> Not at what I was, . . . but at what I wasn't that made me what I was. I . . . saw myself in the morning light, in the gold on my skin, saw myself in my friends, . . . in the faces of my parents and the way my mother smiled or my father yelled—in all that I wasn't I found myself. (Pp. 51–52)

In later chapters, Wil's natural observations expand to give him insights into the larger world as well. Directing students to keep track of the course of events in ways that encourage them to notice the writer's language will increase their comprehension of the plot while laying the groundwork for more complex discussions.

Mapping a Novel's Symbols

Sometimes a story element that becomes a major symbol may suggest itself as a way to chart plot developments. Noting each reference to the hatchet in Gary Paulsen's *Hatchet* (1987, N), followed by Brian's response to it, may help to provide a structure for this book. Recording references to the camera in Patricia MacLachlan's *Journey* (1991, N), followed by a notation of who is using the camera and what is happening at the time, could call attention to this important symbol and provide students with a sequence of plot details at the same time.

Table 4.1.
Major plot developments during Ged's travels in *A Wizard of Earthsea.*

Place	Feat	Motivation
Gont	Makes fog	Protect his village; naive
	Reads spell	Impress a girl
Roke	Summons spirit	Dared by Jasper
Low Torning	Fails to save boy	Friendship for boy's father
Pendor	Outwits dragon (no magic)	Save people of Pendor

On a larger scale and as an aid to later discussion, students can notice symbols that suggest the larger themes of the novels by charting these symbols as they read. For example, the bear that terrorizes the Worthens' cabin in the first chapter of *Lyddie* takes on increasing symbolic weight as the novel progresses. At the end of the book Lyddie realizes that "[t]he bear that she had thought all these years was outside herself . . . was in her own narrow spirit" (p. 181). The teacher could read the first chapter aloud, and after discussion of the incident, students could record any times during the novel that Lyddie seems to be facing down "bears"—that is, any time she has to respond with courage to face difficulties in her life (see table 4.2). In fact, Paterson's novel is so carefully crafted that several other symbolic occurrences could provide mappings as well. Lyddie's mother's misspelled note, "We can still hop"—instead of *hope*—is reprised at several other points in the novel. Since the general movement in *Lyddie* is from hopelessness to hope, recording references to

Table 4.2.
"Bears" that main character has to face in *Lyddie*.

Page	Text	What It Is
1	"Lyddie looked up from the pot of oatmeal . . ., and there in the doorway was a massive black head."	A real bear
19	"She was startled out of her dreaming by a hideous roar."	Stagecoach at Cutler's Tavern
39	"Keeping her eyes on the intruder as though he *were* a bear, she managed to get her left foot across the sill."	Runaway slave Ezekial is in their cabin.
52	"At first she thought it was the bear, clanging the oatmeal pot against the furniture, but then the tiny attic came alive with girls."	Morning in the boardinghouse
126	"In her uneasy sleep she saw the bear again, but, suddenly, in the midst of his clumsy thrashing about, he threw off the pot . . . leaping . . . up into the loft. . . . And she could not stare him down."	Uncle Judah has put her mother in an asylum, has dropped Rachel at the boardinghouse, and is planning to sell the farm.
129	"She tried to stare him down, but her eyes were burning in their sockets."	Mr. Marsden is attacking her.
181	"The bear that she had thought all these years was outside herself, but now, truly, knew was in her own narrow spirit. She would stare down all the bears!"	Lyddie decides to leave for Oberlin College, which "will take a woman just like a man."

the note could provide the basis for an alternative mapping for use later in the discussion of this important theme. Further, this is one of those unusual books with chapter titles which actually give clues to the story. As Sonia Landes (1989) suggests in her discussion of Paterson's *The Bridge to Terabithia* (1977), chapter titles can be used to encourage prediction, to map the story's developments while reading it, and to discuss it afterward. Among Landes's suggestions for using chapter titles are to compare predictions to actual developments, to note which story element (plot, character, setting, theme) is signified by each title, to notice whether each title is literal or ironic, and to make connections between chapters.

Mapping to Understand Character

Teachers who plan to involve students in discussions of characters or connections between characters might provide a basis for these discussions by having groups of students draw up profiles of different characters. As with plot mappings, students should be encouraged to compile their character profiles by pointing out specific passages in the novel by which the author makes these qualities evident. Doing this for the novel *Up from Jericho Tel* (1986, N) helps students to become aware of E. L. Konigsburg's flair for language as they get to know Jeanmarie and Malcolm, two latchkey children, and Tallulah, the spirit of a dead actress. Tallulah's imaginative wit and Malcolm's love of rationality, for instance, are evident in the following conversation between the two:

> "I happen to like math very much, and I happen to be very good at it. It is one of my talents."
> Tallulah took a deep puff of smoke and blew it out before turning to Malcolm to say, "Mathematics is for the dentists of the soul." (P. 26)

The class can consolidate individual mappings during later discussions by using a Venn diagram in order to demonstrate characters' individual qualities as well as the ones they have in common with other characters. A group of students working on *Up from Jericho Tel* began with a line of three circles to depict the characters when class discussion focused on what Tallulah needed from each child, but eventually they developed the circles into a triangular configuration (see figure 4.4) as discussion evolved into the interrelationships among all three of the major characters.

The structure of the novel to be studied and the teacher's general plans for discussion will determine the most appropriate kind of mapping, but the goal of any mapping assigned before reading begins should be to provide students with an organized set of details to use, and even to reorganize, as they begin to interpret and analyze material they have read.

Figure 4.4.
Map of personality
traits and interrela-
tionships among the
three main charac-
ters in *Up from
Jericho Tel.*

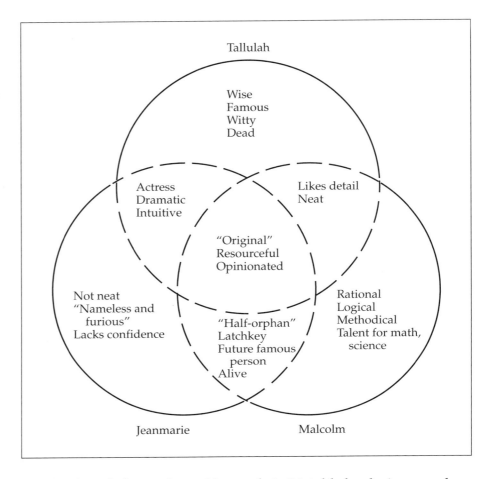

How Authors and Their Characters Highlight Language

As mentioned above, the writing style in Notable books is exemplary in its own right. For instance, students can enjoy the richness of language in Paterson's novel *Lyddie* (1991, N):

> The tumult that had raged inside her damped down more and more as though beat into the muddy earth under the horses' hooves. (P. 176)

They can observe the poetic quality of Fleischman's prose from *Saturnalia* (1990, N):

> It was December of 1681 and tombstone-cracking cold. Having bested fifty previous winters, Mr. Baggot was undeterred by the freezing gust of wind scouring his face and strode powerfully ahead without pause, parting the gale with his hatchet nose. (Pp. 3–4)

They may be stunned by the stark, "Hemingwayesque" economy of Paulsen's *Woodsong* (1990, N):

I began to understand that they are not wrong or right—they just are.

Wolves don't know they are wolves.

That's a name we have put on them, something we have done. I do not know how wolves think of themselves, nor does anybody, but I did know and still know that it was wrong to think they should be the way I wanted them to be.

And with that thought, with that small understanding, came the desire to learn, to know more not just about wolves but about all things in the woods. All the animals, all the dances . . .

And it started with blood. (P. 8)

Furthermore, in many of these novels, writing itself becomes a path to or an indicator of character development. In Beverly Cleary's *Dear Mr. Henshaw* (1983, N), the reader becomes privy to both Leigh's letters and his journal entries as he struggles to deal with his parents' estrangement and his own position as the "new kid" at school. In *Lyddie,* the title character's personal growth parallels her growth in literacy; her newfound fascination with Charles Dickens inspires her to teach another worker to read and write and eventually to pursue a future as a teacher. In *Saturnalia,* William, a Narraganset Indian, comes to appreciate literacy and language in a different way through his apprenticeship as a printer: "He was a rememberer, a preserver. . . . He would become [his tribe's] book" (p. 108). Zilpha Keatley Snyder's *Libby on Wednesday* (1990, N) contains examples of Libby's developing journal writing as well as the creative writing produced by her and the other three members of the writing club in which she reluctantly becomes involved. Wil Neuton in *The Island* observes nature and records his "nonfictional" observations in the style of a talented naturalist. Avi presents *Nothing but the Truth* (1991, N) as a series of memos, newspaper stories, journal entries, letters, and recorded dialogues.

The writing that occurs within these books could be used to map character development, as mentioned previously, or to discuss how writing changes according to purpose and audience. In Sarah's introductory letters to the Wittings in Patricia MacLachlan's *Sarah, Plain and Tall* (1985, N), for example, she writes poetically to Anna about the colors of the sea and the birds her fisherman brother observes; her letter to Caleb is a much more straightforward description of cats and houses and snoring; and to their father, Jacob, she merely writes, "I will come by train. I will wear a yellow bonnet. I am plain and tall," with a brief postscript: "Tell them I sing" (p. 15). Even her signature changes: for Anna she is "Sarah Elisabeth Wheaton," for Caleb she is "Sarah Elisabeth," for Jacob simply "Sarah." Students can be encouraged to notice and discuss the reasons for the various styles of writing, and to try some of the many varieties themselves.

Making Literary Connections

As mentioned previously, several of the Notable novels refer specifically to other writers (Poe, Dickens), and several of the characters in Smith's *Voyages* (1989, N) are gods and goddesses of Norse myth. Teachers can take advantage of these intertextual designs to connect books with other literature as follow-up activities. Or students can compare several books by the same author and develop a sense of how that writer uses language to develop character, plot, or theme. MacLachlan's novels *Sarah, Plain and Tall* (1985, N) and *Journey* (1991, N) make a good pair to compare and contrast. Each is a first-person narrative, one by a girl whose mother has died, the other by a boy whose mother has abandoned him and his sister. *Sarah* is set in the nineteenth century, while *Journey* is much more contemporary. Yet both stories deal with coming to terms with loss and finding renewed joy in life. The dearth of outstanding new fiction for the third- and fourth-grade level makes MacLachlan's work additionally attractive.

Authors whose earlier works might be compared with their recent Notable selections include E. L. Konigsburg and Katherine Paterson. Students who are acquainted with Paterson's *The Great Gilly Hopkins* (1978), for instance, may find characters in *Lyddie* to compare and contrast with Gilly, William Ernest, Mr. Randolph, Courtney, and even Trotter. Those who know *From the Mixed-Up Files of Mrs. Basil E. Frankweiler* (1967) may wish to explore Konigsburg's reprise of the boy-girl quest under the guidance of a wise older woman twenty years later in *Up from Jericho Tel.*

Teachers interested in developing students' awareness of genre might consider focusing an author study on Paul Fleischman, whose Notable books include both novels and poetry. Students might look for hints of Fleischman's narrative style in *Joyful Noise: Poems for Two Voices* (1988, N), or for examples of poetic language in *Saturnalia* (1990, N) or *The Borning Room* (1991, N).

Many of Gary Paulsen's novels have also appeared on the lists of Notable books. Author studies might examine the main characters in such books as *Hatchet* (1987, N), *The Voyage of the Frog* (1989), or *The Island* (1988, N), comparing and contrasting Paulsen's heroes and their quests. Or students might consider the requirements of various literary genres by noting differences between Paulsen's fiction and the episodes of nonfiction in *The Island* or in the autobiographical *Woodsong* (1990, N).

Enhancing Critical Thinking

Under the guidance of the perceptive and sensitive teacher, novels can be a valuable tool for developing critical thinking skills. In "Using Literature to Teach Critical Thinking," Commeyras (1989) lists some of the language skills that can be taught through literature. Many of the activities already suggested, such as mapping to keep track of the story and discussions and expansions afterward, address Commeyras's first three skills: keeping in mind the original or basic concern, withholding judgment when evidence and reasons are insufficient, and seeing similarities and differences. Other critical thinking skills include the ability to investigate by seeking evidence and counterevidence, the disposition and the ability to seek reasons, the ability to judge the credibility of a source or whether an observation is reliable, and the ability to determine whether a generalization is warranted. One key for unlocking the more complex skills, Commeyras suggests, is "careful consideration of alternative interpretation of a story." As Iser suggests in *The Implied Reader* (1974), a reader actively engaged with a text will fill in "gaps" in a text—all the places where it is open to possibility—according to his or her "own faculty for establishing connections." Further, since "one text is potentially capable of several different realizations, . . . no reading can ever exhaust the full potential, for each individual reader will fill the gaps in his [or her] own way" (p. 280). Or, as Bruner so elegantly states in *Actual Minds, Possible Worlds* (1986), "the function of literature as art is to open us to dilemmas, to the hypothetical, to the range of possible worlds that a text can refer to."

Helping students move toward an appreciation of this "range of possible worlds"—that is, toward a consideration of alternatives and connections—can be accomplished at several levels, depending upon the sophistication of the student. For any novel written in the first person, for instance, the teacher could encourage students to consider the story from the point of view of one of the other characters. MacLachlan's *Sarah, Plain and Tall* or *Journey* could be approached in this way. Students could write how Caleb or Sarah might have described Sarah's arrival at the Wittings' prairie house, or how Journey's grandfather might assess his own efforts at photography.

Zilpha Keatley Snyder's *Libby on Wednesday* (1990, N) provides a more complex example of how to generate multiple perspectives. As the novel develops, the reader gets to know Libby and the three other members of the writer's workshop, not only as characters but also as writers. Students could take incidents described by Libby in her journal and rewrite them in the journal of another character. For an extra challenge, students could try to rewrite the story written by one of the student authors in *Libby* in the voice of another character.

Avi's *Nothing but the Truth* (1991, N) provides the most complex, but possibly the most rewarding, use of multiple perspectives. The narrative, in the style of many modern narratives, is actually written from multiple perspectives. Avi's presentation of the story of a ninth grader, Philip, who refuses to stand at "respectful, silent attention" while the Star-Spangled Banner is being played shifts constantly among the viewpoints of all the characters who become affected by Philip's action—his teacher, his parents, his girlfriend, his classmates, the principal, a newspaper reporter, and people who read the newspaper. In addition, the various pieces of narrative vary in format, including letters, formal memos, excerpts from the school policy manual, diary entries, newspaper stories, and transcripts of conversations. Avi's primary consideration here, and the reader's as well, is how many different versions of "truth" are possible, even when only a brief and simple incident is involved.

After students read the transcript of the "incident" as given at the beginning of chapter 11 (pp. 49–50), particular students could then read only those portions of the book that pertain to a specific character. After each character has read his or her part, the students can come together and "justify" themselves to the class as a whole. The class could consider questions such as the following:

> Who makes the best case?
>
> How can you come to an understanding of the whole story?
>
> Does anyone ever know the whole story?
>
> Is there information you still don't know, even after reading the whole book?
>
> What else would you want to know before making a judgment about Philip's behavior?

There is plenty here to open up Bruner's "subjunctive" world, the world of alternatives, of what-ifs, for elementary students and their teachers as well.

Another useful activity for this book would be to trace the growth of the "humming incident" as it escalates from a homeroom encounter and becomes national news. Students could try to pinpoint exactly how and when it gets out of control, whether any of the characters could have stopped it, and what alternatives are left to the major characters by the end of the book.

Conclusion

These are only a few literature-based approaches that might encourage students to notice and interpret textual details in order to move eventually into the world of multiple perspectives, a world that encourages both efferent and aesthetic responses. Responding to this full range of possibilities, according to Bruner (1986), "render[s] the world less fixed, less banal, more susceptible to re-creation. . . . Literature, in this spirit, is an instrument of freedom, lightness, imagination, and yes, reason. It is our only hope against the long gray night" (p. 159).

References

Professional Resources

Alvermann, D. E. 1991. "The Discussion Web: A Graphic Aid for Learning across the Curriculum." *The Reading Teacher* 45 (October): 92–99.

Bruner, J. 1986. *Actual Minds, Possible Worlds.* Cambridge, MA: Harvard University Press.

Commeyras, M. 1989. "Using Literature to Teach Critical Thinking." *Journal of Reading* 32 (May): 703–7.

Davis, Z. T., and M. D. McPherson. 1989. "Story Map Instruction: A Road Map for Reading Comprehension." *The Reading Teacher* 43 (December): 232–40.

Fitzgerald, J. 1989. "Research on Stories: Implications for Teachers." In *Children's Comprehension of Text: Research into Practice,* edited by K. D. Muth. Newark, DE: International Reading Association.

Flender, M. G. 1985. "Charting Book Discussions: A Method of Presenting Literature in the Elementary Grades." *Children's Literature in Education* 16:84–92.

Iser, W. 1974. *The Implied Reader.* Baltimore: Johns Hopkins University Press.

Landes, S. 1989. "The Poetry of Chapter Titles." *The New Advocate* 2 (Summer): 159–68.

Rosenblatt, L. 1983. *Literature as Exploration,* 4th ed. New York: Modern Language Association.

Stott, J. C., and A. Moss. 1986. *The Family of Stories.* Toronto, Ontario: Holt, Rinehart and Winston of Canada.

Children's Literature

Konigsburg, E. L. 1967. *From the Mixed-up Files of Mrs. Basil E. Frankweiler.* New York: Atheneum.

Le Guin, Ursula. 1968. *A Wizard of Earthsea.* New York: Bantam Books.

Paterson, Katherine. 1977. *Bridge to Terabithia.* New York: Thomas Y. Crowell.

———. 1978. *The Great Gilly Hopkins.* New York: Harper and Row.

Paulson, Gary. 1989. *The Voyage of the Frog.* New York: Orchard Books.

See the Bibliography of Notable Books at the end of the book for bibliographic information about cited Notable Books. The Notable titles do not appear in this reference list.

II Responding to the Language of Notable Books

What opportunities can we provide to help children respond enthusiastically and purposefully to an unusual phrase, an innovative format, or a unique language style in a book? Drama as a way of making stories and language come alive, storytelling to capture the essence and magic of language, reading to write with an "author's eye"—these are all enriching and powerful ways to help children become actively engaged with the language of books. They become active members of a literate classroom community, exploring how writers use language purposefully, depending on context and purpose. They also develop an awareness of the ways in which language can shape one's perception and appreciation of story.

Anthony Manna presents exciting improvisational drama sessions from actual classrooms to illustrate how teachers experiment with dramatic activity to foster awareness of the rich language opportunities in books. Inga Kroman-Kelly shows how exposure to books incorporating storytelling language helps children learn its power to evoke emotion, see the world through different lenses, and get in touch with our literary heritage. Yvonne Siu-Runyan clearly describes how reading books "with the eyes of an author" can help children improve and expand upon their own writing, particularly their sense of story structure and their ability to use words effectively and creatively.

5 Language Use through Drama

Anthony L. Manna
Kent State University

When the teacher signaled the tableau to come to life, a tense atmosphere immediately filled the room. To one side a group of angry citizens shifted nervously. Facing this group from the opposite side of the room was another group of citizens. In both groups, several people whispered to one another, but they could barely be heard. Others either stood defiantly, with their arms folded across their chests, or stared at their opponents with disgusted expressions on their faces. Several appeared uncomfortable. Others looked confused. Standing uneasily between the two groups was Maniac Magee. Raising his arms so that they were parallel to the floor, he called the meeting to order.

> *Maniac:* Uh, we have to do something about all the fighting that's going on.
>
> *Citizen 1:* Oh, yeah, sure. Why should we? It's them who always starts it. We can't even walk on their side of town.
>
> *Citizen 2:* Yeah, they, uh, call us names just because our skin's a different color from theirs. Why don't you get them to talk about that?
>
> *Citizen 3:* What about the things you do to us?
>
> *Maniac:* Look, we gotta stop saying these things. Everybody has to stop talking at the same time. When you wanna say something, raise your hand and I'll let you talk.
>
> *Citizen 4:* You always take their side . . . because, uh, you live with them.
>
> *Several citizens:* That's right, you like them better than us.
>
> *Maniac:* Stop yelling! If you keep yelling, what's that gonna prove, huh?

The author wishes to thank Ms. Dona Greene Bolton, of the Childhood Development Center, Kent State University, Ms. Carrie Goddard, fourth-grade teacher at Lake Elementary School, Hartville, Ohio, and their students for graciously welcoming him into their classrooms.

Citizen 5: We'll show them how strong we are. We can beat them any
time! They should stay on their side of town. We don't want them
here.

The scene comes to an end when several citizens from the "white"
side of town storm out of the meeting. Frustrated, Maniac turns his
back to the remaining citizens. Obviously shaken by his failure to
bring the rivals together, he sighs and sits heavily in a chair.

The teacher asks the participants to freeze the action. In the
discussion that follows the drama, the students examine the reasons
for the citizens' distrust and Maniac's role as a mediator.

The fourth-grade students involved in this brief improvised
drama experienced firsthand the theme of racism which Jerry
Spinelli weaves throughout *Maniac Magee* (1990, N). Because a story
told in drama is communicated largely through action, the improvisation allowed these students to demonstrate, rather than only talk
about, their interpretation of the situation which Maniac discovers in
his new town. Through their involvement in drama, these fourth
graders ceased being observers of a conflict in a text and, instead,
became active agents and participants in a very real human dilemma, using language to work toward resolution of that dilemma.

The improvisation of *Maniac Magee* was a significant opportunity for language use. Because dialogue is an important means of
revealing the incidents in a drama, these students needed to search
for and use both physical and verbal language that suited the occasion, the characters they were portraying, and the characters with
whom they were interacting.

In one sense, drama had been an invitation to these students to
"live" an experience in order to make sense of it. Operating as agents
of the problem, they could begin to see in direct and personal ways
how complex and puzzling a human issue can be. As they indicated
in the discussion that followed the drama, their involvement had
convinced them that sometimes there can be no easy solutions to
social problems. For them, drama had become a means of making an
otherwise abstract concept concrete, accessible, and relevant. The
experience supported Bolton's (1985) claim that when students
collaborate on constructing and maintaining a dramatic event, the
process can be a powerful classroom strategy for "making personal
meaning and gaining a sense of universal, abstract, social, moral,
and ethical concepts" (p. 155).

Drama and the Language Arts

Drama itself is a language art, but it is also a learning medium
around which many different language forms and functions can be
experienced within meaningful contexts. In a given drama, students
speak and listen, but they can also be encouraged to read and write

in order to enrich the dramatic situation and to structure and communicate their ideas more effectively. Involved in a rich language network, they can both explore and use a variety of language forms and styles.

Morgan and Saxton (1988) have highlighted some of the opportunities for language development that participation in drama offers students. When teachers and students generate ideas for brief or longer drama experiences and shape these ideas into "playable moments," they can discuss and assess their work during and following the enactment. In doing so, they use both oral and written language "expressively," for the purpose of communicating or even intentionally hiding thoughts, feelings, intentions, and motives. When they search for and share information that is instrumental to planning and maintaining a dramatic situation, they are operating in the language mode which Morgan and Saxton call "informational" (p. 34). In negotiations about the meaning and significance of their ideas, the course of action a drama might take, and the information needed to solve the problems that arise as a particular drama unfolds, the teacher and students are using language in the "interactional" mode (p. 34).

In the brief drama on *Maniac Magee,* the participants experienced each of these modes. They worked with informational language when they reviewed the details in Spinelli's novel to help give form to a scene which does not appear in the story but is suggested by it. In considering and using movement, the strategic placement of characters to show relationships, a variety of gestures and physical stances, and, of course, dialogue, they used expressive language. Finally, in both devising the basic outline of the scene and developing it through the give-and-take of argument, the participants engaged in a decidedly frustrating exchange of sentiments and ideas— a process characterizing the interactional mode.

Literature is a fertile source of the kind of dramatic activity that invites students to cover a wide range of language types. According to Booth (1985), literature-based drama can become a genuine interpretive experience that engenders a rich variety of language "when the teacher uses the issues, themes, characters, mood, conflict, or spirit of the story as a beginning for dramatic exploration" (p. 196). In this type of literature-based drama, the teacher targets a particularly significant concept or conflict in the literature and assists students in developing the context for dramatic action, characters, and dialogue around this specific center of interest. Rather than students acting out each episode in a strictly sequential manner, they have the opportunity to dwell on specific elements in the literature in order to encourage reflective and critical reading. The experience can also steer students toward using language that best expresses the ideas and feelings the literature elicits.

Literature-Based Drama in Action

A literature-based drama based on Emily Arnold McCully's *Picnic* (1985, N) and its sequel, *First Snow* (1985), was the catalyst for this kind of exploration in a recent drama session involving a group of first-grade students. The drama evolved out of the work the children had been doing with their regular teacher in a brief instructional unit designed to address people's emotions, particularly their fears. Since McCully depicts a number of childhood anxieties in her wordless books about the experiences of an extended family of mice, the series seemed particularly suited to the unit's theme as well as its main objective, namely, to give students an opportunity to discuss and perhaps manage their emotions through reading, writing, and speaking about them.

While working through *Picnic* and *First Snow* with a shared-book process, the children were less interested in addressing the young mouse's fears than they were in discussing the dangers in her—and their own—environment and the kinds of precautions she—and they—might take to avoid such threatening situations. Because the issue of safety emerged from our conversations as a very real concern, safety was the topic we pursued in the brief drama that developed around these books. To establish a context for this drama, the children were told that in drama we can pretend to be someone else in a different place and time. "When I move my chair to the other side of the room," I said, "I will pretend to be someone else. Would you like to pretend, too?"

I then took the role of a parent concerned over the increasing number of minor accidents that were occurring in my neighborhood, and the students were invited to join me as my neighbors. At a "meeting," we discussed the kinds of accidents we had heard and read about, and we considered the places where these accidents were happening. One "parent" voiced her concern about a dangerous intersection, while another described in vivid detail the speed with which people drove their cars through our neighborhood, not to mention the pollution caused by such heavy traffic. We also considered the things we might do to inform and protect our children. Maintaining the role of the organizer, I suggested that we try to solve the problem by talking to our mayor and by approaching the principals of our local schools to find out about safety programs. I ended the "meeting" by urging my "neighbors" to help me write a letter to our mayor about the problem, calling ourselves the Jerome Street Safety Committee.

Many other opportunities for both large- and small-group language activities involving drama, reading, and writing could evolve from this initial drama. In subsequent sessions, the Jerome Street Safety Committee might reconvene to prepare for a meeting with the mayor or a principal. The committee members would then visit this official (role-played by the teacher) to discuss their concerns. To create the kind of tension that makes a dramatic situation interesting, the official might be unsympathetic to the committee's cause; he or she might be unable or unwilling to help because of limited funds or lack of interest. In another episode, the teacher, in the role of the committee chair, could organize a meeting at which members of the committee, in response to a principal's request, draft a proposal for a safety program to be implemented in their school. Newspaper reporters (role-played by several children) might interview the committee and selected officials in preparation for the stories they plan to write on the issue.

Similar situations in other trade books could lead to further dramatic exploration of the issue of danger or safety. In *The Ghost-Eye Tree* (1985, N) by Bill Martin Jr. and John Archambault, for example, a brother and sister quake at the thought of having to make a trip to the other side of town to get a bucket of milk because they will have to pass the dreaded tree. Working in pairs to role-play as these siblings, students could discuss their fears: "What's the worst thing that could happen?" asks the teacher to initiate the drama. They could also discuss the tree's history, the legends they have heard about the tree, and ways of confronting its alleged power. A large-group drama on this book could have the brother and sister challenge members of the community who refuse to believe any of the ridiculous stories about the ghost-eye tree. Or the teacher could supply the first line to facilitate dialogue among the participants. Playing one of the disbelieving citizens in the *Ghost-Eye Tree*, the teacher might say: "This is just a lot of nonsense. I've never seen that tree do anything strange!" The siblings and the skeptics would then explain their respective points of view, question their opponents, and provide meaningful details to validate their feelings.

A drama developed around any type of literature can also encourage the particpants to use language to explore specific incidents and elements in a text. For example, consider the following scenarios which could evolve from *Picnic*. The teacher role-plays one of the adults in the story, and the students take the parts of the missing mouse's siblings. They share their feelings and devise a plan for finding her. In pairs, the students meet in the clearing in the woods where the missing mouse can be found. One student is an animal that makes its home in the woods; the other is the missing mouse. What if they meet? What might they say, do, think, and feel? Following this brief improvisation, several pairs volunteer to show their interpretation of the meeting to the rest of the class. The teacher and several students role-play the adult characters, while the other students role-play the mouse children. Together they work through the reunion that unites the family at the conclusion of the story.

Staying in role, the students reflect on the day's events in their journals, writing the entries on the evening of the family's outing.

While this type of literature-based drama does not attempt to lead the participants through every episode in a text, it can enable them to make inferences and to express and act on the personal associations evoked by situations in literature. As teachers relinquish the urge to "cover" the text by rushing from one episode to another in a strictly linear fashion, the participants in this type of improvisational drama are able to linger awhile on one incident, concept, or dilemma so that, as Dorothy Heathcote maintains, they can detect "what lies between people . . . that aura that can be felt in a human situation" (quoted in Wagner 1985, 44–45). By lingering on the danger/safety issue for the duration of the one brief drama session on *Picnic* and *First Snow*, the students and I were able to look closely at the pressures, choices, and alternatives inherent in a situation which truly concerned them. As in most social interaction, once we settled into the drama there was a need for the participants to use both oral and written language to explain, justify, and convince as the event and our common task took shape.

The Teacher's Role: Students and Teacher Collaborate

The teacher's active involvement in this process is a vital link to the quality of student interest, energy, and motivation. It also helps to determine the kinds of risks that students are willing to take in a given dramatic situation. Morgan and Saxton (1985, 1988) have described a number of specific roles which teachers can take throughout the drama process. Depending upon the context being constructed and the desired outcomes of the drama, the teacher can initiate and manage a literature-based drama and build student belief in it in the role of a *narrator,* an *agent* responsible for establishing and changing the atmosphere for a drama, or a *participant* who alters his or her role in response to the needs, tasks, and interests of all those who agreed to participate. Sometimes the distinction among these roles blurs as the teacher moves in and out of the drama as it evolves.

Teacher as Narrator

The teacher can direct a drama as a narrator either outside the action or within the dramatic context. For example, in a climactic moment in one drama based upon *The Green Lion of Zion Street* by Julia Fields (1988, N), the teacher functioned as a facilitator removed from the context but instrumental to its development. She invited the students (as the characters in Fields's story) to gather near the stone lion (which could be either imaginary or shown on a large poster) and to ponder its power by carrying out her instructions:

> It's very cold in this place in the park where the lion stands on its pedestal. Look up at this towering figure. Take in all of its features. You hear the lion's roar in your mind, and now you imagine it moving through the park toward you and your friends. When I place my hand on your shoulder, share your thoughts and feelings with your friends.

In response to this prompt, one student remarked, "He scares me, but he's also awesome. I want to run, I really do, but I feel hypnotized by this towering figure. I can't get my legs to move." As the teacher moved from one participant to another, each echoed the same enticing fear.

To conclude the drama on *The Green Lion of Zion Street*, the teacher, once again removed from the action, prepared the students for a writing activity in which they reflected on the experience in role.

> *Narrator:* The children sat on park benches to talk about what had happened. Worried over being late for school, they wondered what they would tell the principal and their friends.
>
> *Student 1:* I don't care what any of you say, I am not going to school. Like I'll tell them that I met this lion that started to move, and I just couldn't leave, could I? Nobody's going to believe this. And Mrs. Walters will think we've gone crazy.
>
> *Student 2:* I agree.
>
> *Student 3:* Well, I don't. I don't care who believes us.
>
> *Student 4:* I'm freezing. Can't we get something warm to drink?

Students were then asked to write a letter to the principal to explain their late arrival.

In contrast, working more as a participant (while still taking a narrator's role) in *The Green Lion of Zion Street* drama, the teacher started another drama by joining the children as one of the group, trading on the ritualisitic visit to the lion and Fields's tantalizing notion of the difference between reality and illusion. In this role the teacher told the group:

> Now that we have seen the lion, each of us is a little different. So we decide to sit on those benches over there to think and talk about what we just did. We wonder if we had imagined it. We wonder if our minds were playing tricks on us. Did the lion really roar? Did it move? Who would dare to go back to that statue? Who's afraid to go back? And we realize that we better think quickly, on this bitter cold morning, about what we're going to tell Mrs. Walters when we arrive at school. We missed the bus and all.

Teacher as Agent for Establishing Atmosphere

A second role the teacher can assume is that of an agent establishing an atmosphere for the situation by designating a place, time, or climate for a drama. The teacher does this by pulling down the shades, playing a tape of music or sounds students have recorded, rearranging furniture, moving to a different area in the room to assume a role (as in the *Picnic* drama), clustering small groups of students in various areas of the classroom, introducing an object, picture, or piece of clothing that is integral to the literature, or by using another appropriate means of transforming a familiar environment into a place apart.

Each of these changes serves as a sign to the participants that they will be operating in a different place or time. It helps the teacher build student belief in the situation and establish what O'Neill (1989) refers to as the "no-penalty zone," which the dramatic context can become for the participants (p. 157). In this safe place students can experiment and work through a situation without actually having to experience the repercussions or consequences of their actions and decisions—for better or worse. Knowing or sensing this, the participants will be better prepared to move outside the situation from time to time, to consider its meaning, and perhaps to see beyond it to what it reveals about the actual world.

Introducing props is a particularly effective way to establish atmosphere. In one fourth-grade classroom the teacher began a drama on Bill Brittain's *The Wish Giver: Three Tales of Coven Tree* (1983, N) by focusing on one of the cards endowed with magic, which Thaddeus Blinn, the mysterious dealer in wishes, will sell to the skeptical youngsters early in the story.

> In the town of Coven Tree some say this card can grant you *anything* you wish. They say that all you need do is press your thumb on this red dot, and your wish will come true. They know that the card is magical, or so they say, because many years ago some children of Coven Tree tried it and their wishes came true, but they received a lot more than they bargained for.

The students, in the role of the children of Coven Tree, examined the card. Several were skeptical about its power, of course, while others were more accepting. One student commented, "Who says things like this can't really happen, you know?" Another student suggested that they contact this Mr. Blinn just to see if he really exists and if he really is as powerful as they say. In subsequent sessions, the children of Coven Tree confronted Blinn (role-played by a student) who granted them their most important wishes. In a follow-up discussion, one student suggested that the group do a drama around the idea of what would happen if one of the wishes makes a child disappear. The teacher, in the role of the principal of Coven Tree Elementary School, pursued this with the participants.

Other examples of props that can entice students into a drama include a large decorated box containing the kinds of memorabilia that the grandmother shares with her grandson in Eth Clifford's *The Remembering Box* (1985, N), the objects which the family discovers in the woods in Crescent Dragonwagon's *Home Place* (1990, N), Maniac's running shoes in Spinelli's *Maniac Magee* (1990, N), a container of maple sugar to introduce a drama on environmental protection inspired by Kathryn Lasky's *Sugaring Time* (1983, N), and the cat's drum in Ashley Bryan's *The Cat's Purr* (1985, N). Making the most of such props, the teacher might supply students with just enough detail to make them wonder about where and when and how the object might be used. What does the object tell us about the people who own it and use it? If it could come alive, what might it say, think, and do? When the prop is examined at different moments in the ensuing drama, the participants can step out of their roles to add new details, revise their expectations and predictions, and speculate. At any point in a drama, the prop could be described in writing.

Another way to establish a sense of atmosphere is by arranging classroom floor space. To help create an atmosphere for a brief drama with a class of sixth-grade students who ask if they can "act out" *Nothing but the Truth* by Avi (1991, N), the teacher rearranges the room, before the students arrive, for the conference at Harrison High School that will involve Philip Malloy, his parents, his English teacher, several school administrators, and a small group of journalists. The conference develops into a heated debate concerning whose story to believe. It concludes when Mrs. Malloy breaks down, Mr. Malloy accuses the principal of defamation of character, and the superintendent appears ready to assault Mr. Malloy. The students join the journalists in preparing feature stories or editorials on the conflict.

Teacher as Participant

A third teacher role is to become part of a dramatic context to help guide the participants through the situations that arise. O'Neill (1989) writes:

> When a teacher works in role it is an act of conscious self-presentation, but one which invites the watchers—the students—to respond actively, to join in, to oppose or transform what is happening. The teacher-in-role unites the students, acknowledges their feelings of ambivalence and vulnerability and focuses their attention. (P. 156)

When working in role, the teacher is not so much a performer as a guide, a medium for learning.

Teachers can take on major and minor roles. They can either assume a position of authority or become equal members of the group, sharing the same responsibilities and facing the challenge of the same tasks and problems. Endowed with varying degrees of knowledge and power inherent in the various parts they play, teachers use language to interact with the other participants according to their status and skills and the purposes they set for the drama (Morgan and Saxton 1988). Following are some examples of how this would work:

1. In one of the scenes in the drama developed for *The Green Lion of Zion Street,* the teacher becomes the school principal, an authority who needs information, and the students role-play the friends who had the adventure and now face the dilemma of what kind of information to supply.

2. In a drama based on "He Lion, Brush Bear, and Bruh Rabbit," in Virginia Hamilton's *The People Could Fly: American Black Folktales* (1985, N), the teacher takes the role of Lion, who, having been told of Doc Rabbit's skirmish with Bruh Fox in "Doc Rabbit, Brush Fox, and the Tar Baby," decides that it is indeed time to mend Doc Rabbit's nasty ways. Lion therefore organizes a meeting of the community to discuss Rabbit's shameful behavior and what can be done about it. Letters are sent to all of the animals, and name tags are made for the occasion.

3. Assuming a less authoritative role in a drama built around *My Place in Space* by Robin and Sally Hirst (1990, N), the teacher joins the team of reporters (played by a group of students) who have heard reports (from several students in the roles of the bus driver and passengers) of a boy wonder whom they will now interview.

4. In a drama based on Aliki's *The King's Day: Louis XIV of France* (1989, N), the teacher is one of the newly hired courtiers (played by a small group of students) in the service of Louis XIV (played by a student). Like the other courtiers-in-training, the teacher has much to learn about the king and a courtier's responsibilities from those who oversee the palace (played by several students). The first thing the veterans do is introduce the new courtiers to the recorded rules and regulations that govern daily life in the palace.

Variations of these roles can also stimulate much thought and language. Teachers can instill dramatic situations with tension by role-playing persons who attempt to oppose or disrupt the needs, plans, or wishes of the group while either hiding or revealing their real intentions or identities. In one incident in a brief drama based on David Wiesner's *Tuesday* (1991, N), O'Neill (1992) incited a heated debate when she role-played an older stodgy frog who disapproved of the night-time escapades of the younger airborne frogs (played by students). In another incident in this same drama, O'Neill played an arrogant government official and attempted to dissuade a group of citizens (played by students) from attempting to contact the flying aliens who allegedly had landed on the town square. Threatened in these ways, the participating students were motivated to reach for language that would fit the tone and mood of the situation and their changing perspective on it.

Drama and the Search for Meaning

In literature-based drama, students will work hard at making meaning happen when the form the drama takes and the strategies used to engage them in the dramatic event allow them to settle into a situation for a while. With their attention and energy fixed on a particular moment within a text, they will be in a better position to translate the "dense" print on the page into vivid human experience by aligning the text with whatever ideas and feelings the circumstance calls forth (Wagner 1985, 186).

For Rosenblatt (1982), this stance toward a text, a stance she calls "aesthetic reading," is crucial to the way readers make personal sense of literature. Rosenblatt says of her aesthetic reader:

> If . . . the reader seeks a story, a poem, a play his attention will shift inward, will center on what is being created *during* the actual reading. A much broader range of elements will be allowed to rise into consciousness, not simply the abstract concepts that the words point to, but also what those objects or referents stir up of personal feelings, ideas, and attitudes. . . . Out of these ideas and feelings, a new experience, the story or poem, is shaped and lived through. (P. 269)

In literature-based drama, an aesthetic manner of working through a text is encouraged when students are drawn into a dramatic situation that evolves out of some significant issue or circumstance, which they discover when they peer into the world the author has created. This becomes the focus for the action, for roles—and thus the language—appropriate to it, and for the meaning that emerges when the participants pause to reflect on the significance of what is said, done, and felt as the drama develops. "As the elaborate web of the drama is spun out from this single thread," Heathcote contends, "the class is caught in the tension of the moment; through this involvement they get a glimpse into what this time and place would be like" (quoted in Wagner 1985, 187).

The following scenario is an example of how aesthetic response can be created and developed as the drama is played out. The same group of fourth-grade students that worked through a drama for *The Wish Giver* dramatized a tense moment in "A Bad Day for Cats," one of the stories in Cynthia Rylant's *Every Living Thing* (1985, N). In this brief incident, Magda, a seemingly gruff woman, confronts the hostile, unkempt boy she suspects of having found her cat, which he has put up for sale. Operating in this meeting are several dramatic elements which make a situation in literature particularly suitable for dramatic activity. Among these are the anticipation and tension invoked by the questions the reader brings to the incident, questions that center on motive, identity, and attitude:

> Is the cat in the advertisement Magda sees really her cat?
>
> Who is the person who is selling Magda's cat?
>
> Why would he or she want to sell a stray cat?
>
> Given what I now know about Magda and the intensity of her search, how might she react?

In other words, we are searching for what causes these characters to act the way they do and say the things they do.

A drama on "A Bad Day for Cats" was then set up following the teacher's oral reading of the story. The intent was to use drama to address the gaps that remained concerning the characters and their actions and to explore the issues of responsibility and human need raised in the story. The drama spanned three half-hour class sessions, and the teacher, serving as an out-of-role facilitator, moved the participants through a series of improvised episodes.

In the first episode, pairs of students improvised a conversation between Magda and her neighbor or one of the people she meets during her frantic search for her missing cat. This takes place before Magda and the boy meet. Prior to the conversation, the teacher and students quickly reviewed the basic elements of the story, using the heuristic technique (who? what? when? where?) to probe for details. The students were encouraged to center the conversation on Magda's concern over Louis the cat. In a follow-up discussion, the participants stepped out of role to share with the class the information they had learned about Magda and perhaps about the person with whom she had conversed.

In the second episode, the participants faced the more difficult task of exploring the character of the unnamed boy. Rylant offers few clues about this character, but the advertisement he posts and the house in which he lives are cause enough for rich speculation. Students worked in pairs; one student assumed the role of the boy, while the other student, out of role, interviewed the boy in order to prepare his profile. In the discussion that followed, one pair revealed that the boy was a victim of physical abuse at home. Other disclosures revealed that he had no friends, that he was a loner at school, that he hardly ever went to school, that he lived in a foster home, that he came from a very large family, that he lived with a mean uncle, that he used alcohol, that he was lonely, and that he was selling the cat because he was desperate for money.

The third episode brought the boy and Magda together on the day she responds to his advertisement. In this episode, which also appears in the story, Magda and the boy meet at the front door of his home. Drawing on the "freeze frame" technique (Tarlington 1985), the teacher directed pairs of students, in the role of either Magda or the boy, to freeze and remain frozen just at the moment when Magda will knock on the door and the boy will open it. "If Magda and the boy could come alive, I wonder what each of them would say," the teacher posed. "I wonder what they're thinking." The teacher then circulated among the pairs, asking individuals to express their thoughts and feelings.

In one sense the third episode was a "rehearsal" for the final episode. The students, paired as they had been in the previous scene, could now draw on the emotional climate and factual content of episode three to briefly prepare and then present to the rest of the class the meeting between Magda and the boy. Not surprisingly, the interpretations of the meeting varied widely with regard to tone, mood, the quantity and quality of the dialogue, and the clues provided regarding the personal issues that lurked within Magda's and the boy's attachment to the cat. In one of the most memorable of these presentations, as Magda was contesting the boy's right to sell a cat that he did not in fact own, he relaxed his defiant attitude and whispered to Magda, "I didn't want to do it—he made me," to which Magda replied in a similarly, and uncharacteristically, subdued manner, "Who? Who made you do it?"

At this point in the drama, the teacher directed the two students to freeze in their roles and invited the students who were watching the scene to offer the characters suggestions for what they might say and how they might behave, a gesture of support that helps those participating in an episode to sustain a significant moment. What ensued was a complete change in the characters' relationship, with Magda serving as the boy's confidante, and the boy, noticeably reluctant to reveal the details of his situation, describing the difficulties of having to live with his ill-tempered uncle. In light of the gift she weaves for the boy at the end of the story, what if Magda and the boy become friends? What if Magda, suspecting abuse, decides to intervene? What if a group of students, the boy's teacher, or the counselor at his school were given the opportunity, through the medium of a playscript, to reveal aspects of the boy's life at school? What if we could hear the uncle's side of the story? What if the boy, now named, were allowed to make a new life for himself? These questions provide rich opportunities to explore real human issues raised by the story.

Conclusion

Drama will fulfill its potential for promoting language growth and for fostering meaningful encounters with literature when teachers and students collaborate in constructing dramatic events in which they serve as participants and agents of change. As active participants in this creative process, students are better positioned to find and use language for shaping the dramatic context and for engaging in the kind of social interaction that encourages them to reach for and assimilate an increasingly wider, and perhaps more complex, range of language styles, forms, and conventions. Because drama invites students to make sense of situations from literature by living through them, rather than replicating them, students not only re-create the experience in the text but also create a new text for themselves by experimenting with sequence, character, and action and by instilling the situation with feeling, fact, and implication. The type of freedom with a text that the process of drama encourages can help students to sense and value their power as readers, writers, and speakers. Buoyed by this freedom, they are more likely to read critically, openly, and reflectively, and to move far beyond safe and acceptable ways of responding to the human experiences they discover in literature. And they may be that more inclined to keep on reading.

References

Professional Resources

Bolton, G. 1985. "Changes in Thinking about Drama in Education." *Theory into Practice* 24:151–57.

Booth, D. 1985. "'Imaginary Gardens with Real Toads': Reading and Drama in Education." *Theory into Practice* 24:193–98.

Morgan, N., and J. Saxton. 1985. "Working with Drama: A Different Kind of Experience." *Theory into Practice* 24:211–18.

———. 1988. "Enriching Language through Drama." *Language Arts* 65:34–40.

O'Neill, C. 1989. "Dialogue and Drama: The Transformation of Events, Ideas and Teachers." *Language Arts* 66:147–59.

———. 1992. Workshop presented at Kent State University, 20 April, Kent, Ohio.

Rosenblatt, L. 1982. "The Literary Transaction: Evocation and Response." *Theory into Practice* 21:268–77.

Tarlington, C. 1985. "'Dear Mr. Piper . . .': Using Drama to Create Context for Children's Writing." *Theory into Practice* 24:199–204.

See the Bibliography of Notable Books at the end of the book for bibliographic information about cited Notable Books. The Notable titles do not appear in this reference list.

Wagner, B. J. 1985. *Dorothy Heathcote: Drama as a Learning Medium.* Washington, DC: National Education Association.

Children's Literature   McCully, Emily Arnold. 1985. *First Snow.* New York: Harper and Row.

Language of the Storyteller

Inga Kromann-Kelly
Washington State University

Storytelling is a tradition as old as humankind. We tell personal stories to make sense of our daily lives; we listen to stories to make sense of our world in relation to the experiences of others. We also are drawn to the stories from our past as a way to get in touch with our roots. Storytelling's value as a means of transmitting the language and mores of people is what has helped this oral art form endure. It may be even more valuable today, given our preoccupation with television, computers, video games, and other devices that furnish us with visual images rather than encourage us to develop our own. Indeed, there is a growing body of evidence and expert opinion to suggest that one of the greatest values of storytelling is the opportunity it affords to develop one's own images and, by extension, one's imagination (Carlson 1982; Greenfield et al. 1981; Hill 1991). Over the years the Notable lists have included a number of books which evoke the voice of the storyteller or encourage children to adopt a storyteller's stance.

A delightful way to introduce the concept of storytelling is with the Caldecott Award–winning picture book *A Story, a Story* by Gail E. Haley (1970). Ananse is an old man who spins a web up to Nyame, the Sky God, keeper of all stories. The price of his golden box of stories is to bring to him Osebo the leopard, Mmboro the hornet, and Mmoatla the fairy. When Ananse manages to capture all three, Nyame gives him the box and proclaims them Spider Stories. Ananse opens the box and all the stories float out, including the one in the book.

Teachers can begin using this book by asking children: "Suppose there were no stories in the world. What would our lives be like?" Responses from one group of third graders ranged from "We wouldn't know fairy tales like 'Cinderella' or 'Little Red Riding Hood,'" to "I wouldn't know about when my grandpa was a sailor because he told my daddy all about it, and daddy told me."

This book offers many possibilities for storytelling and connections to similar books. The rhythm of language and repetition of phrases ("we do not really mean, we do not really mean") so characteristic of African tales can be chanted and incorporated into the telling of other stories. Students might be asked what language patterns they find in *Why Mosquitos Buzz in People's Ears* by Verna Aardema (1975). Children can discuss the effect of repetitions such as "so sad, so sad, so sad" as well as sounds made by animals such as the iguana ("badamin, badamin, badamin"), the rabbit ("krik, krik, krik"), and others. They can make up sounds of other jungle creatures and compare them with those made by the animals in Aardema's *Who's in Rabbit's House?* (1977). The motif of the gum baby used to capture the fairy can send readers to *The Tales of Uncle Remus* by Julius Lester (1987) for the story of Brer Rabbit and the Tar Baby and can lead to a storytelling session in which the two stories are retold and then compared. The golden box from which the stories float suggests rereading and retelling the myth of Pandora's Box in order to explore similarities and differences between the box motif in a Greek myth and in an American tale.

After reading and discussing other Ananse stories, students can orally share tales of their choice. Some may wish to enhance the rhythmic language through body movement. Or they might want to try adding song and dance. Ashley Bryan's spider tale, *The Dancing Granny* (1977), is an excellent resource for guiding such activities. In that book, Granny Anika raps, drums, taps, and *umms,* but most of all she loves to dance. Lazy Brother Ananse, seeking to steal vegetables from her garden, tempts her with his catchiest tunes; he "sweets" her so much that she takes off down the road, wheeling and cartwheeling until she is miles away. Tired of losing her vegetables, she hooks Ananse's waist with her hoe one day and twirls him along with her for a final turn.

> Dance, Granny! As the lead bends
> The dance goes on, but the story ends. (P. 62)

Storytelling, song, dance, mime, and improvisations beyond the brief text are all ways to enjoy this book. Children can also create their own oral spider tales, traditional or modern, solemn or merry, using story patterns similar to the ones they have read. Put into the oral tradition, students almost intuitively pick up the rhythms and cadences that make storytelling different from oral reading.

Books Showing the Significance of Storytelling in People's Lives

Great Aunt Dew in *The Hundred Penny Box* by Sharon Bell Mathis (1975) has only one possession, the box of one hundred pennies which she brings along when she comes to live with her great-nephew and his wife. Teachers can ask students to discuss the significance of the box not only to Aunt Dew but to her great-nephew's young son. For Aunt Dew, each penny represents a year of her life and the story that goes with it. We hear only a few of Aunt Dew's stories, but their significance to her is clear, as is their impact on the young boy. Although the theme of the book is intergenerational conflict, children can begin to understand how people's stories *are* their lives and that hearing such stories enriches the lives of listeners.

Similarly, in *The Remembering Box* by Eth Clifford (1985, N), we share with Joshua many of his grandmother's stories. Teachers can lead children to speculate with Joshua on the difference between "crying" tears and "remembering" tears. It is an important distinction for him—and readers of the story—to understand. In Susan Roth and Ruth Phang's *Patchwork Tales* (1984, N), a girl's grandmother recounts the family stories that she associates with different blocks of a sampler quilt as it is wrapped around the child's shoulders. Elizabeth Fitzgerald Howard's *Aunt Flossie's Hats (and Crab Cakes Later)* (1991) describes the Sunday afternoon storytelling session two girls have with their great-great-aunt Flossie. As they delve into her collection of hats, she tells a personal story which she associates with each hat. To their delight, she even tells a story which includes them.

Sometimes these memories are steeped in nostalgia, as in Byrd Baylor's *The Best Town in the World* (1983, N), in which a child's father describes his little Texas hometown where everything was perfect. The best cooks lived there, as did the smartest dogs. Summers were the longest, and even the insects were special. Celebrations, of course, were the biggest and best. Told with whimsical exaggeration and gentle humor that are extended with Norman Rockwell–like paintings, this book can inspire children to tell stories in the voice of someone who recollects events fondly, even imperfectly, because they were so "perfect." Students might interview senior citizens in order to seek out nostalgic recollections of their elders and, in the process, enhance their own sensitivity to and appreciation of the value of storing up memories for future storytelling.

Family stories and storytelling are often an integral part of everyday life. In *The Winter Room* by Gary Paulsen (1989, N), two young boys gather every evening in the winter room of their old farm house to hear Uncle David tell stories. Evening after evening, he begins with the tragic story of his young wife, who died in childbirth. But soon the stories change to hero tales of Vikings and of the north woods. This book can lead to a discussion about the role of storytelling in a family. Ask students what role storytelling played for each family member in this novel. One such discussion brought out the importance of family rituals, the therapy of relating a tale of personal tragedy, the stature of being the household storyteller, and the passing on of culture.

Angela Johnson's *Tell Me a Story, Mama* (1989) and Ruth Wallace-Brodeur's *Stories from the Big Chair* (1989, N) are other examples of books in which storytelling is an important part of everyday life. Jan Slepian's *The Broccoli Tapes* (1989, N) is one sixth-grade girl's first-person account, told through the format of an audiotaped journal, of her five months away from her hometown. The book recounts her initial feelings of loneliness and her eventual discovery of friendship. The tape format captures the fresh immediacy of her observations and clearly demonstrates that an ordinary life can be the focus of storytelling. Children can be encouraged to experiment with this mode of storytelling by tape-recording their own personal diaries. Even a dog's life can be the basis for stories, as Susan Meddaugh's hilarious book *Martha Speaks* (1992, N) shows. After reading this book, children could pretend their own pets can talk and tell stories.

One of the richest experiences for children and adults is in answer to the plea, "Tell about when I was born!" Eyes light up, and everyone listens with rapt attention to a tale they have heard so often that they know it by heart. So does the Native American boy in Bill Martin Jr. and John Archambault's *Knots on a Counting Rope* (1987, N), demonstrating the universality of this desire to know. Children who know the story of their own beginnings can share them and perhaps learn the birth stories of other family members. Debra Frasier's *On the Day You Were Born* (1991, N) also prompts children to consider their births in relation to the rest of the world, which welcomes every new member of humankind: "We are so glad you've come!" (unpaged, p. 26). Children can be encouraged to tell the story of what some spot in the world was like on the day they were born.

My Grandmother's Stories by Adéle Geras (1990, N) is a collection of ten Jewish tales for which the context becomes a story in itself. For example, at Passover time, Grandmother tells the history of the Passover and reflects with the grandchild on special food and other rituals associated with the family celebration. Grandmother also tells her grandchild the tale of the overcrowded house, which many readers know as *It Could Always Be Worse* by Margot Zemach (1976). Thus, storytelling becomes associated with family rituals and encourages children who have experienced such rituals to recall them as part of their oral heritage. We also see that although a culture might shape a story, there are some stories that are common to many cultures. Children can be encouraged to keep charts of similar stories across cultures, noting differences and similarities in details and structure.

Oral Personal Histories in Book Form

Fortunate indeed is the youngster who has sat around a family table listening to elders tell about "the olden days." Stories that once might have been told orally come to life for a wider audience through book form. For example, in stark but poetic prose, the grandmother in Ann Turner's *Dakota Dugout* (1985, N) describes life on the prairie as a young bride. Their sod house is cold and dirty; seasons are so extreme that their cattle freeze to death in winter and crops fail from heat and drought. Eventually times improve, and they build a clapboard house with real glass windows and slick floors. Teachers can encourage children to retell the story in the voice of the grandchild, thereby illustrating how oral personal histories often are transmitted in real life.

Brett Harvey's *My Prairie Year: Based on the Diary of Eleanore Plaisted* (1986, N) tells a similar story from a child's perspective. Ann Turner's *Nettie's Trip South* (1987, N) features a young girl describing her trip to the pre–Civil War South. Her eyewitness accounts of her first train ride, everyday life on a plantation, and a slave auction provide a compelling story of the past. After reading or hearing these books, and with some guidance in framing questions and conducting conversations, children can gather oral histories from local residents. Stories that are taped can be shared with the class and edited into individual or collected stories for the library and for the people whose histories have been recorded.

Claudia Louise Lewis in *Long Ago in Oregon* (1987, N) relives her childhood in the Northwest during World War I. In unrhymed verse, she describes recollections of a loving family and their everyday events: the noise of the woodsaw, holidays, neighbors, schools. This book underscores the significance of everyday experiences, those events which connect people to their past in place and time. Children, too, can begin to look back on their lives by asking themselves: What do I remember? Why do those events mean something to me? They can begin to realize that the daily events of their own experience can provide the impetus for storytelling.

Similarly, Cynthia Rylant's *Waiting to Waltz: A Childhood* (1984, N) tells of a young girl growing up in the Appalachian village of Beaver. She describes an era of child sitters, high school cheerleaders, "pet rocks," and the Beatles. We learn how hard it is for a thirteen-year-old to lose a father whom she has not seen since childhood and how announcing his death to her friends makes her feel important. It is embarrassing to have a working mother who is too tired to attend PTA meetings, but gratifying when a classmate faints and everyone turns to the daughter for advice because her mother is a nurse. Rylant's *Soda Jerk* (1990) recounts the same town and era from the perspective of the town soda jerk. His reflections on the jocks, the popular girls, the families, and the others who form a montage of small-town life are witty and insightful. As he puts it, "the tips are good but the secrets are better." Paul Fleischman's *The Borning Room* (1991, N) is another excellent example of oral history told in book form. An Ohio farm woman describes her life through vignettes centering on the family's borning room, a place set aside for the arrival of babies and the departure of the dying. The eloquent first-person account presents a universal picture of the cycle of life. These and other touching experiences that comprise the woof and warp of one life, shared through a storyteller's poetic talents, can serve as a springboard for young people to recollect stories about events in their own lives and retell them to each other. The poetic voice demonstrates that the storyteller's voice can take different forms.

Wordless Books: Stimuli for Storytelling

The narrative qualities of the illustrations in wordless (or nearly wordless) picture books can often stimulate storytelling. *Picnic* by Emily Arnold McCully (1984, N), for example, shows a large family of mice going on an outing. Unfortunately, the youngest one falls out of the truck and has a very different adventure. Young children can tell the main story from the perspective of any one of the family members who reach the picnic grounds and the "inside" story from the perspective of the little lost mouse. Lively illustrations showing a range of emotions could be used as stimuli for sharing the two stories in pantomime, perhaps set to music. Middle-grade children can use the double-story model to tell a new story and put it into wordless-book format for one another or for other classes.

Tomie dePaola's *Sing, Pierrot, Sing: A Picture Book in Mime* (1983, N) uses Renaissance garb and an original ending to tell the classic tale of unrequited love. This is another book which lends itself not only to storytelling but to pantomime, or a combination of the two. Older students, particularly, can put mime to music and seek out the original Pierrot tale for comparison.

Fourteen full pages of unusual and imaginative drawings, each accompanied by a title and a first sentence, comprise the contents of *The Mysteries of Harris Burdick* by Chris Van Allsburg (1984, N). One bizarre drawing shows a nun sitting on a straight-back chair, suspended under a cathedral ceiling. The story, we are told, centers on seven chairs, one of which ends up in France. Students enjoy making up stories which use the pictures as a launching point and then go far beyond them. Stories evoked by the pictures are limited only by the imagination.

Novels That Stimulate Further Reading

Writing a sequel to a popular book is tricky business at best, but there are some outstanding successes. Gary Paulsen's award-winning survival book *Hatchet* (1987, N), about the boy who spends fifty-four days in the Canadian wilderness after a plane crash, has been widely acclaimed. A gripping story of coming of age, it is sure to propel the reader toward its sequel, *The River* (1991). Here we see firsthand how people are shaped by traumatic experiences in a way that is difficult, perhaps impossible, for others to understand. When he is asked by two survival scientists to "do it again" with them, Brian knows he must because survival is a psychological process which can be learned only by experience. The voice is first person, drawing the reader in with a compelling storytelling quality.

Fans of Beverly Cleary's Newbery Award–winning book *Dear Mr. Henshaw* (1983, N), about a boy named Leigh Botts who shares life's ups and downs in letters to his favorite author, will want to read the sequel, *Strider* (1991), about a homeless dog that complicates Leigh's life but also helps him become a star runner. Readers hooked on dog stories will not want to miss *Shiloh* by Phyllis Reynolds Naylor (1991), in which young Marty discovers a badly mistreated beagle that belongs to a harsh and stubborn neighbor. But it is also about making choices, like living a lie, albeit for good reasons, and bargaining for the dog in exchange for silence about poaching. The inner conflicts of a boy caught up in life's hard choices, some of his own making and some not, are also found in *The One-Eyed Cat* by Paula Fox (1984, N). This time the action centers on a wild cat that a boy believes he has accidentally maimed, but the ramifications go far beyond the animal.

Down-home characters, strange and magical happenings, and a generous sprinkling of humor characterize Bill Brittain's tales of Coven Tree, a small New England town named after a huge, twisted tree under which groups of witches used to meet. Beginning with *The Devil's Donkey* (1981), the series continues with *The Wish Giver* (1983, N), *Dr. Dredd's Wagon of Wonders* (1987, N), and, finally, *Professor Popkin's Prodigious Polish* (1990). Middle- and upper-grade readers who like suspense laced with humor can find these stories highly engaging. Also engaging are Avi's two mysteries for upper grades, *The True Confessions of Charlotte Doyle* (1990, N) and *The Man Who Was Poe* (1989). The latter is especially intriguing as motivation for reading about Edgar Allan Poe and his works.

Middle graders who enjoy tall tales, and almost everyone does, may be enticed by the folktale style of the Newbery Award–winning book *Maniac Magee* by Jerry Spinelli (1990, N). Legend has it that Maniac was born in a dump, that his stomach is a cereal box, and that he has an eight-inch cockroach on a leash, but the truth is much more awesome. Tongue-in-cheek exaggeration, humorous dialogue, and a serious theme characterize this contemporary story in tall tale style.

It is said that literature forms a kind of continuum (Purves and Monson 1984), and nowhere is this more evident than in folklore, where universal themes from different cultures and genres can be identified. For young children, *Foolish Rabbit's Big Mistake* by Rafe Martin (1985, N) is an appealing variation of the "Henny-Penny" or "Chicken Little" story. Older children can delve into its Jataka tale origins and discuss the book's artistic attributes. William Hooks's *Peach Boy* (1992) can lead to reading and telling other tales with the theme of a diminutive child acquired at long last by an older couple, such as Hans Christian Andersen's *Thumbelina* (1975). Many of these stories give children an appreciation of the cumulative tale, an element which they can incorporate into their own storytelling.

Variations and motifs from "Cinderella" appear in stories from different cultures, such as the Chinese version *Yeh-Shen: A Cinderella Story from China* by Ai-Ling Louie (1982), which can serve as a springboard for collecting, comparing, and contrasting the many other variations, and then for sharing them orally with the class. The caring versus the uncaring daughter appears in the African tale *Mufaro's Beautiful Daughters* by John Steptoe (1987) as well as in one from the American South, *The Talking Eggs* by Robert San Souci (1989, N). Both picture books can be read by older children to compare motifs, story structure, and deeper levels of meaning. They can then turn to *Moss Gown* by William Hooks (1987, N), which contains elements of both "Cinderella" and *King Lear.* Here Candace is rejected by her father, who misunderstands her love, and by her selfish sisters, who conspire against her, thus providing background for subsequent reading of Shakespeare's play.

Conclusion

Books discussed in this chapter expose children to rich language, stimulating their appreciation for the oral sources of stories. Through storytelling, we come to see the power of story and language to move us intellectually, emotionally, and imaginatively—engaging us in the search to understand our world.

References

Professional Resources

Carlson, K. 1982. "The Measured Reactions of Children to Treatments of Storytelling and Illustrated Books." Master's thesis, University of Toledo.

See the Bibliography of Notable Books at the end of the book for bibliographic information about cited Notable Books. The Notable titles do not appear in this reference list.

Greenfield, P., B. Geber, J. Beagles-Roos, D. Farrar, and I. Gat. 1981. *Television and Radio Experimentally Compared: Effects of the Medium on Imagination and Transmission of Content.* Boston: Society for Research in Child Development.

Hill, L. 1991. "Children's Response to Story in Illustrated and Non-illustrated Text at Three Grade Levels." Ph.D. diss., Washington State University, Pullman.

Purves, A., and D. Monson. 1984. *Experiencing Children's Literature.* Glenview, IL: Scott, Foresman.

Children's Literature

Aardema, Verna. 1975. *Why Mosquitoes Buzz in People's Ears: A West African Tale.* New York: Dial Books.

———. 1977. *Who's in Rabbit's House?* New York: Dial Books.

Andersen, Hans Christian (retold by Amy Ehrlich). 1975. *Thumbelina.* Illustrated by Susan Jeffers. New York: Dial Books.

Avi. 1989. *The Man Who Was Poe.* New York: Orchard Books.

Bryan, Ashley. 1977. *The Dancing Granny.* New York: Atheneum.

Brittain, Bill. 1981. *The Devil's Donkey.* New York: Harper and Row.

———. 1990. *Professor Popkin's Prodigious Polish.* New York: Harper and Row.

Cleary, Beverly. 1991. *Strider.* New York: William Morrow.

Haley, Gail E. 1970. *A Story, a Story.* New York: Macmillan.

Howard, Elizabeth Fitzgerald. 1991. *Aunt Flossie's Hats (and Crab Cakes Later).* Illustrated by James E. Ransome. New York: Clarion Books.

Johnson, Angela. 1991. *Tell Me a Story, Mama.* Illustrated by David Soman. New York: Orchard Books.

Lester, Julius. 1987. *The Tales of Uncle Remus: The Adventures of Brer Rabbit,* vol. 1. Illustrated by Jerry Pinkney. New York: Dial Books.

Louie, Ai-Ling. 1982. *Yeh-Shen: A Cinderella Story from China.* Illustrated by Ed Young. New York: Philomel Books.

Mathis, Sharon Bell. 1975. *The Hundred Penny Box.* New York: Viking.

Naylor, Phyllis Reynolds. 1991. *Shiloh.* New York: Atheneum.

Paulson, Gary. 1991. *The River.* New York: Delacorte Press.

Rylant, Cynthia. 1990. *Soda Jerk.* Illustrated by Peter Catalanotto. New York: Orchard Books.

Steptoe, John. 1987. *Mufaro's Beautiful Daughters: An African Tale.* New York: Lothrop, Lee and Shepard Books.

Zemach, Margot. 1976. *It Could Always Be Worse.* New York: Farrar, Straus and Giroux.

Connecting Writing, Talk, and Literature

Yvonne Siu-Runyan
University of Northern Colorado

> Even though I really like this piece, I put it towards the back [of my literacy portfolio] because I didn't really write this piece. Gary Paulsen really did. I liked the book *Hatchet* [1987] so much that I wanted to rewrite the story. So, I thought of writing an adventure story following Paulsen's style. I think I did a pretty good job of following his style, but I also rewrote his story. So that's why I put this towards the back. . . . I used Paulsen's style of repeating certain words to make it sound almost like a poem.
>
> D. J., sixth-grade student

> I got the idea of using the words "tree gap" in this piece from the book, *Tuck Everlasting* [1975].
>
> Stephanie, fifth-grade student

These students read as writers. They read literature not only for the story itself but also to inform their writing. They read to learn how the authors design or structure their pieces and how they use words to craft and present ideas. As Smith (1983) so aptly states, "To learn to write, children must read in a special kind of way."

When students read with an author's eye, they read deeply and critically. But reading to develop and sharpen one's writing is not something that most students do easily by themselves. Students often need demonstrations and meaningful conversations about how reading and writing are connected in order to learn how to write from reading. Then they need opportunities which encourage them to experiment with and use what was learned about the connections between reading and writing.

Experiences with Literature: A Necessity

Researchers (Eckhoff 1983; DeFord 1981; Mills 1974) have found that students who read literature write more competently than students who do not. After a four-year longitudinal study, Mills reported that the fourth graders who either read or listened to children's literature and then discussed it as a springboard to writing scored significantly higher in their freewriting than the control group who did not use children's literature in this way. Eckhoff's and DeFord's research shows that children's writing reflects the features of the text they have read. Specifically, Eckhoff found that the children's writings reflected the same features of the basal texts they had used. Similarly, DeFord reached three conclusions: (1) students whose reading instruction focused primarily on phonics and who read linguistic readers (*cat, sat, hat,* and so on) wrote stories following this kind of linguistic format; (2) students who read basal readers with controlled vocabularies ("The boy can run. The girl can run. The boy and girl can run.") wrote stories which also reflected the language and syntactic structure of basal readers with a controlled vocabulary format; and (3) students who read literature wrote a consistently higher percentage of well-formed stories using a variety of language structures.

Authors of books for children, adolescents, and adults have known for years that reading affects writing. When asked, "What advice would you give to someone who wants to write?" a typical author response is, "Read, read, read, and write, write, write." From their own experiences, many authors know that to become better at writing, they must do two things—read great literature and write about the things they deeply care for.

But as many teachers know, having students read and discuss wonderful pieces of literature and then giving them opportunities to write about related topics of great importance to them are often not enough to help them develop their writing through reading. Helping students understand the connections between reading and writing requires the following: thoughtful planning, knowledge of children's books, meaningful conversations about books and how reading and writing are connected, a classroom learning context which supports risk taking, and literacy experiences which require students to use reading and writing for real purposes. Thus, this chapter focuses on ways of talking about books to help students make these connections, to help them read with the eye of an author and then to write their own pieces using what they have learned from reading.

Learning to Read with the Eyes of an Author

An important aspect of helping students learn how to read with the eyes of an author is the way in which teachers introduce books and talk about them. Teachers often read books to involve students in the story itself. Or they read so that students will gain some valuable information about specific subject areas. While these are important, if teachers want to connect reading and writing instruction to help students learn about writing from reading, they must talk about books in a different kind of way. The following sections discuss ways of talking and using books to help students (1) find topics for writing, (2) learn about ways to structure their pieces, (3) revise the text, (4) understand the importance of knowing about a subject in order to write well, (5) effectively use stylistic devices such as captivating leads, imagery, metaphor, strong verbs, and specific nouns, and (6) become aware of authors' different writing styles.

Getting Started: Helping Students Find Topics for Writing

Like experienced and published authors, novice writers also find it challenging to select a topic. In fact, many students resort to replaying television violence on paper because this is what they too frequently think makes a good story. And if they do not replay TV plots, then they often choose movies with a lot of action to retell on paper. Many students are under the impression that a good story is one with a lot of action since this is the kind of story they see on television, videos, and films. While in one sense they are right— many stories have fast-forward action—they also need to understand that many stories are about quite different aspects of life, like impressions and feelings, relationships, unique experiences, unique observations about the world, and other more quiet topics. Figure 7.1 lists categories of topics and suggests books that could be shared to illustrate each topic.

To encourage students to explore the range of possibilities about which they can write, teachers should read a wide variety of books with them, discuss the author's topic in each book, and record the information on a class chart. This shows students the range of subject matter about which authors write, and the chart can become a reference and a place to record additional information about this topic.

Because Cynthia Rylant writes about ordinary events in such an extraordinary way, a good starting place for showing children that all stories need not be action-packed is to read aloud *The Relatives Came* (1985), followed by Rylant's *Night in the Country* (1986, N), *When I Was Young in the Mountains* (1982), and *Appalachia: The Voices of Sleeping Birds* (1991, N). After reading each book, invite students to share the remembrances that the books sparked for them. Teachers could demonstrate how to generate ideas for writing from reading books by listing on the chalkboard the ordinary things from their lives that could become writing topics. Then ask students to prepare their own lists of topics and to share their lists with one another. This kind of activity generates interaction and exchange of ideas as well as ideas for writing.

Another starting point could be Jane Yolen's books because she writes in different genres about a wide variety of subjects. A favorite Yolen book titled *Bird Watch* (1990, N) contains poems about fourteen well-known species of birds. Read each poem out loud so

Figure 7.1.
Writing topics and
suggested readings.

Impressions and Feelings

Byrd Baylor, *I'm in Charge of Celebrations* (1986, N)

Nancy White Carlstrom, *Goodbye Geese* (1991, N)

Crescent Dragonwagon, *Home Place* (1990, N)

Paul Fleischman, *Rondo in C* (1988)

Bill Martin Jr. and John Archambault, *Listen to the Rain* (1988, N)

Joanne Ryder, *Mockingbird Morning* (1989)

People and Relationships

Eve Bunting, *The Wednesday Surprise* (1987, N)

Mem Fox, *Night Noises* (1989, N)

Gloria Houston, *My Great-Aunt Arizona* (1992, N)

Bijou Le Tord, *My Grandma Leonie* (1987)

Myra Cohn Livingston, *There Was a Place, and Other Poems* (1988, N)

Patricia MacLachlan, *Through Grandpa's Eyes* (1980) and *Journey* (1991, N)

Katherine Shelley Orr, *My Grandpa and the Sea* (1990, N)

Carolyn Reeder, *Shades of Gray* (1989, N)

Unique Experiences

Jane Chelsea Aragon, *Salt Hands* (1989)

Marc Harshman, *A Little Excitement* (1989)

Laura Lattig-Ehlers, *Canoeing* (1986)

Robert Munsch, *Thomas' Snowsuit* (1985)

Gary Paulsen, *Woodsong* (1990, N)

Helena Clare Pittman, *Once When I Was Scared* (1988)

Joanne Ryder, *Mockingbird Morning* (1989)

Susan Talanda, *Dad Told Me Not To* (1983)

Ways of Knowing about Our World

Raymond Bial, *Corn Belt Harvest* (1991, N)

William T. George, *Box Turtle at Long Pond* (1989)

Brenda Guiberson, *Cactus Hotel* (1991, N)

Loreen Leedy, *The Furry News: How to Make a Newspaper* (1990, N)

Joan Lowery Nixon, *If You Were a Writer* (1988, N)

Diane Siebert, *Heartland* (1989, N)

Observations

Burton Albert, *Where Does the Trail Lead?* (1991)

Deborah Chandra, *Balloons, and Other Poems* (1990, N)

Denise Fleming, *In the Tall, Tall Grass* (1991, N)

Peter Parnall, *Quiet* (1989, N)

Ruth Yaffe Radin, *A Winter Place* (1982)

Joanne Ryder, *Under Your Feet* (1990)

Diane Siebert, *Heartland* (1989, N)

A Slice of Life

Eve Bunting, *The Wall* (1990, N) and *Fly Away Home* (1991)

Barbara Shook Hazen, *Tight Times* (1979)

Ron Hirschi, *Harvest Song* (1991)

David McPhail, *Farm Morning* (1985, N)

Linda Lowe Morris, *Morning Milking* (1991)

Patricia Polacco, *Thunder Cake* (1990, N)

Bonnie Pryor, *Greenbrook Farm* (1991)

that students can hear the metaphor-rich language. For example, in her poem "Woodpecker," Yolen compares this bird and the "ratatatatat" sound it makes with numerous objects:

> His swift
> ratatatatat
> is
> as casual as a jackhammer
> on a city street,
> as thorough as an oil drill
> on an Oklahoma wellsite,
> as fine as a needle
> in a record groove,
> as cleansing as a dentist's probe
> in a mouthful of cavities,
> as final as a park attendant's stick
> on a lawn of litter. (Unpaged, p. 8)

After reading the poems, talk about the images that each poem creates. Then ask students to think about the animals, insects, and other objects in nature about which they could write and the comparisons they could make.

Students could then be introduced to Yolen's exquisite book *Owl Moon* (1987), which has a completely different feel from *Bird Watch*. After hearing this story about a father and daughter who walk through the woods on a moonlit night in hopes of spotting an owl, students could discuss the special occasions they have had with important people in their lives. Again, encourage the students to jot possible writing topics down on their developing lists.

Next, as a change of pace, read Yolen's *Dove Isabeau* (1986, N), a humorous version of the traditional tale "Snow White." A discussion about the similarities between the original tale and Yolen's version and about how authors draw from original tales to create new versions can demonstrate to children how folklore can provide ideas for writing, as in Jon Scieszka's *The Frog Prince, Continued* (1991) and *The True Story of the Three Little Pigs by A. Wolf* (1989).

Discussions which focus on books read, the authors' topics, and the writing ideas suggested by reading and discussing these books should go on throughout the school year. In this way students will discover the many literate occasions (Graves 1990) about which they could write.

Knowing Their Topics

Once students become conscious of the many possible writing topics, teachers can help them focus on the ideas about which they have some knowledge. Many novice writers often abandon a writing project because they do not have enough information to develop their ideas in depth. After reading a book, teachers may want to ask students, "What do you suppose the author had to know in order to write this piece?" Teachers may want to start with personal narratives like Gary Paulsen's chapter book *Woodsong* (1990, N) or Linda Lowe Morris's picture book *Morning Milking* (1991) and then move to stories about special people, such as Gloria Houston's *My Great-Aunt Arizona* (1992, N), and informational books, such as Brenda Guiberson's *Cactus Hotel* (1991, N), Patricia Lauber's *The News about Dinosaurs* (1989, N), Diane Siebert's *Heartland* (1989, N), and Raymond Bial's *Corn Belt Harvest* (1991, N). Finally, teachers might read works of historical fiction and discuss the research done by each author in order to write the story. Some excellent books from this genre to share are Katherine Paterson's *Lyddie* (1991, N), Paul Fleischman's *The Borning Room* (1991, N), and Jan Hudson's *Sweetgrass* (1989, N).

This strategy paid off when Geoff, one of my sixth-grade students, decided he was going to write a piece about a Vietnam veteran who went to sleep, had a flashback dream, woke up, and killed himself. Although I was bothered by his topic selection, I said, "Great idea, Geoff. That is a very important topic which deserves attention. Now then, what do you know about the Vietnam War and the veterans who fought in that war that will help you write your piece?"

Geoff dropped his eyes, shuffled his feet, and mumbled, "Well, not very much."

"That's okay," I encouraged. "Remember what authors do when they need information?"

"They do research," responded Geoff.

"Right," I answered. "We have quite a few books on Vietnam in our library, and there are some Vietnam veterans who live here. You could do some library research and interview some of the veterans. What do you think?"

Because Geoff's original intention for writing this story was to put blood and gore on paper and to replay this movie plot on paper, he decided for himself that he did not have enough information to write this piece. Instead, Geoff settled on writing a piece about his own dreams.

What about Design and Structure?

After topic choice, design becomes a concern. When teachers first introduce ways of structuring a piece with novice writers, it is often helpful to select personal narratives with obvious structures. An old favorite enjoyed by students of all ages is Caroline Feller Bauer's *My Mom Travels a Lot* (1981), which uses an opposites design pattern. The young narrator, discussing how his mother's job requires her to travel, alternately relates "The good thing about it" and "The bad thing about it" several times, ending with, "But the best thing about it is. . . ." After reading the book and discussing its design, teachers might orally engage students in making up new stories following the book's structure before they actually write their own stories. This kind of rehearsal provides the scaffolding many inexperienced writers need before they feel comfortable using this design in their own writings.

After experiencing the opposites design structure in literature, discussion, and writing, students can then move on to other, more complex structures, such as circle or turn-around plot, story-within-a-story, parallel plot, flashback, sequential pattern, cumulative or add-on pattern, interlocking pattern, question/answer format, repeated refrain, surprise ending, and patterns of three.

Knowing about text structures facilitates not only writing development but reading and thinking development as well. For example, Tommy, a fifth grader, was having trouble organizing and sequencing his stories. After I read aloud Laura Joffe Numeroff's *If You Give a Mouse a Cookie* (1985), Tommy decided he would try the circle or turn-around plot structure in the next three pieces he wrote: "If You Give a Chipmunk a Peanut Butter Bread," "If You Give a Goat Some Grass," and "If You Give a Bear Some Crumbs." Because each event builds on the previous one until the end of story, which brings the reader back to the beginning, Tommy had to think about the sequences of events for each of the three pieces. Both Tommy's special education teacher and I noticed that after he used this structure in his stories, he was better able to organize and sequence other writings. By using the tight design and sequence of the circle plot stories, Tommy learned how to organize his ideas.

In another instance, after I read aloud Miller's *My Grandmother's Cookie Jar* (1987), D. J., a sixth grader, decided to use the story-within-a-story structure used in Miller's book. He eagerly told me: "I got the idea for Mesa Verde after you read us a book about an Indian grandmother. We talked about the plot structure of the book and how the author used the story-within-a-story design. . . . After we talked about this, I was getting ready to write a piece, and I thought why not try it out?"

When students know various ways of organizing the text, they can more easily choose an appropriate design to use when writing. For this purpose, using picture books or short chapter books may make it easier for students to see the structure. Figure 7.2 lists some specific structures and suggests sample books in each category.

Revision: Beyond Topic Choice and Design

Once students are aware of how reading and discussing literature can help them consider topics for writing and designs for organizing their writing, teachers can help them notice the more subtle connections between reading and writing.

Figure 7.2.
Specific plot struc-
tures and suggested
readings.

Circle or Turn-Around Plot (the story begins and ends at the same place):

Lark Carrier, *There Was a Hill* (1985)

Paul Fleischman, *Coming-and-Going Men: Four Tales* (1985, N)

Anita Lobel, *Alison's Zinnia* (1990, N)

Laura Joffe Numeroff, *If You Give a Mouse a Cookie* (1985) and *If You Give a Moose a Muffin* (1991)

Chris Van Allsburg, *Jumanji* (1981)

Story-Within-a-Story (there are two stories; one is the vehicle for telling the other):

Mem Fox, *Night Noises* (1989, N)

Patricia MacLachlan, *Mama One, Mama Two* (1982)

Bill Martin Jr. and John Archambault, *Knots on a Counting Rope* (1987, N)

Margaret Miller, *My Grandmother's Cookie Jar* (1987)

Marisabina Russo, *A Visit to Oma* (1991)

Susan Talanda, *Dad Told Me Not To* (1983)

Parallel Plot (two simultaneous stories):

Lorna Balian, *Humbug Rabbit* (1974)

John Burningham, *Come Away from the Water, Shirley* (1977)

John S. Goodall, *Above and below the Stairs* (1983, N)

Trinka Hakes Noble, *Meanwhile Back at the Ranch* (1987)

Flashback (a main character in the present tells a story about the past):

Karen Ackerman, *Song and Dance Man* (1989)

Eth Clifford, *The Remembering Box* (1985, N)

Ina R. Friedman, *How My Parents Learned to Eat* (1984)

Magan McDonald, *The Potato Man* (1991)

Chuck Thurman, *A Time for Remembering* (1989)

Ann Turner, *Dakota Dugout* (1985, N)

Sequential Plot (one event follows another):

Keith Baker, *The Dove's Letter* (1988, N)

Robert J. Blake, *The Perfect Spot* (1992)

Janina Domanska, *Busy Monday Morning* (1985, N)

Norah Dooley, *Everybody Cooks Rice* (1991)

Paul Fleischman, *Time Train* (1991)

Florence Parry Heide and Judith Heide Gilliland, *The Day of Ahmed's Secret* (1990, N)

William Joyce, *A Day with Wilbur Robinson* (1990)

Rafe Martin, *Foolish Rabbit's Big Mistake* (1985, N)

Paul Rogers and Emma Rogers, *Zoe's Tower* (1991)

Cumulative or Add-On Structure (each event is repeated in order of occurrence each time a new event is added):

Verna Aardema, *Bringing the Rain to Kapiti Plain* (1981)

Mem Fox, *Hattie and the Fox* (1987, N) and *Shoes from Grandpa* (1989)

Paul Galdone, *Henny Penny* (1968) and *The Gingerbread Boy* (1975)

Nonny Hogrogian, *One Fine Day* (1971) and *The Cat Who Loved to Sing* (1989, N)

Susan Ramsay Hoguet, *I Unpacked My Grandmother's Trunk* (1983, N)

Arnold Lobel, *The Rose in My Garden* (1984, N)

Nadine Bernard Westcott, *The Lady with the Alligator Purse* (1988)

Figure 7.2. (cont.)
Specific plot structures and suggested readings.

Audrey Wood, *The Napping House* (1984)

Interlocking Plot (the answer for one response becomes the beginning for the next sentence):

Tedd Arnold, *Ollie Forgot* (1988)

Bill Martin Jr., *Brown Bear, Brown Bear, What Do You See?* (1970) and *Polar Bear, Polar Bear, What Do You Hear?* (1991, N)

Sue Williams, *I Went Walking* (1990)

Question/Answer (a question is asked, followed by a response):

Pamela Allen, *Who Sank the Boat?* (1983)

Ruth B. Gross, *What's on My Plate?* (1990)

Deborah Guarino, *Is Your Mama a Llama?* (1989)

Montzalee Miller, *Whose Shoe?* (1991)

Susan Sussman and Robert James Sussman, *Lies (People Believe) about Animals* (1987)

Masayuki Yabuuchi, *Whose Baby?* (1985) and *Whose Footprints?* (1985)

Repeated Refrain (a phrase is repeated throughout the story):

Ruth Brown, *Ladybug, Ladybug* (1988)

Eric Carle, *The Very Busy Spider* (1984) and *The Very Quiet Cricket* (1990)

Alhambra G. Deming, *Who Is Tapping at My Window?* (1988, N)

Michael Flanders and Donald Swann, *The Hippopotamus Song* (1991)

Robert Michal Koontz, *This Old Man: The Counting Song* (1988, N)

Bill Martin Jr. and John Archambault, *Chicka Chicka Boom Boom* (1989, N)

Michael Rosen, *We're Going on a Bear Hunt* (1989, N)

Nancy Van Laan, *Possum Come a-Knockin'* (1990, N)

Judith Viorst, *Alexander and the Terrible, Horrible, No Good, Very Bad Day* (1972)

Surprise Ending (the end of the story is unexpected):

Lisa Campbell Ernst, *Sam Johnson and the Blue Ribbon Quilt* (1983)

Mercer Mayer, *There's a Nightmare in My Closet* (1968)

Inga Moore, *Six-Dinner Sid* (1991, N)

Patterns of Three (there may be three characters, three tasks, or three things to overcome throughout the story):

Virginia Haviland, *The Talking Pot* (1990)

John W. Ivimey, *The Complete Story of the Three Blind Mice* (1987, N)

Robert D. San Souci, *The Talking Eggs: A Folktale from the American South* (1989, N)

Ruth Sanderson, *The Enchanted Wood* (1990)

Claus Stamm, *Three Strong Women: A Tall Tale from Japan* (1990)

Familiar Sequences (stories are built around familiar sequences, such as months of the year, days of the week, holidays; stories capitalize on children's familiarity with sequences that are part of their daily lives):

Eric Carle, *The Very Hungry Caterpillar* (1983)

Maurice Sendak, *Chicken Soup with Rice* (1962)

Uri Shulevitz, *One Monday Morning* (1967)

While students may enjoy putting their ideas down on paper, the vast majority do not enjoy revising their writing and often confuse revision with editing. They do not understand that revision involves relooking at or reseeing their writing through a fresh perspective and that revision is an opportunity to explore and make clearer one's message, not a "punishment for failure" (Murray 1991), as many students think.

For students to understand that (1) revision occurs in many areas, not only in writing but also in reading, and that (2) revision is an opportunity to rethink, resee, and rediscover, they need to develop a broad meaning of the term *revision.* Teachers may want to demonstrate that we revise not only in writing but also in reading and talking.

As teachers write, read, view films, and converse with others, they might find it helpful to notice the ways in which they revise their own ideas, leading to a discussion of the kinds of changes or modifications they make. That is, talk about how new information alters our perceptions and original notions. Then invite students to share the revisions they made when they encountered new information and took a fresh look at their original ideas.

For example, after reading Gary Paulsen's *Woodsong* (1990, N), Travis stated, "I like to hunt and kill animals. After reading this book, I realize that all animals have a right to live. I don't know if I'm going hunting again. I need to think about this some more."

Like Travis, Stephanie had to revise her thinking after the teacher read Russell Freedman's *Lincoln: A Photobiography* (1987): "I didn't know that Lincoln was a Republican. I always thought he was a Democrat. And I didn't know that Lincoln was also a family man. I didn't realize he had all those children and that one of them died. No wonder he was so compassionate."

After reading Katherine Paterson's *Lyddie* (1991, N), Daniel remarked: "Wow, I didn't know that they treated females like slaves back then. I thought that only blacks were treated that way. I guess revision is revision whether in writing or reading. Now I understand that revision means thinking again about something I thought was one way."

When students share the revisions they made in their thinking after reading a certain book, they gradually come to understand that revision in writing is the same as revision in thinking—that they too can make discoveries and go beyond what they originally said when they wrote their drafts.

When first using this technique with students, it is important to select books carefully in order to give students something different to think about. The books listed in figure 7.3 are particularly powerful in helping students rethink, resee, and ultimately revise previously held notions.

Figure 7.3.
Book that are models
for revision.

For Students Ages 5–9:	For Students of All Ages:
Norah Dooley, *Everybody Cooks Rice* (1991)	Byrd Baylor and Peter Parnall, *The Other Way to Listen* (1978)
Gail Gibbons, *Sharks* (1992)	Diane Hoyt-Goldsmith, *Hoang Anh: A Vietnamese-American Boy* (1992)
Florence Parry Heide and Judith Heide Gilliland, *The Day of Ahmed's Secret* (1990, N)	Robert Ingpen and Margaret Dunkle, *Conservation* (1988)
Bernard Most, *The Cow That Went OINK* (1990)	Patricia Lauber, *The News about Dinosaurs* (1989, N)
For Students Ages 10 and up:	Joan Lowery Nixon, *If You Were a Writer* (1988, N)
Claude Clément, *The Voice of the Wood* (1989)	Katherine Scholes, *Peace Begins with You* (1990)
Drew Nelson, *Wild Voices* (1991, N)	Susan Sussman and Robert James Sussman, *Lies (People Believe) about Animals* (1987)
Doris Buchanan Smith, *Voyages* (1989, N)	
Jerry Spinelli, *Maniac Magee* (1990, N)	

Paying attention to copyright dates in informational books is another avenue to discussing revision. An engaging activity is to have students explore a topic, particularly one that is scientific in nature, by looking at past and current books, noting the copyright dates. This can lead to a discussion of how scientific information has changed over time, how scientists and authors had to revise their thinking about the topic, and why copyright dates are important information when doing any kind of research. An excellent book to use for this kind of reflection is Patricia Lauber's *The News about Dinosaurs* (1989, N).

Stylistic Concerns: Using Works like a Writer

Leads

In his book *A Writer Teaches Writing*, Murray (1985) describes the various kinds of leads and why they are important: "We know that a reader takes three to five seconds—or less—to decide to read an article. Professional writers know how quickly they have to capture the reader, and the journalistic term 'lead' comes from the need to lead the reader into the story" (p. 27). To help students understand the importance of leads, select about two dozen books. Read each lead sentence, and ask the students if they are interested in the book. Put the books in two piles—ones they would like to read and ones they are not interested in reading. Discuss why they made their decisions. Then engage the students in a conversation about the importance of leads and the kinds of information they provide. Avi begins his chapter book *The True Confessions of Charlotte Doyle* (1991, N) with an "important warning" to the reader. One cannot read this without wanting to finish the book:

Not every thirteen-year-old girl is accused of murder, brought to trial, and found guilty. But I was just such a girl, and my story is worth relating even if it did happen years ago. Be warned, however, this is no *Story of a Bad Boy*, no *What Katy Did*. If strong ideas and action offend you, read no more. Find another companion to share your idle hours. For my part I intend to tell the truth as *I* lived it. (P. 1)

An example of a descriptive lead which takes an entire chapter is the "Tuning," or prologue, to Gary Paulsen's *The Winter Room* (1989, N). Paulsen skillfully involves the reader in the smells, sights, and sounds of a Minnesota farm:

If books could be more, could show more, could own more, this book would have smells. . . .
It would have the smells of old farms; the sweet smell of new-mown hay as it falls off the oiled sickle blade when the horses pull the mower through the field, and the sour smell of manure steaming in a winter barn. It would have the sticky-slick smell of birth when the calves come and they suck for the first time on the rich, new milk; the dusty smell of winter hay dried and stored in the loft waiting to be dropped down to the cattle; the pungent fermented smell of the chopped corn silage when it is brought into the manger on the silage fork. This book would have the smell of new potatoes sliced and frying in light pepper on a woodstove burning dry pine, the damp smell of leather mittens, steaming on the back of the stovetop, and the acrid smell of the slop bucket by the door when the lid is lifted and the potato peelings are dumped in—but it can't.
Books can't have smells. . . .
If books could have more, give more, be more, show more, they would still need readers, who bring to them sound and smell and light and all the rest that can't be in books.
The book needs you. (Pp. 1–3)

Patricia MacLachlan, on the other hand, begins her book *Journey* (1991, N) with a lead which introduces all the characters on the first page of chapter one:

My grandfather is belly down in the meadow with his camera, taking a close-up of a cow pie. He has, in the weeks since Mama left, taken many photographs—one of our least trustworthy cow, Mary Louise, standing up to her hocks in meadow muck; one of my grandmother in the pantry, reading a book while bees, drawn to her currant wine, surround her head in a small halo; and many of himself, taken with the self-timer device he's not yet figured out. The pictures of himself fascinate him. They line the back of the barn wall in a series of my grandfather in flight, dressed in overalls, caught in the moment of entering the picture, or leaving it; some with grand dimwitted smiles, his hair flying; one of a long, work-worn hand stretched out gracefully, the only part of him able to make it into the frame before the camera clicks. (Pp. 2–3)

Discussing leads and showing examples of the various kinds of leads will move students away from the "Once upon a time" and "This is a story about" leads they typically write and will encourage them to write leads that entice and intrigue a reader to continue reading.

Imagery, Metaphor, and Sound

As Denman (1991) indicates, "Written images found in stories provide a finishing polish that adds luster and brilliance to a description" (p. 135). Images of sound, sight, taste, touch, and smell bring the reader into the piece; they evoke responses to the story and allow the reader to experience the tale and react to it. The poetic text and strong imagery in Nancy White Carlstrom's *Goodbye Geese* (1991, N) make it an excellent book to use for this purpose. Read this lovely picture book about winter, discuss the sensory images the author creates, and ask students to think about new ways to explain and describe winter.

Students will quickly notice the use of metaphors in Audrey and Don Wood's *Quick as a Cricket* (1982). After reading this lyrical book, engage the students in creating their own metaphors. Start off by giving them a stem, such as, "I am as loud as," and ask them to complete it. Be advised, however, to resist the temptation to put this kind of language play exercise on a worksheet. It is important for children to play around with metaphors verbally and hear what others have created. In this way, the students are teaching one another, and the atmosphere is one of experimentation and risk. Two other metaphor-filled books which teachers may find helpful for this activity are Robert San Souci's *The Talking Eggs: A Folktale from the American South* (1989, N) and Judi Barrett's *A Snake Is Totally Tail* (1983, N).

Novels can also provide excellent examples of imagery. In Thomas A. Barron's *The Ancient One* (1992), a dramatic fantasy about the deforestation of the ancient redwood trees in the Pacific Northwest, the author engages the reader by using crisp imagery throughout. When Barron writes, "The great redwoods swayed back and forth in the wind, creaking and groaning like wrathful beasts," it is difficult not to be swept into this tale of intrigue and mystery. This captivating chapter book for students ten and older is filled with images of sound, sight, smell, touch, and feelings and is an excellent read-aloud. As the students listen to the story, they might jot down those images that grab them, and then talk about how the images enhanced the story.

Strong Verbs and Nouns

Start mini-lessons on strong verbs by reading all the sentences in which the students used the word *said*. Ask students exactly how their characters said what they were saying. "Did the person say this in a quiet voice, an angry voice, a concerned voice?" After this discussion, point out that authors often use other words for *said,* such as *screamed, whispered, grumbled, muttered.* These alternatives paint pictures for the readers and make the stories more interesting. Follow the discussion by asking students to listen for and jot down alternative words for *said* in the stories read aloud. Books that are especially helpful for making this point are Natalie Babbitt's *Tuck Everlasting* (1975), Tololwa Mollel's *The Orphan Boy* (1990, N), Nicolas van Pallandt's *The Butterfly Night of Old Brown Bear* (1992), and Eric Carle's *The Very Busy Spider* (1984) and *The Very Quiet Cricket* (1990).

Once students are comfortable using other words for the word *said,* discuss alternatives for the words *got* and *went,* which students frequently overuse. Again, start by reading books and asking students to listen for the words the author uses instead of *got* and *went.*

At this point, students usually understand that using strong verbs is better than modifying weak verbs with adverbs. Discuss the value of using precise verbs and encourage students to notice the verbs in the literature they are reading. Some particularly excellent books for this exercise are Bill Martin Jr. and John Archambault's *Listen to the Rain* (1988, N), Denise Fleming's *In the Tall, Tall Grass* (1991, N), Barbara Booth's *Mandy* (1991), Claire Ewart's *One Cold Night* (1992), and Jim Arnosky's *Otters under Water* (1992, N).

Using specific nouns is another stylistic device to point out. Because writing nonfiction books demands that careful wording be used to explain the information, these books are useful in demonstrating to students the importance of the stylistic device. Megan McDonald's *Is This a House for Hermit Crab?* (1990, N) and William George's *Box Turtle at Long Pond* (1989) and *Fishing at Long Pond* (1991) use specific nouns throughout. When these books are read aloud, students might listen for interesting or powerful nouns like *driftwood, burrow,* and *spine* in *Is This a House for Hermit Crab?* which provide readers with a specific image, or nouns like *paloverde, seedling, jackrabbit,* and *Gila woodpecker* in Brenda Guiberson's *Cactus Hotel* (1991, N).

Application   An important aspect of learning how to write enticing leads, to incorporate evocative imagery, and to use strong verbs and nouns is to encourage students to apply this information to their own writing. Ask students to look for places in their own stories which would be improved by using these techniques. Have students share the original and revised sections and explain why they made those changes. Students might select a sentence and show the revisions that this one sentence underwent. Student authors could write the variations of that sentence on a large chart so that the other students can actually see all the changes. In this way, all the students become teachers and learners. Students need to use the information they learn through mini-lessons and discussions if they are to make the techniques their own.

Becoming Aware of an Author's Different Styles

Many students are unaware that an author's style of language may vary from book to book, depending on the tone and mood he or she wants to create in the story. To help young readers and writers become knowledgeable about this important aspect of writing, teachers may want to involve students in an examination of one writer's books. Because upper-elementary and middle school or junior high students typically enjoy Gary Paulsen's books, his work provides a good starting place for examining different writing styles. For example, Paulsen uses a concise, terse style in *Dogsong* (1985), *Hatchet* (1987, N), and *Canyons* (1990). In *Canyons*, he writes:

> His horse tried to keep running without stepping on him but could not and veered off into a circle fighting away from the body.
> The body.
> Magpie.
> Magpie was a body.
> He must untie the rope holding him to the straw-colored horse. He fumbled with the knot, jerked, finally pulled it free. Only twenty good leaps to the canyon mouth, to the trail, to safety, to life.
> Magpie was a body.
> He slammed his heels into the horse, asking for more, still more speed. Behind him there was more gunfire. The bluebellies reloaded as they rode, shot again and again and still the bullets missed.
> Ten leaps.
> Now five. (P. 71)

In *The Island* (1988, N), on the other hand, Paulsen writes in a more descriptive style, using longer and more complex sentences:

> He did not know what awakened him. One second he was asleep, and the next his eyes were open and he was staring at the ceiling, not realizing where he was or how he got there. The sun was streaming through the windows and cooking his head. He had been sleeping flat on his back, hard and down, without moving and with his mouth open, and now he was awake to a taste that can come only from sleeping with your mouth open after eating half-warm beans and franks, and he couldn't think of where he had packed his toothbrush. He turned his head sideways and saw a face looking at him through the window—a face so ugly it drove him off the bed and down along the wall. (P. 12)

Readers will appreciate the difference in style between *Canyons* and *The Island* and will easily notice that Paulsen's groundbreaking *Nightjohn* (1993) is unlike anything else he has ever written. Paulsen effectively uses dialect to communicate time and setting, develop his characters, and achieve a particular mood.

This is a story about Nightjohn. I guess in some ways it is a story about me just as much because I am in it and I know what happened and some of it happened to me but it still seems to be most about him.

Nightjohn.

There's some to say I brought him with witchin', brought Nightjohn because he came to be talking to me alone but it ain't so. I knew he was coming but it wasn't witchin', just listening. (P. 13)

All I know for a mammy is the one that raised me, old Delie, and she be the one who raises all the young. Breeders don't get to keep their own babies because they be spending all their time raising babies and not working. So when they're born babies go to the wet nurse and she feeds them and then old Delie gets them and they don't live with their birthing mammies again even if they aren't sold off. (P. 16)

Discussing the various styles one author uses can help young writers take risks and experiment with different styles in their own writing. Such experimentation will in turn help students develop and focus their ability to read to learn about writing style. When students select particular authors as their mentors and study the authors' various styles, they become aware that words and their placement in sentences work synergistically to create mood and tone, communicate time and setting, and develop characters. Students can then use this information to work consciously on developing a range of writing styles.

Books about Children as Writers

Children are curious about and often identify with the children they encounter in books, so teachers might introduce them to books which portray students as writers. Picture books such as Dale Gottlieb's *My Stories by Hildy Calpurinia Rose* (1991), Pat Brisson's *Kate on the Coast* (1992), and Joan Lowery Nixon's *If You Were a Writer* (1988, N) and chapter books like Karen Hesse's *Letters from Rifka* (1993), Avi's *Nothing but the Truth* (1991, N), Gary Paulsen's *The Island* (1988, N), and Carla Stevens's *A Book of Your Own: Keeping a Diary or Journal* (1993) can provide excellent models and guidance about writing. When sharing these books with students, teachers might discuss the characters' intentions for writing and why they might have selected the forms they did to communicate. Such discussions can help children understand that form of writing is determined by one's purposes.

Cautions and Considerations

Students can learn about writing through reading works of literature. But rather than controlling our students' writing by using literature as the new story starter, we must encourage students to experiment with various writing formats and styles and then share these with others. This means that we teachers must write alongside students and show them how we learn about writing from the books and stories we read.

Of course, when students are grappling and struggling, and the writing energy of the class begins to dissipate, it may be necessary for the teacher to step in and give some direct assistance. While giving students time to read and write are important aspects of any literacy program, knowing what to teach, how to teach, when to step in and give direct assistance, and when to stand back and allow children to explore and make their own mistakes involves proper timing. "Timing is important because unless the student is able and ready to receive the information, any attempt at teaching concepts, strategies, or skills may be in vain" (Siu-Runyan 1991, p. 103).

References

Professional Resources

DeFord, D. 1981. "Literacy: Reading, Writing and Other Essentials." *Language Arts* 58:652–58.

Denman, G. A. 1991. *Sit Tight, and I'll Swing You a Tail . . .: Using and Writing Stories with Young People*. Portsmouth, NH: Heinemann.

Eckhoff, B. 1983. "How Reading Affects Children's Writing." *Language Arts* 60:607–16.

Graves, D. H. 1990. *Discover Your Own Literacy*. Portsmouth, NH: Heinemann.

Mills, E. 1974. "Children's Literature and Teaching Written Composition. *Elementary English* 51:971–73.

Murray, D. M. 1985. *A Writer Teaches Writing*. Boston: Houghton Mifflin.

———. 1991. *The Craft of Revision*. New York: Henry Holt.

Siu-Runyan, Y. 1991. "Learning from Students: An Important Aspect of Classroom Organization. *Language Arts* 68:100–107.

Smith, F. 1983. "Reading like a Writer." *Language Arts* 60:558–67.

Children's Literature

Aardema, Verna. 1981. *Bringing the Rain to Kapiti Plain: A Nandi Tale*. Illustrated by Beatriz Vidal. New York: Dial Books.

Ackerman, Karen. 1989. *Song and Dance Man*. Illustrated by Stephen Gammell. New York: Alfred A. Knopf.

Albert, Burton. 1991. *Where Does the Trail Lead?* Illustrated by Brian Pinkney. New York: Simon and Schuster.

Allen, Pamela. 1982. *Who Sank the Boat?* New York: Coward-McCann.

See the Bibliography of Notable Books at the end of the book for bibliographic information about cited Notable Books. The Notable titles do not appear in this reference list.

Aragon, Jane Chelsea. 1989. *Salt Hands.* Illustrated by Ted Rand. New York: E. P. Dutton.

Arnold, Tedd. 1988. *Ollie Forgot.* New York: Dial Books.

Babbitt, Natalie. 1975. *Tuck Everlasting.* New York: Farrar, Strauss and Giroux.

Balian, Lorna. 1974. *Humbug Rabbit.* Nashville, TN: Abingdon Press.

Barron, Thomas A. 1992. *The Ancient One.* New York: Philomel Books.

Bauer, Caroline Feller. 1985. *My Mom Travels a Lot.* Illustrated by Nancy Winslow Parker. New York: Frederick Warne.

Baylor, Byrd, and Peter Parnall. 1978. *The Other Way to Listen.* New York: Macmillan.

Blake, Robert J. 1992. *The Perfect Spot.* New York: Philomel Books.

Booth, Barbara D. 1991. *Mandy.* Illustrated by Jim LaMarche. New York: Lothrop, Lee and Shepard Books.

Brown, Ruth. 1988. *Ladybug, Ladybug.* New York: E. P. Dutton.

Brisson, Pat. 1992. *Kate on the Coast.* Illustrated by Rick Brown. New York: Bradbury Press.

Bunting, Eve. 1991. *Fly Away Home.* Illustrated by Ronald Himler. New York: Clarion Books.

Burningham, John. 1977. *Come Away from the Water, Shirley.* New York: Thomas Y. Crowell.

Carle, Eric. 1969. *The Very Hungry Caterpillar.* New York: Philomel Books.

———. 1984. *The Very Busy Spider.* New York: Philomel Books.

———. 1990. *The Very Quiet Cricket.* New York: Philomel Books.

Carrier, Lark. 1985. *There Was a Hill.* Saxonville, MA: Picture Book Studio.

Clément, Claude (trans. by Lenny Hort). 1989. *The Voice of the Wood.* Illustrated by Frédéric Clement. New York: Dial Books.

Dooley, Norah. 1991. *Everybody Cooks Rice.* Illustrated by Peter J. Thornton. Minneapolis: Carolrhoda Books.

Ernst, Lisa Campbell. 1983. *Sam Johnson and the Blue Ribbon Quilt.* New York: Lothrop, Lee and Shepard Books.

Ewart, Claire. 1992. *One Cold Night.* New York: G. P. Putnam's Sons.

Flanders, Michael, and Donald Swann. 1991. *The Hippopotamus Song: A Muddy Love Story.* Illustrated by Nadine Bernard Westcott. Boston: Little, Brown.

Fleischman, Paul. 1988. *Rondo in C.* Illustrated by Janet Wentworth. New York: Harper and Row.

———. 1991. *Time Train.* Illustrated by Claire Ewart. New York: HarperCollins.

Fox, Mem. 1989. *Shoes from Grandpa.* Illustrated by Patricia Mullins. New York: Orchard Books.

Freedman, Russell. 1987. *Lincoln: A Photobiography.* New York: Clarion Books.

Friedman, Ina R. 1984. *How My Parents Learned to Eat.* Illustrated by Allen Say. Boston: Houghton Mifflin.

Galdone, Paul. 1968. *Henny Penny.* New York: Seabury Press.

———. 1975. *The Gingerbread Boy.* New York: Seabury Press.

George, William T. 1989. *Box Turtle at Long Pond.* Illustrated by Lindsay Barrett George. New York: Greenwillow Books.

———. 1991. *Fishing at Long Pond.* Illustrated by Lindsay Barrett George. New York: Greenwillow Books.

Gibbons, Gail. 1992. *Sharks.* New York: Holiday House.

Gottlieb, Dale. 1991. *My Stories by Hildy Calpurnia Rose.* New York: Alfred A. Knopf.

Gross, Ruth B. 1990. *What's on My Plate?* Illustrated by Isadore Seltzer. New York: Macmillan.

Guarino, Deborah. 1989. *Is Your Mama a Llama?* Illustrated by Steven Kellogg. New York: Scholastic.

Harshman, Marc. 1989. *A Little Excitement.* Illustrated by Ted Rand. New York: E. P. Dutton.

Haviland, Virginia. 1990. *The Talking Pot: A Danish Folktale.* Illustrated by Melissa Sweet. Boston: Little, Brown.

Hazen, Barbara Shook. 1979. *Tight Times.* Illustrated by Tina Schart Hyman. New York: Penguin.

Hesse, Karen. *Letters from Rifka.* New York: Henry Holt.

Hirschi, Ron. 1991. *Harvest Song.* Illustrated by D. Haeffele. New York: E. P. Dutton.

Hogrogrian, Nonny. 1971. *One Fine Day.* New York: Macmillan.

Hoyt-Goldsmith, Diane. 1992. *Hoang Anh: A Vietnamese-American Boy.* Photographs by Lawrence Migdale. New York: Holiday House.

Ingpen, Robert, and Margaret Dunkle. 1988. *Conservation.* Toronto, Ontario: Macmillan of Canada.

Joyce, William. 1990. *A Day with Wilbur Robinson.* New York: Harper and Row.

Lattig-Ehlers, Laura. 1986. *Canoeing.* Illustrated by I. Gantschev. Saxonville, MA: Picture Book Studio.

Le Tord, Bijon. 1987. *My Grandma Leonie.* New York: Bradbury Press.

MacLachlan, Patricia. 1980. *Through Grandpa's Eyes.* Illustrated by Deborah Kogan Ray. New York: Harper and Row.

———. 1982. *Mama One, Mama Two.* New York: Harper and Row.

Martin, Bill, Jr. 1970. *Brown Bear, Brown Bear, What Do You See?* Illustrated by Eric Carle. New York: Holt, Rinehart and Winston.

Mayer, Mercer. 1968. *There's a Nightmare in My Closet.* New York: Dial Press.

McDonald, Megan. 1991. *The Potato Man.* Illustrated by Ted Lewin. New York: Orchard Books.

Miller, Montzalee. 1987. *My Grandmother's Cookie Jar.* Illustrated by Katherine Potter. Los Angeles: Price Stern Sloan.

———. 1991. *Whose Shoe?* New York: Greenwillow Books.

Morris, Linda Lowe. 1991. *Morning Milking.* Illustrated by David Deran. Saxonville, MA: Picture Book Studio.

Most, Bernard. 1990. *The Cow That Went Oink.* San Diego: Harcourt Brace Jovanovich.

Munsch, Robert. 1985. *Thomas' Snowsuit.* Illustrated by Michael Martchenko. Toronto, Ontario: Annick Press.

Noble, Trinka Hakes. 1987. *Meanwhile Back at the Ranch.* Illustrated by Tony Ross. New York: Dial Books.

Numeroff, Laura Joffe. 1985. *If You Give a Mouse a Cookie.* Illustrated by Felicia Bond. New York: Harper and Row.

———. 1991. *If You Give a Moose a Muffin.* Illustrated by Felicia Bond. New York: HarperCollins.

Paulson, Gary. 1985. *Dogsong.* New York: Bradbury Press.

———. 1990. *Canyons.* New York: Delacorte Press.

———. 1993. *Nightjohn.* New York: Delacorte Press.

Pittman, Helena C. 1988. *Once When I Was Scared.* Illustrated by Ted Rand. New York: E. P. Dutton.

Pryor, Bonnie. 1991. *Greenbrook Farm.* Illustrated by Mark Graham. New York: Simon and Schuster.

Radin, Ruth Yaffe. 1982. *A Winter Place.* Illustrated by M. L. O'Kelley. Boston: Little, Brown.

Rogers, Paul, and Emma Rogers. 1991. *Zoe's Tower.* Illustrated by R. B. Corfield. New York: Simon and Schuster.

Russo, Marisabina. 1991. *A Visit to Oma.* New York: Greenwillow Books.

Ryder, Joanne. 1989. *Mockingbird Morning.* Illustrated by Dennis Nolan. New York: Macmillan.

———. 1990. *Under Your Feet.* Illustrated by Dennis Nolan. New York: Macmillan.

Rylant, Cynthia. 1982. *When I Was Young in the Mountains.* Illustrated by Diane Goode. New York: E. P. Dutton.

———. 1985. *The Relatives Came.* Illustrated by Steven Kellogg. New York: Bradbury Press.

Sanderson, Ruth. 1991. *The Enchanted Wood: An Original Fairy Tale.* Boston: Little, Brown.

Scieszka, Jon. 1989. *The True Story of the Three Little Pigs by A. Wolf.* Illustrated by Lane Smith. New York: Viking.

———. 1991. *The Frog Prince, Continued.* Illustrated by Steve Johnson. New York: Viking.

Scholes, Katherine. 1989. *Peace Begins with You.* Illustrated by Robert Ingpen. Boston: Little, Brown.

Sendak, Maurice. 1962. *Chicken Soup with Rice.* New York: Holt, Rinehart and Winston.

Shulevitz, Uri. 1962. *One Monday Morning.* New York: Charles Scribner's Sons.

Stamm, Claus. 1990. *Three Strong Women: A Tall Tale from Japan.* Illustrated by Jean and Mou-Sien Tseng. New York: Viking.

Stevens, Carla. 1993. *A Book of Your Own: Keeping a Diary or Journal.* New York: Clarion Books.

Sussman, Susan, and Robert James Sussman. 1987. *Lies (People Believe) about Animals.* Photographs by F. Leavitt. Niles, IL: Albert Whitman.

Talanda, Susan. 1983. *Dad Told Me Not To.* Illustrated by Cindy Wheeler. Milwaukee: Raintree Press.

Thurman, Chuck. 1981. *A Time for Remembering.* Illustrated by Elizabeth Sayles. New York: Simon and Schuster.

Van Allsburg, Chris. 1981. *Jumanji.* Boston: Houghton Mifflin.

van Pallandt, Nicolas. 1992. *The Butterfly Night of Old Brown Bear.* New York: Farrar, Strauss and Giroux.

Viorst, Judith. 1972. *Alexander and the Terrible, Horrible, No Good, Very Bad Day.* Illustrated by R. Cruz. New York: Atheneum.

Westcott, Nadine Bernard. 1988. *The Lady with the Alligator Purse.* Boston: Little, Brown.

Williams, Sue. 1990. *I Went Walking.* Illustrated by Julie Vivas. San Diego: Harcourt Brace Jovanovich.

Wood, Audrey. 1982. *Quick as a Cricket.* Illustrated by Don Wood. Singapore: Child's Play.

———. 1984. *The Napping House.* Illustrated by Don Wood. San Diego: Harcourt Brace Jovanovich.

Yabuuchi, Masayuki. 1985. *Whose Baby?* New York: Philomel Books.

———. 1985. *Whose Footprints?* New York: Philomel Books.

Yolen, Jane. 1987. *Owl Moon.* Illustrated by John Schoenherr. New York: Philomel Books.

III Developing an Appreciation for Language Diversity

Books written about a culture reflect the language of that culture. In well-written multicultural literature the language is natural and blends with the story line, yet it also is crafted to lend authenticity and flavor to the story, resonating with the cadences and rhythms of the culture from which it is drawn.

Children need to become aware of language diversity and how language differs across cultures. They must learn to respect this diversity and become sensitive to language that characterizes a particular culture. This is true not only for children who are members of a particular cultural group but for all children.

Jon Stott addresses this issue by showing how trickster tales from many cultures demonstrate the subtle uses and misuses of language while also teaching children an appreciation for the unique qualities of stories from that culture. He also offers suggestions for authentic activities which help children discover these connections. Deborah Thompson explores the language and structure of stories from one culture. She shows how teachers can help children appreciate dialect, unusual words, colorful phrases, storytelling styles, and major writers of that culture. Although she uses African American literature to ground her discussion, the ideas are applicable to a focused study of literature from other cultures. Carl Tomlinson then expands the discussion of language and culture, describing how international books can introduce children to unusual words, provocative language, and new insights on how language and culture are intertwined.

8 How to Do Things with Words: Trickster Stories, Multicultural Awareness, and Language Arts

Jon C. Stott
University of Alberta

It is eleven o'clock in the morning on April 1. The grade-four class is curious and expectant as I walk into the room. For the last month we have been studying trickster stories together—tales from around the world about such characters as the Gingerbread Boy's fox, Robin Hood, Coyote, Ananse, and Rabbit. One of the synonyms we have developed for this type of character is the "irony-maker." Tricksters are successful when what they do is a surprise; it is ironic—not what the victims expect. Familiar with the definition of *irony* as something that is not what you or the characters expect, the students have become comfortable with the synonym. During the preceding classes, I had frequently played the role of irony-maker or trickster, saying or doing things that were not what the students expected. After each incident we discussed my actions and words in relation to the types of stories being considered.

As this class continued and we laughed at the events of the story and discussed the manipulative behavior of the central character, many of the looks of curiosity and expectancy changed to puzzlement and concern. Finally, in the last few minutes of the

The description of classroom activities in this chapter represents a composite account of work done in three Edmonton, Alberta, schools between 1976 and 1991. I am particularly grateful to Norma Youngberg of Belgravia Elementary School, Gladys Vogel and Marie Whelan of Holy Family School, and Maureen Duguay of St. Michael School for opening their classrooms to me and providing valuable feedback and suggestions for further development of the activities.

lesson, one child raised her hand and shook it urgently. When she began to speak, she almost blurted out her words: "But, but!—it's April Fools' Day, it's Irony Day!" (This was another of the class's synonyms.) "Yes," I replied, "I know! What did you expect?" "You haven't played a trick," she replied, and you have in every other class." I paused for a few moments before replying: "So that's what you expected. Did I do what you expected?" Another pause, and then another member of the class exclaimed: "You did play a trick— we expected a trick, and the surprise was that we didn't get one. That was the April Fool!" I was very pleased; the children had obviously understood the nature of the trickster stories we had read and had been able to relate the stories to this day's classroom experience. (As it was, I did have a real trick to play on them. But what it was is a secret—I may want to use it another time!)

Found in cultures around the world, the trickster figure not only reveals the specific social, moral, and religious beliefs of the tremendously different groups who tell stories about him; he also illustrates humanity's ability to use and misuse its special gift of language. Children in the middle- and upper-elementary grades who are introduced to a range of trickster stories will gain a greater sense of the multicultural nature of the world as they study the various incarnations of this almost universal character. By paying careful attention to his use of language, they will also gain a fuller understanding of the subtle effects language can produce when it comes from the tongue of a clever, skilled practitioner.

Psychologists, anthropologists, folklorists, and literary critics have studied the trickster figure extensively, noticing the common qualities he shares in all the geographical regions in which he is found. Nearly always he is male, a fact which some feminists have suggested reflects the negative character traits found in men everywhere. More likely, however, is the contention that being male gives him the freedom necessary to rove about and experience many adventures. He is a complex, divided being. Sometimes he is a creator, involved in making the world and giving the landscape and animals the distinctive features they possess to this day. At other times, he is a vulnerable individual who must use his wits to defeat physically superior enemies. Often he is purely selfish, tricking others to gratify his desires. At the extreme, he is an evil being, employing his abilities to destroy goodness and bring sorrow to others. And in some cultures, he can be all of these at different times. Nanabush, the Ojibway (Chippewa) trickster, not only rebuilds the world after a great flood, rewarding and punishing various creatures as they deserve, but he also uses his devious wiles to gluttonize and to seduce young women.

In some stories, the trickster is female. She generally does not possess the negative qualities of her male counterpart. Most frequently, she must use her wiles to escape from dangerous situations in which she is in conflict with physically superior opponents. Usually her actions are undertaken for the benefit of others as well as herself.

Diamond has called the trickster the "*personification* of ambivalence" (quoted in Radin 1972, xiii). Jung stated that he is "a faithful copy of an absolutely undifferentiated human consciousness, corresponding to a psyche that has hardly left the animal level" (p. 200). Canadian Ojibway storyteller and anthropologist Johnston (1983) believes that the trickster "symbolizes mankind and womankind in all their aspirations and accomplishments, or in all their foibles and misadventures" (p. 44). As such, stories of the trickster have been an important component of "children's literature" around the world, implicitly providing young listeners with the moral lessons and cultural values of the people telling the stories. Laughter has been an essential part of the response to these tales. "Yet it is difficult to say," Radin (1972) writes, "whether the audience is laughing at him, at the tricks he plays on others, or at the implications his behaviour and activities have for them" (p. xxiv).

In structure, trickster stories follow a remarkably similar pattern. A tale usually begins with the main character facing a problem which will require all his wits to solve. The obstacle he must overcome can be internal (his laziness, for example) or external (such as difficulties in the way of reaching his goal or other characters who present a danger to him). Planning is essential, but even with careful planning the achievement of the goal is not certain, for the forces or individuals that the trickster must confront are frequently of sufficient magnitude to make defeat possible. The action of the story involves using his abilities in the face of opposition. Success is usually the result of the trickster's skill at understanding his opponent and taking advantage of his awareness of his adversary's weakness. Defeat often comes when the trickster fails to take into account his own flaws, the four most important of which are his ego, his greed, his lust, and his laziness.

Within this general structural pattern, there are many potential variations in details, thus making possible the trickster story cycles, or collections of adventures of a specific character, that are found in many cultural groups. More important, details can be varied to reflect the cultural specifics of the societies telling the stories. What the trickster wants to do, the explicit strengths and weaknesses he reveals, and the nature of his opponents and opposing forces all cast light on the moral, religious, and social environment out of which each story emerges.

Given the humor of the tales, it is not surprising that many have been adapted and written as children's stories. As children's perceptions of the absurd and of situational and verbal ironies grow during the middle-elementary years, they are more receptive to comic adventures and misadventures. Moreover, as they also begin to perceive cultural differences in the people around them and the world at large, they can appreciate and respect the culture-specific values the trickster both embodies and violates. In the pages that follow, I outline the ways in which I have presented a number of trickster stories to fourth- and fifth-grade students in Edmonton, Alberta, and how they have used their study of these tales to increase their understanding of the implicit nature of literary language, their respect for other cultures, and their use of and response to language in a variety of situations. The stories are discussed here in the order in which they were presented in the classroom, an order which encouraged a cumulative development of the students' literary skills and cultural understanding.

A Story, a Story (1970), Gail E. Haley's Caldecott Medal–winning adaptation of the Ashanti (West African) tale about the origin of stories, takes readers back to an era that most will find hard to envision, a time when stories did not exist. People possessed language, but not its supreme vehicle of expression: literature. Ananse, the weak and small old man who seeks stories from the Sky God, Nyame, must perform three seemingly impossible tasks. Readers' interest in the tale is not on *if* he will be successful, but *how*. Faced with capturing a fierce leopard, a swarm of stinging hornets, and an invisible fairy, Ananse uses language to trick his physically more able opponents. Knowing the leopard's fondness for games, Ananse suggests one which ends with the leopard tied up. Understanding the hornets' fear of rain, he pours water on their nest and lies about a rainstorm. Recognizing the fairy's temper, he holds his tongue, causing her to become angry at his silence and thus to entrap herself. Ananse deserves the reward of stories, for he has demonstrated that he possesses the language skills necessary to appreciate them. He is also a hero to the Ashanti people, for whom the communal event of storytelling was a socially binding ritual.

Our class discussion of *A Story, a Story* focused on the obstacles Ananse faces, both his own physical limitations and the apparently superior characteristics of the animals, and the value of his language skills in his success. We considered the differences between the stated and intended meaning of his conversation with the leopard, the success of his misrepresentations to the hornets, and the appropriateness of his silence toward the fairy. I asked students:

> Why didn't Ananse object when the leopard said the old man would be his lunch, instead suggesting that they play a game?

Did he know something important about the leopard?

How did he use words to achieve his goal of capturing the leopard?

Students replied:

He didn't want the leopard to get angry by trying to run away!

He knew the leopard wasn't very smart.

The leopard liked games. He thought Ananse would untie him and that he'd be able to tie the man up and then eat him.

Then the students created sentences expressing what Ananse was thinking rather than what he was saying: "Boy, are you ever stupid, Osebo. You think I'm doing what you want." One child said, "One down, two to go!" We then discussed how Ananse's behavior and his ability with words reveal that he is the worthy recipient of stories. Finally, we examined the importance of story as a learning tool for traditional and modern Ashanti children and considered the lessons contained in other *anansesem,* as collections of Ananse stories are called. In an extended language arts activity, students compared Ananse's use of language with that of modern advertisers. Like the trickster hero, advertisers use their knowledge of consumers to shape language to fulfill their own needs, not always those of the consumers. The students reported on the language of commercials they watched during Saturday morning cartoons.

Many of the West African trickster stories were carried to the New World, where they were adapted to the new and terrible conditions of the slaves. Those about Ananse are found most frequently in the Caribbean; those about the rabbit resurfaced as tales about Br'er, Bo, or Mr. Rabbit. In the United States, Rabbit became a symbol of the slaves, surviving and occasionally thriving through clever dissembling.

"Mr. Rabbit and Mr. Bear," in *The Knee-High Man, and Other Stories* by African American author Julius Lester (1972), presents the trickster as a victor in a repressive society which would exclude him from sharing in its bounty. A lover of lettuce, Mr. Rabbit discovers that the farmer has surrounded his acres of lettuce by a wire fence. Too lazy to dig under, he talks a little girl into letting him in, lying when he says that the farmer wanted her to do so. Captured by the angry farmer, who hangs him by one leg from a tree, Mr. Rabbit does not panic; he begins immediately to plan his escape. When the slow-footed and slow-witted Mr. Bear comes by, the hero uses his linguistic skills to effect his release, telling his friend that he is enjoying his situation, a new and wonderful position for resting, and expressing reluctance to trade his place with the now envious Mr. Bear.

The students discussed Mr. Rabbit's creative solutions to two problems: getting into the garden and then getting out of the trap.

Concentrating on his dialogue, we considered the effect of what he said on his victims. The children recognized that he had flattered the little girl and created a sense of trust. He made the bear envious by appearing to be unwilling to trade places. The most enjoyable follow-up language activity began with an examination of the adjectives used to describe the lettuce: "delicious, scrumptious, crispy, luscious, delectable, exquisite, ambrosial, nectareous" (p. 13). We talked about the meanings of the words and then created similar ones to describe food the students liked: *juicy* (for hamburgers), *crunchy* (for popcorn), and *stringy* (for cheese topping on pizza). Then we devised linguistic strategies for getting people to eat something they did not like. The children first listed the foods they particularly detested and then recalled what adults had said to make them eat, but which did not work. The most universally suggested negative phrase was, "It's good for you!" Now we became tricksters of language, creating adjectives to make the disliked food items appear attractive: *crisp broccoli, creamy porridge,* and *crackling crackers.* Finally, each child role-played, pretending to be an adult enticing a younger child to eat the "stuff."

While the best-known trickster stories deal with males, there are many about females. In studying these, readers can ponder the question of whether gender influences the nature and motivation of the trickster's actions. The next two stories deal with brave and clever female tricksters who use their wits to escape dangerous, threatening situations. Each is no physical match for her opponent; survival, a safe arrival at her destination, and fulfillment of a mission on behalf of others depend on successful execution of plans, one aspect of which involves fast talking.

Flossie and the Fox by Patricia McKissack (1986, N) is an African American version of the traditional tale of the sly fox and his unsuspecting victim. Delivering eggs to a neighbor whose henhouse has suffered from the raids of a fox, Flossie uses language to thwart the fox's intentions to steal the eggs, and she arrives safely at her destination. Perceiving the creature's pride in himself as a fox, she suggests that his physical features could mean that he is a rabbit, a rat, a cat, or a squirrel, thereby lessening his self-esteem. Confident at first, he later "shouts," "gasps," "howls," "pleads," and finally "cries" like a baby. On a more culture-specific level, Flossie may represent the young, Southern, rural, African American female who is successful dealing with an adult male whose speech patterns early in the story are not unlike those of a white, Northern carpetbagger. The students studied the success of the heroine's tactics by tracing the changing speech patterns of the fox. They suggested that when the fox said to her, "My dear child . . . of course I'm a fox. A little girl like you should be simply terrified of me. Whatever do they teach children these days?" (unnumbered, p. 12), he was talking like a snobbish and bossy adult. When asked to be more specific, they suggested older aunts and uncles who had never had children and some teachers they remembered. One child recalled a clergyman he disliked. They noted that the fox frequently used big words because he thought that Flossie was not smart enough to understand them. "He's losing it now," one student remarked about the fox's stammering responses later in the story.

Canadian author/illustrator Robin Muller's version of the English folktale *Mollie Whuppie and the Giant* (1982) presents a familiar theme: the triumph of the youngest sister. Mollie's actions lead to the escape of three girls from both a cannibalistic giant and the poverty which had initially caused their parents to abandon them in the deep woods. After she has brought them safely to the palace of a king with three unmarried sons, Mollie procures royal husbands for her two sisters and then for herself by returning three times to the giant's home to retrieve treasure he had stolen. She reveals her cleverness and courage most fully on the third and most dangerous trip, when, imprisoned by the giant in a sack, she piques the curiosity of the giant's wife by saying that there are wondrous things to be seen in the sack, but refusing to tell what they are. When the woman opens the sack and lets Mollie out so that she herself can get in, Mollie sews up the sack and escapes. The happy-ever-after ending for the three girls represents a kind of wish fulfillment for poor English girls of times gone by. With virtually no hope of social advancement, most could only look forward to a life of drudgery and subservience in marriage. Not only does Mollie acquire wealth, power, and equality in her royal marriage, but she controls her own destiny by revealing a cleverness which most people of that time would not have believed a female could possess.

In examining the language of the story, the students compared the dialogue of Mollie and her sisters to see how the speeches of each revealed aspects of character. They then compiled a list of adjectives to describe the girls' characters, making sure that each word was an adjective by seeing if it would fit naturally into the blank space in the words "a (or an) _____ person." Suggested answers ranged from fairly obvious and general—*brave* and *smart*—to more precise—*resourceful, daring,* and *considerate.* We accepted all the adjectives, requiring only that students explain their reasons for choosing certain words. Some students observed that several adjectives chosen were quite similar in meaning, which led to a discussion of synonyms and to a listing of synonyms for some of the other previously suggested adjectives. Mollie's successful manipulation of the giant's wife was compared to similar situations in earlier stories, particularly Flossie's encounter with the fox and Ananse's meeting with the leopard. Finally, we noticed that this retelling is particularly rich in metaphorical comparisons. For example, as the girls wander lost in the woods, "The trees became as black as crows' wings" (p. 2). The students discussed the appropriateness of both the color and shape of the metaphor. One student said that crows eat dead meat and felt that this association made the forest seem more dangerous and frightening to her. We then made new metaphors for other details in the story. Beaten by her husband, the giant's wife screamed like "a tired baby," "an angry cat," and "a skidding car."

Whereas Flossie and Mollie help others while extricating themselves from dangerous situations, the female trickster of Gail E. Haley's *Birdsong* (1984) uses her wiles for selfish and evil purposes. Jorinella, an old woman who has lost her ability to snare the wild birds she sells, notices how Birdsong, a poor young girl, draws birds to her by playing her pipes. After enticing the girl to her cabin with promises of happiness, food, and shelter, Jorinella deceives Birdsong into attracting birds by her pipe playing and then captures the birds. Learning the truth, Birdsong liberates the captives, who carry her away to a distant kingdom where she lives a happy life. Jorinella, the villain, is the type of folklore character known as the *crone*: an old woman who should use her wisdom to help young women achieve maturity. However, she is an *anti-crone*, deceptively tricking the girl for her own selfish and evil purposes. While this story is not culture specific, it belongs to the European tradition of stories about evil witches.

In executing her deceptions, Jorinella practices irony, creating false expectations in Birdsong. Listening to the story a second time, the students noticed how her words deceived the girl. "Come with me, help me with my chores, and you can have all that I own" (unpaged, p. 9) she says, recognizing the young woman's hunger, poverty, and loneliness and creating hopes of a home. She makes Birdsong feel useful by asking her to play the pipes in order to keep her from straying too far; in fact, Jorinella is using the girl's talents for her own ends. Students compared the two italicized passages in the book, relating what the birds sang to Birdsong, and listed the opposites these contained: dawn–night, birth–death, joy–sorrow. Students considered how these opposites related to Birdsong and Jorinella and gradually understood that like the birds that sing to her, Birdsong represents youth, life, freedom, and happiness; Jorinella, the reverse. The relationship between the characters and the themes of freedom and imprisonment were then discussed.

One of the best-known tricksters in world mythology is Loki, the Norse god/giant whose character has many similarities to the biblical Satan. A member of a race which was in constant battle with the gods, Loki had nonetheless befriended the gods, who enjoyed his quick wit and fun-loving mischievousness. However, this mischie-vousness gradually turned to malice, as he set about to gratify his selfishness at his friends' expense. His actions and those of his fellow giants symbolized the difficulties faced by the Norse people in a rugged, harsh, and unpredictable environment. In *Iduna and the Magic Apples* (1988), retold by Marianna Mayer, Loki attempts to save himself from the wicked giant Thiassi by kidnapping Iduna, keeper of an orchard containing the fruits the gods must eat to prevent aging and death. However, when Loki begins to age along with the gods and they discover his treachery, he must set out alone to rescue Iduna.

One of the most interesting aspects of the story to explore is Loki's creative problem solving. To escape from the clutches of Thiassi, he agrees to perform an extremely difficult task: abduction of Iduna from her protective garden. As Loki talks to her, the narra-tor states that he "knew the power of his words." In the classroom we examined Loki's dialogue, noticing how each speech reveals his knowledge of Iduna's character weaknesses. The students created alternative dialogue for each of these speeches, presenting Loki's thoughts, rather than his spoken words. When Loki tells Iduna that she will be sorry if people stop coming to her garden, one student suggested, he is really thinking, "But you'll be even sorrier if you believe me and leave it yourself."

Loki's trick backfires, as do those of many other evil tricksters, two of the most notable being the Sheriff of Nottingham (from the English Robin Hood legends) and Coyote, the Native American character of the Great Plains nations. For personal gain, both violate the moral and social codes of their cultures. Robin Hood was un-justly deprived of his private property by the Sheriff of Nottingham, who was as much interested in his own gain as he was in the pur-poses of his superior, Prince John. Leader of a vastly outnumbered group of similarly dispossessed people and constantly in danger for his life, Robin fought for what was his by right of English law. In the story "Robin Hood Plays Butcher," retold by the nineteenth-century American author/illustrator Howard Pyle (1946), Robin and the sheriff seek to trick each other, but for different reasons: Robin seeks revenge on the sheriff as well as some of that man's ill-gotten gold, whereas the sheriff wishes to outwit for personal gain someone he considers a wealthy simpleton. Each must practice deception in order to succeed. Robin disguises himself as a butcher to enter the town and then assumes the role of a fool easily fleeced of his money so that he can gain admittance to the home of the greedy sheriff, whom he then entices into his own domain, Sherwood Forest. The sheriff, in truth an inhospitable person who hates to be generous with his own possessions, plays the affable host, hoping thereby to trick Robin out of the cattle the hero says he possesses. Pleased with his cleverness and his head filled with thoughts of the easy acquisition of more wealth, the sheriff is victimized by his intended victim, who leads him into a place where he is most vulnerable.

Students began discussion of this story by noticing the goals of each of the characters and the ironic nature of the plans they formulate. The success or failures of the intentions of each were then examined, with students noting the effectiveness of each step of the two strategies. Attention focused on the dialogue of each character, with discussion of the intended result of each speech. Because Pyle sometimes used archaic language to enhance the medieval atmosphere of the story, students made a list of unfamiliar words, looked up dictionary definitions, and considered how Pyle's choice of these words enhanced or detracted from their appreciation of the story. In this activity, students concerned themselves with the role of style in contributing to the total effect of a story.

The trickster figure is also pervasive in Native American mythology—Raven on the Northwest Coast, Nanabush and Glooscap in the Eastern Woodlands, Rabbit in the Southeast, and Coyote across much of the Plains and Western Plateau. He is a complex figure; he is sometimes a helper; and his frequently selfish tricks often backfire. Stories dealing with this aspect of his character were told to children as a means of reenforcing accepted moral and social values of the specific culture. The trickster was held up as a ludicrous, negative example. Such is the case in the story "Coyote Loses his Dinner," retold by Hettie Jones (1974). Always a glutton, Coyote sees a pond of geese and devises a plan to kill, with minimal effort and much trickery on his part, as many as possible. In addition to being lazy and deceitful, he is violating the code prohibiting the killing of more birds than needed. Later, while he is cooking the geese, he is approached by a fox who wishes to share the feast, but Coyote refuses, breaking the law of hospitality. Noticing that the fox is lame, he challenges her to a race. However, the fox, who has been feigning, easily wins the race and devours all the birds before Coyote returns. The trickster has been out-tricked, and it serves him right.

Before reading the story aloud, I discussed with the class the fact that traditional native peoples, as well as many contemporary ones, told stories to children to teach them about acceptable and unacceptable behavior. I asked them to imagine that they were a Lakota (Sioux) boy or girl hearing the story some 150 years ago. What would they learn about appropriate conduct from it? After discussing the cultural aspects, we examined the dialogue, noticing the difference between what the characters say and what they mean. This story has been retold in many forms by many different Native American peoples. By examining some of these versions, such as

Paul Goble's *Iktomi and the Ducks* (1990), from the Sioux; Fran Fraser's "The Old Man and the Ducks" (1959), from the Blackfoot; and the Coatsworths' "Nanabush and the Ducks" (1979), from the Ojibway; we noticed the basic pattern underlying each story and specific differences between them. We pondered whether these differences suggested different cultural backgrounds.

Conclusion

This survey has considered only a small group of trickster stories from different cultures. They could be supplemented or replaced by hundreds of others: further tales of Ananse, Rabbit, Robin Hood, Loki, and Coyote; and trickster tales of different cultures, such as the Polynesian Maui, the biblical Satan, or the Greek god Hermes (Mercury). Whatever texts are selected, a trickster unit can be a valuable component of literature, reading, language arts, and other curriculum programs. Not only are the stories enjoyable and entertaining in their own right, but they can introduce students in the middle- and upper-elementary grades to two important aspects of literary study: (1) the idea that groups of tales share many common elements, that there are genres, or families of stories, and that awareness of the characteristics of each genre can help people in reading each new story in the genre; and (2) that each story is a unique variant within the genre. Stories should be studied both individually and in relation to each other. Moreover, since literature represents a highly specialized and skilled use of language, and since tricksters are extremely clever in their employment of words, reading trickster stories provides excellent training in the transmission and reception of words. Finally, because trickster stories are reflections of the specific and different cultures which create them, a study of these stories is an excellent introduction into the wonderfully varied world in which we live. If we understand the stories of many cultures, we will be better able to understand, appreciate, and respect the people who tell them.

References
Professional Resources

Johnston, B. 1983. "Nanabush." In *Canadian Children's Literature* 31/32:41–45.

Radin, P. 1972. *The Trickster: A Study in American Indian Mythology*. New York: Schocken Books.

See the Bibliography of Notable Books at the end of the book for bibliographic information about cited Notable Books. The Notable titles do not appear in this reference list.

Children's Literature

Aardema, Verna. 1960. "Tricksy Rabbit." In *Tales from the Story Hat.* Illustrated by Elton Fax. New York: Coward-McCann. (Reprinted in J. C. Stott and A. Moss, eds. 1986. *The Family of Stories: An Anthology of Children's Literature.* Toronto, Ontario: Holt, Rinehart and Winston of Canada.)

Coatsworth, Emerson, and David Coatsworth. 1979. *The Adventures of Nanabush: Ojibway Indian Stories.* Toronto, Ontario: Doubleday of Canada.

Fraser, Fran. 1959. *The Bear Who Stole the Chinook, and Other Stories.* Toronto, Ontario: Macmillan of Canada.

Goble, Paul. 1990. *Iktomi and the Ducks.* New York: Orchard Books.

Haley, Gail E. 1970. *A Story, a Story.* New York: Atheneum.

———. 1984. *Birdsong.* New York: Crown.

Jones, Hettie. 1974. "Coyote Loses His Dinner." In *Coyote Tales.* Illustrated by Louis Mofsie. New York: Holt, Rinehart, and Winston. (Reprinted in J. C. Stott and A. Moss, eds. 1986. *The Family of Stories: An Anthology of Children's Literature.* Toronto, Ontario: Holt, Rinehart and Winston of Canada.)

Lester, Julius. 1972. "Mr. Rabbit and Mr. Bear." In *The Knee-High Man, and Other Stories.* Illustrated by Ralph Pinto. New York: Dial Books.

Mayer, Marianna. 1988. *Iduna and the Magic Apples.* New York: Macmillan.

Muller, Robin. 1982. *Mollie Whuppie and the Giant.* Richmond Hill, Ontario: North Winds Press.

Pyle, Howard. 1946. "Robin Hood Plays Butcher." In *The Merry Adventures of Robin Hood.* New York: Charles Scribner's Sons. (Reprinted in J. C. Stott and A. Moss, eds. 1986. *The Family of Stories: An Anthology of Children's Literature.* Toronto, Ontario: Holt, Rinehart and Winston of Canada.)

Diversity in Language: Using Notable African American Children's Literature in the Classroom

Deborah Thompson
American University

A portion of a K-T-L science log entry on spiders from one of Kay Magness's second graders reads as follows:

Know

I no that spiders make their own web.

They have long legs.

Think

I think they all have hair.

They have teeth.

They live in the zoo.

Learn

They lay eggs.

They live in dark places.

They like yams.

They eat flies.

Yams? Spiders? A West African folktale, *Anansi and the Moss-Covered Rock* by Eric Kimmel (1988), influenced this student's log. Magness introduced and shared this tale with her class during read-

The research reported here was funded by a grant from the Tonelson Teaching and Learning Center at Old Dominion University, Norfolk, VA. The author thanks Kay Magness and her second-grade students at James Monroe Elementary School in Norfolk, VA, for allowing her to share in their adventures in good reading.

aloud time. Throughout the school year, she provided her students with a wealth of multiethnic children's books, from folktales to poetry. Students used these books as models for writing and oral retellings and a number of other language extensions. They were knowledgeable about these books and "talked the talk" of their favorite authors with confidence.

Magness's use of multiethnic literature, specifically African American literature for children, grew from the knowledge and understanding she had of her students. She provided them with literature that was fun to read aloud or dramatize, or that led to other language activities as a way to extend their understandings of the stories.

Why Use African American Literature in the Classroom?

There are numerous reasons for using African American literature for children in the classroom. First of all, it is the most readily available of all the ethnic literature (Bishop 1992). Because of this availability, it is not unusual to find teachers who know many more titles by and about African Americans than titles by and about other ethnic groups, such as Hispanics or Asian Americans (Thompson and Hager 1991). Two equally important reasons for using African American literature for children are characters who serve as positive role models, such as Grace in *Amazing Grace* by Mary Hoffman (1991, N) or Sam in *My Friend Jacob* by Lucille Clifton (1980), and the cultural enrichment that enlightens all students, such as learning about Kwanzaa in *Seven Candles for Kwanzaa* by Andrea D. Pinkney (1993) or about the migration of African Americans from the South to the North in the earlier part of this century in *The Great Migration: An American Story* by Jacob Lawrence (1993).

Further, many African American writers have contributed stories rich in the unique rhythms and cadences of language of the oral tradition. Finally, African American literature for children also addresses universal themes, such as life and death, family, and love, that connect readers through common experiences, emotions, needs, and desires (Bishop 1987).

Notable Storytellers

Everyone has a favorite story that has been told by a parent, grandparent, or elder relative. Often these stories have been in the family for many generations. Instead of relying on written stories, these family members tap memories of exciting times, people, and places through oral retellings, or storytelling. With each retelling, the unique memories of a storyteller frame the events conveyed through the magic of words.

The rich and textured stories highlighted in this section are framed by talented storytellers who celebrate the contributions of

African Americans to the body of children's literature. These stories
—folktales, biographies, and historical fiction—picture books,
chapter books, and anthologies—entertain, inform, and inspire
readers through powerful language that evokes vivid images.

Perhaps the easiest introduction to any genre is the anthology.
Anthologies of African American folktales are accessible and include
many award-winning titles that should prove popular with students.
For example, *The People Could Fly: American Black Folktales* by Virginia
Hamilton (1985, N) is a well-known collection of folktales from the
American South. The colorful adventures and dialect of Bruh Rabbit,
Bruh Bear, and He Lion are excellent for reading aloud. Notice
Hamilton's skillful use of the Sea Island dialect, Gullah, in this
section from "Bruh Alligator Meets Trouble":

> Bruh Rabbit has words with Bruh Gator on account Bruh Gator can't
> keep he mouth shut. He tell Bruh Rabbit one day, tellum say, "We
> gators live in the river and my chil'ren smart cause of that. Bruh
> Rabbit, I can't see how *oonuh* can live *pontop* the hard land. Can't
> stand the land, myself." Say all that to Bruh Rabbit, and the rabbit
> dint think much of gator for it.
>   Bruh Rabbit just say, "Mebbe you right, Bruh Gator. We on the
> land seein a lot of trouble."
>   "What Trouble is?" asked Bruh Gator. (P. 35)

At the end of this tale, Hamilton includes a glossary for the
Gullah terms and gives a brief history of the dialect. Those who do
not feel comfortable reading the tales aloud will delight in hearing
the stories read (on tape) by James Earl Jones, whose mellifluous
tones complement Hamilton's well-written text. The language of
each folktale is both colorful and challenging, and the characters'
adventures lead naturally to dramatization. In addition to reading
aloud and listening to the tales, other extensions are possible. For
example, students could make their own personal dictionaries of
Gullah vocabulary and sayings. They could also compare these
African American folktales with other ethnic tales, such as the Jack
tales, Grandfather tales, or Coyote tales.

Teachers who enjoy *The People Could Fly* may also find
Hamilton's *The All Jahdu Storybook* (1991) useful for stimulating
language-oriented response activities. Hamilton created a trickster
hero who was "born in an old oven beside two loaves of baking
bread," and he is always "running along" (p. 11). Students can
compare Jahdu with other tricksters, such as Anansi or Bruh Rabbit,
to discover how cultural, linguistic, and regional differences are
embodied in each character.

Hamilton also writes novels from an African American perspective, which provides students with opportunities to explore
more subtle nuances of dialect and culture. *The Magical Adventures of*

Pretty Pearl (1983, N), a modern fantasy with historical overtones, showcases the feats and adventures of Pretty Pearl and her brothers and fellow African deities, High John the Conqueror and John Henry Roustabout, who travel from Mount Kenya to intermingle with the "Inside People." In the biography *Anthony Burns: The Defeat and Triumph of a Fugitive Slave* (1988, N), Hamilton uses language effectively to weave a narrative pattern that intertwines past and present events:

May 24, 1854

"Hold on, boy!" A harsh voice called to him from the dim light on Brattle Street.

He held himself in and managed to sound calm when he asked, "What do you want of me?"

"They say a boy broke into the jewelry store," the man said, and walked nearer. "About twenty hours ago it was that a boy took a valuable piece of silver. And you look like the same boy." (P. 3)

Just as the readers prepare themselves for further events in 1854, Hamilton abruptly pitches them into the past:

Spring 1839

He awakened with his raggedy self curled upon the dirt floor. Around him were his sister's children, deep asleep. He was smaller than the others at the age of five, but he had the children in his charge from dusk to dawn. His sister had told him so.

"Anthony," she had said, "you will get them up and you will put them to bed."

"I makin' 'em resters," he told his sister. But the children didn't want his pillow resters. On lying down they shunned all contact with him. They despised him because he never had to work hard. (P. 8)

This unusual yet compelling narrative style, coupled with the use of dialect, makes Burns's life become real to readers. Students could construct time lines that indicate the events in the country and the world that occurred during Anthony Burns's lifetime. The novel can be a springboard for numerous oral language activities; for example, the court scenes can be dramatized, or students could debate the complexities of the laws that allowed Charles Suttle to lay a legal claim to Anthony Burns.

Julius Lester, another gifted writer, has compiled selections that are from two cultures: African American and Jewish American. In *How Many Spots Does a Leopard Have? and Other Tales* (1989), Lester includes trickster tales as well as pourquoi stories—tales that ancient peoples told to explain customs, characteristics, or natural phenomenon. In one pourquoi tale, "Why the Sun and Moon Live in the Sky," Lester explains an unusual friendship:

> In the time of the beginning of the beginnings, everything and everyone lived on earth. If you had been living in those times, you could've sat on your porch in the evening and watched the Sun, the Moon and the Stars taking a stroll and chatting with all the neighbors.
>
> The Sun had many friends, but his best friend in all the universe was Water. Every day Sun visited Water and they talked about this and that and enjoyed each other's company, which is what friends do.
>
> There was one thing wrong with their friendship, however. Water never came to visit Sun at his house. That hurt Sun's feelings. (P. 1)

Like Virginia Hamilton, Julius Lester uses his broad knowledge of the oral tradition to enrich his stories. Each story invites children to read aloud, do oral retellings, or perform choral readings or creative drama. Students can write their own pourquoi tales explaining why animals have certain characteristics or why some natural phenomenon exists, such as how colors came to the rainbow or why rabbits have cotton tails. What teachers often discover is that children incorporate into their own writings the cadences and phrases they have heard in stories read aloud.

One of the qualities of a Notable title is the skillful use of evocative language. William Hooks's conjure tale from the Piedmont region, *The Ballad of Belle Dorcas* (1990, N) is filled with such language and strong images. In this story, Hooks relates the story of Belle Dorcas, a free-issue woman who is in love with the slave Joshua:

> Belle Dorcas loved Joshua. Always had, for as long as she could remember. But Joshua was a slave. And a highly prized slave at that. Joshua was the hardest-working man on the plantation and the best fiddle player in the county. . . . He dreamed that someday he would have enough saved to buy his freedom and marry Belle.
>
> When the rains of fall had settled the dust on the Wilmington road and Belle Dorcas had chosen no free-issue man, she spoke with her mama.
>
> "Dear Mama, I'm breaking your heart, and you are crushing mine. I'd rather live with Joshua as a slave than as a free issue with another man. It's him I'll marry or die." (Unpaged, p. 10)

Not only is this a well-written story, but it is also a powerful history lesson. Students can read how slavery destroyed black family life on even the most "benevolent" plantations. By comparing this tale to Hamilton's *Anthony Burns*, students can construct a picture of American slavery that counters the argument that enslavement was a time when blacks were happy and satisfied to live near the "Massa." They can also study how Hooks uses language to create a mood ("Belle Dorcas was frantic. She could think of no way to save Joshua."), or evoke emotions ("Belle Dorcas pleaded with the master.

'Spare Joshua, sir, I pray you.' But her pleas did not move him."
[unpaged, p. 15]). Each turn of the page draws the reader compellingly into this story of love and sacrifice, and it is the language
which makes the difference.

Patricia McKissack's storytelling skills, honed at her
grandfather's knee, are as prodigious as those of Hamilton, Lester,
and Hooks. These skills have been put to good use in her many very
readable stories. Students who read *Flossie and the Fox* (1986, N),
Mirandy and Brother Wind (1988), *Nettie Jo's Friends* (1989), and *A
Million Fish . . . More or Less* (1992, N) find memorable characters,
great plots twists, and colorful language. All are treasure troves of
historical tidbits giving readers glimpses into African American life
during the nineteenth and early twentieth centuries.

Perhaps McKissack's most enduring character is Flossie Finley,
a spunky little girl who outwits Mr. Fox so she can get her basket of
eggs safely "over to Miz Viola." As she starts on her way, she immediately encounters the fox:

> Flossie commenced to skip along, when she come upon a critter
> she couldn't recollect ever seeing. He was sittin' 'side the road like he
> was expectin' somebody. Flossie skipped right up to him and nod-
> ded a greeting the way she'd been taught to do.
> "Top of the morning to you, Little Missy," the critter replied.
> "And what is your name?"
> "I be Flossie Finley," she answered with a proper curtsy. "I reckon
> I don't know who you be either." (Unpaged, p. 11)

After a series of give and take encounters, the fox tries a final time to
convince Flossie that he is a fox:

> Fox tried not to whimper, but his voice was real unsteady-like.
> "I–I have sharp teeth and I can run exceedingly fast." He waited for
> Flossie to say something.
> Slowly the girl rocked from heel to toe . . . back and forward.
> "You know," she finally said, smiling, "it don't make much differ-
> ence what I think anymore."
> "What?" asked Fox. "Why?"
> "Cause there's one of Mr. J. W. McCutchin's hounds behind you.
> He's got sharp teeth and can run fast too. And, by the way that
> hound's lookin', it's all over for you!" (Unpaged, p. 28)

Not to worry, the fox does escape, but not before Flossie has thor-
oughly "outfoxed" him with her verbal feints and parries.
McKissack has created in Flossie the ultimate character with
"moxie," and the girl's exploits are always fresh and exciting.
McKissack's other books also provide opportunities for children to
experience a well-told story with characters whose escapades provide hours of linguistic delights.

I receive many requests from teachers to read the story of Flossie aloud to their students. Children of all ethnic origins find Flossie's story worth hearing over and over. One third-grade class loved to recite certain parts of the story for their peers. Especially popular was Fox's attempt to convince Flossie he was a fox because of his long pointed nose:

> Fox came up to her and said, "I have a long pointed nose. Now that should be proof enough."
> "Don't prove a thing to me." Flossie picked some wild flowers. "Come to think of it," she said matter-of-fact-like, "rats got long pointed noses." She snapped her fingers. "That's it! You a rat trying to pass yo'self off as a fox." (Unpaged, p. 18)

Teachers do enjoy hearing the story read aloud, but some are uncomfortable with the dialect. My advice to these teachers is not to focus on Flossie's dialect until they have acquired their "storytelling voices." When their "storytelling voices" are in place, teachers will discover the dialect enhances Flossie's escapade.

Well-Known Poets of Color

Many teachers have found that children love poetry and have favorite poets. One special favorite is Eloise Greenfield. Children love the rhythmic *Night on Neighborhood Street* (1991, N), the soothing *Africa Dream* (1979), the melodious *Under the Sunday Tree* (1988), and the provocative *Daydreamers* (1981). A gifted wordsmith, Greenfield delights readers of all ages with the cadence of the harmonious rhythms of the Caribbean in *Under the Sunday Tree*. The silent and powerful strength of dreams and thoughts pervades *Daydreamers*. And the Mother Continent beckons in *Africa Dream*:

> I went all the way to Africa
> In a dream one night
> I crossed over the ocean
> In a slow, smooth jump
> And landed in Africa
> Long-ago Africa (Unpaged, pp. 7–9)

Another poet with "kid appeal" is Nikki Giovanni, whose poems celebrate the joys of being alive. In *Vacation Time: Poems for Children* (1978), Giovanni uses vivid imagery to capture the special moments of childhood, focusing on the delight of observing snowflakes, the fun of getting kisses, and the pleasures of chocolate, as shown in the poem "The Reason I Like Chocolate":

> The reason I like chocolate
> is I can lick my fingers
> and nobody tells me I'm not polite . . .

and I like books
for all those reasons
but mostly 'cause they just make me
happy
and I really like
to be happy (P. 49)

In *Spin a Soft Black Song* (1971), Giovanni tells her readers that she wrote this volume of poems because no such volumes existed for children of color when she was a child. In the following excerpt from a poem titled "ten years old," a book has excited a young boy so much so that he desperately wants to explore it further. Giovanni's use of words to accentuate the librarian's disdain for the boy's not having a library card, the boy's plea for the book, and the bystander's grasp of the situation's greater import makes for a superb read-aloud:

and i got off on time and walked
past the lions and the guard straight
up to the desk and said
    "dr. doolittle steroscope please"
and this really old woman said
    "Do You Have A Library Card?"
and i said
    "i live here up the street"
and she said
    "Do You Have a LIBRARY Card?"
and i said
    "this is the only place i can use the steroscope
     for
    dr. dooolittle miss washington brought us here
    this spring
    to see it"
and another lady said
    "GIVE THE BOY WHAT HE WANT. HE
    WANT TO LEAD THE RACE"
and i said
    "no ma'am i want to see dr. dooolittle"
and she said "same thang son same thang" (Pp. 42–43)

Sharon Bell Mathis is noted for her outstanding novels for middle-grade and adolescent readers. In *Red Dog, Blue Fly* (1991), she has crafted a book of action-packed football poems for all sports fans. The title poem, "Red Dog/Blue Fly," is a football term familiar to the millions of fans who view football either in person or on TV each fall weekend:

signals red, signals blue
stuck up in my mind like glue

red dog/blue dog
signals for the defense
trying to remember them
keeps me tense
red fly/blue fly
signals for offense
gotta keep them straight
so they make some sense . . . (P. 1)

In addition to being excellent selections for reading aloud, these poems can lead children to explore the language of sports.

Coconut Kind of Day: Island Poems by Lynn Joseph (1990) contains enough fresh and vivid poetry to enliven everyone's vocabulary and expose children to the language patterns and culture of African Caribbeans, as shown in the poem "Morning Songs":

"Coc-a-toodle-too," from the galvanized gate.
"Whoo-too-too," from the sea.
"G'mornin' Miz Rosie," from the ebony man
selling mangoes and papaws
in the street. (Unpaged, p. 7)

Students who read these lyrical poems will encounter such terms as *soursop, mangoes cricket* (the game), *manicou, mongoose,* and *palet man.* Each term invites the readers to research and make discoveries about the culture and language of the Caribbean islands. Other books of poetry that celebrate the language and culture of the Caribbean are *Caribbean Canvas* by Frané Lessac (1987) and *Not a Copper Penny in Me House* by Monica Gunning (1993):

Early Saturday morning
the market bus us a moving farm
going into Kingston Town
baskets in the aisle
bursting with breadfruits
coconuts bumping against jackfruits
passion fruits sitting on pumpkins
roll with the bus along country roads (Gunning, p. 22)

Much of Lucille Clifton's poetry celebrates the joys of family life. Her very popular Everett Anderson series highlights the life of a small African American boy. Each book is a poetic celebration showing readers how words work beautifully together. In *Everett Anderson's Friend* (1976), Everett Anderson discovers a new family has moved into apartment 13A:

Someone new has come to stay
in 13A, in 13A
and Everett Anderson's Mama and he
can't wait to see, can't wait to see

whether it's girls or
whether it's boys and
how are their books and
how are their toys and
where they've been and
where they go and
who are their friends and
the people they know,
oh, someone new has come to stay
next door in 13A. (Unpaged, p. 6)

In *Everett Anderson's Goodbye* (1983), Everett Anderson has to deal with the trauma of the loss of his father:

Everett Anderson tries to sleep
but it is too hard and
the hurt is too deep.

Everett Anderson likes his food
but how can a dinner
do any good?

Everett Anderson just sits staring,
wondering what's the use of caring. (Unpaged, p. 15)

The poems in Joyce Carol Thomas's *Brown Honey and Broomwheat Tea* (1993) create a kaleidoscope of words that also accent family life. Thomas's words evoke images of mellow earth tones that curl around the tongue and warm the ears of the listener, as in "Cherish Me":

I sprang up from mother earth
    She clothed me in her own colors
I was nourished by father sun
    He glazed the pottery of my skin (Unpaged, p. 6)

Nikki Grimes's *Something on My Mind* (1978) contains poems that reflect universal concerns of children. The following poem focuses on a dilemma teachers and students constantly encounter—what constitutes authentic writing?

My summer vacation . . .
went to Jones Beach with Jo Jo's family.
Jimmy got out of jail.
I sneaked into the pool across town twice.
Daddy lost his second job.
Mama said don't worry,
but he did.
Sharon's sister hit the number.
That makes the fourth times.

Teacher don't want to hear that.
What can I write?
Went to Jones Beach . . . (P. 21)

The language of all the poems in this section invite children to read, perform, imitate, and share. The rhythms, repetitive patterns, and colorful phrases of the poems can assist students as they engage in oral or written language activities.

Books about Africa

Many notable titles highlight the diversity of the African continent. These titles introduce students to a varied continent, serving as healthy antidotes to the stereotypes of Africa and Africans too often portrayed on TV and in the movies. For example, *Galimoto* by Karen Lynn Williams (1990, N) traces one day in the life of Kondi, a young boy from Malawi. A very determined Kondi collects pieces of wire so that he can make a *galimoto* (a wire car). A story with a similar theme is *Charlie's House* by Reviva Schermbrucker (1989). Charlie, a South African child, collects popsicle sticks, mud, bottle caps, and other debris around his compound in order to build a small house—the house of his dreams, where each member of his family can live in comfort, warmth, and privacy. Reading and comparing these books exposes children to the language and culture of a continent which influences the culture of African Americans and African Caribbeans.

South Africa is also the setting for the gentle story of Malusi and his grandmother, Gogo, in *Not So Fast, Songololo* by Niki Daly (1985). The two take a day trip to town on a very important shopping trip:

There was a shoe shop next. Tackies!
Malusi looked down at his old tackies and then at the shoes in the window.
They were bright red with stripes down one side.
"What are you looking at? asked Gogo, when she caught up at last.
"Look Gogo," said Malusi, "bright red tackies!"
Gogo looked at the new tackies and then she looked at Malusi's old ones and she clicked her tongue. (P. 17)

The happy surprise at the end gives the book its title. Students can familiarize themselves with the vocabulary of a different culture as they compare a day of shopping with their loved ones with the shopping trip of Malusi and Gogo.

The Orphan Boy by Tololwa Mollel (1991, N) is a folktale from the Masai. This story of a child who suddenly appears and helps a farmer become prosperous is similar to *The Crane Wife* by Sumiko Yagawa (1981) and *Dawn* by Molly Bang (1982):

As he had done every night of his life, the old man gazed deep into the heavens. He spent so much time scanning the night sky that he knew every star it held. . . .

Tonight, he noticed, one of the stars was missing.

Like a worried father, the old man searched the darkness for his missing star. Just then he heard footsteps.

Startled, the old man looked down, and there before him stood a boy. "Who are you?" he asked.

"My name is Kileken," replied the boy. "I am an orphan and I've travelled countless miles in search of a home." (Unpaged, pp. 3–4)

Students could construct comparison/contrast charts with these tales, using language to analyze and synthesize their ideas. They can also search for and share tales from other cultures with the same theme.

Rachel Isadora has written two beautiful and informative picture storybooks about life in the same region: *At the Crossroads* (1991) and *Over the Green Hills* (1992). In both stories, Isadora uses powerful words and images to portray the effects apartheid has on black South African children. In *At the Crossroads,* Isadora makes the wait that the children have to endure as anticipatory and tense for the reader as for the characters in the story. With the chant, "Our fathers are coming home! Our fathers are coming home!" she makes their waiting (and our reading) more tolerable. In *Over the Green Hills,* she gives the reader a panoramic view of Zolani's Transkei trek:

They stop to rest by the side of the road. Zolani's mother feeds Noma and shares a mango with Zolani. "Look, there is an ostrich!" she says.

Zolani has never seen one. He runs to get a closer look, but the ostrich speeds away.

"They are the largest birds, but they cannot fly," says Zolani's mother.

"But they can run very fast," says Zolani, out of breath. (Unpaged, pp. 18–19)

A close reading of this book gives the reader a feel for the life of young Zolani, a life that students in this country can compare in terms of daily chores, native foods, and animal and plant life. Zolani's South African extended family could also be compared with family life in the United States.

In a series of three picture storybooks about the Central African nation Cameroon, *The Village of Round and Square Houses* (1986), *Darkness and the Butterfly* (1987, N), and *Osa's Pride* (1990), Anne Grifalconi tells of Osa and her village, Tos. The three books give the reader a glimpse into Osa's life and the revelation that children of all cultures have similar fears and joys. *The Village of Round and Square*

Houses is a delightful story that explains why the women in the village of Tos live in round houses and the men in square ones. Students might enjoy dramatizing the consequences of the volcano's eruption (called Mother Naka by the villagers):

> "But when they came to the burned-out village,
>   Only two houses were left standing:
> One SQUARE—　　　　And one ROUND! . . .
> "But the village chief had no time
>   For such questions—. . .
> "He pointed to the ash-covered people:
>   'YOU! TALL GRAY THINGS!
> You go live in the SQUARE house!'
> "'And you! ROUND GRAY THINGS—
>   Go live in the ROUND house!' (Unpaged, pp. 23–25)

In *Darkness and the Butterfly,* Osa confronts her fear of the dark, a familiar fear to many children; in *Osa's Pride,* she learns the pitfalls of having too much pride. Both books invite children to engage in meaningful discussions about fears and attitudes that are universal to us all.

Several nonfiction titles use photos to give the reader a true picture of the different faces of the African continent. *Africa Journey* by John Chiasson (1987) is a breathtaking photo-essay in which the author/photographer shares his travels to six different areas of this awesome continent. Senegal, on Africa's west coast, is a mosaic of sights, sounds, and smells, and a clash of the old and the new:

> Dakar is a major African port where big ocean freighters unload and take on cargo daily. It is a modern city with neon lights, buses, and billboards. Even with these Western touches, Dakar is unmistakably African. . . . In the stalls of the open-air markets in the city's center, Wolof, Toucouleur, and Serer tribesmen sell locally-grown foods, traditional medicines, hand-woven fabrics, and artwork. (Pp. 23–24)

An exciting activity would be to examine the contributions that African languages have made to our lexicon, such as *gris-gris* (charm) and *pirogue* (flat-bottomed boats).

Tanzania is the backdrop for the story of young Rehema in *Rehema's Journey* by Barbara Margolies (1990). She takes her first day tour to the Ngorongoro Crater with her father to see the magnificent wildlife:

> Early the next day we stop at the market to buy food for our ride to the crater. The market is colorful and very crowded. Looked at the piles of salt!
>
> Here is a bundle of sticks called miswaki. We use miswaki to clean our teeth. When I chew on the end of miswaki, it becomes a brush!

I have just enough time to buy a pineapple and some mangoes before we begin the long drive to Ngorongoro. (Pp. 15–16)

Sahara: Vanishing Cultures by Jan Reynolds (1991) is a stunning look at the Tuaregs, a nomadic tribe with many ancient traditions, including the oral stories told by tribal members of long ago.

As the sun drops behind the Hoggar Mountains in the center of the Sahara, the largest desert on earth, a young boy named Manda asks his father to tell him a story about their tribe, the Tuareg.

Evening breezes sweep across the hot sands, cooling the desert. Manda creeps closer to the fire, and his father begins his tale.

"Long ago, Tuareg men rode proudly on their camels. They covered their faces with cloth veils so only their eyes could be seen, making them look fierce and noble. They were called the Blue Men because the dark blue dye in their robes would rub off on their skin. The Tuareg rode camels in caravans, carrying wonderful things like ostrich feathers, salt, parrots, and even ivory and gold." (Unpaged, pp. 4–7)

In these three books, as well as in the others cited in this section, American students are exposed to lifestyles of children on a far-off continent who share daily experiences with their families and friends. These richly written books use dialect, interesting vocabulary, and vivid descriptions to show students, and teachers, that this is indeed a small, small world.

Using African American Literature in the Classroom

As you enter Kay Magness's small but cozy second-grade classroom, your eyes are drawn to the children's work and colorful book posters that adorn the walls, the shelves filled with children's literature, and the display center of books written by the students. If you time your arrival correctly, you see an animated Magness reading aloud to a group of excited second graders. On this day, she is reading *Anansi and the Moss-Covered Rock* by Eric Kimmel (1988). As she continues the story, the children lean forward, gesturing and warning characters to beware of Anansi's tricks. One eagle-eyed student has already spied Little Bush Deer in the corner of one page, observing Anansi's prank. Soon all the students have discovered Little Bush Deer's presence in each picture, and they wait with anticipation to see the trickster "get tricked." When Little Bush Deer "turns the tables" on Anansi and snares him in his own trap, the students are happy and relieved. They relax and savor the story's turn of events—what just desserts for Anansi to be caught in his own snare! But, alas, the story has ended too soon, so the students plead with Magness to read it again. As she does, they join in:

> "Lion! Look! Do you see what I see?"
>
> "Oh, yes, Anansi!" said Lion. "Isn't this a strange moss-covered rock!"
>
> KPOM! Down fell Lion. Anansi ran back to Lion's house and made off with Lion's yams. (Unpaged, pp. 10–11)

Giggles and laughs abound as the students enjoy the adventures of Anansi once again.

Three years ago, Kay Magness began converting her Chapter 1 class from the plethora of worksheets and skill drills to one in which reading and writing were the foundation. She decided her inner-city students needed to be exposed to a variety of quality children's literature, especially African American literature. She also wanted to add more literature-based language response activities to her program. So with exemplary titles from different genres added to the class library and with a reading/writing workshop in place, Magness and her students were off on many literary adventures.

The Kimmel story was one of several Anansi tales Magness used in her year-long unit, Folktales around the World—Africa. For example, Magness had her students examine the differences in Anansi's character as he is portrayed in Kimmel's story versus how he is portrayed in *A Story, a Story* by Gail Haley (1970), *Anansi the Spider* by Gerald McDermott (1979), *The Adventures of Spider: West African Folk Tales* by Joyce Arkhurst (1964), *How Anansi Obtained the Sky God's Stories* by Janice Skivington (1991), and *Anansi Goes Fishing* by Eric Kimmel (1992). Each of these tales served as fertile ground for other oral and written activities as well. The students extended the adventures of their favorite arachnid in model stories, pourquoi tales, science logs, songs, poetry, drama, or rap. For example, Kevin (a pseudonym, as are the names of other children in this chapter) produced a very long, but unfinished, tale filling three notebook pages in which he relates a new Anansi adventure, "Anansi Goes to the Store." In the rough draft of his first page, he wrote:

> One day Anansi whent to the store and he brought cereal, pancakes, fish, and pumking, pie, and he whent to the chash redisder and all together was $14.99 but he had $13.99 but he steal can bye it. So he whent home and cooked the food. But when he was going to eat it his friend the lion came with a huge watermelon.

Mary, too, was interested in getting Anansi into new adventures, so she wrote about Anansi's taking a walk through the woods with friends:

> The Anansi was walking throw the woods and he saw pig and he side do you won't to go in the woods why yes side pig I will like to.

Pig and Anansi saw Rabbit and ask Rabbit he side yes I will like to.
And they saw leo and he sade yes I will like to.

The natural connection between Anansi the folk character and spiders in nature provided a springboard to science. There were also mini-science units on spiders and the foods animals eat. During these units, students were motivated to write and read for purposes of discovery, explanation, description, and problem solving. No fear of spiders here; Magness's students eagerly constructed 3-D models of spiders, and they read and wrote about the many facets of spider life and their environment. Elements from Kimmel's Anansi tales, as well as material from informational books such as *Spiders* by Illa Podendorf (1982), found their way into the students' science logs and transitional writing. Nikki's transitional piece on spiders has both personal and expository elements in it:

I like spder.
They have 2 body parts
And they have 6 lags
spide lay egg and
they have 8 legs
And they have long legs
And they eat bess
And crwt on people and
it tickles
And they stig bess
And they have two pars
All have hair Spider
dong have Teeth
THE END

Sharon's transitional piece on spiders also conveys information:

I like spider.
They have 2 body parts
They have 8 legs.
Spidders live in cornners.
It have 2 eyes.
It is alot of spider.

Ria's science log entry shows the influence of Anansi folktales and informational reading:

Spiders lay egg and they have
8 legs and some spiders are big and
small they have long legs
and crawl on people and it tickles
And they can hide eneywere
And you can not see ther webs
And some spiders have hair and

some spiders oley come out at nitghtime
And they eat yams

Mary incorporated material from the folktales and informational books into a K-T-L chart:

Know
Spider have 8 lags
spider spend webs
spider lay eggs
spider like yams

Think
I think that spiders eat bees
spiders eat flies
spider have 4 parts
long legs

Learn
8 or 6 eyes
eat raches
live in a ground web

As Magness introduced each new title in the folktale unit, she found her students were eager to offer their predictions and share interesting observations or book details. They particularly loved books such as *McBungle's African Safari* by Parkes (1987), with its repetitive rhythms, bouncy refrains, and colorful and unique use of language:

. . . And that very night they decided to get
A simply
    STUPENDOUS
    SPLENDIFEROUS pet . . .

McBungle searched far.
McBungle searched near.
He searched ALL the places
Where crocodiles appear.
"Oh, dear! Oh, dear!
No crocodiles here!" (Pp. 7–8)

Every book generated many requests to be read aloud. Extension activities were completed with relish. During silent reading (SSR and DEAR) students often selected stories that had been read aloud in class.

When Magness and I began working together, we targeted the second grade only. However, Magness was so successful at getting her second graders to read and write that she decided to use the same books and some of the same strategies with her fourth graders. What she discovered was a group of students hungry for good literature and meaningful language activities.

With her older students, Magness took the approach of intro-
ducing them to positive role models in African American literature.
Nathaniel in the poem "Nathaniel's Rap" from *Nathaniel Talking* by
Eloise Greenfield (1988) was a good place to start:

> "It's Nathaniel talking
> And Nathaniel's me
> I'm talking about
> My philosophy . . ." (P. 2)

Magness found that her students, especially the boys, often rapped
the poem. As with her second graders, she inundated her fourth
graders with lots of quality literature during reading and writing
workshop time. Through sharing poetry she discovered that her
fourth graders loved this genre, particularly poems written by Eloise
Greenfield. Those in *Nathaniel Talking* (1988) and *Honey, I Love, and
Other Poems* (1978) were special favorites. Students loved to memo-
rize and recite the title poem in the latter volume and to rap many of
the poems in the former. Magness also found that pleasurable
rhythms of Greenfield's poetry led the fourth graders to turn some of
the poems into choral reading selections.

Magness also developed many language-based response
activities for the Anansi stories. Where the second graders were
interested in Anansi's adventures as models for writing, the fourth
graders enjoyed comparing the different authors' treatments of the
character of Anansi. They read and recorded the types of capers in
which Anansi was engaged and the results of his mischief making,
such as the moon goes to reside in the sky, the Sky God loses his
stories, the Sky God renames his stories the "spider stories." The
better readers among the group got their first experiences with
chapter books through Arkhurst's two volumes of Anansi tales.

Magness discovered that these reluctant fourth-grade readers
were often drawn to literature with clever characters who were like
them. For example, Mary Hoffman's *Amazing Grace* (1991, N) was
read over and over, first as a read-aloud, then as a favorite selection
during DEAR or partner reading. When Magness first introduced
Patricia McKissack's *Flossie and the Fox* (1986, N), the students did
not like the book very much and felt Flossie was not very smart. As
Magness reread the tale, she asked the students to look closely at the
illustrations and to listen carefully to the dialogue between Flossie
and the fox. To their surprise and delight, the students discovered
Flossie was indeed a very clever girl. Students were so pleased at
making such a discovery that Flossie's cleverness served as a springboard for many writing and dramatic activities.

Other exemplary titles that proved to be just as inviting to
students included *Tar Beach* by Faith Ringgold (1991, N), a story with

fantasy elements that appealed to the imagination ("I will always remember when the stars fell down around me and lifted me up above the George Washington Bridge" [unpaged, p. 7]); *Mufaro's Beautiful Daughters: An African Tale* by John Steptoe (1987), a popular story that was a natural for impromptu drama; and *Why Mosquitoes Buzz in People's Ears* by Verna Aardema (1975), a funny cumulative folktale from West Africa filled with colorful words ("At last King Lion called a meeting of the animals. They came and sat down, *pem, pem, pem,* around a council fire" [unpaged, p. 14]. "King Lion called the python, who came slithering, *wasawusu, wasawusu,* past the other animals" [p. 23]). Other fourth-grade favorites were *The Talking Eggs: A Folktale of the American South* by Robert San Souci (1989, N), *The Black Snowman* by Phil Mendez (1989), and *Willie's Not the Hugging Kind* by Joyce Durham Barrett (1991).

It was exciting to see students who usually did not find reading to be a positive experience become excited at the introduction of a new book of poetry by Eloise Greenfield, an Anansi adventure, or a collection of African American folktales. Magness found that her students were starved for good literature. By nurturing the reader-writer in each student, she slowly helped her students become lovers of quality literature. Magness provided her second graders and fourth graders with the keys to literacy by acknowledging them as readers-writers and by using literature that included the celebratory language of their culture.

References

Professional Resources

Bishop, R. S. 1987. "Extending Multicultural Understanding through Children's Books." In *Children's Literature in the Reading Program,* edited by B. E. Cullinan. Newark, DE: International Reading Association.

———. 1992. "Multi-cultural Literature for Children: Making Informed Choices." In *Teaching Multicultural Literature in Grades K–8,* edited by V. J. Harris. Norwood, MA: Christopher Gordon.

Thompson, D. L., and J. M. Hager. 1991. "Assessing Teachers' Knowledge of Multi-ethnic Literature." In *Literacy: International, National, State and Local,* edited by B. L. Hayes and K. Camperell. Eleventh Yearbook of the American Reading Forum. Logan: Utah State University, College of Education.

Children's Literature

Aardema, Verna. 1975. *Why Mosquitoes Buzz in People's Ears: A West African Tale.* New York: Dial Books.

Arkhurst, Joyce C. 1964. *The Adventures of Spider: West African Folk Tales.* Boston: Little, Brown.

Bang, Molly. 1982. *Dawn.* New York: Lothrop, Lee and Shepard Books.

Barrett, Joyce Durham. 1989. *Willie's Not the Hugging Kind.* New York: HarperCollins.

Chiasson, John. 1987. *Africa Journey.* New York: Bradbury Press.

Clifton, Lucille. 1976. *Everett Anderson's Friend.* New York: Holt, Rinehart and Winston.

———. 1980. *My Friend Jacob.* New York: E. P. Dutton.

———. 1983. *Everett Anderson's Goodbye.* New York: Henry Holt.

Daly, Niki. 1985. *Not So Fast, Songololo.* New York: Margaret K. McElderry Books.

Giovanni, Nikki. 1971. *Spin a Soft Black Song.* New York: Hill and Wang.

———. 1980. *Vacation Time: Poems for Children.* New York: William Morrow.

Greenfield, Eloise. 1977. *Africa Dream.* New York: Harper and Row.

———. 1978. *Honey, I Love, and Other Poems.* New York: Harper and Row.

———. 1981. *Daydreamers.* New York: Dial Books.

———. 1988. *Nathaniel Talking.* New York: Black Butterfly Children's Books.

———. 1988. *Under the Sunday Tree.* New York: Harper and Row.

Grifalconi, Anne. 1986. *Village of Round and Square Houses.* Boston: Little, Brown.

———. 1990. *Osa's Pride.* Boston: Little, Brown.

Grimes, Nikki. 1978. *Something on My Mind.* New York: Dial Books.

Gunning, Monica. 1993. *Not a Copper Penny in Me House: Poems from the Caribbean.* Honesdale, PA: Boyds Mills Press.

Haley, Gail E. 1970. *A Story, a Story.* New York: Atheneum.

Hamilton, Virginia. 1991. *The All Jahdu Storybook.* San Diego: Harcourt Brace Jovanovich.

Isadora, Rachel. 1991. *At the Crossroads.* New York: Greenwillow Books.

———. 1992. *Over the Green Hills.* New York: Greenwillow Books.

Joseph, Lynn. 1990. *Coconut Kind of Day: Island Poems.* New York: Lothrop, Lee and Shepard Books.

Kimmel, Eric A. 1988. *Anansi and the Moss-Covered Rock.* New York: Scholastic.

———. 1992. *Anansi Goes Fishing.* New York: Holiday House.

Lawrence, Jacob. 1993. *The Great Migration: An American Story.* New York: HarperCollins.

Lessac, Frané. 1987. *Caribbean Canvas.* New York: J. B. Lippincott.

See the Bibliography of Notable Books at the end of the book for bibliographic information about cited Notable Books. The Notable titles do not appear in this reference list.

Lester, Julius. 1989. *How Many Spots Does a Leopard Have? and Other Tales.* New York: Scholastic.

McDermott, Gerald. 1972. *Anansi, the Spider.* New York: Holt, Rinehart and Winston.

McKissack, Patricia. 1988. *Mirandy and Brother Wind.* New York: Alfred A. Knopf.

———. 1989. *Nettie Jo's Friends.* New York: Alfred A. Knopf.

———. 1992. *A Million Fish . . . More or Less.* New York: Alfred A. Knopf.

Margolies, Barbara A. 1990. *Rehema's Journey: A Visit in Tanzania.* New York: Scholastic.

Mathis, Sharon Bell. 1991. *Red Dog, Blue Fly: Football Poems.* New York: Viking.

Mendez, Phil. 1989. *The Black Snowman.* New York: Scholastic.

Parkes, Brenda. 1987. *McBungle's African Safari.* Crystal Lake, IL: Rigby Education.

Pinkney, Andrea D. 1993. *Seven Candles for Kwanzaa.* New York: Dial Books.

Podendorf, Illa. 1982. *Spiders.* Chicago: Children's Press.

Reynolds, Jan. 1991. *Sahara: Vanishing Cultures.* San Diego: Harcourt, Brace, Jovanovich.

Schermbrucker, Reviva. 1989. *Charlie's House.* New York: Viking.

Skivington, Janice. 1991. *How Anansi Obtained the Sky God's Stories.* Chicago: Children's Press.

Steptoe, John. 1987. *Mufaro's Beautiful Daughters: An African Tale.* New York: Lothrop, Lee and Shepard Books.

Thomas, Joyce Carol. 1993. *Brown Honey and Bloomwheat Tea.* New York: HarperCollins.

Yagawa, Sumiko (trans. by Katherine Paterson). 1981. *The Crane Wife.* New York: William Morrow.

International Books and the Language Arts

Carl M. Tomlinson
Northern Illinois University

U sing international children's trade books with students presents a rich opportunity to expand their cultural awareness and language growth. In this chapter, international children's trade books are defined as those books written by non–U.S. citizens, originally published in a country other than the United States for a child audience other than U.S. children, subsequently translated into English, if necessary, and published in the United States. A less strict definition also includes those books written by U.S. citizens for a U.S. child audience, but set in a country other than the United States. Although only a few studies related to international children's books and the school curriculum have been done, results show agreement on several important points:

- international children's literature provides an excellent source of information about countries, people, and cultures outside the United States
- this literature gives young readers an emotional experience of "living in" other countries
- these stories present believable characters and show how events and environment affect their lives
- this literature is interesting to young readers because it is rich in the details of characters' everyday lives (Schluck 1989; Tomlinson and Lynch-Brown 1989; Monson, Howe, and Greenlee 1989).

These studies show that high-quality international literature can stimulate children to think and talk about people, places, ideas, issues, and situations that are new and intriguing to them. Through this literature they meet and use interesting and strange new words for the first time; they use known words in new ways and contexts; and, inevitably, they compare and contrast their lives and cultures

The author acknowledges the contributions of Tina Frese, Balfour Elementary School, Thomasville, GA, and Jane Orchard, Tudor First School, London, England.

with the lives and cultures of story characters.

Language development in such a context is a natural outgrowth, particularly as regards heuristic, informative, and personal language—that is, the language used when discovering new information, when telling others about it, and when reflecting on how this new knowledge changes oneself. This chapter focuses on opportunities for language development provided by international children's literature.

Involvement with books from other countries has two other related benefits for children: it provides enjoyment and promotes international understanding. Although this chapter focuses on ways global literature can support children's language growth, it has been developed with the understanding that students must first be allowed to enjoy international literature before the stories are extended, and that the social growth and language development to be derived from this literature are of equal consequence.

Awareness of Foreign Languages

Young children are naturally curious about language and, when given the opportunity, seem remarkably adept at learning foreign languages. Recognizing this, many primary- and intermediate-grade teachers have found that bilingual books—books printed in two languages—offer students many opportunities for language development. At the most basic level, this can mean a child's introduction to the simple fact that there are languages other than English. Bilingual books enable children to see other languages in print and to compare the written forms of these languages to their own. Seeing the pictographic characters of Asiatic languages, as in Fumiko Takeshita's *The Park Bench* (1988), translated from Japanese, or the "almost familiar" letters of the Cyrillic alphabet, as in Vladimir Vagin and Frank Asch's Russian–U.S. coproduction, *Here Comes the Cat!* (1989), broadens a child's appreciation for the variety and richness of language.

Bilingual books also can be used to bring children to higher levels of language awareness by providing opportunities for them to hear foreign languages spoken and then to learn the foreign-language equivalent of selected English words. After reading aloud *Here Comes the Cat!* and explaining that the Russian text has the same meaning as the English text, a second-grade teacher found her students' interest in the foreign language aspect of the book was so high that she located some English-Spanish bilingual stories in order to take advantage of her rudimentary knowledge of Spanish. Harriet Rohmer's *Uncle Nacho's Hat/El sombrero del tío Nacho* (1989), adapted from a Nicaraguan folktale with text in English and Spanish, proved an excellent choice. After first allowing her students to enjoy the story in English as a read-aloud, the teacher listed on chart paper several Spanish words in the story and their English equivalents. She then read aloud *Uncle Nacho's Hat* again, this time substituting Spanish for the selected English words, pointing to the word on the chart as she did so. By the third reading, the students were supplying the Spanish words in chorus.

Following up on one child's observation that the Spanish word *escuela* sounds a little like the English word *school*, the teacher introduced her students to the concept of etymology, or word origin, during the next several days. Using dictionaries with partners, and with their teacher guiding them, these second graders discovered for themselves why, for example, the Spanish word *flores* is so similar to the English word *flower*.

In the following weeks these students listened to other bilingual books, such as Alejandro Martinez's *The Woman Who Outshone the Sun/La mujer que brillaba aún más que el sol* (1987), and to English-language stories in which other languages are woven, such as Arthur Dorros's *Abuela* (1991) and Maria Cristina Brusca's *On the Pampas* (1991), both with Spanish elements, and Roch Carrier's *The Boxing Champion* (1991), with French Canadian elements. In addition, the teacher encouraged her students to use the foreign words they learned, thereby involving them in a unique form of wordplay.

Such relatively simple classroom activities as those described above can have surprisingly important and long-lasting effects on students' language development. Not only did the teacher's simple introduction to foreign languages show her students that different languages are interesting, rather than weird or scary, but it also broadened the children's concept or schema of language by revealing a few of its many possible forms. Learning about word origins can deepen children's understanding of how language lives and grows. In addition, children begin to feel a kinship with their peers in other countries after learning that they are interested in and generally talk about many of the same things that American children do.

Opportunities for Vocabulary Growth

Authors from other English-speaking countries often use words that are unfamiliar to American readers to name or describe familiar objects. The familiar grain *corn*, for example, is referred to as *maize* in Malawi, as in Karen Lynn Williams's *Galimoto* (1990, N), and *mielie* in South Africa, as in Norman Silver's *No Tigers in Africa* (1992). Some international books include a glossary of terms as a comprehension aid, as is the case in Duncan Williamson's Scottish book, *Fireside Tales of the Traveller Children* (1983, N), and Nadia Wheatley's Australian book, *My Place* (1989). These books present opportunities for vocabulary and writing development. A fourth-grade teacher, for example, began his booktalk of *My Place* (1989) by explaining that American and Australian English differ slightly, such as the Australian *bloke* for the American *guy* and *flat* for *apartment.* Two students showed particular interest in Australian English and asked for more Australian books. Later, these two produced their own "Dictionary of Australian Terms," which was added to the class bookshelves. The teacher reported that several students subsequently wrote fictional pieces with Australian settings or characters just so they could use terms like *mate, petrol,* and *pub.* From their experiences with Australian fiction and their knowledge of a few Australian terms, these students discovered how idiomatic language can be used to create a sense of place or to give authenticity to characterization.

International books also introduce and provide contexts for understanding new words that have been assimilated into American English. For example, it is one thing to recognize the word *apartheid* when it is heard on television newscasts and to be able to relate the word to events and policies in South Africa. But to experience the human degradation and injustice that are the results of apartheid through reading such books as Hazel Rochman's short stories in *Somehow Tenderness Survives* (1988) and Beverley Naidoo's *Journey to Jo'burg* (1985) is to understand the implications of the term for people's lives. A fifth-grade teacher's encouragement of her students as they hotly decry the civil rights injustices encountered in *Journey to Jo'burg* suggests a potent opportunity for language development. These students could explore their anger in their literature logs and then look for and document evidence of civil rights injustices in this country. Such activities go far beyond the "I knew something was wrong, but it wasn't important to me" stance and produce concerned involvement. Today an understanding of words like *yen, glasnost,* and *apartheid* is essential to an understanding of current events. It is for this reason that many teachers purposely include several international books in their literature programs.

Opportunities to Gain New Knowledge

International books contain worlds of information. This is expected in works of nonfiction, such as the Australian picture book by Robin and Sally Hirst titled *My Place in Space* (1990, N), the Italian picture book by Piero Ventura titled *Great Painters* (1984, N), and the British picture book by Helen Cowcher titled *Antarctica,* (1990), but works of realistic fiction can also be important resource books. Not only do they provide accurate, firsthand information about countries and cultures, but they also acquaint U.S. children with their peers in other lands. In Otto Svend's charming picture book set in China, *Children of the Yangtze River* (1982), for example, young readers can see houses, multigenerational families, clothing, schools, favorite snacks, pets, occupations, modes of transportation, and handwriting, to name a few of the many details included in the illustrations.

Many people in this country, children and adults alike, avoid international books, thinking that the characters and situations will be so unfamiliar as to make the story either boring or incomprehensible. People who have read good international books agree, however, that although there are differences, the similarities between themselves and the characters in the books are even greater. Teachers can take advantage of the natural tendency of most readers to compare themselves to book characters by asking their students to compare their lives with the lives of the story characters in international books. This activity promotes students' ability to formulate and articulate comparisons and contrasts, an essential aspect of their language development. A third-grade teacher's experience with Cecil Bödker's *The Leopard* (1975) provides an excellent example. During the first several days of reading aloud this adventure story about a young Ethiopian shepherd, the teacher reported that her students just giggled and "ugh-ed" at the characters' strangeness. The lives, the work, and even the clothing of the story characters were so unusual that they were at first unacceptable to these young listeners. But as the plot developed, the students began to share the shepherd's suspicions and then his fears as he is kidnapped by an evil medicine man. Then they began to applaud his pluck and good humor in the face of danger.

At this point the teacher suggested that her students chart the similarities and differences between themselves and the children in *The Leopard.* She provided a simple chart that had one column for students to list how their lives were similar and a second column to list differences. To the students' surprise, they found as many similarities as differences. One student, summarizing the similarities and differences she had charted, wrote, "Tibeso and Sokineh [the boy and girl in the story] live diffrent than we do, but they're just people like us." On one level, this student's statement signals important growth in language development—an ability to make an intelligent statement of comparison and contrast. On another and equally important level, her statement signals a remarkable and valuable awakening to a concept that lies at the heart of international understanding.

Language development is also supported when teachers weave several international books into a thematic teaching unit to introduce a global perspective. For example, primary-grade children involved in a unit on Toys and Games could investigate such picture books as Mary Hoffman's *Amazing Grace* (1991, N), Sonia Appiah's *Amoko and Efua Bear*, (1989), Karen Lynn Williams's *Galimoto* (1990, N), and Ann Tompert's *Grandfather Tang's Story* (1990, N) to discover toys and games new to them and to chart similarities and differences between their favorite toys and games and those of their peers in England, Ghana, Malawi, and China.

Children can take such an idea far. A British first-grade class that was studying toys and games and that had numerous picture books from around the world to consult accomplished all of the following language-related activities in one month:

- drew and labeled pictures of toys in other lands
- described the toys in writing
- discussed the similarities and differences in these toys and games and their own favorites
- reported on their findings to other groups and classes
- tried building some of the toys described in the books (and kept a log of the project)
- developed a list of characteristics common to favored toys around the world
- designed an original toy with universal child appeal

An eavesdropper in this classroom would have heard and seen marvelous examples of heuristic, informative, and personal language being used, extended, and developed through reading, talking, writing, planning, and reporting.

Sometimes an international book can serve to correct misinformation or stereotyped notions of a group of people or a place. It is safe to say, for example, that many U.S. schoolchildren think of Africa in terms of lions and elephants and tribal groups dressed in cloths or skins and roaming endless savannas. Several primary-grade teachers have used Ingrid Mennen and Niki Daly's excellent picture book *Somewhere in Africa* (1992) to dispel this stereotyped image of a remarkably diverse continent. In this book young readers meet Ashraf, who lives, not in the Africa of crocodiles and zebras, but in a large, bustling African city with traffic lights, tall buildings, and public libraries. There is a supermarket, too, but next to the supermarket musicians play drums, marimbas, and horns, and the townspeople dance. What a good example of cultural difference (street music and dancing) within a more fundamental similarity (food stores) this scene provides for young children. The reader is shown the city as Ashraf, dressed in jeans and a striped T-shirt, goes to the library to renew his favorite book, the subject of which is as exotic and exciting to this *African* boy as it is to millions of children around the world—the Africa of wild animals and untamed jungles and savannas. Many teachers encourage their students to document their learning by suggesting that students write in their logs what they know or think about a concept or topic prior to a learning experience and then to write again after the learning experience. One second grader, after hearing a number of books such as *Somewhere in Africa* read aloud, wrote, "I thought Africans were sick and hungry. I didn't want to go to Africa, but now I think I might." Such activities promote the simultaneous development of both heuristic and personal language.

Somewhere in Africa can be grouped with other excellent picture books to give students an idea of the diversity of African life and topography. Florence Parry Heide and Judith Heide Gilliland's *The Day of Ahmed's Secret* (1990, N) is set in Cairo, Egypt, and Rachel Isadora's *At the Crossroads* (1991) is set in a shantytown in South Africa. The more traditional view of Africans is presented in Tololwa Mollel's *The Orphan Boy* (1990, N), as befits a timeless Maasai folktale from Tanzania. One teacher followed up an investigation of these books by involving her students in writing and producing a theater piece consisting of "snapshots" of various African cultures and landscapes. Skits representing typical activities, games, or work of children in various African tribes were written and presented before student-drawn backdrops depicting appropriate landscapes. An alternative follow-up activity would be to encourage students to translate their newfound knowledge into a class book about the many African cultures represented in Africa. A child or group of children could each be responsible for the text and illustrations of a two- or three-page chapter giving details about the language, work, clothing, food, and homes of an African culture encountered in reading trade books. Both activities encourage students to rethink, confirm, and organize their newfound knowledge while exercising and developing their speaking and writing skills.

Opportunities to Gain New Insights and Perspectives

As children move into the upper-elementary and middle school grades, their growing sense of independence and increased physical and mental abilities are mirrored in their reading interests. These children like plots in which children their age struggle successfully for survival against great odds. They understand and enjoy stories set in the past or the future. They are also mature enough to deal with many of the unpleasant aspects of life, such as war, homelessness, poverty, prejudice, and intolerance. The corpus of international books available in this country is particularly rich in books like this, since so many European, Middle Eastern, and Asian children's book authors writing today had firsthand experiences with war when they were children. Novels on these topics rarely fail to cause young readers to think about the issues involved, to gain a deeper understanding, and to react.

Although the ten- to fourteen-year-olds for whom these books are intended should be competent readers, they also derive great benefit and pleasure from being read to. Hearing these books read aloud by a good reader might, in fact, increase their impact. Furthermore, the shared reading experience would make class discussion possible and would be one way to ensure that children stick with those excellent stories that begin slowly.

Following are some of the topics explored in international books for readers in fifth to eighth grade and some exemplary titles under each topic:

- *The effects of war and alternatives to war.* Ruth Minsky Sender's *To Life* (1988, N), Minfong Ho's *The Clay Marble* (1990, N), Peter Dickinson's *AK* (1990), and Robert Westall's *The Kingdom by the Sea* (1990) make evident war's terrible effects on children. Christophe Gallaz and Roberto Innocenti's picture book for older children, *Rose Blanche* (1985, N), which includes graphic illustrations of children in German concentration camps, makes the horror and injustice of war particularly real.

- *Homelessness.* Patricia Wrightson's *Night Outside* (1985, N) reveals that homelessness is a global issue.

- *The destructive effects of prejudice.* For more mature readers (this book contains strong language), Norman Silver's *No Tigers in Africa* (1992) allows the reader to witness a young South African's awakening to his own deep-seated racial prejudices. Hans Richter's *Friedrich* (1970) shows the insidious growth of anti-Semitism in Germany in the 1930s and 1940s and does so from a child's point of view, which makes it particularly effective in helping young readers understand one of the powerful forces behind the Holocaust. Prejudice grows, too, in a village in western England in Bel Mooney's *A Flower of Jet* (1991) when a coal workers' strike turns friends into bitter enemies.

Because novels such as these set up situations in which young protagonists are forced to defend or question their opinions or actions, question the decisions of others, and seek alternatives, they make excellent prompts for critical thinking and authentic stimuli for explanatory, persuasive, argumentative, and evaluative language. As teachers read these books aloud, they can stop at pivotal points to ask questions such as the following:

Was this character's decision right or wrong? Why?

Why did this character act as he or she did?

What were this character's alternatives?

Given the same situation, would you have done the same thing as this character? Why?

What might have happened if this character had acted differently?

Writing, debating, or dramatizing responses to questions such as these would force children to come to grips with the issues, to become aware of their own values, and to begin to articulate these values. Moreover, they would have the opportunity to put language to serious use in expressing themselves, arguing or defending a position, and evaluating others' opinions or arguments. To enable children to gain a clearer notion of who they are and what they stand for and to guide them toward articulating their ideas are worthy aims for children's book authors and teachers alike.

Conclusion

The objective of the international children's literature movement is to promote world peace by using books to build bridges of understanding among the children of the world. When teachers provide children with good books from other countries and encourage them to learn about each other in this way, these teachers contribute to this noble objective. At the same time, they provide their students with excellent opportunities for language growth.

References
Professional Resources

Monson, D. L., K. Howe, and A. Greenlee. 1989. "Helping Children Develop Cross-Cultural Understanding with Children's Books." *Early Child Development and Care* 48 (special issue): 3–8.

Schluck, C. G. 1989. "Using International Children's Literature in the Content Areas." *Early Child Development and Care* 48 (special issue): 9–18.

Tomlinson, C. M., and C. Lynch-Brown. 1989. "Adventuring with International Literature: One Teacher's Experience." *The New Advocate* 2 (3): 169–78.

Children's Literature

Appiah, Sonia. 1989. *Amoko and Efua Bear.* Illustrated by C. Easmon. New York: Macmillan.

Bödker, Cecil (translated by G. Poulsen). 1975. *The Leopard.* New York: Atheneum.

Brusca, Maria Cristina. 1991. *On the Pampas.* New York: Henry Holt.

Carrier, Roch (translated by S. Fischman). 1991. *The Boxing Champion.* Illustrated by S. Cohen. Plattsburgh, NY: Tundra Books.

Cowcher, Helen. 1990. *Antarctica.* New York: Farrar, Straus and Giroux.

Dickinson, Peter. 1990. *AK.* New York: Delacorte Press.

Dorros, Arthur. 1991. *Abuela.* Illustrated by Elisa Kleven. New York: E. P. Dutton.

Isadora, Rachel. 1991. *At the Crossroads.* New York: Greenwillow Books.

Martinez, Alejandro C. 1987. *The Woman Who Outshone the Sun/La mujer que brillaba aún más que el sol.* Illustrated by F. Olivera. San Francisco: Children's Book Press.

Mennen, Ingrid, and Niki Daly. 1992. *Somewhere in Africa.* Illustrated by Nicolaas Maritz. New York: E. P. Dutton.

Mooney, Bel. 1991. *A Flower of Jet.* London: Puffin.

Naidoo, Beverley. 1985. *Journey to Jo'burg: A South African Story.* Illustrated by Eric Velasquez. New York: J. B. Lippincott.

Richter, Hans P. 1970. *Friedrich.* New York: Henry Holt.

Rochman, Hazel, comp. 1988. *Somehow Tenderness Survives: Stories of Southern Africa.* New York: Harper and Row.

Rohmer, Harriet, adapter. 1989. *Uncle Nacho's Hat/El sombrero del tío Nacho.* Illustrated by Veg Reisberg. San Francisco: Children's Book Press.

Silver, Norman. 1992. *No Tigers in Africa.* New York: E. P. Dutton.

Svend, Otto S. (translated by J. Tate). 1982. *Children of the Yangtze River.* London: Pelham.

Takeshita, Fumiko (translated by Ruth A. Kanagy). 1988. *The Park Bench.* Illustrated by M. Suzuki. Brooklyn, NY: Kane/Miller.

Vagin, Vladimir, and Frank Asch. 1989. *Here Comes the Cat!* New York: Scholastic.

Westall, Robert. 1990. *The Kingdom by the Sea.* London: Methuen.

Wheatley, Nadia. 1989. *My Place.* Long Beach, CA: Australia in Print.

IV Putting It All Together

What are exciting ways teachers and children can explore to connect books and experiences and create new understandings? Barbara Chatton and Susan Hepler weave a rich tapestry of powerful suggestions for developing thematic units, including linking curriculum areas, studying authors and illustrators, genre studies, and other avenues in their chapter, "Linking Literature and Language Use through Thematic Units." Chatton and Hepler identify ways to develop authentic literature-based units that challenge students to investigate literature as a means to finding out about their world.

11 Linking Literature and Language Use through Thematic Units

Barbara Chatton
University of Wyoming

Susan Hepler
Alexandria, Virginia

In the book-filled classroom, the focused inquiry and provocative activities of thematic units let children use language to ask and answer questions, investigate and share knowledge, collaborate and negotiate, master and use related vocabulary, and rehearse new learning orally. Children who "study something" in this large context take pride in their own and others' efforts to create and master knowledge. Every student, no matter what learning style or capability, can participate in thematic units. In fact, children often help each other to levels of understanding that a teacher did not think possible. Teacher Marci El-Baba's second graders, for example, explored Chinese culture through a thematic unit. El-Baba read aloud Margaret Leaf's *Eyes of the Dragon* (1987, N), a folktale in which a dragon painted on the village wall comes alive and destroys the wall because of a magistrate's pride. In the discussion that followed, children commented on walls, dragons, the story's theme, the Chinese lettering in the story, and illustrator Ed Young's use of pastels. Darcy Pattison's literary folktale *The River Dragon* (1991), with illustrations by the Tsengs, showed children some specific characteristics of Chinese dragons which contrast with more familiar Western dragons. One child noted that a dragon she purchased during Chinese New Year celebrations had a pearl in its mouth, like the River Dragon. After reading Margaret Mahy's *The Seven Chinese Brothers* (1990), also illustrated by the Tsengs, children raised questions about

We would like to thank Marci El-Baba, whose second graders did the units on China and birds, and Susan Steinberg, whose fifth and sixth graders worked on the units on the ABC's and Chris Van Allsburg. Both teach at George Mason Elementary School, Alexandria City Public Schools, Alexandria, VA.

the Great Wall, which sent them to Leonard Everett Fisher's *The Great Wall of China* (1986). When several sources disagreed on how long it took to build the wall, a small group of children began to investigate the Great Wall. Other groups explored pandas, dragons, and other topics that had been raised.

A school employee originally from China was invited to the classroom to answer questions. He brought pictures, money, and magazines, and taught the class to count in Chinese from 1 to 10. Later, some students made a chart of Chinese numbers and their pronunciation. Some children wrote silly and cheerful fortunes (such as, "Your little brother will bug you forever" and "You will always have many friends"), and parents baked the nontraditional but essential fortune cookies for a snack. After one group of students wrote directions for papermaking, parent volunteers helped children make paper to reinforce the idea that the first papermakers were Chinese. Some children made kites to go with Jane Yolen's *The Emperor and the Kite* (1967).

The illustrations by Chinese American Ed Young for *Lon Po Po: A Red Riding Hood Story from China* (1989) and Ai-Ling Louie's *Yeh Shen: A Cinderella Story from China* (1988) were used to introduce some of the techniques and styles of Chinese art. Students were invited to compare these variants with the more familiar stories of "Little Red Riding Hood" and "Cinderella." Peggy Thompson's *City Kids in China* (1991) gave children a glimpse of contemporary life in a Chinese city.

Throughout this thematic study, these second graders linked books and experiences together to build a wider understanding of different aspects of Chinese culture. They practiced research skills; helped each other produce charts, directions, explanations, and reports; collaborated on murals and map work; and reread many of the books on display throughout the classroom. When the results of this short study of China were displayed, adults were amazed at the quality of work the seven-year-olds could produce. Through the teacher's planning and skillful manipulation of language use in the classroom, these children had become experts on China.

What Is a Thematic Unit?

A thematic unit, such as El-Baba's unit on China, is a planned curriculum that begins with a central idea or concept. The teacher helps children discover and enlarge upon that idea or concept by introducing books and activities that invite children to use reading, writing, talking, and thinking to make meaning. A well-planned thematic unit gives children time to consider ideas, to examine them in light of new evidence, to discover the patterns which underlie and unify a theme, and to double back to previous reading and experiences to confirm, clarify, or redefine their previous conceptions.

In *The Unschooled Mind: How Children Think and How Schools Should Teach* (1991), Howard Gardner points out that the natural redundancy of information present in a thematic unit is a key element in children's learning:

> [A] central subject at least makes it possible for teachers to point up the relationships among various facets of a many-sided topic and for students to begin to relate in their own minds the often disparate shards of knowledge encountered in the course of the school day so that they can begin to examine it from several perspectives. . . . [T]he by-product is often a more critical stance toward receiving opinions about various realms of knowledge. (P. 214)

Teachers can create thematic units in several different ways. Subject matter for themes can arise from a specific topic required by the curriculum guidelines at a particular grade level. For instance, topics such as Outer Space or Plants, typically found in the science curriculum, or Cultural Diversity or Family Life in social studies, can become cornerstones for units. Other units can arise from concepts or themes that cut across the curriculum, such as Seeing, Imagination, or Journeys. Thematic units also can start with language arts–related themes such as Wordplay, or with studying an author, illustrator, single book, or an aspect of a literary genre such as Wish Tales or ABC Books.

Papas, Kiefer, and Levstik (1990) counsel teachers who are choosing a theme to pick one that is broad enough to incorporate many types of books, resources, and activities, but not so broad that children lose sight of the connections that exist among the areas to be explored. The key to any thematic unit's success, however, is the teacher's careful collection of related books and the thoughtful consideration of what classroom experiences might enhance children's realms of knowledge. Different classrooms and teachers will produce many varieties of curriculum from the same list of books. To suggest how a teacher might move around in a theme, we are including sample thematic units. The sample units here draw heavily on selections from the Notables list because of their rich language and their ability to evoke responses in children. These sample units are merely "jumping off" points for the creation of your own thematic units.

Beginning with a Curriculum Area

Thematic units lifted directly from a topic listed on a district's curriculum allow a teacher to build upon available resources. The teacher does not need to develop a rationale and objectives, as they are already present. However, as a teacher assembles books and materials, the basic curriculum inevitably broadens. Different perspectives are considered, updated information can be included, and new links with other curriculum areas are often forged. For example, the science topic of Outer Space, normally limited to the study of facts in a textbook, can be enriched by works of poetry, nonfiction, science fiction, folktales, and biography. Myra Cohn Livingston's moving poems in *Sky Songs* (1984, N) give us a sense of the mysteries of space. The vast perspectives of Robin and Sally Hirst's *My Place in Space* (1990, N) and the humorous format of Joanna Cole and Bruce Degen's *The Magic School Bus Lost in the Solar System* (1990, N) provide entertainment as well as knowledge. Jill Paton Walsh's *The Green Book* (1982) is a brief science fiction novel which speculates about travel to a new planet, and Sally Ride's autobiography, *To Space and Back* (1992), tells of her actual experiences in space. Tololwa Mollel's *The Orphan Boy* (1991, N), a Maasai myth which explains the origins of the morning star, Venus, introduces children to one of the ways people have considered the heavens in traditional literature. With the use of these varied resources, thematic planning moves easily beyond the boundaries of the science slot but always returns to it.

Sometimes a teacher may consciously plan a topic which spans several curriculum areas concurrently. For example, second-grade science objectives might include the skills of observation and inference, while a math topic might be the making and reading of graphs, and a social studies topic at this level might include Natural Diversity. A teacher could choose the topic of Birds to bridge these parts of three curriculum areas. The poems in Jane Yolen's *Birdwatch* (1990, N) and in Paul Fleischman's *I Am Phoenix: Poems for Two Voices* (1985, N) might introduce this topic. Lois Ehlert's humorous *Feathers for Lunch* (1990, N) focuses on the birds (cut to scale in vibrant collage) that a cat unsuccessfully tries to catch. Children might set up a feeder, observe birds in their neighborhood, and draw them to scale as Ehlert does. They might describe the life cycle and activities of a bird or birds as Joanne Ryder does in *Dancers in the Garden* (1993, N). Jennifer Dewey's *Clem: The Story of a Raven* (1986, N), in journal form, suggests that children might keep their own close observations of a particular bird, species, or action at the feeder. They might graph the appearances of sparrows, pigeons, grackles, or other common birds and compare their frequency with rarer ones such as titmice or cardinals.

The theme of Families is usually addressed in language arts, science, and social studies in some way in kindergarten through third-grade classrooms. Alma Flor Ada (1991) suggests that many children come to school feeling as if their own stories and those of their families do not have the value of the stories they hear in school. Teachers might use a selection of books which invite children in their classrooms to investigate, listen to, and honor the stories of their own families. When children write their own family stories, illustrating them with drawings and family photographs, and share these stories with family members and classmates, they can change their perceptions about themselves and about their place in school.

Families can be studied in a variety of ways. We might look at different kinds of families, at what families do together, or family history (genealogy). We might focus on specific members of families, on brothers and sisters or other special relatives. Figure 11.1, a web for a thematic unit on Grandparents, features their stories, memories, and other gifts they give us as well as gifts we may be able to give back to them. While the unit is aimed at a primary audience, it might also be a provocative starting point for older children. Questions, activities, and many of the books are appropriate for most elementary students. In addition, books for older readers such as Cynthia Rylant's *Missing May* (1992, N) can provide an impetus for discussions on the topic What Makes a Family.

Studying an Author, Illustrator, or a Single Book

A classroom study of an author or illustrator gives children a chance to know the breadth and depth of a single creator's work. It also provides a finite content from which children can generalize about that person's choice of subjects, literary or artistic style, and other patterns. These studies can culminate during Children's Book Week, which is usually the second week of November, or they can take place anytime in the school year. Artists and authors on the Notables list such as Mitsumasa Anno, Avi, Lois Ehlert, Peter Parnall, Gary Paulsen, Cynthia Rylant, Chris Van Allsburg, Vera B. Williams, and Jane Yolen have each published a large enough body of books to invite children to think about books and their creators.

One teacher led a sixth-grade group through a chronological study of Chris Van Allsburg's books. While not all illustrators and authors lend themselves to this chronological approach, Van Allsburg is particularly interesting because his books have changed over the course of his career. The teacher began by reading aloud *The Garden of Abdul Gasazi* (1979) and *Jumanji* (1981) and asking children what they noticed. They commented on his dramatic use of black and white, the way the perspective shifts from eye level to higher or lower viewpoints, and the appearance of the same dog Fritz (a Boston bull terrier, they later discovered in library research). Some children also noted that Van Allsburg has surprises in his endings. These patterns were confirmed when children dispersed to work on other Van Allsburg titles in small groups. The teacher continued to read aloud his books, and a picture of each cover was placed on a time line in the hall. She read excerpts from Van Allsburg's Caldecott acceptance speech for *The Polar Express* (1985) and David Macaulay's

Figure 11.1. Web for thematic unit on Grandparents.

Gifts We Can Give Our Grandparents

What gifts do the children in these books give to older people?
What gifts could you give to older people who live in your community?
Write one of your memories of an older person as a story and give it to that person.

Books
Eve Bunting, *The Wednesday Surprise* (1989, N)
Mavis Jukes, *Blackberries in the Dark* (1985)
Patricia Polacco, *Chicken Sunday* (1992)

Gifts Our Grandparents Give Us: Tangibles

Draw a picture of something special given to you by a grandparent or someone older. Write or tell about your picture.
Write a letter to a grandparent or someone older telling them something special you appreciate about them.

Books
Judith Caseley, *Dear Annie* (1991)
Lucille Clifton, *The Lucky Stone* (1986)
Margarette S. Reid, *The Button Box* (1990)

Gifts Our Grandparents Give Us: Intangibles

What ideas or values are the grandparents passing on in these stories?
Tell a story about something that you heard from an older person.

Books
Choi, Sook N., *Halmoni and the Picnic* (1993)
Arthur Dorros, *Abuela* (1991)
Mary Hoffman, *Amazing Grace* (1991, N)
Patricia MacLachlan, *Through Grandpa's Eyes* (1980)
Patricia Polacco, *Thunder Cake* (1990, N)
Mary Stolz, *Go Fish* (1991)

Growing Older

What are some of the good things that happen as you grow older? What are some of the different things?
How can you benefit from knowing an older person?

Books
Aliki, *The Two of Them* (1979)
George Ancona, *Growing Older* (1978)
Eve Bunting, *Sunshine Home* (1994)
Helen Griffith, *Georgia Music* (1986)
Vaunda Micheaus Nelson, *Always Grandma* (1988, N)
Charlotte Zolotow, *I Know a Lady* (1984)

Humorous Stories

Tell a tall tale about you and some member of your family.
Create a story or picture collage of items you might unpack from a grandparent's trunk.

Books
Susan Ramsay Hoguet, *I Unpacked My Grandmother's Trunk: A Picture Book Game* (1983, N)
James Stevenson, *Could Be Worse!* (1977)

Resource Readings

D. Rife, *A Family History Handbook* (1985)
D. Weitzman, *My Backyard History Book* (1975)

GRANDPARENTS

What is important about grandparents?
What do they do for us?
What is it like to grow older?
How do families show their love for each other?

Grandparents' Stories and Memories

Interview a grandparent or other older person about his or her childhood. You might ask about celebrations, trips, summer fun, school, chores, or games.

Books
Eth Clifford, *The Remembering Box* (1985, N)
Adéle Geras, *My Grandmother's Stories: A Collection of Jewish Folk Tales* (1990, N)
Elizabeth Fitzgerald Howard, *Aunt Flossie's Hats (and Crabcakes Later)* (1991)
Bill Martin Jr. and John Archambault, *Knots on a Counting Rope* (1987, N)
Joanne Robertson, *Sea Witches* (1991, N)
Allen Say, *Grandfather's Journey* (1993)

tribute to Van Allsburg (1986). Each child selected one of the unfinished stories in *The Mysteries of Harris Burdick* (1984, N) and completed the story. As children worked with Van Allsburg's more recent titles, such as *Just a Dream* (1990), *The Wretched Stone* (1991), and *The Widow's Broom* (1992), they noticed that later books seemed to be more obviously focused on a message.

A final assignment was to write an essay summarizing the work of this author. Most eleven-year-olds would find this a challenge, but because of their knowledge built on class discussion and careful observation, these children were able to make generalizations and support them with good examples from Van Allsburg's books. Petra, a sixth grader, wrote:

> Chris Van Allsburg isn't your average writer. [He] sort of has a technique that he used in most of his books. What he does is he gets everything fixed in the book. Then he puts a twist in and ends the book so it leaves you puzzled.
>
> He doesn't exactly write for children. He writes for himself. Children can understand his books, but he puts bits of humor in the book that children either don't notice or won't understand. For instance, in his book, *Jumanji*, there is a piano and it is labeled Baldway, instead of Steinway or Baldwin. . . .
>
> Also in a few of his books he has messages. For instance, in *Just a Dream* it showed you clearly not to pollute our earth because a good thing can't last forever.
>
> The most appealing thing to me about Chris Van Allsburg is that in all of the eleven books he has published there is a dog that relatively looks like Spuds McKenzie. Fritz (the dog) was introduced to the readers in his first book *The Garden of Abdul Gasazi*. . . .

Single books may also become the center of study. However, other books usually enter into the discussion as well, so single books often become the key book in a wider theme. *Galimoto* by Karen Lynn Williams (1990, N) shows in story and pictures how Kondi, a boy who lives along the shores of Lake Malawi, barters, earns, trades, and connives enough wire to make a toy car, a *galimoto,* out of wire. The book lends itself to a variety of activities. Children might discuss and emulate Kondi's resourcefulness, find pieces of wire, and then collaborate in groups to construct their own wire toys. Sources might include a neighborhood construction site, Mom or Dad's toolbox, the telephone repair person's scraps, and so forth. Children might write lists of the sources of their wire samples, directions for making a *galimoto,* or about problems the group encountered and how they were solved (Huck, Hepler, and Hickman 1993a). *Galimoto* also connects to themes of living in a community, inventions, life in Eastern Africa, and self-reliance. It could serve as the key book to introduce a thematic unit on any of these subjects.

Avi's *The True Confessions of Charlotte Doyle* (1990, N), a novel about an eighteen-century girl's harrowing crossing from England to America during a mutiny on board her ship, is written in diary form and is a good novel to use as the center of a thematic study. Older readers who like this style may want to search out other historical novels written in diary form, such as Diane Glaser's *The Diary of Trilby Frost* (1976) or Joan Blos's *A Gathering of Days: A New England Girl's Journal, 1830–32* (1979), to read and compare. Avi's novel raises questions about the restrictions on young women in a earlier time. Students may want to read historical works to consider the accuracy of this portrait and to decide whether they think Avi's ending is realistic. Students might also find out more about life in this time period by reading other novels and nonfiction which might give them new insights. A wise teacher realizes that a good book has within its covers a myriad of possible connections to other good literature and to the lives of children. While the teacher may lead children into deep study of a single book, it is also important to let children choose links to other books and topics based on their interest and response.

Studying an Aspect of a Literary Genre

Genres of children's literature, such as fantasy, historical fiction, picture storybooks, or folktales, are too large an area for children and teachers to study. However, smaller, well-defined chunks—such as animal fantasy or time-travel fantasy, historical fiction about the Civil War or immigration, alphabet or counting books, and pourquoi tales or cumulative tales—allow teachers and students to focus more tightly on the patterns found in each of these types of stories.

One fifth-grade teacher took a surprising tack with her class by bringing in about fifty alphabet books. Under protests that "We already know the alphabet" from these ten-year-olds (to which the teacher replied, "Well, I should hope so"), she asked small groups to decide which books were easy, which books were harder, and why this was so. Next, she asked them to regroup and read other books to see if they could discover the organizing principles of ABC books. Their list of principles, along with books which are examples of each, are listed below. (Some books might fall into more than one category.)

- *Simple words, picture or letter identification*
  Tana Hoban, *26 Letters and 99 Cents* (1987)
  Laura Rankin, *The Handmade Alphabet* (1991, N)

- *Stories*
  Jim Aylesworth, *Old Black Fly* (1992, N)
  Arthur Geisert, *Pigs from A to Z* (1986, N)
  Bill Martin Jr. and John Archambault, *Chicka Chicka Boom Boom* (1989, N)

- *Riddles and puzzles*
  Suse MacDonald, *Alphabatics* (1986, N)
  Chris Van Allsburg, *The Z Was Zapped: A Play in Twenty-Six Acts* (1987, N)

- *Topics or themes*
  Jim Aylesworth, *The Folks in the Valley: A Pennsylvania Dutch ABC* (1992)
  Lois Ehlert, *Eating the Alphabet* (1989, N)
  Anita Lobel, *Allison's Zinnia* (1990, N)
  Eve Merriam, *Halloween ABC* (1987, N)

- *Alliteration and wordplay*
  Crescent Dragonwagon, *Alligator Arrived with Apples: A Potluck Alphabet Feast* (1987, N)
  Susan Purviance and Marcia O'Shell, *Alphabet Annie Announces an All-American Album* (1988, N)
  Graeme Base, *Animalia* (1987, N)

When children were then asked to produce their own alphabet books, their products showed remarkable diversity. From ABC's of fish, sports, and occupations to alliterative stories and lift-the-flap riddles, the depth of their texts and detail in their artwork showed their appreciation of alphabet bookmaking as a thoughtful and complicated process.

Thematic Units around an Idea

Sometimes interesting units arise out of an idea or question that occurs to children and teachers as they work together in the classroom. A group of students, for example, who listened to Bill Martin Jr. and John Archambault's *Knots on a Counting Rope* (1987, N) might raise a question which is subtly posed by these authors: "What does it mean to see?" In this story, clearly the young character sees even though he is blind. This kind of "sight" is also apparent to readers of Patricia MacLachlan's *Through Grandpa's Eyes* (1980). This question can lead to others:

What are other ways of seeing?

How can we begin to observe the world more closely?

Does our point of view influence what we see?

Do artists and photographers "see" differently?

An entire unit can emerge from this small insight, one which explores the many ways of seeing. Figure 11.2, a web of Seeing Things, lists readings and activities around this idea.

Themes across the Curriculum

Previously mentioned themes, such as China or Birds, began with aspects of preexisting curriculum. Some thematic units, however, begin with a topic and spread naturally across the curriculum.

Figure 11.2. Web for thematic unit on Seeing Things.

What Is the Artist's Eye?

What does the artist see?
How do artists tell stories with pictures?
Is a picture worth a thousand words?

Books
Barbara Cooney, *Hattie and the Wild Waves* (1990)
Pat Cummings, *Talking with Artists* (1992, N)
Beverly Gherman, *Georgia O'Keeffe: The Wideness and Wonder of Her World* (1986, N)
M. B. Goffstein, *An Artist* (1980)
Cynthia Rylant, *The Dreamer* (1993)
Piero Ventura, *Great Painters* (1984, N)

Taking a Different Point of View

Who can you think of who might see a situation from a different point of view? Illustrate a book showing that point of view.
How do people above and below the stairs and in different roles in the family see life differently in Goodall's book?
What does the cat see that the humans don't in Wolff's book?

Books
John S. Goodall, *Above and below the Stairs* (1983, N)
Jon Scieszka, *The True Story of the Three Little Pigs by A. Wolf* (1989)
Chris Van Allsburg, *Two Bad Ants* (1988)
Ashley Wolff, *Only the Cat Saw* (1985, N)

How Do We Observe the Natural World?

Create a careful log of your own observations of a natural environment. What do you see? How can you describe it so others will see it, too? If you like, add sounds, smells, textures, visuals, and tastes to your log to help your readers really *see* this place.

Books
Byrd Baylor, *I'm in Charge of Celebrations* (1986, N)
Jean Craighead George, *One Day in the Alpine Tundra* (1984, N)
Peter Parnall, *Quiet* (1989, N)
Gary Paulsen, *The Island* (1988, N)
Terry Tempest Williams, *Between Cattails* (1985, N)

SEEING THINGS

What does it mean to see?
How can we develop an observing eye?
Do artists develop special ways of seeing?

What Are Other Ways of Seeing?

How do the deaf "see" language? Learn to sign the letters of the alphabet from Rankin's book.
What messages do Martin and Archambault and MacLachlan give us about "seeing"?

Books
Patricia MacLachlan, *Through Grandpa's Eyes* (1980)
Bill Martin Jr. and John Archambault, *Knots on a Counting Rope* (1987, N)
Laura Rankin, *The Handmade Alphabet* (1991, N)

Resource Readings

M. Bang, *Picture This: Perception and Composition* (1991)
"Picture This Web: Perception and Composition" (*The Web*, 1990)

What Does the Camera See?

How do photographers help you see the world in a new way?
Why do you think MacLachlan uses images from photography to help tell her story? Make a paper frame which you can place over pictures you have taken or found. Have others guess what your picture shows by its texture.

Books
Tana Hoban, *Take Another Look* (1981)
Patricia MacLachlan, *Journey* (1991, N)
Milton Meltzer, *Dorothea Lange: Life through the Camera* (1985, N)

Visual Storytelling

What stories do these books tell? How much of the story is in the pictures? Chart the references you find in pictures to children's books, painting, history, people, and so forth.

Books
Mitsumasa Anno, *Anno's U.S.A.* (1983, N)
Graeme Base, *The Eleventh Hour: A Curious Mystery* (1989, N)
Fulvio Testa, *If You Look around You* (1983, N)
Chris Van Allsburg, *The Mysteries of Harris Burdick* (1984, N)

Various aspects of the curriculum come into play as books and activities suggest them. For example, a number of Notable books might be used in a unit on Cities in the upper-elementary grades. As demonstrated by the books and activities included in the web in figure 11.3, this topic allows students to explore urban communities in a number of different ways. The unit might begin with a focus on the literary element of setting. A middle school teacher might have as one objective to increase children's awareness of how setting affects character and plot. Realistic novels such as *Maniac Magee* by Jerry Spinelli (1990, N), *The Mouse Rap* by Walter Dean Myers (1990), or Virginia Hamilton's *The Planet of Junior Brown* (1971) show life in eastern urban areas. Paula Fox's *Monkey Island* (1991), a portrait of a homeless boy in the city, or Felice Holman's *Secret City, U.S.A.* (1990), about a group of boys who build themselves a home in an abandoned neighborhood of a city, present problems which occur in modern cities. *Saturnalia* by Paul Fleischman (1990, N), set in seventeenth-century Boston, and Leon Garfield's many novels set in eighteenth-century England look historically at city life. Students could compare the images of life in the mill town of Lowell, Massachusetts, in the nineteenth century in Katherine Paterson's *Lyddie* (1991, N) and in Bernice Selden's *The Mill Girls: Lucy Larcom, Harriet Hanson Robinson, Sarah E. Bagley* (1983, N).

As they read historical novels, students may want to learn more about how cities have changed over time. Even such simple picture books as Virginia Lee Burton's classic, *The Little House* (1942), can be used to begin this discussion. Students might read novels which show cities of the future, such as John Christopher's *City of Gold and Lead* (1967) or H. M. Hoover's *This Time of Darkness* (1980). They might look at the ways a city changes over vast periods of time as Grace Chetwin does in *Collidescope* (1990). Students might elect to read one of these key novels and discuss it in a small group. The teacher might reserve one book as the key book to read aloud and pose the "overarching questions" for the thematic unit (listed in the center of the web).

While reading novels to consider how setting is portrayed, students may begin to ask questions about the city. Why, for example, are so many portraits of the city negative? If students reread the old fable of *The Town Mouse and the Country Mouse,* retold by Janet Stevens (1987, N), they can see that this message was given even in this traditional story. What do nonfiction sources reveal? Who are the city lovers? Why? What's good about living in the city? All of these questions can be explored through reading, study, interviews, surveys, letter writing, and other forms of research.

Picture books can enrich thematic study in the upper-elementary grades by allowing students to see artists' interpretations of

Figure 11.3. Web for thematic unit on Cities.

CITIES

City versus Country

What living place would you choose? Why? What does the fable of the town mouse and the city mouse say about life in the city? Is this true? How do you know?

Books

Lilian Moore, *I'll Meet You at the Cucumbers* (1988, N)

Tom Paxton, "The Town Mouse and the Country Mouse," in *Belling the Cat and Other Aesop's Fables* (1990)

Janet Stevens, *The Town Mouse and the Country Mouse* (1987, N)

Then and Now

Consider change. How does each setting change? Which changes are good? Which aren't? What does each book say about the past?

Investigate an older part of town. What used to go on here? How can you tell? How has it changed? Why?

Become the voice for an old house in your neighborhood. Write about what "you" have seen over the years.

Make a picture of your home, put a flap over part of it as Goodall did, and draw what it might have been like 100 years ago or what it might be like 100 years from now. Look out the window and make a collage illustration of what you see.

Books

Jeannie Baker, *Window* (1991)

Virginia Lee Burton, *The Little House* (1942)

John S. Goodall, *The Story of an English Village* (1979)

Alice Provenson and Martin Provenson, *Shaker Lane* (1990)

Uri Shulevitz, *Toddlecreek Post Office* (1991)

Ann Turner, *Heron Street* (1989)

Renata Von Tscharner and Ronald L. Fleming, *New Providence: A Changing Cityscape* (1987)

Resource Readings

"Grand Constructions" Web (*The Web*, 1989)

U. Shulevitz, "The Inside Story: *Toddlecreek Post Office*" (*Booklinks*, 1991)

D. Weitzman, *My Backyard History Book* (1975)

The City in Novels

Read one of the novels about the city in the future. What might lead the author to predict that the city will be as it is described?

Books

Grace Chetwin, *Collidescope* (1990)

John Christopher, *City of Gold and Lead* (1967)

Paul Fleischman, *Saturnalia* (1990, N)

Paula Fox, *Monkey Island* (1991)

Virginia Hamilton, *The Planet of Junior Brown* (1971)

F. Holman, *Secret City, U.S.A.* (1990)

H. M. Hoover, *This Time of Darkness* (1985)

Walter Dean Myers, *The Mouse Rap* (1990)

Katherine Paterson, *Lyddie* (1991, N)

Bernice Selden, *The Mill Girls: Lucy Larcom, Harriet Hanson Robinson, Sarah G. Bagley* (1983, N)

George Selden, *The Cricket in Times Square* (1960)

Jerry Spinelli, *Maniac Magee* (1990, N)

How does the main character live in the city? How does living there affect the character's outlook and values?

What is the image created of the city? What is the author or illustrator's attitude toward urban life?

How do cities and attitudes toward cities change?

Examining Your Own Community

What is your city or town like? What makes it distinctive?

Make a travel brochure for your own town which persuades tourists to visit.

Interview someone who has lived in your town a long time. Prepare your questions beforehand.

Using Baylor's book as a guide, describe the ways in which you live in the "best town in the world."

Make an "inside-outside" book of your own community patterned after Munro's book. Draw an aerial view of your community.

Books

Byrd Baylor, *The Best Town in the World* (1983, N)

Roxie Munro, *The Inside-Outside Book of New York City* (1985, N)

Are Cities in Other Countries Different from American Cities?

How do children live in these cities? How does the city affect them?

Books

Nina Bawden, *The Finding* (1985)

Ann Cameron, *The Most Beautiful Place in the World* (1988, N)

Niki Daly, *Not So Fast, Songololo* (1986)

Florence Parry Heide and Judith Heide Gilliland, *The Day of Ahmed's Secret* (1990, N) and *Sami and the Time of Troubles* (1992)

Beverley Naidoo, *Journey to Jo'burg* (1985)

themes and ideas as well as those presented in the written texts of novels and nonfiction. Picture books which illustrate modern city life using various media, styles, and tones can be brought in and considered. What do these illustrators show us about how they feel about life in the city? Picture books also show life in other times and places, and the artistic representation of these cities can be considered as well. The poems in Eloise Greenfield's *Night on Neighborhood Street* (1991, N), which show some of the harshness of city life as well as its blessings, can be compared with those in Lee Bennett Hopkins's *A Song in Stone: City Poems* (1983, N). How do the poets feel about the city? What do word choices, rhythms, and sounds reveal about their attitudes?

This unit merely touches on aspects of cities and city life. Teachers can tailor the unit to the communities from which their students come because one outcome of this unit might be for children to see their own lives and situations more clearly. A unit for rural children might take a different direction from a unit for urban children. The use of different novels, nonfiction works, picture books, and poems about the city could enrich the unit and change the questions which are posed here.

Thematic Unit Planning

In planning for thematic units, teachers must take into account a number of different factors. They need to consider their curriculum: what topics, themes, or skills do they want students to know, and what are stimulating ways in which these can be presented and developed? Teachers need to consider resources: what novels, stories, picture books, poems, and nonfiction are available which could pique interest in, highlight aspects of, stimulate questions about, and introduce the language or ideas of this thematic area? Thematic units should do more than simply present a subject or theme. Instead, units should invite teachers and students to ask significant questions, to think critically about the world and their place in it. Units should also provide focused study rather than an attempt to merely cover a topic or theme. As Silva and Delgado-Larocco (1993) point out, thematic unit planning should "focus on the identification of concepts and universal generalizations rather than activities." In selecting books, teachers should identify a set of "conceptually related books that allow students to arrive at and test universal generalizations" (p. 473). The overarching questions provided in each of the units discussed here were generated from our reading of the books selected for inclusion in the unit. They are intended to provide unifying ideas and a focused perspective on these materials. Teachers also need to consider their students as they plan for units. The length of a unit and the activities generated for it will depend upon the needs and interests of students. There is no one "right" unit which will emerge from this interaction. Different books, different teachers, and different groups of children will influence planning and the directions in which a unit will grow.

Not all unit planning happens before the unit begins. As teachers and students begin reading, writing, and talking about a topic or theme, new questions arise and new directions can be followed. Units used in one context may be adapted for use in another. The Then and Now section of the thematic unit on Cities in this chapter, for example, might also be used as part of a unit on the environment or a unit on Change. The principles used in planning the unit on China in this chapter might be adapted for units of study of other geographic areas. Over time, new books and new questions can be added to broaden units, or single aspects of units may be borrowed for "mini-units" which highlight a single small theme or subject.

There are many ways for children to learn and a variety of language uses which can be generated through thematic units. In these units children talk over, talk about, and talk through their ideas. They listen to and interact with each other and with adults. Talk and writing are used to explore, entertain, inquire, organize, inform, review, and create. Children read for different purposes, and their reading matter is diverse, crossing genres and ability levels. Children's writings become part of the text of the thematic unit. The books they read, especially those which feature notable uses of language, influence their own writing. The vocabulary, style, and content of their readings is reflected in their writing and talk. Literature and language are linked, and the skills of language arts are put to real use, for authentic purposes rather than as ends in themselves. Throughout, language and learners are alive and thriving.

References
Professional Resources

Ada, A. F. 1991. Speech on family stories. Delivered at the Conference of the International Reading Association, Las Vegas, NV.

Bang, M. 1991. *Picture This: Perception and Composition.* Boston: Little, Brown.

Book Links. Chicago: American Library Association.

Cummings, P. 1992. *Talking with Artists.* New York: Bradbury Press.

Gardner, H. 1991. *The Unschooled Mind: How Children Think and How Schools Should Teach.* New York: Basic Books/HarperCollins.

"Grand Constructions" Web. 1989. *The Web* (Fall): 12–17.

Huck, C. S., S. Hepler, and J. Hickman. 1993a. "A Guide for *Galimoto.*" In *Children's Literature in the Elementary School,* 5th ed. San Diego: Harcourt Brace Jovanovich.

————. 1993b. "Resources for Teaching: Author Autobiographies." In *Children's Literature in the Elementary School*, 5th ed. San Diego: Harcourt Brace Jovanovich.

Kiefer, B. Z., ed. 1992. *Getting to Know You: Profiles of Children's Authors Featured in Language Arts, 1985–90*. Urbana, IL: National Council of Teachers of English.

Laughlin, M. K., and S. W. Letty. 1986. *Developing Learning Skills through Children's Literature*. Phoenix, AZ: Oryx.

Macaulay, D. 1986. "Appreciation." *The Horn Book Magazine* (July / August): 420.

Pappas, C. C., B. Z. Kiefer, and L. S. Levstik. 1990. *An Integrated Language Perspective in the Elementary School: Theory into Action*. White Plains, NY: Longman.

"Picture This" Web: Perception and Composition. 1990. *The Web* (Winter): 12.

Rife, D. 1985. *A Family History Handbook*. Logan, IA: Perfection Form Company.

Shulevitz, U. 1991. "The Inside Story: *Toddlecreek Post Office*." *Booklist* (January 15): 1030–34.

Silva, C., and E. L. Delgado-Larocco. 1993. "Facilitating Learning through Interconnections: A Concept Approach to Core Literature Units." *Language Arts* 70:469–74.

Weitzman, D. 1975. *My Backyard History Book*. Boston: Little, Brown.

Children's Literature

Aliki. 1979. *The Two of Them*. New York: Greenwillow Books.

Ancona, George. 1978. *Growing Older*. New York: E. P. Dutton.

Aylesworth, Jim. 1992. *The Folks in the Valley: A Pennsylvania Dutch ABC*. Illustrated by Stefano Vitale. New York: HarperCollins.

Baker, Jeannie. 1991. *Window*. New York: Greenwillow Books.

Bawden, Nina. 1985. *The Finding*. New York: Lothrop, Lee and Shepard Books.

Blos, Joan W. 1979. *A Gathering of Days: A New England Girl's Journal, 1830–32*. New York: Charles Scribner's Sons.

Bunting, Eve. 1994. *Sunshine Home*. Illustrated by Diane de Groat. New York: Clarion Books.

Burton, Virginia Lee. 1942. *The Little House*. Boston: Houghton Mifflin.

Caseley, Judith. 1991. *Dear Annie*. New York: Greenwillow Books.

Chetwin, Grace. 1990. *Collidescope*. New York: Bradbury Press.

Choi, Sook N. 1993. *Halmoni and the Picnic*. Illustrated by K. M. Dugan. Boston: Houghton Mifflin.

Christopher, John. 1967. *The City of Gold and Lead*. New York: Macmillan.

Clifton, Lucille. 1986. *The Lucky Stone.* New York: Delacorte Press.

Cooney, Barbara. 1990. *Hattie and the Wild Waves.* New York: Viking.

Daly, Niki. 1986. *Not So Fast, Songololo.* New York: Clarion Books.

Dorros, Arthur. 1991. *Abuela.* Illustrated by Elisa Kleven. New York: E. P. Dutton.

Fisher, Leonard Everett. 1986. *The Great Wall of China.* New York: Macmillan.

Fox, Paula. 1991. *Monkey Island.* New York: Orchard Books.

Glaser, Diane. 1976. *The Diary of Trilby Frost.* New York: Holiday House.

Goffstein, M. B. 1980. *An Artist.* New York: Harper and Row.

Goodall, John S. 1979. *The Story of an English Village.* New York: Macmillan.

Griffith, Helen. 1986. *Georgia Music.* Illustrated by James Stevenson. New York: Greenwillow Books.

Hamilton, Virginia. 1971. *The Planet of Junior Brown.* New York: Macmillan.

Heide, Florence Parry, and Judith Heide Gilliland. 1992. *Sami and the Time of Troubles.* Illustrated by Ted Lewin. New York: Clarion Books.

Hoban, Tana. 1981. *Take Another Look.* New York: Greenwillow Books.

———. 1987. *Twenty-Six Letters and Ninety Cents.* New York: Greenwillow Books.

Holman, Felice. 1990. *Secret City, U.S.A.* New York: Charles Scribners' Sons.

Hoover, H. M. 1980. *This Time of Darkness.* New York: Viking.

Howard, Elizabeth Fitzgerald. 1991. *Aunt Flossie's Hats (and Crabcakes Later).* Illustrated by James E. Ransome. New York: Clarion Books.

Jukes, Mavis. 1985. *Blackberries in the Dark.* Illustrated by Thomas B. Allen. New York: Alfred A. Knopf.

Louie, Ai-Ling. 1988. *Yeh-Shen: A Cinderella Story from China.* Illustrated by Ed Young. New York: Philomel Books.

MacLachlan, Patricia. 1980. *Through Grandpa's Eyes.* Illustrated by Deborah Kogan Ray. New York: Harper and Row.

Mahy, Margaret. 1990. *The Seven Chinese Brothers.* Illustrated by Jean and Mou-Sien Tseng. New York: Scholastic.

Myers, Walter Dean. 1990. *The Mouse Rap.* New York: Harper and Row.

Naidoo, Beverley. 1985. *Journey to Jo'burg: A South African Story.* Illustrated by Eric Velasquez. New York: J. B. Lippincott.

Pattison, Darcy. 1991. *The River Dragon.* Illustrated by Jean and Mou-Sien Tseng. New York: Lothrop, Lee and Shepard Books.

Paxton, Tom. 1990. "The Town Mouse and the Country Mouse," in *Belling the Cat, and Other Aesop's Fables.* New York: William Morrow.

Polacco, Patricia. 1992. *Chicken Sunday.* New York: Philomel Books.

Provensen, Alice, and Martin Provenson. 1990. *Shaker Lane.* New York: Viking.

Reid, Margarette S. 1990. *The Button Box.* Illustrated by Sarah Chamberlain. New York: E. P. Dutton.

Ride, Sally, and Susan Okie. 1985. *To Space and Back.* New York: Lothrop, Lee and Shepard Books.

Rylant, Cynthia. 1993. *The Dreamer.* Illustrated by Barry Moser. New York: Scholastic.

Say, Allen. 1993. *Grandfather's Journey.* Boston: Houghton Mifflin.

Scieszka, Jon. 1989. *The True Story of the Three Little Pigs by A. Wolf.* Illustrated by Lane Smith. New York: Viking.

Selden, George. 1960. *The Cricket in Times Square.* Illustrated by Garth Williams. New York: Farrar, Straus and Giroux.

Shulevitz, Uri. 1990. *Toddlecreek Post Office.* New York: Farrar, Straus and Giroux.

Stevenson, James. 1977. *Could Be Worse!* New York: Greenwillow Books.

Stolz, Mary. 1991. *Go Fish.* Illustrated by Pat Cummings. New York: HarperCollins.

Thompson, Peggy. 1991. *City Kids in China.* Photographs by Paul S. Conklin. New York: HarperCollins.

Turner, Ann. 1989. *Heron Street.* New York: Harper and Row.

Van Allsburg, Chris. 1979. *The Garden of Abdul Gasazi.* Boston: Houghton Mifflin.

———. 1981. *Jumanji.* Boston: Houghton Mifflin.

———. 1985. *The Polar Express.* Boston: Houghton Mifflin.

———. 1988. *Two Bad Ants.* Boston: Houghton Mifflin.

———. 1990. *Just a Dream.* Boston: Houghton Mifflin.

———. 1991. *The Wretched Stone.* Boston: Houghton Mifflin.

———. 1992. *The Widow's Broom.* Boston: Houghton Mifflin.

Von Tscharner, Renata, and Ronald L. Fleming. 1987. *New Providence: A Changing Cityscape.* New York: Harper and Row.

Walsh, Jill Paton. 1982. *The Green Book.* Illustrated by Lloyd Bloom. New York: Farrar, Straus and Giroux.

Yolen, Jane. 1967. *The Emperor and the Kite.* Illustrated by Ed Young. New York: World.

Young, Ed. 1989. *Lon Po Po: A Red Riding Hood Story from China.* New York: G. P. Putnam's Sons.

Zolotow, Charlotte. 1984. *I Know a Lady.* New York: Greenwillow Books.

V Authors' Voices: Perspectives of Notable Authors on Wordcrafting

There is something special about getting to know the person behind the words in a story. Writers can speak to their readers not only through the images and ideas in their books but also through comments on how they view the world and the craft of writing. As children get inside an author's head, they become more aware of how writers strive to select the best possible words and then arrange those words in a way that pleases the ear and conveys the intended meaning. They learn that writing is a deliberate act and that language, the tool of writers, can be shaped to the writer's purposes.

Several common ideas resonate throughout the essays in this section. First, the authors indicate that writing is hard work, requiring much thought and diligence. Eve Bunting, in particular, makes this point when she recalls in wonder how she spent hours subtly crafting a half-dozen words for a fairly lengthy novel. William Hooks also spends enormous time experimenting with words to discover the precise language and cadences that "give wings to [his] words."

Second, the comments demonstrate that writers particularly ponder over the language of stories. The authors of these essays continually make the point that language use is not casual or careless but rather quite deliberate. For example, Jerry Spinelli tells how he struggled with finding the best words to effectively show someone learning to read in *Maniac Magee.* After searching through sounds and combining them in various ways, he came up with a simple simile which effectively captured his image. Tony Johnston demonstrates how she tried to make her phrases sway lyrically to imitate "the sway of whales on long journeys, the sway of seaweeds, the sway of swells on the sea" for *Whale Song.* Words for her are wonderful "piles of beads" waiting to be sorted through in order to find just the right ones for a story.

Third, the authors of the essays emphasize that revision is a critical part of the process. As Katherine Paterson states, "Revising is where the fun and artistry begin." Peter and Connie Roop describe the decisions they make as they shape the initial draft of a story written for beginning readers. They tell how they deliberately work to make the language flow yet keep it accessible for a child who is just becoming an independent reader. Avi recounts how he always "reads and revises with my readers in mind."

Fourth and most importantly, these writers share a universal love for language and its power to shape thought and story. Bill Brittain calls it "the greatest plaything in the world." Eleanor Cameron relates how she was "besotted with words" as a child. Jan Slepian probably echoes them all when she says, "The joy . . . is in the way I say a thing, and when I know it's right, there's nothing like it. It's the greatest."

The authors of these essays write in different genres and from many different perspectives. Their thoughts can be used in conjunction with reading their work or used as commentary on the writing process.

The Language of My Books

Aliki

My first book, *My Five Senses* (which was actually my second book), just happened. I wrote the words effortlessly, and the pictures emerged in the same way. Before that time, I had no other desire than to be an artist; to spend my life drawing. The idea then struck me that if I wrote another book, it would provide a reason to draw illustrations. Five books later, I received a shock when someone referred to me as an "author." By then I was hooked.

But how do I now explain writing (or illustrating, for that matter, since they are so similar)? Goals are easier to define than the way to reach them.

The challenge of writing nonfiction is to achieve a message that is correct, clear, and concise. Added to that is the quest to reach the soul of one's voice. Facts without emotion—without playfulness, humor, or harmony—are as colorless as a weather report. If I manage to do this, I do so with pain, because rewriting is what I do most.

In a thirty-two-page picture book, text and illustrations are shared, so space is limited. I like to keep the main text as short and as accessible as possible, so as not to turn off a reluctant reader (like myself). That is why, in some books, I use captions or speech balloons. They are my subtle way of packing in more information that is either necessary or so fascinating to me that it has to be told.

> Each favored courtier woke at dawn, dressed, and prepared for his long day. He would hover near the King, so Louis might toss him a favor—a free meal, a title, or an exemption from paying taxes. To get to the King's apartment for the *Lever,* he made his way down dark staircases and through a maze of corridors and chambers. (*The King's Day: Louis XIV of France,* unpaged, p. 13)

(A caption needs so much revising, it takes on a life of its own.) Also, when dealing with a serious subject, speech bubbles may be the only written way to lighten it and inject humor:

> This is a little fella.
> One swat of his tail would show you *how* little.
> (*Digging Up Dinosaurs,* unpaged, p. 8)

> I'm halfway there.
> I wonder how the world is doing.
> (*How a Book Is Made,* unpaged, p. 15)

Captions and speech balloons provide an extension of the text for the more fluent or curious reader, and I hope they turn reading a book into a more dimensional digging process.

Long before I ever thought I would write books, I have been fascinated by words—perhaps due to my bilingual (Greek and American) background or my strong musicality. I love finding choices for words, weaving them together, searching for the clearest meaning, the truest sound or feeling. Words do more than describe. Their sounds can grate, punctuate, or console.

> There was nothing to do without Peter.
> There was no one to play with.
> There was no one to share with.
> There was no one to fight with.
> Not the way best friends fight.
> There was no fun anymore.
> "I'll bet Peter doesn't even remember me,"
>   said Robert.
> "It's a good thing he's not here.
> I'd have to punch him one."
> (*We Are Best Friends,* unpaged, pp. 9–12)

Like music, words create mood, atmosphere, and color.

> We tried to catch the bat rays, gliding like pancakes in their own shallow pool. (*My Visit to the Aquarium,* unpaged)

They can activate all the senses. That is the difficult challenge of writing—mixing fact with feeling.

Long before I begin to write, I steep myself in research and become familiar with it, as does an actor who learns his lines before he knows how he will speak them.

Establishing my first paragraph is essential. It introduces the subject, provides the flavor, and sets the mood.

> I like books.
> I like the way a book feels.
> I like the way a book smells.
> I like to turn each page,
> read each word,
> look at the pictures.
> (*How a Book Is Made,* unpaged, p. 3)

It is the anchor to which the second and subsequent paragraphs will link. Part of me is still in the Dark Ages, so I write in longhand, over and over, changing words and phrasing, until the Great Break-through comes, when words begin to flow, towed out on a thread of thought. *The King's Day* was so hard that I wrote three different versions, and only the first paragraph remains intact.

> Louis XIV
> was every inch a King.
> He wore the curliest wigs,
> the richest robes, the rarest jewels,
> and the fanciest shoes in all of France. (P. 5)

Finding my voice in fiction—which I call my "feeling" books—is easier and more natural. Usually, the story comes out easily, with its own language, in a flow, such as with *At Mary Bloom's* and *The Two of Them.* Sometimes it takes years to find the voice. (*Welcome, Little Baby* took ten years.) There are surprises. After years of trying to write a story about twins, *Jack and Jake* emerged in verse—frightening to anyone who thinks few things are worse than bad verse. Another surprise was *Christmas Tree Memories,* which flowed out in four voices, with no break for quotes. I didn't want to disconnect the interrupting voices by piercing them with "he says" and "she says."

> There is my heart of dough.
>
> You were only two when you made it.
> That was the year of the blizzard. Remember?
>
> There was no water or electricity, and we boiled
> snow for soup and told stories by the fire. (Unpaged, p. 8)

I love language and words, and try to use them in a respectful way. I use colloquial expressions in quotes, in speech bubbles, or if a character is speaking in dialect. I would not make words easier for children. On the contrary, in the revised edition of *My Hands,* I was thrilled that I thought to add the word *ambidextrous.*

When I titled one of my books *Communication,* I was told I'd have to find an easier word. But there was no clearer one, and I decided that if children can pronounce (and spell!) *Tyrannosaurus,* they can cope with *Communication.* (The new "snippet re-language" of today, used in many magazines for those who no longer have time to read a whole sentence, is like ice on my teeth.)

I correct my words, trying to read with fresh eyes, until the book goes to press. Then I hope it is the best I can do.

References   Aliki. 1962. *My Hands.* New York: Thomas Y. Crowell.

————. 1976. *At Mary Bloom's.* New York: Greenwillow Books.

————. 1979. *The Two of Them.* New York: Greenwillow Books.

————. 1981. *Digging Up Dinosaurs.* New York: Thomas Y. Crowell.

————. 1982. *We Are Best Friends.* New York: Greenwillow Books.

————. 1986. *How a Book Is Made.* New York: Thomas Y. Crowell.

————. 1986. *Jack and Jake.* New York: Greenwillow Books.

————. 1987. *Welcome, Little Baby.* New York: Greenwillow Books.

————. 1989. *The King's Day: Louis XIV of France.* New York: Thomas Y. Crowell.

————. 1991. *Christmas Tree Memories.* New York: HarperCollins.

————. 1993. *Communication.* New York: Greenwillow Books.

————. 1993. *My Visit to the Aquarium.* New York: HarperCollins.

The Hardest Part of Writing

Avi

"What is the hardest part of writing?" That is a question I am often asked. What I say is, "The hardest part of writing is—reading." Let me explain.

When you read one of my books—or by one of my many gifted colleagues—more often than not you find it reads smoothly, with few flaws. "How do *they* write so well?" you ask yourself. The next thing you say to yourself is, "What I just wrote seems so poor in comparison."

But what you are *not* seeing is that the text you read was probably *rewritten* many times. You do not see the rough drafts. You see the final work. Speaking for myself, I rewrite my books between forty to fifty times. Of course not all sentences get rewritten, just as there are those key sentences (like the opening line of a story) that I may rewrite a hundred times. (I've already rewritten this short piece twelve times!)

The question is, *why* do professional writers rewrite so much? It is because a writer like myself writes for readers, not for myself. When you write a diary you have (you hope!) but one reader, your-self. You know what you mean. When you write a letter you do have another reader, but usually that reader knows who you are, perhaps even what you are trying to say. But when you write for people who have no idea who you are, what you are thinking, or what you are trying to say, you must make sure that reader understands your meanings, ideas, emotions, and so forth.

As a consequence, I am constantly reading what I have writ-ten, trying to judge it from the point of the reader. Of course, it matters that I understand it. In the end, however, it is more impor-tant that my readers understand it. Having read through my work—critically—I become a writer again and make changes, only to be-come a reader again, making critical judgments. This critical read-ing—making judgments about what I am writing—is the hard part of writing.

Please notice that unless you read a lot of things by other people, it is very hard to do this kind of critical reading. If you do read a lot, you can develop an inner sense—*a reader's ear and eye*—for what makes a good piece of writing.

In other words, *the best way to learn to write is to read a lot.* Unless you are a reader, you cannot become a writer. The more you read, the better your writing will be.

Need a simple way to keep this in mind? Try this: a writer does not write writing. A writer writes reading. Better yet: Want to write? Read!

Words That Make Music

Natalie Babbitt

For me, the process of writing is always as much a listening exercise as anything else. For even when you are reading to yourself, you hear the words in your head while you're seeing them on the page, and how they sound is every bit as important as what they mean.

There are always many different ways to say the same thing and convey the same meaning, but the way you choose has everything to do with whether you will make good music as well as good sense. I use the term *music* deliberately. Rhythm is very much involved—in prose as in poetry—and there is harmony, and there is the setting of a mood.

Readers sometimes ask me why, in my story *Tuck Everlasting,* the man in the yellow suit wears a yellow suit. And I tell them that since the phrase "the man in the yellow suit" is used so often, it was especially important that the words make good music. This means that the color I chose had to have two syllables, not one. "The man in the black suit" has a blunt, abrupt sound, as would any other one-syllable color, whereas "the man in the yellow suit" sounds more fluent and graceful, and gives a far more pleasing rhythm to the phrase.

There are many ways to enhance the sound of a sentence. You need to think about numbers of syllables in a given word, as in the example above, and you also need to think about whether word and phrase repetitions will help or hinder, and whether alliteration will add or detract. In *The Devil's Other Storybook,* there is lots of alliteration because I thought it sounded right, phrases like "its body was broken to bits" and "shuffling and snuffling" being only two examples. And there is phrase repetition, too, where it seems right, like "quite red in the face" in "The Signpost," or the combination of "a walrus" and "several roosters" in "The Rise and Fall of Bathbone."

But the biggest consideration of all, in stories like the ones in *The Devil's Other Storybook,* is simply whether or not the chosen words are funny to the ear. I don't presume to imagine that everyone will agree about what's funny. Senses of humor come in all shapes and sizes. But to me certain words are always funny, words like *turnip* and *walrus,* and certain phrases are always funny, like *worn to a frazzle.* In the story "Justice", the phrase "pounding through the wild parts" is funnier by far to me than would be "running through the underbrush." I don't know why. Similarly, in "Wishes," to "chop bamboo" in Borneo is funnier than, for instance, "to pick coconuts" in the Tropics. This has nothing whatever to do with the meaning; it's all in the listening.

So I have always told writing students, "Listen to what you are saying, not for the meaning—we will take for granted you are saying clearly what you mean—but for the sound." And then I refer them to Charles Dickens's *A Christmas Carol,* and how he tells the reader, at the beginning and again at the end, about the weather. Dickens doesn't say, "It was below freezing" and leave it at that. He makes wonderful music out of both descriptions. At the beginning: "It was cold, bleak, biting weather . . . he could hear the people . . . wheezing up and down, . . . stamping their feet upon the pavement-stones to warm them" (p. 4). At the end: "clear, bright, jovial, stirring, cold; cold, piping for the blood to dance to" (p. 117). Needless to say, there's only one Dickens, but we can all learn from him. We have, after all, the same language, all the same wonderful words, at our disposal. All we have to do is listen.

References

Babbitt, Natalie. 1975. *Tuck Everlasting.* New York: Farrar, Straus and Giroux.

———. 1987. *The Devil's Other Storybook.* New York: Farrar, Straus and Giroux.

Words, Words, Words!

Tom Birdseye

As a kid, I often wondered where the words in books came from. I knew that a person called a writer was responsible for them. But to me writers were more mythical than real, living in wild and exotic places, far from the stubbed-toe, tree-climbing, gotta-set-the-table reality of my Greensboro, North Carolina, world. Words just came to them, I figured, spiraling ever-so-perfectly into their gifted minds, then through some miraculous dipsy-doodle onto the page as a bonafide marvel for me to read.

This that I imagined was a far cry from my own experience at school. Convinced that my writing should sound like someone else's—preferably a professor of English grammar—I wrestled my words out of any natural vocabulary or cadence and then penned the new "right" version into awkward submission. Panting with the effort of producing such masterpieces as "My Summer Vacation," "George Washington—Our First President!" and "The Life Cycle of a Pinto Bean," I thanked my lucky stars when the 3:10 bell rang and I was pardoned—WHEW!—until the next day. How writers pulled off what they did, I didn't have a clue. It was all literary hocus-pocus to me.

And yet time slipped on by, the right teacher came along at the right time, and to the surprise of many (including myself), I became a writer.

A little hocus-pocus of my own? No, nothing so magical. I wrote and rewrote, sweating over plot, place, and people in my stories, struggling with my poor spelling and punctuation skills. I spent years getting better . . . s-l-o-w-l-y.

But in the process of that slow learning, something more than a passable story began to emerge. At first it was muffled, like Beethoven played in a bucket of mud. But over time it grew stronger and stronger, until finally it rang out clear. It was my writer's voice, the lilt and rhythm of where I've lived, who I've known, what I've done. With that voice, I began to sing.

Words, words, words. For me, they are the notes of storytelling, and they are *everywhere*. In fact, there are so many that I have to carry a small notebook in my back pocket just to keep track. If Aunt Dana says, "The mosquitoes were so big they made the cats pay rent to sleep in the barn," I write it down. Or if Opa Holsclaw says, "Those guys are so crooked they have to screw their socks on every morning," I write that down also. Or if I see some kids playing tag on a summer evening and I remember doing the same thing years ago—running after a friend yelling, "I'm gonna' open up a can of gotcha and send you airmail to the moon!"—those words go into my notebook, too. They float around in my brain and on my tongue, becoming part of who I am. Then, just as sure as pigs like mud, they come out again when I start writing. They come out shouting, "Why just say it, when you can make it really live!"

Just the other day, my four-year-old daughter, Amy, looked out the window at an afternoon storm and said, "The world is a big dog that shakes when it rains."

Raining words, I thought, wonderful, wonderful words.

The Greatest Plaything in the World

Bill Brittain

As a writer of books for young people, I guess I'm expected to be reasonably adept in using language. Sure, I know that names begin with capital letters (unless the name is e. e. cummings), and every sentence must end with a period (except for those that don't), and the plural of *goose* is *geese,* but the plural of *moose* is not *meese.*

But when I address a group of teachers, librarians, or young people and describe the English language as "the greatest plaything in the world," I get looks that silently but eloquently question at the very least my common sense, and perhaps my sanity.

I'm sorry, but to me, our language is fun to play with. It's a magnificent toy that's a constant source of amusement and wonder, and I don't even have to purchase it at the department store. As a child I learned a goodly supply of words, which are the basic building blocks of language. Throughout my life I've been adding to my supply of blocks, as well as discovering new and intriguing things about them.

I was delighted, for example, to learn at some time that our word *muscle* comes from the Latin word for *mouse.* Just watch some well-endowed athlete rippling his biceps or pectorals and then tell me it doesn't remind you of tiny rodents skittering around beneath the blankets.

What fun to find *pneumonoultramicroscopicsilicovolcanoconiosis* marching all the way across one of the columns of *Webster's Seventh New Collegiate Dictionary.* Who cares what it means? It's one humongous word. And it's about five times as long as *humongous* itself.

A challenge: try writing a short paragraph with the following guidelines. It must be exactly twenty-six words long. It must make some kind of sense, no matter how weird or exotic. And finally, the first word must begin with A, the second with B, and so on, right down through the alphabet. A pox on you athletic types who can hit baseballs and practically fly in a basketball arena. Can any one of you write such a paragraph? Without help? I thought not. Hah!

I once heard a fellow writer describe the yarn he was writing as "a movie being shown inside my head." I, too, tend to see my stories as movies. And those movies have a sound track. What fun it is to play with the sounds of words.

Who was the poetic genius who ended a rhyme with the burning question: "Is it harder to toot or to tutor two tooters to toot?" Magnificent!

Who wrote the incredible oath given to Captain Hook in the Mary Martin production of *Peter Pan*? We've read of pirates swearing "by the great horn spoon," or "by the blood of my ancestors." But Hook's "Now, bi-carbonate of soda!" is a monument to the art of punning.

I want my readers to share my delight in playing with the language. In my first Coven Tree tale, *Devil's Donkey*, Old Magda the witch begins one of her spells. Oh, the spell is perfectly straightforward:

> *"Who sheds . . . his blood by . . . Coven Tree . . .*
> *Under Old Magda's . . . spell will be."* (P. 14)

But Old Magda's age is more than three centuries. Surely in that vast time, dry rot has set in among at least a few of her brain cells. So, she has difficulties.

> *"Who spreads his bed . . ."* (P. 13)

No. Try again, Magda.

> *"Who spoils his bread . . ."* (P. 13)

Still not quite right. Suffice it to say, the old girl is finally successful. But in the meantime, both I and the reader have had a little fun with words.

Roll the name of almost any Charles Dickens character over your tongue, and you'll know at once what that person is like. "Ebenezer Scrooge." Can't you hear the crackling and wrinkling of bills as the old skinflint grasps them greedily? "Wilkins McCawber." What else could he be but a blowhard? And try to imagine Uriah Heep as anything but the obsequious villain that he is.

I do my best to follow in Mr. Dickens's footsteps. Mr. Beel—for Beelzebub—is my devil. Although Beel is the most wicked, Dr. Dredd isn't anybody to fool around with either. And why do I call the village blacksmith Sven Hensen? I guess it just sounds like the name a blacksmith should have.

Other characters in present or future books include Stewart Meade, or, as he's better known, Stew Meat. There are a couple of knights, Sir Prize (who always attacks when least expected) and Sir Render (an errant coward), as well as Walpurgia, another witch. And

I hope at least a few baseball fans will appreciate Twi-Nite, my two-headed witch.

We're all familiar with the FBI, the CIA, and the initials of other undercover Washington agencies. In one story, *My Buddy, the King*, I needed my own super-secret spy organization. So I came up with the "Security Intelligence Service, Bureau of Operational Methods, Beginning-Agent Headquarters." Does anyone really believe the acronym for this group—SIS-BOOM-BAH—is just an accident? No way.

I've been asked if King Tokab of Mokobway in the same story is a real person from a real country. No. But the fact that I was asked shows that my combination of letters at least *sounds* convincing.

Yeah, in my stories, I have a lot of fun with words—both the real ones and those I make up. Playing with the English language is fun.

I hope my readers agree.

References   Brittain, Bill. 1981. *Devil's Donkey.* New York: Harper and Row.

————. 1989. *My Buddy, the King.* New York: Harper and Row.

The Sound of the Voice in the Printed Word

Ashley Bryan

To hear a storyteller is a special experience. To read that story in a book is another kind of special experience. The stories of all people were, initially, oral. With the creation of written languages, these stories from the oral tradition have come down to us in books.

The literal taking down of a story does not always work in book form. The writer is challenged to create a written voice for the oral tradition that will keep the story alive.

The African and Caribbean folktales from which I work are generally brief. They document story motifs. Often they are taken from the direct English translations of the hundreds of African tribal languages from which they come. With only simple grammatical corrections, they appear in anthologies of African tales in this form. They lack the spirit of storytelling from which they came. I take these motifs and become the storyteller. I explore the suggestions for adventure as I develop the tale. I listen for a written equivalent of the tale by using devices that open *the sound of the voice in the printed word.*

To achieve this, I work from poetry. Poetry is an oral art. Hearing a poem is as necessary to the art of poetry as hearing a song is necessary to the art of song. To know song only from sight-singing music is as limited an experience as knowing poetry only from sight-reading the words.

I practise reading aloud from the black American poets. This is the voice that informs my retelling of the African tales. Through the vocal play that the words and meanings suggest, I bring to life the voice in the printed words. The poem now speaks to me, and I can then offer it to others.

This practise relates to the whole literature of English and American poetry. It is the only way that poetry, of whatever age, becomes meaningful and lives in the present.

I apply the devices of poetry to my retelling of African and Caribbean tales. I hope thereby to invoke the presence of the storyteller while one is reading from the book, even when one is reading silently.

It is to this re-creation of the oral tradition in written form that books of poetry and story aspire. I am pleased when the reader of my stories exclaims, "I can hear the sound of the voice of the story-teller in your written story!"

The Power of Words

Eve Bunting

Early I learned the value of words through the poetry my father read to me. Sometimes the meaning escaped me, but never the beauty. I was a child who read and reread descriptive passages in the books I loved. Now, as a writer myself, I have to be careful not to go overboard with description. The temptation is there, but I try to limit myself to one or two lines to set the scene or portray the place. It isn't easy. The world is filled with wonderful words. It is foolhardy for me to start looking through my battered thesaurus. When I start, I can't stop reading. For me those magical words can be disastrous, catastrophic, ruinous, cataclysmic, grievous, fatal, not to mention deadly!

It always astonishes me how one descriptive word can change an entire mental image. When I taught a class at U.C.L.A., I once gave my students a sentence: *The dog walked across the road*. I asked them to substitute another "walking" verb; then, as each new sentence was read aloud, we pondered the new concept. How did the change of verb change our view of the dog?

The dog *sauntered* across the road. (Cool pooch)

The dog *hobbled* across the road. (Injured pooch)

The dog *dashed* across the road. (Dog in a hurry)

The dog *limped* across the road. (Sore paw)

The dog *scurried* across the road. (Dog with a guilty secret)

The dog *pranced* across the road. (Frisky dog—dog in love?)

Change the generic *dog* to a definite breed, and the picture is transformed once more. Isn't it amazing what one word can do?

One of my favorite *Peanuts* cartoons shows Snoopy at his typewriter. "Suddenly a shot rang out," he types. Lucy reads the sentence. She tells Snoopy that it is important to select the perfect words. She wonders if *suddenly* is quite right. Snoopy considers, then types his new sentence. "Gradually a shot rang out." It *is* amazing what one word can do!

I always read my work aloud, making myself aware of how it sounds. Do the words flow pleasantly? Do they evoke vibrant images? I check for overwriting. Does the dialogue sound real? I have written, "I know I am well loved." I, the author, might say that.

But would my protagonist, the one who is speaking in my book? He's a fourteen-year-old boy. Come on, Eve. Get real!

Recently I had a problem that was new for me. I was writing a middle-grade novel set in an Irish boarding school in 1942. The story is based partly on my own experiences and partly on my imagination. I knew the way we talked then, the words we used. I knew what I meant when I wrote *torch* (flashlight). But would my reader know? Would my reader know that a *counterpane* is a quilt? that a *girdle* is a kind of sash or belt? My editor, Jim Biblin, and I spent hours going over this problem. What to do? Should we have a glossary? Too formal. Should we use the word that is familiar to American children but actually dishonest for that time and place? I hated that idea. Should we use the familiar version the first time the word came up and revert to the 1942 Irish word from then on? That seemed confusing. Probably we will try to subtly define each unfamiliar word the first time it is used. "She took her torch from the drawer, checked that the batteries were still strong and switched it on. The beam of light. . . ." I think this will work. Isn't it remarkable that in a fairly long novel we should spend so much time and effort on a half-dozen words? Yes, because each word has its own importance.

Perhaps it was Mark Twain who said: "The difference between the right word and the nearly right word is like the difference between lightning and the lightning bug." Whoever said it was right. Lightning bugs glow. But it is the lightning that has the power.

Imagination and Language

Ann Cameron

Learning to write fiction is a lot like learning to dance. At first you feel awkward. You try the steps. You think everybody is looking at you, even when you're completely alone. Later, when you know the steps, it doesn't matter who is looking: your whole body has turned into music.

Henry James said that the purpose of fiction is "above all, to make us feel." To do that, fiction must construct a series of events that focus and intensify our emotions. Fiction's means to enhancing feelings is the dramatic use of language.

As an author, I try to express what is essential to a character's life as simply, clearly, and specifically as I can, using the fewest words possible. If I succeed, each word carries maximum emotional impact, and every incident in the story will contribute to its strength. In the second stage of my writing—after I finish a first draft—I read every sentence carefully, looking for unnecessary words and for places that aren't clear, places where I need more words to create a picture in the reader's mind or to make a situation more dramatic.

What do I mean about dramatizing a situation? A Guatemalan boy who is my neighbor told me many of the main events in *The Most Beautiful Place in the World*. He told me, for instance, about going to his mother's house and hiding under the bed. To dramatize that scene and intensify its emotion, I invented the part about the little rug that covers Juan. The dialogue used makes the dramatization more real and the outcome more unpredictable.

When I reread my work, I especially look for what I call "blanket words." A blanket word is a general word that's thrown over a situation and hides it. For instance, taken by itself, "She sells excellent food at the market" is a boring sentence because it creates no picture. As one would expect, right in the middle of it are blanket words: *excellent food.* What is under that blanket? Hot dogs roasted over an open fire? Caviar? I try to specify—so readers are in a world that they can see, hear, taste, feel, and touch. If there's not much in a story that a reader can see, hear, taste, feel, and touch, it's a bad, boring story. On the other hand, if too much detail is put in at the wrong time, that makes a muddled story (just as a painting can be muddled if it has a whole lot of figures that don't form a unified composition). For instance, if we're waiting to hear what is in the teacher's note that Juan brought home, and instead we hear what the family had for dinner, then we get confused, because that is not where our interest has been focused. What makes a writer an artist is the ability to invent exactly the right details to focus and intensify emotion.

In my book *The Most Beautiful Place in the World,* Juan might say his stepfather is a mean man—but *mean* would be just a blanket word. Readers would know Juan doesn't like his stepfather, but they wouldn't have any idea of how his stepfather behaves. There wouldn't be anything for readers to puzzle about. What makes life interesting is trying to figure out why people do what they do and how it affects others. By describing people's words and behavior exactly, we make stories as interesting as life—stories we go on thinking about after they're over. Just saying someone is mean doesn't begin to describe him. There are so many kinds of *mean*! And so many kinds of *nice*! As many as there are people in the world.

To highlight what kind of mean man Juan's stepfather is, I have his first words to Juan's mother be about Juan ("what a handsome little boy you have!"), and then, a few pages later, Juan learns that the man who is to be his stepfather really doesn't want him at all. With my language I try to "show, not tell" what happens to characters. I want my readers to live the story, side by side with the characters. I want them to be scared when my hero is scared, and to rejoice when he does. I want them to see through his eyes and hear through his ears.

Because Juan is a young boy, I have him use run-on sentences (the kind teachers teach us not to write!). When he's feeling comfortable and optimistic, his sentences are long—the sentence that opens the paragraph beginning "After my mom and I moved back to my grandmother's house" has 115 words!

When events or actions are sad and hurt Juan a lot, his sentences are short, full of one-syllable words, and flat as his disappointment. For instance, when Juan's mother leaves him because the stepfather won't take the boy, he says: "But I couldn't go with her. He didn't want me. He wanted his own children. He didn't have the money for me." A teacher might want to have children experiment with turning all those sentences into one. When I do it, it becomes, "I couldn't go with her because he didn't want me and just wanted his own children, and besides that he didn't have money for me"—a confusing sentence with no pauses for the bad news to sink in, no time out for the pain. A sentence like this would make us feel that what was happening was not very important to Juan.

In a first draft my choice of language is mostly unconscious (or rather, the harvest of earlier learning and a lifetime of listening to real people talk). I don't feel that I select a word; I feel that the word "comes to me." I don't consciously work on the rhythm and flow of sentences and paragraphs. That, too, "comes to me." I have only one guideline in writing dialogue: the characters' speech must reflect who they are and be within the reader's capacity for understanding.

The business of ideas and language "just coming" to writers is the hardest for nonwriters to understand. It sounds like writers don't have to work! And in a way, that's true: often the harder one works, the worse the writing is. And the more one "considers" language, "selects" words, and "tries to establish" rhythms, the worse they get.

Rather, the language of writing is very like the language of living. It comes spontaneously from depth (or shallowness) of feeling. For all of us there are times in life when we have something to say that we know is important, and we want to say it right. At those times we are in a state of grace: our words and speech rhythms are one, not because we choose them self-consciously bit by bit, but because strong emotion and much thought integrate them.

It's very important that child writers are not made too self-conscious about language techniques—because the most important aspect of story writing is imagination and feeling. If the writer can imagine vividly what happens in someone else's life and how the character feels about it, good language will follow.

I don't—I can't!—visualize characters fully before I begin a story; rather, the visualizing and the writing happen together. I become the character Juan. Juan is going to talk to American children. American children don't know anything about small-town Guatemala, so the first thing Juan has to talk about is the place where he lives and, by implication, how he feels about it. "Where do you live?" I ask Juan. I wait for him to answer and write down what he says. The language comes out right, not only because of my intensity of concentration, but also because many Guatemalan children are my friends and talk to me about their lives. I am guided by their voices and their eyes.

How do I know "Juan" is speaking to me? I'm never sure. I use the piece of paper to scrawl down whatever "comes to me." I avoid thinking of the piece of paper as "my" story or "my" manuscript, or as an arena where I am measured by anyone, even me. The paper is only the humble servant of the story. I, too, am only its servant.

I keep on scrawling things down without any self-criticism. (How can "what comes to me" be my fault or my achievement, either one? It's just what comes.) Finally some words get written down that have passion and conviction. They sound right, sound like the kids I know. They are a tiny grain of truth—one honest word or phrase or sentence which will attract more truth to it.

I could make it clear that Juan is living in another country and make the story exotic by having him use Spanish words—he could call his grandmother *abuela* or *abuelita,* for instance. I decide not to do that, because I want American children to feel they are Juan, to feel all they have in common with him. Using Spanish would distance many of them from his inner world of feeling. (For the same reason, I use standard English in my books about Julian, even though dialect expression can be so rich. Learning to read is hard enough at the beginning without introducing variant words and spellings.)

Juan meets his stepfather for the first time. I ask the stepfather how he feels. He tells me he has no interest in Juan—he'll use the boy for a minute to get his mother's attention. And then I write down what the stepfather says to Juan's mother. And so I continue, becoming all the people in my story, making them from aspects of many people I've known around me in four years of living in Guatemala and a lifetime of living many places.

I've written all the first drafts of my books in restaurants. That's not where Ann Cameron lives, so when I'm in one I can forget about Ann Cameron—the dust on her table, the plant that needs water, the concerns Ann Cameron has about herself and her house. I stop being Ann Cameron. I'm free. I can be a dog, a bird, an octogenarian, or a three-year-old child. I become so involved with the character I am imagining that sometimes I laugh out loud or tears run down my face. I cried when I wrote the part where Juan's mother leaves him. What was happening to him was at that moment my reality.

I am concerned about what effect we'll have on children as we teach them to be conscious of the language of the stories they read. If we do it gently, they will appreciate literature more. We could start by asking them what part of a book they liked especially, and how it made them feel. If we instruct them about what language they should like, we will turn them into junior graduate students, distanced from the books they read and their own emotions, parroting off one more right answer.

There is no right answer. A good work of fiction is a jewel with many facets. Which ones shine depends on where you're standing. We need to make sure children understand all the language in a book. We don't need to grade it for them.

I experiment with language as I write, but I don't write to experiment with language. I write to portray the life I see around me, to express the spirit that enables some people to live it well, even nobly. I write to give myself courage.

I hope that when teachers use my book, they'll raise moral questions with children. What do they think of the mother in the book? Are there any excuses for her? for the stepfather? Were they too young to be starting families? What makes a good person? a good mother? What are the qualities Juan has that help him to survive?

I worked with language to make *The Most Beautiful Place in the World* easy to read. It is very easy to read, but emotionally it is difficult for children. Many of them, even if not so poor as Juan, are neglected or abandoned by a parent. Talking about Juan gives them a way to express their own pain and affirm their own values, without having to share more than they want to. In some primary school classes, I've pointed out that Juan and his mother never talk things through. I've suggested that the children become Juan and his mother and write down what they should say to each other. (Or they might invent the lines the grandmother should say to her daughter and the daughter's response.) The story can be changed to work out the way the readers wish it would work out.

When one little girl found this hard to do, I told her I'd be the mother, and she could be Juan.

> "I want you to live with me, but if you come live with me, he'll hit you," I said.
> "If you stay with him, he'll hit you, too," she said. "You should come back home and live with grandma."
> "You're right," I said. "I'm sorry. I will come back."
> "We'll go to his place right now!" she said. "Come on! Let's go get your clothes!"

When we help children participate in the stories they read, we're helping them to heal themselves and grow as human beings, to understand the world as it is, and to imagine a better world. If we encourage children to express what they think and feel and to write down the worlds they can imagine, their language will show us wonders.

Reference   Cameron, Ann. 1988. *The Most Beautiful Place in the World.* Illustrated by Thomas B. Allen. New York: Alfred A. Knopf.

A Child Besotted with Words

Eleanor Cameron

As I was a child who turned into the woman who wrote about her own childhood in the Julia Redfern books, I thought I might look through *A Room Made of Windows* (the first in the series to be written, but Julia is twelve here in *Room*, and the books begin when she is six) for a sense of Julia's commitment to words. Though I myself never kept a journal, except for the years spent on *The Seed and the Vision*, which is all about words and writing, I know that Julia's idea is the right one, as well as the title she chose, for the *Book of Strangenesses*. For the world is full of strangenesses, and the novelist is unusually aware of them and searches for the exact words that will hold these strangenesses in the reader's mind in a certain, singular way that comes as near as possible to satisfying the writer's private vision.

I wondered if I had sufficiently conveyed to the reader that Julia is a child besotted with words. Because I *was* Julia, as I am any child I write of, I trusted now that her nature would have naturally expressed itself as one who, at the age of twelve, was already aware of the fascination of words, how they could be combined to give the most satisfaction, the most vivid picture, the greatest depth of emotion. I myself might not be able to do it as I saw Alcott and London doing it, but I had the strongest compulsion to try. And early on in *Room* I find Julia adding to lists in her journal of most beautiful and most detested words. Under the beautiful ones, which begin with *Mediterranean* and *quiver* and *undulating* and *lapis lazuli* and *empyrion*, she puts *mellifluous.* And in the detested column she adds *intestines* to *rutabaga, larva, mucus,* and *okra.* Her brother Greg says that she's all mixed up and that it isn't the words themselves she can't stand but their meaning or the object they bring to mind. She strenuously disagrees, because it's the *sound* she can't abide as well as the picture in her mind. For instance, an old woman had once told Julia she got great support from that comfortable word *Mesopotamia,* and Julia finds this is almost what she feels about *Mediterranean.*

> All I have to do is say to myself, the vast blue Mediterranean, and I get a feeling I don't know how to describe. I see this enormous sea all moving and trembling and glittering, the deepest blue you can

ever imagine with light splintered across it, and I have a feeling of its being quaking and fathomless. Not the real Mediterranean, maybe—but *what* Mediterranean? And I say it over and over to myself because of what the saying does to me. (P. 139)

When Julia and her friend Mrs. Moore stand in the garden one evening, they become aware of "a multitude of tiny voices," high overhead,

> a continuous faraway music made up of bell-like chirruping that called to one another without cease. On and on they went, as though an endless cloud were passing over, and together with this faint, urging communion could be sensed—or was it heard?—an indescribable swiftness: the rush of innumerable wings in the distant sky. (P. 32)

I had heard these sounds years before the writing of *Room*, and they had moved me so, for some indefinable reasons, that I went in at once, after they'd faded away, and tried to put my feelings into words.

> "Little birds like bubbles of glass fly to other Americas"—Western tanagers—yes, flying up from South America. . . . We've had an epiphany, you and I, Julia. Do you know what the word means? (P. 33)

Julia does not. It means, says Mrs. Moore, an illumination, an understanding brought about by some brief happening, but for her it's come to mean as well any sort of rare moment, any treasurable combination of events never to be forgotten. A moment of being. Yes, because Julia had been taken right out of herself into a sense of heightened wonderment and delight. She, too, goes into the house to write in her *Book of Strangenesses* her experience of "The Night of the Birds." She wants to try to grasp it immediately.

Another time, in a moment of rage at being frustrated and reproved in front of her mother's friend in a restaurant, she bursts out, "You wouldn't treat Greg like this. . . . I'm just a scrapegoat, that's what I am," and her mother's face suddenly sparkles. "Scapegoat, dear." But, no! What kind of word is *that?* It doesn't mean *any*thing, because she *did* feel scraped, absolutely scraped to the bone, bloodied.

Julia has been sending her poetry and stories to the *Berkeley Daily Gazette* for the Children's Page, and they have been accepted by the editor, Mrs. Penhallow. When Julia is invited up to Dr. and Mrs. Penhallow's house for a talk about her newest story, not yet published, Mrs. Penhallow says there is a gift Julia has that any writer must have in order to amount to anything, and that's the gift of seeing. She so much likes the way Julia had described in one word the tall, dark house in her dream as looking *warped.* Julia might have said *frightening* or *ugly* or *looming,* and yet *warped* was more unexpected and gave much more the sense of something seen in a nightmare, the dreamer's sight twisting the ordinary into the grotesque. "You must always see clearly the object or scene or person you're describing and find precisely the right words to explain what you feel and see." She does, says Julia, especially before she goes to sleep at night, when she makes stories come alive. Then she sees everything down to the smallest detail.

(When a friend of mine pointed out to me the meaning of the name I had quite unconsciously given the editor, Penhallow, I was reminded of Julia's mistaking the actual name of a neighborhood doctor, Mendenhall, as being Dr. Mendenheal; the mistake was a great disappointment, as what she'd thought she heard was a perfect name for a doctor.)

The evening of the day Julia had gone to the Penhallows and told Greg and her mother what Mrs. Penhallow had said, Celia Redfern asks Julia to look at her and close her eyes, and then to describe the trunk of the oak outside their window. Julia says that it is big and gray, that the trunk is leaning toward their neighbor's house on the left, that the limbs don't begin until higher up because the tree is so old, that the limbs are all crooked and bending, that some have sharp elbows, that the trunk and limbs are rough with little roughnesses, and that the leaves are small, like little clawed paws. Is the trunk pure gray? asks her mother. Yes, pure gray. Well, look, then, says Mrs. Redfern. And the trunk wasn't pure gray but in places cast over with the faintest, palest, pinkish-orange wash of color, and scattered over the trunk are splotches of grayish white. Both are lichens, and—oh, thinks Julia, not *lich-ens,* then, but *like-ens.* And, just at this moment, the limbs up there aren't gray, but the richest amber, a kind of rosy amber in the sunset light, and luminous on their undersides because of the reflection from other limbs. And the roughnesses aren't all small roughnesses, but large open splits as well as narrow cracks running lengthwise, some long and some short and some wavering.

There are times when Julia's aunt is her nemesis, though Julia doesn't come to that word until later. Aunt Alex is heavy and loves food. To Julia her beautiful face is like a large, ripe, golden peach, and when she relates a treasured recipe and says, "Take a cup of butter," Julia, who has a sensitive stomach, feels like going and eating celery. And Aunt Alex is always telling recipes, her plump, smooth hands, with their rosy nails, moving in the air as though, thinks Julia, she was shaping each spoonful and carrying it lovingly to the bowl.

But Aunt Alex isn't always a nemesis. She takes Julia to a theater in San Francisco to hear her son Oren as the pianist in a concert. And when the music begins, Julia can hear Mrs. Penhallow's words about seeing

> and she began noticing how the conductor seemed to mold the music he was drawing from all those instruments, quieting it, smoothing it, putting his fingers to his lips, then calling it up again in full force with vigorous, powerful movements of the arms. The violinists and cellists, the men with their big double basses on the side, swept their bows, stopped, looked up quickly, then *swept* again. And every once in a while there came a majestic flood from all the strings together, welling and pouring out in a wave that was almost too much for Julia. (P. 227)

What material for her journal!

In *The Private Worlds of Julia Redfern,* in which she is fifteen, Julia has the part of Juliet in that year's play at high school. She writes in her journal:

> Strangely, I've learned something about writing from being in this play. It's silent acting. I didn't realize it consciously until now, though I think I knew it in my mind. As I'm writing, I'm hearing and seeing it all—the story—and it's like a play, because there's the dialogue and you're listening inside your head to just how a person would say something. You have to hear the tone and the way of saying and the rhythm according to the person, just as you do onstage when you're rehearsing your lines. And you're *seeing* it all happen. If you can't, how could you know what each character is doing every moment, in relation to the others, just how they're sitting or standing or turning and moving off the stage in your scene. It's all so fascinating and unexpected—the way the play experience has fitted in with the writing. (Pp. 193–94)

But it isn't only seeing that is of utmost importance, seeing that calls up the rich play of imagination, but the writer's responses to all the senses. Julia must go out and feel the trunk of the old oak, feel it as if she were a blind person, an act which would tell her at once that all those roughnesses weren't small, but some knobbly, some sharp, indented into the tree at a slant, and here's a large round smooth place where a limb has either fallen off or been cut away and the tree has healed its wound. It is sound, late at night, that brings to her the sense "of an indescribable swiftness: the rush of innumerable wings in the distant sky," and that these are small birds because of the "multitude of tiny voices," "a continuous faraway music made up of bell-like chirrupings," that "faint, urging communion" that brings her a heightened wonderment and delight.

Virginia Woolf wrote of the enormous difficulty of fusing what the eye sees with what one feels about each perception, and of finding words which will convey, arrow-like, both sight and feeling.

References   Cameron, Eleanor. 1971. *A Room Made of Windows.* New York: Atlantic Monthly Press.

————. 1988. *The Private Worlds of Julia Redfern.* New York: E. P. Dutton.

————. 1993. *The Seed and the Vision: On the Writing and Appreciation of Children's Books.* New York: Dutton.

Of Memory and Language That Sings with Young Children

Nancy White Carlstrom

We were all children once. Sometimes we choose not to look back. But as a writer for young children, I make use of my memories of Child Past. At times I am very much aware of this and can remember the exhilaration of rolling down a grassy hill, as in this excerpt from *Wild Wild Sunflower Child Anna*:

> Rolling Anna rolling
> down the sweet smelling hill
> Sky
> Yard
> Sky
> Yard
> Which will it be?
> Anna Anna floating
> on a grass green sea. (Unpaged, p. 22)

At other times Child Past creeps in without knowing it. During our first autumn in Fairbanks, Alaska, I was struck by the sense of urgency as all of nature—bird, beast, and humankind—prepared for winter. Out of my own emotional response, I wrote a poem entitled *Goodbye Geese*. Now I thought all of this was the Child Present in me, or for that matter, the adult, as it certainly grew out of what I was then experiencing. But as I read over what I had written, I was struck with the image of winter trying to get in through the cracks, because she had not learned to turn the doorknob.

> Papa, is winter coming?
> Yes, and when winter comes she'll touch every living thing.
> Does winter have fingers?
> Yes, her frosty grip will tire the flowers, Winter puts the whole garden to bed and covers it with a fresh white blanket.
> Does winter have hands?
> Yes, but she never learned to turn the doorknob.
> Winter tries to walk in through the cracks. (Unpaged)

As I reread it, I heard my mother's voice telling me, her ten-year-old, that the night before I had been sleepwalking. She followed me out to the living room where I then tried to open the door, prying at the crack, as if I hadn't learned to turn the doorknob. I don't know if my mother ever said those words or not, but for over thirty years I have associated the phrase with the memory. When I wrote it down as a line in the poem I was only conscious of the fact it was an apt description for winter, trying to get in through the cracks.

In the biography *Margaret Wise Brown: Awakened by the Moon* (1991), author Leonard Marcus says,

> Margaret later observed that memory, the ultimate source of her creative works, is a "wild and private place," a place to which "we return truly only by accident"—the writer's craft. Whatever the method or the path, she was convinced that "as you write, memory will come out in its true form." (P. 7)

Many of my poems and books spring from a "wild and private place," sometimes waking me up at night as a tapping on the window, or mysteriously arising with me as if from a dream I can't shake. However, even these "inspired ones" are refined by way of the "beaten path of the writer's craft," and many are coaxed into actual birth by the arduous labor of writing and rewriting and rewriting some more.

When writing, I usually begin with many more words than I need, and so my rewriting becomes a cutting-away process, as I get down to the spare, bare bones of what I want to say.

And to say it, I often sing it! Language is a musical experience for me. Rhythm, rhyme, and cadence all become an important part of the process. I love the way a young child, just learning language, rolls a word around on her tongue and, if she likes the sound of it, may chant it over and over.

I want my poems and stories to roll off the reader's tongue in such a way as to invite him or her to participate in this wonderful game of language.

The use of questions as a framework for my books is another way to gain participation. *Where Does the Night Hide? How Does the Wind Walk? What Does the Rain Play? Does God Know How to Tie Shoes?* Questions such as these (all titles of published books) are easily transferred to children's own imagination and can carry them to spontaneous and limitless possibilities, some of which end up being far more clever than my own.

Onomatopoeia. A big word, seldom used, for something so common and close to the ways of young children learning language. They respond wholeheartedly to invented words, especially sound words. As I've shared *Baby-O*, one of my books that really must be sung, children have joined in with delight as the sounds with a calypso beat grow, culminating in the bus named Baby-O arriving at the market where all the family members sell their various goods.

> Chuka Chuka, Wusha Wusha, Tomatoma, Kongada
> Pika Pika, Plesh Plesh, Dippa Dippa
> Putta Putta Clank Clank
> Putta Putta Clank Clank
> Listen to the way the Baby goes,
> Baby Baby Baby-O. (Unpaged, pp. 32–34)

After all, making up their own words is what young children do, too, and I might add, their creations are often quite logical. My son, at age three, used the word *yesternight* to refer to the previous night, while a friend's granddaughter had the same idea when she coined the word *lasterday*. As Kornei Chukovsky (1968) said in his marvelous book *From Two to Five*, "poetry is the natural language of the young child."

Whether I draw upon my own memories of Child Past or Child Present, or make use of the child's natural bent toward music, questions, and sound, writing poetic picture books for the receptive audience is, indeed, a privilege. For young children participate in the poems I write, and so make these poems their own. Could any poet ask for more?

References

Carlstrom, Nancy White. 1988. *Wild Wild Sunflower Child Anna.* Illustrated by Jerry Pinkney. New York: Macmillan.

———. 1990. *Where Does the Night Hide?* Illustrated by Thomas B. and Laura Allen. New York: Macmillan.

———. 1991. *Goodbye Geese.* Illustrated by Ed Young. New York: Philomel Books.

———. 1992. *Baby-O.* Illustrated by Suçie Stevenson. Boston: Little, Brown.

———. 1993. *Does God Know How to Tie Shoes?* Illustrated by Lori McElrath-Eslick. Grand Rapids, MI: William B. Eerdmans.

———. 1993. *How Does the Wind Walk?* New York: Macmillan.

———. 1993. *What Does the Rain Play?* New York: Macmillan.

Chukovsky, Kornei. 1968. *From Two to Five.* Berkeley: University of California Press.

Marcus, Leonard. 1991. *Margaret Wise Brown: Awakened by the Moon.* Boston: Beacon.

The Alchemy of Sound

Deborah Chandra

Our language conveys many hidden meanings through its speech sounds. In poetry these sounds tend to cluster and affect one another. Their interplay and variation serve to create texture in language that can emphasize a thought, evoke emotion, and "goosebump" our aural imaginations. It is then that the phonetic aspects of language blend with and become inseparable from its meaning, and through some mysterious alchemy of sound, transform language into a living thing.

In my own work, I often choose a particular word because of its ability to combine with other words and form a relationship of sounds that symbolize a certain quality of meaning. There are three broad ways in which I have used sound symbolism.

Phonetic Intensives

These are speech sounds that suggest meaning. For example, the emotional connotation of a long resonant "o" can be one of melancholy. I chose words containing that sound to create a forlorn and gloomy creature in the first stanza of the poem "Fog."

> An *o*ld c*o*ld-blooded creature,
> Sl*o*w and tired, glides—
> Out of the *o*cean's twilight deeps,
> Up from the endless tides—
> (*Balloons, and Other Poems*, p. 32)

Different sounds have different powers of suggestion. The harsh "c" and "ck" sound can have a clattering, clanging effect, and I used it to give the impression of stark, unyielding cliffs in the first stanza of the poem "The Sea." It is followed by the sound of "sl," which often begins words meaning "smoothly wet," and also by the sound of softened "s." The sounds are arranged from "c" to "sl" and "s" to suggest the clashing of the sea against the land and then its sliding retreat.

> *C*lutching at the ro*ck*y *c*liffs,
>   The dis*c*ontented *s*ea
> *Sl*ides *sl*owly back into it*s*elf
>   On *sl*ippery hand*s* and knee*s*. (P. 19)

Onomatopoeia

These are speech sounds that imitate the natural sounds associated with an object or action. To imitate the sustained satisfaction of a purring cat, I deliberately repeated the soft nasal sound of "m" in the lines "Swi*m*s a war*m m*ouse-flavored/'*m*eow.'" This also indirectly suggests the "Mmmmm!" we make when tasting something as delectable to us as mousemeat must be to a cat. The phonetic energy of a word may not only give the suggestion of a sound but also the movement that produced it. I tried to use it that way when I described balloons as

> Bumping and rubbing along the walls
> Until they feel their *fat backs*
> *Bob* against the ceiling. (P. 3)

An initial "b" introducing a word gives the sense of impact, and the "b's" in this passage animate one another, but it is the sequence of the three words "fat backs bob" that creates an effect analogous to the short jerky motion of balloons bobbing against a ceiling.

Articulation

This is the way sounds have been arranged to make them easy or difficult to say. In the poem "Mama's Song," I needed soft sounds that could evoke the effortless sway of the sea, a rocking chair, a lullaby. While I was playing with words, what began to make itself noticed was a vibration of "m's" and "ng's." I supported them with the liquid sounds of "v" and quiet "f." They are all easy to say in relationship to one another.

> *M*a*m*a hu*m*s a sea-so*ng* with her eyes,
> A deep blue risi*ng* sea-so*ng*,
>   *m*ovi*ng* as her eyes *m*ove,
>   wea*v*i*ng f*oam across *m*y *f*ace.
>
> White gulls whirl overhead,
> The sun washes back and forth,
>   and I am rocki*ng* . . .
>   rocki*ng* . . .
>   like a boat
>   in the wa*v*es
>   of her so*ng*. (P. 13)

All the sounds of our human speech, either because of their intrinsic rightness or because of long association, have inner vitalities. They can evoke emotion, reinforce meaning, fuse the elements of experience—and when they do, language jumps to life.

Reference

Chandra, Deborah. 1990. *Balloons, and Other Poems.* Illustrated by Leslie W. Bowman. New York: Farrar, Straus and Giroux.

The Magic of Language

Eth Clifford

A question frequently put to me is, "Where do you get your ideas?" and it is often most difficult to explain. How does one pinpoint the creative process? Ideas can become full-blown in the mind apparently out of nowhere, as was the case with my book *Help! I'm a Prisoner in the Library.* The title sprang into my mind when I wasn't thinking about a story at all. I was so taken with the title, however, that I deliberately built a story around it. This is writing the hard way. Ideas can simmer on a back burner for a long while, some to drift eventually into oblivion, others to take firm root and demand to be written. I postponed writing *The Remembering Box* until several other of my books were published, and then it demanded, literally, to be brought into being. Who would want to read, I asked myself, a book with essentially only two characters, with disparate ages and backgrounds and lifestyles—a simple tale of love? Would such a story appeal to young readers? How would they respond to the dialogue? It was imperative that the dialogue—the intonations and speech patterns, for example—not come across as broad caricature but with overtones of thought and language expressed by one whose native tongue was not English. I loved the boy and the grandmother and consequently saw them not as characters but as real people who might walk through my front door at any moment.

When I wrote the dialogue, I could hear the cadence of their speech. I observed how they interacted with one another. As a grandmother myself, I understood and cherished the love they shared.

The writing style I used in *The Remembering Box* was unique to that story. It would have been totally inappropriate in other books I have had published. I remember one critic complaining that I had no recognizable style. But it is precisely the option of changing one's style to suit a particular story that is both fascinating and challenging to me. For example, I wrote a book called *The Wild One.* It was a fictionalized, partial biography of a famous Spanish scientist. How, I asked myself, could I convey to the reader the feeling and taste and atmosphere of a bygone era and still have the young adult reader understand that growing up can be painful and sometimes destructive in any culture and age? To capture that spirit, I wrote the manuscript in an English that a Spaniard might speak in a tongue that was not his own. Stories told in the first person require special attention, for all action, reaction, dialogue, descriptions, and so on are restricted to that individual's perceptions. In this story, Santiago, the protagonist, reveals his innermost feelings by explaining himself in relation to others around him. For example, he loved the tranquility of the woods, to which he fled when troubled. He confides in the reader:

> I have a need often to be alone, to sort out my ideas, to *own* myself. This my friends and parents do not comprehend. How shall I explain this to you? When someone speaks to you, then you must reply, is it not so? The words fly back and forth between you. Words provoke thoughts and emotions and perhaps memories you may not wish to think or feel or remember. In conversation, your mind is engaged by someone else. Alone, your mind is free. (P. 39)

Sensitivity and introspection seem disregarded by many, but teenagers, even in today's raucous world, need time to sort out their emotions unhampered by the pressure of others.

I depend a great deal on dialogue in all my books, whether they are serious or in good fun. Dialogue can move a story, exploit adventure, create atmosphere, tickle the funny bone. Younger children, I believe, respond to dialogue rather than text. It is easier to read, more natural to hear, and makes the characters more believable. I don't always make a conscious effort to choose particular words, but I hear them clearly in my mind as the way the character would naturally speak. When I read what I have written, I do find some words haven't the look on the page I am aiming for, in which case I immediately make changes and substitutions.

Some aspiring authors have difficulty fleshing out their characters, in which case the reader cannot see them or empathize with them, or care what happens to them. Unfortunately, no book is better than the people an author puts into it. There have to be descriptions, of course, but they can be brief and still visual. For example, in my book *The Curse of the Moonraker*, a single sentence describes the cook aboard the *Moonraker*:

> Slush was a thin, spare man, sun-wrinkled and sun-shriveled, with small, hard, raisin eyes, pinched lips, and a habit of twitching his head about like a dog sniffing a strange scent on the wind. (P. 2)

Another example, from *The Dastardly Murder of Dirty Pete*, shows a concise description:

> One day there was a new face in town. It belonged to Sorehead Jones, a man with silver hair and blue eyes that burned like the sky

on fire. A scar like forked lightning ran down one side of his face, from his eyebrow to his chin. No one dared ask how he got that strange scar. (P. 52)

It helps to make characters stay in a reader's mind if they are given a quirk or habit that singles them out. In *Help! I'm a Prisoner in the Library*, Miss Finton, the librarian, peppers her speech with old-fashioned, long out-of-date phrases. This worked well for Jo-Beth as well, a most imaginative child. When Miss Finton exclaims, "Well, if that doesn't beat buttered parsnips," Jo-Beth reacts by thinking: What a strange thing to say. What was a parsnip, anyway? It sounded like a little animal with short sharp claws and tiny beady eyes. But why, Jo-Beth wondered, would anyone want to butter it?

For younger readers, I paragraph often so that the page doesn't seem formidable. Lots of dialogue and open space help the younger reader approach a book with less trepidation. Good readers take this in stride; slower readers begin to achieve pride in progress.

I have several series books going because I loved such books when I was a child, always eager to know what happened next, after the story was over. Evidently today's kids feel the same way, for my book *Help! I'm a Prisoner in the Library* has been in continuous hard-back publication for more than fourteen years. I myself am partial to Jo-Beth, one of the two main characters, because there is a lot of me in her. In their latest adventure, *Never Hit a Ghost with a Baseball Bat*, Mary Rose and Jo-Beth are pursuing a child who has a way of vanishing. They are in a trolley museum. In one of the trolleys, there is a coffin, and Mary Rose wants it open, while eight-year-old Jo-Beth objects.

"What are you afraid of," Mary Rose wants to know. Jo-Beth replies, after being assured the coffin is empty, "If it's empty, why do we have to open it? I don't like opening coffins," Jo-Beth sobbed. "I'm not supposed to open coffins. I'm too little." (P. 63)

I sometimes feel my characters are writing the stories. All I have to do is sit back and let it happen!

References   Clifford, Eth. 1974. *The Wild One.* Boston: Houghton Mifflin.

———. 1977. *The Curse of the Moonraker: A Tale of Survival.* Boston: Houghton Mifflin.

———. 1979. *Help! I'm a Prisoner in the Library.* Boston: Houghton Mifflin.

———. 1981. *The Dastardly Murder of Dirty Pete.* Boston: Houghton Mifflin.

———. 1985. *The Remembering Box.* Illustrated by Donna Diamond. Boston: Houghton Mifflin.

———. 1993. *Never Hit a Ghost with a Baseball Bat.* Boston: Houghton Mifflin.

Finding Words That Ring True

Paula Fox

What novelists and poets try to imagine is the truth. Truth is like the light that falls upon us all without prejudice or judgment.

Words are like notes of music. They, too, have tempo and color and innate sequence. But they can be elusive, and a writer has to struggle to find the right words for the story she wants to tell.

Words are not the things they name. They are things in themselves, and they can wake us up, arouse our interest—at times, our fears—make us laugh, and make us sad. Even though language has such power, it is fragile; there's a great deal of jargon on television, in the newspapers, even in books, that we can use when we don't really want to think about something, when we want to sum it up and forget it.

But a real writer doesn't want to sum it up and forget it. When you write, you want to remember and to think. It's hard work. It's a lot easier to grab up the popular catch-words of the day.

When I begin a story, I am often uncertain of what I'm going to say. Part of the work of being a writer is to learn to live with that uncertainty and not rush to cover it over with words one doesn't mean.

Living language suggests the real moments of our lives. There is a mystery no one has been able to solve about the way in which a story can help us recognize what we have not actually experienced ourselves.

The very word *novel* means news! And the Greek word for reading means *recognition.*

Setting the Story Free

Mary Hoffman

It's only a metaphor, but I see the stories I write as already existing. Like the slaves and apostles which Michelangelo saw inside the blocks of Carrera marble delivered to his workshop, the story is already there waiting to be brought into the world for others to recognize. My job is to find it, to release it, by choosing the best language and format for presenting it to others.

A story for me begins in one of three ways:

- It starts with a character. Grace in *Amazing Grace* and *Boundless Grace* and Nancy in *Nancy No-Size* are characters who took up residence in my brain and gave me no peace until their stories were told.

- A title appears in my mind. The books *Dracula's Daughter* and *The Second-Hand Ghost* (not published in the United States), for example, started this way. Writing then becomes a process of internal question and answer: How do you acquire a ghost second-hand? . . .

- It is generated by an incident or phrase. *Henry's Baby* began at a party when a friend told me how much her oldest son and all his friends were enjoying the family's new baby.

If I am lucky, and this is a gift that Margaret Mahy once told me was one of her greatest assets, the story brings with it a sense of its proper format. I know whether it will work as a thirty-two-page picture book, a junior series book of 3,000 words or so, or a novel in one of the conventional lengths of 12,000 or 25,000 words or more. This means I have a strong sense of audience because the target age of the reader is a first measure of length.

However, I am particularly interested in less conventional formats, like the picture book for older readers, which is what *Henry's Baby* is, or the highly line-illustrated short text designed to appeal to junior readers whose reading skills are not fully developed. This is what *Cyril M.C.* (not yet available in the United States) is—a rap for juniors, with lots of black-and-white illustrations and unconventionally designed typefaces.

All these decisions are made before a word is written, and since I now have the experience of producing over fifty books for children, they can be made quite quickly. The next stage also takes place in the head. I can live with an idea for months, sometimes years. Other ideas insist on being turned into books quite fast.

But when the actual business of writing starts, whether on the word processor (picture books and short stories) or in longhand with a pen on a lined pad (novels), something strange happens. The very act of writing generates new characters, plot incidents, and dialogue. Then, more than ever, do I feel like a medium through which a story is transmitted, rather than like an originator.

All of my books, whether for younger or older children, are designed to be read aloud. I read every sentence either actually out loud or in my head. How it sounds, the music of each sentence, is of prime importance to me. Was it T. S. Eliot who said, "Take care of the sounds and the sense will take care of itself"? Whoever it was has my complete agreement.

A picture book is like a poem. Each word in this short text is carefully chosen, so that you cannot make changes piecemeal. A word changed on the first page may throw off the rhythm several pages later. I also care passionately about the *filo,* that is, the thread of the story which makes one page follow inevitably from the previous one. Words and pictures must also be closely allied and complement one another.

When I use dialect forms, as I did in *Amazing Grace* for the dialogue of the grandmother, I will check for authenticity with a speaker of that dialect. But that is a very rare case. A story should be self-contained and dictate its own authenticity. However, I did spend a weekend in Edinburgh to check the settings for *The Four-Legged Ghosts.* This trip was completely wasted as far as the American reader is concerned, because the book was Americanized by my U.S. publisher and all those references were carefully removed!

In the two "Grace" books, there were two main considerations that come to mind. Firstly, I wanted both books to refer to lots of other stories. I think this is a component that teachers have appreciated because it facilitates plenty of extension work in classrooms. When I wrote the first draft of *Amazing Grace,* I included references to Superman, *Flat Stanley, The Shrinking of Treehorn,* and *Burglar Bill.* Superman was the first victim, because my British publishers feared we might have to pay huge sums to the copyright owners in order to use the name and a picture of Grace in costume. It appeared there might be copyright considerations, too, about other contemporary references.

I gave way on this, bowing to their superior experience, but it did change the texture of my story. I had wanted Grace to be as familiar with contemporary stories as with traditional ones, and in both books I have had to limit her scale of literary reference. This is an example of how external considerations can prevent a writer from using her preferred words or phrases.

The second consideration was the sayings that Nana uses to encourage and support Grace. "You can be anything you want if you put your mind to it" is something I strongly believe to be true, and it felt right in that character's mouth. In the second book there are two: "Families are what you make them" and "a family with you in it is your family," both said by Nana. Again I believe in both of these sentiments. Yet the strange thing is, this is not the kind of thing I would say in my own voice. It feels right for Nana but not for me.

In recent years, one of the hardest experiences I have had with regard to language has been having changes made for American editions of my books. It was a conscious decision made by my U.S. publisher to allow the reader to feel that Grace was an African American child, something which has clearly paid off in terms of sales and popularity. But it was agonizing for me to lose references to British pantomimes and Hannibal, and I had to fight quite hard to keep Mowgli.

One of the great things about being a writer of fiction is being able to give characters appropriate names. I have always been fascinated by names and did in fact write a book about their social and psychological significance—*Our Names Our Selves* (1983), written under the pseudonym Mary Lassiter.

We have so few opportunities in our own lifetimes to bestow names—a few children, maybe a dozen pets, a house—that writing fiction allows a name-addict like me a whole new freedom. Sometimes they have a personal significance that no reader could know. Natalie, for example, was the name of a child in my middle daughter's primary school class, who had been affected by the racist attitudes of her parents. So the child who says, "You can't be Peter Pan. He wasn't Black," in *Amazing Grace* was an obvious Natalie for me, even though I did not intend that remark to be understood as intentionally racist, just a statement of fact as that child saw it.

All writers are word people, I'm sure. In my case, words are active components of my daily life. I can get quite "high" on individual words and become furious with politicians, journalists, and writers of pulp fiction who use words carelessly or in clichés. I do the *Times* crossword, rejoice in an apt pun, love the writing of James Joyce and Terry Pratchett, and can forgive my teenage daughters, when I am in full spate of scolding them, if they just come up with a telling phrase in their justification.

When my oldest daughter, who writes poetry, was very small, she asked, "What rhymes with *mouthful*?" and I ignorantly said "nothing." She commented with scorn, "What about *fouthful* and *gouthful*?" and I realized, as I frequently do, how much children have to teach adults about preconceptions of language. Keeping in touch with that freshness of approach, and with the strength of imagination of children, which in most people atrophies with age, is a vital aspect of writing children's literature.

References

Hoffman, Mary. 1987. *Nancy No-Size.* Illustrated by Jennifer Northway. London: Methuen Books; New York: Oxford University Press.

———. 1991. *Amazing Grace.* Illustrated by Caroline Binch. New York: Dial Books.

———. 1993. *The Four-Legged Ghosts.* New York: Dial Books.

———. 1993. *Henry's Baby.* Illustrated by Susan Winter. London: Dorling Kindersley; Boston: Houghton Mifflin.

———. 1995. *Boundless Grace.* New York: Dial Books.

———. *Cyril M.C.* (Not published in U.S.)

———. *Dracula's Daughter.* (Not published in U.S.)

———. *The Second-Hand Ghost.* (Not published in U.S.)

Lassiter, Mary (pseud.) 1983. *Our Names Our Selves.* Portsmouth, NH: Heinemann.

Searching for the Voice

William H. Hooks

O nce the idea for a story has finally settled in my head, the search is on for the right voice for telling the tale. This quest, for me, is far more complicated than whether to spin out the story in first or third person. I need to know specifically who the storyteller is, how the storyteller uses language, and, most important of all, how the storyteller communicates with the reader/listener. Getting this voice clarified will influence the rhythm, descriptive language, dialogue, and flow of the story in such a way that I can reveal the wonder, mystery, adventure, and, yes, even the magic that inhabit all good stories.

Sometimes I identify the storyteller, as in *Mean Jake and the Devils,* a retelling of several Jack tales from my English-Irish heritage. Here GranAnna tells the story to a young boy in her distinctive voice that captures both the mystery and humor of the tales. She transports the boy to a magical world by chanting:

> Out of time and into grace
> We enter now a magic place.
> Protect us as we venture far
> And speak of things that never were
> But always are. (P. 12)

GranAnna's voice is as rich in imagery as it is loaded with humor. Her trio of devils have names: Big Daddy Devil, D.J., who is a devil junior, and Baby Deviline, a wicked little girl devil. When Big Daddy's reputation as the meanest person in the world is called into question by Mean Jake, it is D.J. who shouts, "It burns me up Big Daddy. That Jake's trying to steal your reputation." And Baby Deviline retorts, "It scorches me too, Big Daddy. Nobody can be as mean as my sweet Daddy Devil!" This kind of language feels more comfortable to me when spoken by the narrator, GranAnna, and assuming her persona determines the choice of words, especially the descriptive adjectives that give color and roundness to the dialogue.

In *The Legend of the White Doe,* which recounts the fate of Virginia Dare, the first English child born in America, I have again used a distinctive storyteller's voice. Although the narrator in this case is unnamed, I have him firmly fixed in my head—he is a living descendant of the intermarriage of the local Indians with the members of Sir Walter Raleigh's "lost colony." It feels right for him to tell the story in slightly archaic language: "Long ago a great boat with white wings, carrying strange men with pale skins and hair the color of corn silk came to our shores." It is his storyteller's voice that convinces the reader that, "In the depths of the wild, mysterious Great Dismal Swamp there roams a ghost deer. A night creature, shining in the starlight, shimmering like a silvery phantom, the white doe is none other than the living spirit of Ulalee [Virginia Dare's Indian name]."

In *A Flight of Dazzle Angels* I felt the need for two voices to tell the story of Annie Earle Roland, an adolescent girl who is lame from a club foot, but who makes her stab for freedom and a full life as she approaches her fifteenth summer. The author uses the third person to set the scenes, painting them with vivid colors to make the year 1908 glow with a you-are-there presence. Contrasting this, Annie Earle's most private inner thoughts are rendered in first person, revealing a wide range of emotions that she would never have dared utter aloud. The trick here is to make these very different voices harmonize. Here is a sample of the third-person omniscient author voice:

> She was running. Running. Something she'd never experienced before, even in dreams. Running as light as dandelion fluff, barely skimming the ground, keeping stride with someone by her side. They were accompanied by a host of dazzle angels, which blinded her with bursts of light like celestial fireflies. She couldn't see the face beside her, but the flaming mane of red hair flickering in the flashing lights belonged to Achilles McPherson. They gathered speed, he reached for her hand and she no longer felt the earth, only the tips of grass brushing the bottoms of her barefeet. Then they soared up, up into a pure blueness, leaving the sparkling dazzle angels flickering far below. (P. 95)

And the counterpart is Annie Earle's first-person interior dialogue:

> I wonder if Achilles feels this. How could this charge be so strong unless it's shared? Annie Earle, how can you sit here enjoying the contact of the flesh. It's against all the Sunday School lessons you've been fed since you can remember. Move your leg girl, pull it away like any well-brought-up girl would do. Shut up, Annie Earle, hold your peace. You're free and ready to fly! (Pp. 147–48)

Other stories demanded other voices, some that needed to deal with dialect. The oral versions that I had heard since childhood of both *The Three Little Pigs and the Fox* and *The Ballad of Belle Dorcas* were told in regional dialect: *The Three Little Pigs and the Fox* utilizing an Appalachian mountain dialect, and *The Ballad of Belle Dorcas* employing Carolina low-country speech patterns. In each case the decision was to tell the story in fairly standard English that was sprinkled with enough colloquialisms to color the language and give the reader a taste of the distinctive flavor that pervades these tales. Also, I was careful to try to capture the unique syntax and sentence structure that underpins the rhythms of each of these dialects. To reach beyond a parochial audience one needs to find this balance where flavor, rhythm, and essence are preserved, but the reader is not mired in a slavish devotion to precisely rendered dialect.

There are times when the appropriate voice demands a form closer to song than spoken prose. This was true in the telling of *Moss Gown,* a story that combines elements of both *King Lear* and "Cinderella." The book was written in phrases and broken lines that look and often read like blank verse. The inherent lyricism of the story needs a singing voice to spin out the tale, as shown by this taste of the *Moss Gown* voice:

> A slender green-eyed witch woman,
> black and sleek as a velvet cat,
> sat at the foot of her moss bed.
> In her hand she held a gossamer gown
> that glistened in the moonlight.
> The black woman sang:
>
>> *Gris-gris woman work all night,*
>> *weave a gown so fine,*
>> *stitch in stars and pale moonlight,*
>> *Gris-gris, gris-gris, grine.* (P. 16)

For every book there is a voice that makes your story sing. Find that voice, journey with it, and it will give wings to your words.

References   Hooks, William H. 1981. *Mean Jake and the Devils.* Illustrated by Dirk Zimmer. New York: Dial Books.

———. 1987. *Moss Gown.* Illustrated by Donald Carrick. New York: Clarion Books.

———. 1988. *A Flight of Dazzle Angels.* New York: Macmillan.

———. 1988. *The Legend of the White Doe.* Illustrated by Dennis Nolan. New York: Macmillan.

———. 1989. *The Three Little Pigs and the Fox.* Illustrated by S. D. Schindler. New York: Macmillan.

———. 1990. *The Ballad of Belle Dorcas.* Illustrated by Brian Pinkney. New York: Alfred A. Knopf.

Starting with Celery; or, How to Toss a Verbal Salad

James Howe

I grew up in a house of words. Jokes, often bad jokes, were a staple of the day's conversational diet, as were riddles, puns, and general banter. Words were playthings, balls bounced through the air in an endless game of verbal toss. Words were crossword puzzles and games of Scrabble that were an almost daily part of our after-dinner lives. In a family of four brothers, words were crucial to our particular version of one-upmanship. In short, even when my brothers had stopped practicing their one trumpet and two tubas, ours was not a quiet house.

I suppose that's why books often start for me with words. Some writers get hooked by a character or story idea. While I've been known to get started in these more conventional ways, it isn't unusual for a simple word or string of them to set me in motion.

Take *The Celery Stalks at Midnight*. After a friend had read *Bunnicula,* the tale of a vegetarian vampire rabbit, she asked, "So what happens to those vegetables Bunnicula attacks? Do they become vampires, too?" That was all I needed to hear. Two titles popped into my head: *The Tell-Tale Artichoke Heart* and *The Celery Stalks at Midnight*. Never mind that it took me several years to come up with a story to go with the latter title. I loved those words, and I had to use them!

But a string of clever words between covers is nothing but a joke book. Put a little meat on its bones and maybe you have a good collection of after-dinner speeches. You still need characters, and you still need a story. Ah, but here is where the fun begins.

What *language* best suits this story? this character? this moment in this story? this moment in this character's life?

In my Bunnicula books, the main characters—Harold, Chester, and Howie—banter and bicker and wisecrack pretty much the way my brothers, my father, and I did. (My mother was always, you should pardon the expression, the straight man of the family. Straight woman? Straight person.) Since I was the youngest brother, I was the one who had to work the hardest in order to impress the older members of the clan. So I'm Howie: the eager pup always running around with his tongue wagging, making jokes, and panting, "Get it, Pop? Get it, Uncle Harold? Get it, huh? Get it?"

Because the Bunnicula books are often about language as much as anything else, there are frequent digressions from the plot, where one of the characters gets hung up on a word . . . or another character (usually Chester) misunderstands a word and makes a mess of everything because of it . . . or the author has become so determined to work in a clever pun that he allows one of the characters to go on and on in a lengthy aside until the punch line is delivered with all the dramatic timing of a major climactic development. (Personally, I see nothing wrong with this. After all, one of my primary goals as a writer is to infect as many people as possible with the same love of words that has had me hooked my whole life.)

Of course, words serve many functions. In the Bunnicula stories, they make the reader laugh and think about language itself; in my Sebastian Barth mysteries, the intent of language is to "goose-bump" the reader and keep him or her turning the pages! (I put "him" first in that sentence because I consciously created the Sebastian Barth series with the hope of keeping boys reading.) Sentences, paragraphs, and chapters themselves are shorter and punchier than in my other books. The mystery writer Gregory McDonald, whose Fletch and Flynn books served as something of a model for me, has made reference to himself as a "postcinematic writer." He meant that he writes for readers who have seen so much film and television they can easily fill in visual details. In consciously leaving words out, the author creates a nice tension between what is said and what isn't. Writing and reading become truly collaborative, as author and reader work together to make the story complete.

I think I'm something of a postcinematic writer myself. Or maybe I'm rationalizing my preference for dialogue over narrative. When I wrote some television scripts a couple of years back, I was shocked to discover how relieved I was not to have to write description at all. It probably has nothing to do with being postcinematic and everything to do with my interest in character over scene. In art, for example, I am almost always drawn to the figure and portrait over still life and landscape. I use dialogue, the words spoken *by* a character, to reveal that character as much or more than anything I might write *about* the character.

Ultimately, of course, language reveals as much about the author behind the words as it does about the character he or she creates. The artist Alexander Calder's statement that "Above all, I feel art should be happy" is clearly reflected in the lines and colors of his work. Calder took delight in the very act of creating and in the materials he used. I would like to think my writing reflects a similar delight, for words are to me what wire and string and paint and metal were to Calder.

References   Howe, Deborah, and James Howe. 1979. *Bunnicula: A Rabbit Tale of Mystery.* Illustrated by Alan Daniel. New York: Atheneum.

Howe, James. 1983. *The Celery Stalks at Midnight.* Illustrated by Leslie Morrill. New York: Atheneum.

Stories by Firelight

Shirley Hughes

I loved working on *Stories by Firelight*. I have always wanted to do a combination of prose, verse, and paintings which expressed a central theme, and this was to be a celebration of the winter season.

I collected ideas like bits of silk for a patchwork for about three years before embarking on the finished artwork. Most of them were visual ideas at the start, very strong pictures in my head to which rhythmic phrases seemed immediately to attach themselves.

Only when I began to forge the individual stories and verses together into a rough dummy for the book did I realize I was going to open up new horizons for myself, as well as (I hope) for the children who read it. I was aiming to reach an audience of children who are beginning to move on from the picture storybook stage, for which *Dogger* and the "Alfie" books are designed, and who are ready for something a bit more adventurous in terms of word and image. They are already visually highly literate, wonderfully quick to pick up narrative clues in the illustrations. They can use this skilled response as a springboard into poetry or more advanced fiction.

One story, "Sea Singing," is taken from the age-old Gaelic myth of a selkie, or seal woman, who comes to live among humans, but who, in the end, is drawn back into the sea. I set this as a "story within a story" into a contemporary seascape with an intergenerational relationship involving a young girl convalescing with her mother's friend, a female artist, who is the storyteller. I found I could use shifts of color, tone, and the design of the page to signal the move back into the past, a visual way of introducing young readers to a literary device which may be new to them.

"Burning the Tree" was inspired by one stunning image I saw through the window: a man and his little grandson outlined against a blazing Christmas tree on a bonfire. The tree itself, in that rather flat time when you take it down and strip it of all its finery, has its last moment of glory as it burns and is all lit up with festive sparks and flames. In the story, William's grandpa is prompted to burn the remnant reminders of the past, too, because this is also a time for clearing out the old wood and making a fresh beginning of renewed hope.

In the worldless story "A Midwinter Night's Dream," the underground netherworld my small hero encounters (but somehow never completely sees) is partly inspired by my own wanderings, armed with a sketchbook, around medieval buildings in Italy, France, and the British Isles. Those wildly fantastic carvings lurking there in the gloom seem to be rooted more in the sculptor's imaginings than in any particular dogma. They struck me as a powerful metaphor for that world, not of magic exactly, but the "otherness" we see out of the corner of our eyes, the world just outside the firelight. And children, of course, are rapturously aware of it.

Parents and grandparents of my own generation reading some of these verses aloud may discover echoes of the poetry we learned by heart when we were young—by Hardy, Tennyson, de la Mare, Milton, and Keats. Since I was steeped in it at an early age, rhythm and meter have been as important as the visual imagery which provides the main focus. Whatever the age range—the wider the better—I would like to think of readers being drawn into a narrative by their enjoyment of the pictures, the mood set by color, tone, a leisurely exploration of detail, a telling gesture, an expressive face. This would give me almost as much pleasure as I had in the making of the book itself.

References   Hughes, Shirley. 1977. *Dogger*. London: Bodley Head; New York: Mulberry, 1993.

———. 1993. *Stories by Firelight*. London: Bodley Head.

On Writing *Whale Song*

Tony Johnston

Once, years ago, I learned that whales communicate with each other beneath the oceans, mile on watery mile. I was so struck by this idea that I wrote *Whale Song*. Although in it whales count out *one* through *ten,* this is not a counting book, but my paean to nature. Numbers were simply a device, a framework for the tale.

Rather than using straight storytelling, the book chose its own form—a lyrical line that carried it along. My aim was to use a loose underlying beat to draw the reader into the rhythm that I feel so strongly in the natural world. I intended the sway of words to imitate the sway of whales on long journeys, the sway of seaweeds, the sway of swells on the sea.

Though *Whale Song* is not a poem in the strict sense, I relied heavily on poetic elements, images, for example, to paint pictures for the reader. Throughout the story, whales are many things—islands, opera singers, a pod of peas, the Universal Mother, boats "crusty with barnacles," a choir, with all its implications and connotations.

Rhythmic line, strong underlying beat, images, connotations, implications. That is fine. But for me as writer, the basic element that everything rests upon is the *word.*

I like to think of words as piles of beads in a wonderfully cluttered shop. When I begin to write a story, all the words are available to me—bins and barrels and basins of them to run my hands through. Then the choices come.

Robert Frost once wrote, *"The ear does it.* The ear is the only true writer and the only true reader." I believe that absolutely. I write with my ear.

And so, in the word-bead shop, I listen to the sound each makes alone. I select carefully. Then one by one I begin to string my word beads, holding them to the light now and then, slipping one off, adding another, listening to the taps and clicks they make as they roll against each other, until at last they are strung into sentences, paragraphs, a book.

For *Whale Song,* I chose "size words" such as *wide, far, great, big, colossal, mighty, tremendous, stupendous* to show the vast expanse of oceans, the vast size of whales. But I also chose *colossal* for the way it rolls off the tongue; and *tremendous* and *stupendous* for that plus the way they roll against each other. Echoing the numbers throughout the text added to the feeling of vastness, I think.

In creating a necklace of sound, it is easy to make it too opulent—to get caught up in the "gorgeosity" of sounds (I love inventing words). I had to restrain myself from choosing too many fancy words like *locomotive* and *smacking* and *crusty with barnacles* so that those few could truly shine. Simplicity is a key to strong writing. As shown by the work of Emily Dickinson, the purity of simple words can convey the strongest feelings.

Sometimes I set unexpected words next to each other. And so, one whale sings out "in a great, big, frosty voice." The reader was probably not prepared to hear *frosty* in this sequence of words. It's fun to do the unexpected, to try to open up the possibilities of language and imagination.

Sometimes I chose word combinations that rhyme, such as "fishes hide inside" or "higher and higher, an uncle choir"; or I used off-rhyme, a similar sound but not exactly the same, like *ice* and *voice*. Not always. Sometimes. A predictable rhyme pattern would have given this piece a restricted feeling. I wanted to imitate Nature's freedom.

I used lots of words with "l" to fill the pages with the liquid sound of the sea. The page where a whale sings out "ONE!" is built around six "l" words; number "TWO!" also uses six; number "FIVE!" has eight—*rumbles, like, locomotive, whale* (twice), *lulling, sleep, softly*.

On the spread of "THREE!" and "FOUR!" with the repetition of *singing* and *rolling* and *over and over* and with the inversion of these words, I tried to roll them off of each other, both to paint a word picture and to capture the feeling of whales in motion.

And it was no accident that at the story's high point I chose to use the word *wonder*.

In trying to analyze *Whale Song* now, this is what I find. But I confess that when I was immersed in writing it, I was caught up in my feelings. Dragged along by my ear. What I wrote was not a carefully plotted work, but a combination of passion, practice, and instinct—thanks to Mother Nature.

Reference   Johnston, Tony. 1987. *Whale Song: A Celebration of Counting.* Illustrated by Ed Young. New York: G. P. Putnam's Sons.

The Surprises of Rime

X. J. Kennedy

In devising verse for children, I've always found that the most essential ingredient has to be *rime.* Most people and most dictionaries prefer to spell the word *rhyme,* but as a teacher I've noticed that students—even college students—find *rhyme* harder than *rime* and confuse it with *rhythm.* So I spell it *rime* in my college textbook, *An Introduction to Poetry.* I believe it helps students keep things straight. Others, however, may not care to join me in this eccentricity.

For a riming poet, rime is the principal generator of ideas. Children ask me, "Where do you get ideas for your poetry?" Then I have to admit that oftentimes when I begin writing a poem, I don't have a thought in my head. All I'll have, to start with, is a couple of words that rime. As the poem takes shape, its subject and its events will emerge along with the rimes. Those rimes cannot possibly be planned or predicted in advance, and therefore to write in rime is continually to take yourself by surprise. Rime, as the poet Rolfe Humphries once remarked, "makes you think of better things than you could think of all by yourself."

Writing in rime is like walking across a series of stepping-stones on a pitch-dark night, with a feeble flashlight in your hand that can illuminate only the next stone—that is, the next possible riming word. You know your next step, but not where you'll end up. As you walk along, stepping from stone to stone (or proceeding from rime to rime), your destination gradually becomes clear to you. I find this a tremendously exciting pursuit. It is also quite crazy, a little bit frightening, and perhaps even closely akin to the primal chaos that spawned the universe.

That is a tall claim, but let me try to be specific. The poet may fully intend to write, let's say, a birthday ode to a poodle. Intending to write a riming poem, he or she begins with a line ending with the word *poodle*—and then what happens? All sorts of tempting possibilities will occur: *doodle, noodle, oodle, apple strudel, kit and kaboodle,* and more. The poet might select *noodle* or *strudel* as the next riming word, and, moving on in that direction, may find the matter of the poem shifting from a dog to a food. Since one riming word leads to another, pretty soon that original poodle might be forgotten altogether. In writing a riming poem, it is often difficult or impossible to write the poem you intend. But, with any luck, you will write a better and more surprising poem than you had meant to do. This process is exhilarating—like riding a roller coaster when you're unable to see past the next looming hill until you're helplessly roaring down over it.

Once upon a time I used to think that to use a riming dictionary was cheating. I believed that to find a suitable riming word all you needed to do was tool through the alphabet. And I thought that far-out, belabored words, such as you'd find in a riming dictionary, would stand out in a poem unnaturally, like a walnut in the belly of a gartersnake. But as I grow older and my brain cells continue to slow, I find myself stuck for a rime more often than when I was a pup. When in a bind, I now resort to a marvelous book: Willard R. Espy's *Words to Rhyme With* (1986), the best and most ample riming dictionary I know. Its storehouse of 80,000 words includes some things that I wouldn't ever think of in a million years. Still, I turn to Espy only as a desperate last resort.

Some poets, it's true, get carried away by their rimes. The need to complete a line will lead them to say things that make no sense whatsoever, and that aren't even comprehensible nonsense. That must have been the problem faced by the little girl who wrote a poem ending with the lines "When you are alone / it keeps you capone." (Those lines became the title of an excellent book on creative writing with children by Myra Cohn Livingston [1973].) In this case, evidently the poet had heard the mysterious name of Al Capone and had become intrigued by it. She didn't know who Capone was nor did she know the sinister connotations of his name, but that didn't stop her for a minute.

In a way, I rather admire the child's reckless daring. That kind of riming bothers us, though, because it seems too obviously striven for. The rime in the child's couplet is like a big dog dragging her along for a walk. A more practiced poet (and riming does take practice, like any other learnable skill) would play around with different possibilities until she discovered one that would seem to have occurred naturally. Or she would have added words to make the word Capone seem to fit: "When you're alone / And feeling mean as gangster Al Capone. . . ." To the fullest extent, the riming poet, whether unskilled or skilled, puts into practice what E. M. Forster said about his own writing (of prose): "How can I tell what I have to say until I see what it is I've said?"

Thinking, no doubt, of the vexing problems that rime can present to both teachers and students, Kenneth Koch in his influential *Wishes, Lies, and Dreams* (1970) encourages teachers to tell their charges not to rime. But to forbid children to rime seems a shame to me. Some children will never get the hang of riming, and that's all right—maybe the Good Lord didn't intend the American nation to consist entirely of riming poets. But other children, especially if they have read some riming poetry and found it enjoyable, will want to try their hands at this wild and exciting game. I am all for letting them take a healthy whack at it.

On visits to classrooms, I've been shown hundreds of riming poems that children have written, some of these poems a little rough around the edges, but scores of them startlingly good and fresh and crackling with surprise. One child I met discovered a connection between *aroma* and *Oklahoma* and wrote a poem that beautifully linked both words. That is the profoundest kind of language play I know.

References   Espy, Willard R. 1986. *Words to Rhyme With.* New York: Facts on File.

Kennedy, X. J., and Dana Gioia. 1994. *An Introduction to Poetry,* 8th ed. New York: HarperCollins.

Koch, Kenneth. 1970. *Wishes, Lies and Dreams: Teaching Children to Write Poetry.* New York: Harper and Row.

Livingston, Myra Cohn. 1973. *When You Are Alone / It Keeps You Capone: An Approach to Creative Writing with Children.* New York: Atheneum.

Ships Sailed the Seas

Patricia Lauber

Once upon a time, when I was fresh out of college and learning the children's field as a staff writer on *Junior Scholastic*, I had an editor who was fond of citing a sentence from Hendrick van Loon, describing the great age of exploration that was part of the Renaissance. A lesser writer (one of those on the editor's staff) might have said, "Several nations sent out ships on voyages of exploration." Van Loon cut to the heart of the matter and said, "Ships sailed the seas." The sentence is noteworthy not so much for its alliteration as for the simplicity with which it expresses an idea and the mental pictures it evokes of small ships of sail on a blue ocean. It has long served me as a touchstone. At times when I'm struggling to express some difficult scientific concept in terms that are both accurate and understandable, I often stop, stare at the offending sentence on the computer screen, and repeat silently, "Ships sailed the seas." Usually I am then able to write myself out of whatever terrible sentence I've written myself into.

As a touchstone, the sentence fits nicely with the several factors that have influenced the way I write nonfiction. The most important of these is probably an early immersion in and love of poetry. I teethed on nursery rhymes read aloud by my mother. Once I had learned to print and to spell a few words, I began writing my own poems. I memorized much of *Poems Every Child Should Know*, and competed on rainy afternoons with similarly smitten friends to see who could learn the most lines. By my early teens, having advanced in the poets I was reading, I yearned to be the next Edna St. Vincent Millay.

Although this was not to be (I do only light verse on occasion), my years with the poets taught me that a person writing a poem must be economical in use of words, must find words that evoke pictures and distill meaning, so that a handful of words conveys what someone else might take a page or more to say. The same person must be able to hear (with the mind's ear) the internal rhythms created as word falls upon word, phrase upon phrase, sentence upon sentence, and these rhythms must somehow add to the reader's comprehension and pleasure.

Drawing on a vocabulary built by years of omnivorous reading, I try to use strong verbs and nouns and avoid weak ones buttressed by adverbs and adjectives. I like words with Anglo-Saxon roots, which seem meatier than those derived from Latin.

And, of course, I try to build a nonfiction book around a narrative line—to show connections, to build suspense, to make the reader want to turn the page.

Just *how* I do any of these things, I don't know, except that there seems to be a collaboration between the conscious and subconscious minds. The conscious mind is, for example, considering a reference that says winds gusting to 120 miles an hour occurred and that shows a photograph of a town devastated by a hurricane. The subconscious mind starts making suggestions of what the wind did . . . ripped the roofs off houses, snapped telephone poles, toppled trees, hurled automobiles across the street, crumpled trailer homes as if they were soda cans . . . then swirled on, leaving people stripped of their belongings and hopes.

Perhaps because I grew up in a pretelevision age, reading books with few illustrations and listening to radio, I have always made my own mental pictures, and I feel that a reader (or listener) who does this becomes much more involved, experiences more, than a person who is being shown what things look like. I want to draw the reader in by offering the details needed to form mental pictures, to make the text at least as interesting as its illustrations, and, to whatever extent possible, to follow in the wake of van Loon's "Ships sailed the seas."

Voice, Form, Style, and Craft: An Afterword

Myra Cohn Livingston

Writing presents any number of challenges to an individual; certainly the longer one writes, the more exacting the demands seem to be. Any attempt to explain how I use language, rhythm, and sound is based, of course, on a certain amount of hindsight and does not adequately describe the long thinking process, the trial and error of finding a voice and form suitable to a given work. In looking back over my four Notable books chosen by NCTE, however, I find that each is written in a totally different voice and form, which seemed prescribed by the subject matter, the mood of the book, and the effect that I hoped to create.

A Learical Lexicon is, obviously, an homage to Edward Lear, who loved to invent ridiculous words and phrases, a book offering "boshlobberbosh" and "phun" in an array of phrases and words with unorthodox or phonetic spellings which I compiled in the hope that children might enjoy inventing their own strange words and spellings. In this case the humorous language of the book, its dialect, and its rhythms are those of Lear. All that is required here of a writer is to recognize the possibilities for a book in selecting the odd phrases and amusing ideas and in arranging them in a form which happily turned out to be a simple alphabet. Actually, the only purely original writing is in the title, subtitle, and introduction, which is written in a narrative voice, incorporating some of the invented words Lear used. Narrative writing is, obviously, the most simple and direct form of informing readers what to expect in a book. It is therefore recognition of the fun of language, research, and organization, rather than any sort of "creative" writing, which characterizes this lexicon.

Sky Songs is a totally different sort of work, based on a poetic, often metaphoric, apostrophe to the sky. Because the poems address the sky directly, ascribing to it an animism, the poems all speak in a voice characteristic of either young children or—at the other end of the spectrum—poets. Each poem in the book is a triple cinquain, a form I favor and use for a number of reasons. One cinquain did not allow enough for the ideas I wished to convey. In addition, I felt that an apostrophe in rhyme, in a series of poems addressed to the sky, would come out reminiscent of the Taylors' "Twinkle, twinkle, little star," and this rhyming of couplets *(star/are, high/sky)* has already been done. A cinquain gave me room to move around and yet not go off into an endless frenzy of free verse, which I have always avoided as too unstructured for the music I believe poetry should always contain.

The voice is that of a young child addressing the sky in that simple, matter-of-fact way in which children often regard nature. I have long been fascinated by the Assiniboin Indian ideas of the moon, and it is this quasi-primitive viewpoint which I use in addressing the stars, planets, storms, and all else. Personification assumes importance. Lightning has legs, sunset wears beautiful colored scarves, smog makes a city sick, tornadoes dress in green billows, a storm raises a roof of clouds, the snow makes a sleeping bag of snowflakes, ad infinitum. As the words must fit into the cinquain syllabic pattern, the total effect is one of tight containment. Of course, my hope is always that the readers will make up their own new kinds of personification, simile, and metaphor, once introduced to it in this fashion. (I might add that although no one has caught it as yet, to my knowledge, I do feel there is a double-apostrophe lurking in the pages; a group of questions and statements not only asked of the sky, but of God, which, I suppose, gives me away as a transcendentalist!)

The poems in *Earth Songs* certainly might have been squeezed into a quatrain or extended into a triple cinquain form, but it would have been a poor choice, insofar as I am concerned, given the subject for the idea of earth speaking. Using a mask, imagining that earth itself speaks, presupposes a voice that must resonate strength. To achieve this I wanted a heavy falling rhythm as well as strong assonance, consonance, and rich sound. After a number of futile attempts to go back to the cinquain, quatrain, couplet, tercet, and other patterns, I evolved a five-line pattern of my own which I felt carried the weight I needed by adding an extra measure of sound. Because the last word of the first line rhymes with the first word in the next line, and so on through line 4, where there is a triple rhyme on the last sound, this strength seems to be achieved.

There is a touch of the dramatic voice, as well as the mask, in the beginning and the end, where the writer/reader addresses "Little O, small earth," and "great" earth begins its answer. The "secrets" are obviously the features of earth which we all know. Again, as in *Sky Songs*, there is a good deal of personification: waters bathe, deserts sleep, volcanoes breathe. The book ends with the roles reversed; the reader becomes aware of the greatness of the planet, whereas earth itself relegates itself to a small place in the total universe.

There Was a Place is totally different from any of the other three books in style, form, and voice. Because the subject matter is highly emotional and contemporary—children from broken homes, children feeling the pain of alienation, divorce, changing relationships in their lives—the language had to be as simple and direct as possible. The voice is lyrical yet avoids a confessional or complaining tone—for such a voice is largely untrue to childhood. Rather, the voice shows the child facing the circumstances of life and accepting a difficult situation to a degree, but also spending some time wishing that things were different. It is also a voice of everyday contemporary speech pattern, the forms varying from simple couplets to quatrains, and often in rhyme. There are a few allegorical poems suggesting that it is not only humans who suffer and become caught in strange webs or volcanic eruptions; there are also several poems at the end pointing to the hope of new relationships and new friends.

All of the books above represent a totally different approach, for the subject and content demand something of each which took much thought and time to develop. The suitability can be more easily understood if one were to think, for example, how ridiculous it would have been if *There Was a Place* had been written in limericks, *A Learical Lexicon* as a conversation, *Earth Songs* in anapestic trimeter, or *Sky Songs* as a ballad.

The use of language is always, for me, grounded in and part of a craft which must be learned and practiced, for without knowing this craft there can be no control over language; and whereas, occasionally, a bit of writing may be successful without attention to craft, it is unlikely that this will happen often. Certainly I have explained in *The Child as Poet: Myth or Reality?*, *Climb into the Bell Tower*, and *Poem-Making: Ways to Begin Writing Poetry* how deeply I believe in teaching children something of the craft of writing, according them respect by believing that they not only are capable of understanding but actually are excited to learn that good writing is an art with rules that must be learned before they are broken.

References

Livingston, Myra Cohn. 1984. *The Child as Poet: Myth or Reality?* Boston: Horn Book.

————. 1984. *Sky Songs.* Illustrated by Leonard Everett Fisher. New York: Holiday House.

————. 1985. *A Learical Lexicon: From the Works of Edward Lear.* Illustrated by Joseph Low. New York: Atheneum.

————. 1986. *Earth Songs*. Illustrated by Leonard Everett Fisher. New York: Holiday House.

————. 1988. *There Was a Place, and Other Poems*. New York: Margaret K. McElderry Books.

————. 1990. *Climb into the Bell Tower: Essays on Poetry*. New York: Harper and Row.

————. 1991. *Poem-Making: Ways to Begin Writing Poetry*. New York: HarperCollins.

Words, Words, Words . . . and Pictures

Anita Lobel

I have been involved with picture books for almost thirty years. Primarily as a picture maker. The fundamental reason for my sustained interest in the genre is the opportunity to use and expand upon the chiseled, focused, and playful use of language. I delight in the reciprocity that happens when pictures enlarge on what the words say and words serve to string pictures in a continuity that can only take place in a carefully maneuvered and structured narrative form.

At the age of three or four, sometime just before the war began, I had learned how to read in Polish, my first language. *Olek i Ola majal jajko* ("Olek and Ola have an egg"). To this day, I remember the sentence in the flimsy paperback reader. The text was primitively alliterative, printed in large scripted letters. In the schematic drawing, a boy and a girl were contemplating an egg in an egg cup.

The war came. I don't remember reading any stories. I didn't go to school. Aside from church prayer books and psalteries, I had no storybooks.

When I was ten years old, I was recuperating from the war in a sanatorium in the south of Sweden. Seven Swedish little girls in the ward were fascinated by the stranger with the shaved head who had been thrust in their midst from a distant place. A stranger who couldn't speak to them. They giggled and whispered. They tried to help, but without language, I was a dark lump in exile.

Children learn. I don't know how. With the help of lots of pointing and gestures, one Swedish word after another—*bröd* ("bread"), *mössa* ("cap"), *skör* ("shoes"), *blommor* ("flowers"), *ont i magen* ("stomach ache")—began to become familiar, and the words accumulated. The magic of half a phrase, a whole sentence. The delicious taste of several words able to follow each other obediently, crowding, pushing, eager and ready to fall from my tongue. Communication. Like breathing freely after suffocating with illness.

The Swedish sanatorium had a small lending library. From there I borrowed my first big book. I lay in my bed turning the pages of the heavy tome. Held captive behind brambles and thorns, the mysterious words in my new language were not unlike sleeping beauties. Very gradually, they began to wake, creep forward from under their thorny underbrush, and shed their moss. If I didn't know the meaning of every word in a sentence, the word placed next to it would send a clue. In this way, I guessed and deciphered. The mystery of the tale and the mystery of the language began to dance. The book I was reading was a drama of religion and romance. My later, more worldly self learned that at the age of eleven, my first hint of the pleasure and challenge of literature began with a translation from English of *The Robe,* a book written in the language that in itself was soon to become a romance and a challenge.

At last, I went to school. I read a lot and wrote well in Swedish. Soon English classes (required in Sweden even then at an early age) began. The English teacher misguidedly tried to entice the unruly class with *Winnie the Pooh* as the text of choice, with disastrous results. "Tiddely pom" and other "Poohisms" didn't go over very well with fourteen-year-olds in Stockholm, Sweden. Eventually, when I was the mother of small American children, Winnie of course became a shared delight.

Lawrence Olivier was Hamlet at the cinema. I fell madly in love with the tortured Dane. I asked the English teacher to help me learn "To be or not to be." Words like *contumely, quietus,* and *bodkin* were acquisitions to be added to all the rich vocabulary I had already layered down in Swedish and was now going to overlay with another grown-up language. A language not as yet necessary for my everyday communications. A luxury, ever present in American music and movies that I and my friends couldn't live without.

When I came to America, I was once again distanced by language. I could make myself understood just fine. I could understand well enough to get by. But language doesn't belong to one until one can play and dance with it. Until one can luxuriate in its twists and turns and sommersaults. Until one can use it to tease and to gossip and to play, language is a stilted and solemn business. A foreigner with a new language swings between humility and aggression. On the telephone, the voice rises into a scream for fear of being misunderstood. Not until one can whisper elegantly or tell a joke well or laugh on cue at the theater can one breathe easily and presume that one approaches fluency.

Perversely, after having been a struggling novice trying to accumulate living, breathing vocabularies in several foreign languages, it is because I like words so much that I enjoy permitting myself a kind of rich austerity that the language in picture books invites. In a picture book, one needs only to tell part of the story. The pictures will become the rest of the narrative, speaking a choreographed language of gestures to support the language of the words.

I have written decent texts for several conventional picture book stories. It is thrilling for me to arrive at a stage where, on twenty-six pages of an alphabet book, I have twenty-six different ways to express a variation on one thought. In *Alison's Zinnia* I play with a minimal text from which all the fat has been trimmed.

From A to Z, each page contains a large painting of a flower. Underneath a line of text there is a picture of a girl depicting an activity involving the flower. The actions hum along, carried forward by twenty-six verbs. The girl's name, the verb, and the flower all start with the same letter of the alphabet. However, no matter how you look at it, the words fundamentally, schematically, repeat only one thought twenty-six different ways: "A 'had' or 'got' a flower for B."

There is also playing with alliteration and subtext, as in "Crystal cut a Chrysanthemum. . . ." There are lots of "C" names. I could have used *Cathy* or *Celia.* But *Crystal* suggested an edge, the sharpness of a cut. The end of the phrase is then softened with the more liquid name *Dawn,* which leads into the next page.

The name *Emily* for some reason suggests humility to me. That is why I have the girl on her knees scrubbing, working to earn the Easter lily. That, in turn, suggests Christianity and, again, humility.

In "Gloria grew a Gaillardia for Heather," it is the "r" sounds that string the whole phrase together. In "Irene inked an Iris for Jane," the flower dictated the content of the picture. The Iris abounds in Japanese art. I made the little girl Japanese. In the picture she holds a brush to ink an Iris in calligraphic style. "L's" are important in "Kathleen kept a Kalmia for Leslie." "S's" are important in "Leslie left a Lady's slipper for Maryssa."

Some of the phrases are purely tongue-in-cheek. "Jane jarred a Jack-in-the-pulpit for Kathleen", for instance, could be translated as "Jane trapped a fellow for Kathleen."

Then there is "Ursula uprooted an Urtica for Virginia." An Urtica is a weed, a nettle. To uproot it seems like a good thing to do. Nettles were used in witches' brews. I have Ursula uprooting the Urtica at night by moonlight.

It seems redundant to wash a water lily for Xantippa or anyone. But the only Xantippa I have ever heard of was Socrates' shrewish wife. If one were to have offered her a water lily she might have demanded that it was spanking clean. Thus, "Wendy washed a Water lily for Xantippa." "Quaker ladies" are humble northern flowers, and quilting is a very New England thing to do. Hence, "Queenie quilted a Quaker-lady for Regina." On the last page, "Zena zeroed in on a Zinnia for Alison," and the wreath of girls and flowers is complete.

Looking at the last phrase, I am fascinated by the configuration of the way the three short words *in on a* have to follow each other in order to make the action of *zeroing* a grammatical sentence. How taken for granted without a second thought now! But how difficult it would have been to string those three little words together when I was acquiring the rudiments of English.

Hamlet, in his famous speech to the players, said: "Suit the action to the words, the words to the action." There would be no purpose for me to produce pictures, no matter how rich and pretty, without the support of a well-thought-out text; it would result in a collection of images without a backbone. I would like to think that the child who is turning the pages of a picture book such as *Alison's Zinnia* might be inspired to make further aesthetic connections between words and pictures.

Reference   Lobel, Anita. 1990. *Alison's Zinnia*. New York: Greenwillow Books.

The Wonderful World of Verbs

Joan Lowery Nixon

Sometimes I tell young writers-to-be, "Action verbs are the best words of description a writer can use—not adjectives, not adverbs, but action verbs. One well-chosen verb can paint a complete picture in readers' minds. Writers don't tell readers what is happening. Writers open a door and *show* their characters in action as the stories take place, and they do this primarily through action verbs."

The children and I make up short sentences to illustrate:

- Don't write, "The man was angry when he came into the room." Write instead, "He *stomped* into the room."
- Don't write, "She didn't want her mother to know she was there." Write instead, "She *slipped* into the room, *slid* behind the rocker, and *peeked* through the slats at her mother."

Even giggly youngsters who have never been taught the parts of speech and know a verb only as a "do word" quickly get the idea and have great fun choosing exciting, intriguing, interesting action verbs.

In *Will You Give Me a Dream?*, my companion book to *If You Were a Writer*, a small boy asks his mother to give him a dream to help him get to sleep. She carries him into his dream on the back of

> a sea gull with wings that spread wider than your arms can reach. . . . His silver feathers gleam in the moonlight and sparkle back at the stars. (Unpaged)

Together Mother and Matthew use familiar objects to create the story that will lead him into sleep, inspiring many other parents and children to create their own dreams in the same way.

Matthew's sea gull brings him to a ship with a broken mast and a crew of dogs who are in tears. Matthew, of course, is strong enough to repair the ship and save the grateful dogs.

> The captain was happy to let Matthew wear his crown and steer the ship. He settled comfortably into a deck chair with a cup of hot cocoa. "Where are we going?" he asked.

The sea gull swooped toward the south, and Matthew spun the wheel to follow. "To magical places," Matthew told the captain. "Wait and see." (Unpaged)

Magical places . . . the essence of any story. And how do we get there? As I wrote in *If You Were a Writer,*

you would let the story mix and grow with the words in your mind. Together they'd zing and zap and explode into sentences you'd taste and feel and hear. Then you'd know it was time to write down the story so it would never be lost. (Unpaged, p. 31)

I live with my stories while I'm writing them, and I try to show these stories vividly to my readers as I transport them to places every bit as magical as Matthew's. Long ago I discovered the best way to do this is to plunge with excitement and delight into the wonderful world of verbs.

References   Nixon, Joan Lowery. 1988. *If You Were a Writer.* Illustrated by Bruce Degen. New York: Four Winds Press.

————. 1994. *Will You Give Me a Dream?* New York: Four Winds Press.

Revising *Lyddie*

Katherine Paterson

To me, writing a first draft is like lifting a huge hunk of marble out of the quarry. Once I have the hunk out, I can begin to carve it into a statue. Revising is where the fun and the artistry of writing begin.

I don't think I've ever rewritten a book as much as I rewrote *Lyddie*. Historical fiction always takes massive revisions. In the early drafts of the book, all those months of research stick out like lumps in poorly mashed potatoes. I have to keep writing until the research is invisible, simply the texture of the story I am trying to tell.

Students ask me about imagery, as though once the story is written, the author goes back and sticks in the metaphors and similes like raisins on a gingerbread man. But to have power, imagery must grow out of the story itself. The bear in *Lyddie* appears in the first chapter. I certainly knew he was there, but I was hardly conscious of the fact that he reappears all through the book until I began to revise. When I realized that this central image had emerged, I took especial pains with those passages. I wanted the image to serve the story without dominating it.

I remember quite well the final reference to the bear because I rewrote that scene over and over again. How could Luke become the bear that must be stared down without making him undesirable? First I wanted to give a hint that Lyddie would come to love the young Quaker someday, although at the moment he was an obstacle in her path:

> She . . . saw in his bent shoulders the shade of an old man in a funny broad Quaker hat—the gentle old man that he would someday become and that she would love. (P. 181)

How I labored over that one sentence. The word which became *shade* was the key. I tried *form, shadow, image,* but none seemed quite right. I settled at last on *shade* in the sense of ghost or spirit. A one-syllable word seemed to fit best the rhythm of the sentence, and the word *shade* sounded stronger to my ear than *form*.

Once I had foreshadowed the future, I needed to show that for the present Luke is one more bear who must be stared down.

> "Do I frighten thee?" he asked gently.
> "Ey?"
> "Thee was staring at me something fierce." (P. 182)

Then finally, when I had them both laughing, Lyddie because she realizes she has made Luke into the bear, and Luke because he is infected by her merriment, I could echo the one running joke of the book.

We can stil hop, Luke Stevens, Lyddie said, but not aloud. (P. 182)

Originally this sentence read "Thee can stil hop. . . ." But as I reread the story I saw that the hope was for us all and revised accordingly.

Reference   Paterson, Katherine. 1991. *Lyddie*. New York: E. P. Dutton.

Dancing with Words

Gary Paulsen

Language, really, is a dance for me. I long ago decided that I would do anything possible to make a story work right—including sometimes getting fast and loose with grammar. Story is all, and language is a tool to make the story work right and should, I think, be kept flexible to fit needs.

In *Nightjohn*, for instance, the language—pace, focus, rhythm—is more suited to a slave girl in the 1850s, using dialect and hesitation; even the thought or feel behind the language in *Nightjohn* is kept that way, simple as opposed to complex and almost antique in its form.

In *Woodsong* the language was slightly different, slightly more active in a modern sense, lending itself to humor and outdoor adventure. In *The Winter Room* there is again an old-fashioned air to it, mixed with a poetic cadence . . .

The main thing is that language must change, must follow what Michener calls "the loop and whorl" of words on paper that go into making a story.

References

Paulsen, Gary. 1989. *The Winter Room*. New York: Orchard Books.

———. 1990. *Woodsong*. Illustrated by Ruth Wright Paulsen. New York: Bradbury Press.

———. 1993. *Nightjohn*. New York: Delacorte Press.

Easy to Read, But Hard to Write

Peter and Connie Roop

E asy-to-read" books, enjoyed by so many beginning readers, are easy to read, but they are also hard to write. Throughout the creative process, as with any story, numerous decisions are made. But the easy-to-read format requires additional questions:

> Is this story suitable for the easy-to-read format?

> Will the story be interesting to beginning readers?

> How do we choose just the right words to tell the story, hold a reader's interest, and stay within the length requirements (around 1,000 words)?

> How much will the context enable the reader to decipher a story-specific word?

> How much repetition should there be and which phrases would bear repeating?

> How much detail will the illustrations convey, details that we can leave out of the text?

The list goes on. Each book presents a unique set of circumstances and dictates its own problems that need resolution.

By no means do we sit with such a list as we write. But these questions repeatedly arise as we go through draft after draft, discussing and rewriting. (We read every draft out loud several times.)

In *Keep the Lights Burning, Abbie,* the decision-making process lasted from the first draft through the tenth. *Abbie* had its own parameters, as we were writing about an actual person and series of events. The first decision was whether or not to create a fictional work by taking only the highlights of Abbie Burgess's heroic actions in single-handedly keeping two lighthouses burning and by fashioning a story with those elements. When we wrote the first draft that way it didn't ring true. Anna (Abbie) did the same things as the real Abbie, but there was no sense of verisimilitude.

For the second draft we stayed with Anna and decided to try a Maine dialect. Having heard the "downeast" accent for years, we thought we could use it to bring Anna to life. Halfway through the draft we realized that, as Midwesterners, we had no real grasp of the dialect and that it would be an impediment to our young readers.

At this point we returned to our research and discovered some actual quotes from Abbie. Armed with the new material, we began the third draft, one which almost wrote itself. Two drafts later we submitted the manuscript to our editor.

Her response was prompt. Yes, we had a story. Yes, the approach was right. Would she publish it? No, not yet. It needed more work, and she would send us a word list to guide our thinking.

Reluctant to use a word list, we wrote two more drafts before glancing at the list. During this stage we honed the story to its basic elements and simplified the language by selecting evocative and active words over static ones (*raced* instead of *ran, steered* instead of *turned*). We also decided to use dialogue to explain the lighthouse terminology necessary for understanding the story and to keep the story moving forward. This decision proved invaluable, as it enabled us to incorporate actual quotes from Abbie's sisters in several places. Quotes like "Oh, look! Look there! The sea is coming!" provide a sense of authenticity that we could not create. (And they were on the word list!)

Dialogue also helped us answer two more questions as we dealt with Abbie's need to know how to keep the lights burning without ever having done so herself. We solved this by having Papa tell her, "You have trimmed the wicks before. You have cleaned the lamps and put in the oil." These words were then used several more times to incorporate an element of repetition: "She trimmed each wick. She cleaned each lamp. She put in more oil."

The final decisions came during the editorial give-and-take, where we changed uncommon words (*locomotive* to *train*) to enhance the story's flow but fought to keep others for the enjoyment of the reader. For example, "The wind put whitecaps on the waves," was slated for cutting, but we kept it over "The strong wind made high waves."

Throughout the whole process we kept eliminating descriptive details, hoping our illustrator, Peter Hanson, would put them in his pictures. Unbeknownst to us, as we whittled each draft, our editor had been giving previous drafts to Peter so he could include what we had cut.

Writing a story is a problem-solving activity. Questions are posed, answers sought, and decisions made. Easy-to-read books require all of the elements of a good story but demand that the author ask and answer unique questions, too. The answers to these questions do help make the story easier to read, just as they make it harder to write.

Reference   Roop, Peter, and Connie Roop. 1985. *Keep the Lights Burning, Abbie.* Illustrated by Peter E. Hanson. Minneapolis: Carolrhoda Books.

Syllables and Songs: Making Words Sing

Diane Siebert

When I write, I think in terms of music rather than poetry. The words that end up as a poem are actually written as a song, with each work composed of time signature, measures, notes, and so on. The rhythms come naturally; they are everywhere: in the rising and setting of the sun, in the changing of the seasons, in the cycles of life and death, in motors and machines, in the sound of my own breathing and in my footsteps as I run with my dogs each morning through canyons, beside rivers, and down quiet dirt trails. These rhythms are infused, like heartbeats, into my writing to give it life. And because the rhythm of a piece is important to me, I pay close attention to each beat. There is no way that I can substitute a quarter note for an eighth note without destroying the rhythm, and this means that words often require a good deal of manipulation. So, after trying to choose words with sounds that suit the subject and finding words that rhyme perfectly, I move them around individually, as phrases, or as whole lines, turning them every which way in order to compress the ideas and incorporate them into the text of a thirty-two-page picture book. On a good day, the pieces of the puzzle fall into place easily, and whole sections may be completed in a matter of hours. On the other hand, I once spent three months on eight lines of text. For although I usually know exactly what I want to say, my brain, and the English language, sometimes refuse to accommodate me. Those are the times when my imagination, my flexibility, my research material, my rhyming dictionary, and my thesaurus seem to let me down. How frustrating to find out that *death* is the only real word that rhymes with *breath!* How annoying to discover, just when I am looking for a word to rhyme with *head,* that a particular animal is always blue and never red!

I'm sometimes tempted to fudge just a little—cheat on a rhyme here, add an extra beat there—but in the same way that every single note and sign in a piece of music plays a vital role, each syllable and word in my poetry is important to the overall effect.

I strive to create poetry that is musical and memorable. Like a good song or a catchy jingle, I want my poetry to stick in the mind and be understandable. And when I hear a child "humming a few bars" of my work by reciting lines of my poetry from memory, I know I've succeeded in turning words into music.

To Bop or Not to Bop: Writing *Turtle in July*

Marilyn Singer

I have always loved words. I got to appreciate them first in the books my mother read me, the songs my dad sang, and, especially, in the stories my Romanian grandmother told me. When I was in elementary school, I made lists of words—words for colors, words for birds, girls' names, boys' names, anything that struck my fancy. I still make lists today. For me, *logophilia* is one of the reasons I became a writer.

Coleridge said that prose is words in the best order and poetry is the *best* words in the best order. I like that idea. I'm constantly looking for the best words to use in my poetry (and, frankly, in my prose, too, but there I'm more concerned with the bigger picture, not the perfect cameo). When I'm working on a poem, I play around with words a lot. If the words I initially choose don't sound like the best ones to me, I try others until I find the words that do. The same goes for their order. I arrange and rearrange phrases until they sound just right.

Order has a lot to do with sound and rhythm. I read each of my poems aloud to myself and ask, does it sing? I don't mean the way a song does. A friend of mine said that a poem has a different music than a song, and I agree with him. I listen for the poetic music.

A lot of my poems are about character. Different words and rhythms fit different characters. I'm not talking about mere description, but about word sounds, shades of meaning, rhythms. This is important if the poem is in the author's voice, and doubly so, I believe, if it is a character's voice. I'm constantly concerned about whether or not the words and phrasing fit the character. This is something else I pay attention to.

To illustrate, let me give you a few examples. When I was working on my collection of animal poems, *Turtle in July,* I was very clear about my intention—I wanted to write poems for each month of the year, plus the four seasons, in the voices of different animals. I wanted each poem to sound like the animal would, if it could speak English.

For the month of February, I decided to write two poems—one about an owl out hunting and the other about its prey, in this case a deer mouse. Deer mice spend much of the winter in their burrows, emerging only to get food and then hurry back in. I pictured a mouse scurrying out of its home, skittering across the snow, and I wanted to get across that swift, syncopated motion in words. To capture the mouse's movement, I chose the word *bop.* I also decided to use spacing and line breaks the way a composer uses musical note values, rests, and measures. The opening of the first draft of the poem read:

> Bop
>   Out of the nest
> Bop bop bop
>   Into the cold
> Bop bop
>   Stop
>   Sniff
>   Seeds under the snow?
>   Bugs under the snow?
>   Bugs beneath the bark?
> Bop bop bop
>   Hustle
>   Don't let your feet rustle

Now I have a kind of personal buzzer in my gut. It goes off when something isn't working. I pay it great heed because it hasn't let me down yet. So when that buzzer went off after I read that draft, I knew something wasn't right. I had to think about the mouse's goals to figure out what it was. I had to realize that the poem was about both motion and *need.* The mouse's need to leave the nest, to find food, to be wary, and, above all, the need to do all of that as quickly as it possibly could. *Bop* was too cute and jolly a word, and also something leisurely. The right word, I found, was *get.* When I discovered that, the rest of the poem fell into place:

> get   get get get   get
>   get
>   out of the nest
>   get
>   into the cold
> get   get get get
>   get
>   food
>   lots of food
>   get
>   seeds
>   berries
>   nuts
>   bugs
>   bark

get enough to last
get enough to store
get more
get get get get   get
    get going
        move
            hustle
don't rustle
don't squeak
            beware
            danger in the air
get busy
get done
get get get get
    get out of here
            run (Unpaged)

For the title poem in my collection, one of the earliest poems I wrote for it, I chose to portray a turtle, chilling out under the hot summer sun. I spent a lot of time watching turtles. Long observation made me feel that a turtle, if it could speak, would talk in short sentences, so as not to waste energy. These, however, would not be the staccato sentences of the deer mouse, but the laconic language of a slow being, one almost too pleasantly tired to speak.

My first draft of the poem read:

Heavy and hot
The air hangs
A thick blanket of wool
But nose high
    in fresh mud
I lie
    very still
    very collected
    very cool
And I think
How fine to be a turtle in July

Although I liked the image of the air hanging like a thick blanket of wool and the wordplay of "very collected, very cool," I felt, in reading over the poem, that it sounded like the author speaking and not the turtle. I wanted something even more spare and, if you will, Zen-like. I also felt that a turtle would be plainspoken and not lyrical, as, say, a deer might be. Colloquialisms such as *icky* would be acceptable to a turtle. With all that in mind, I rewrote the poem as follows:

Heavy
Heavy hot
Heavy hot hangs
Thick sticky
Icky
But I lie
Nose high
Cool pool
No fool
A turtle in July (Unpaged)

Writing, and particularly writing poetry, is full of many such "eurekas." For me, when something doesn't work in a poem, I hold the thought that soon I will discover what will. I find that philosophy comforting, sustaining. Now if only I could apply it to the rest of my life, what a wise and happy person I'd be!

Reference   Singer, Marilyn. 1989. *Turtle in July.* Illustrated by Jerry Pinkney. New York: Macmillan.

The Way You Say a Thing

Jan Slepian

In thinking about how I create the working language in my books, I made an extraordinary discovery. Because I tried to separate my use of words from the other aspects of making a novel, I came to realize that for me, the biggest thrill in writing my books is in the language itself—finding just the right word or the right phrase, the right sentence to say what I want to say.

For some writers a rousing story may give the most pleasure, the working out of a good plot. For others the big thrill might be in developing a character so that he or she jumps to life on the page. When the book is done, it's almost impossible to separate out which aspect of writing gave the most pleasure. But if I had to choose, I would absolutely say along with the poet Robert Frost, "The fun is in the way you say a thing."

As I think back, it has always been like that for me. When I was in grade school we wrote "compositions" for English. The composition I wrote for Mr. Pargot, my sixth-grade teacher, is still vivid to me because it showed me something I hadn't known before. We were reading a book called *Arrowsmith* by Sinclair Lewis. I dimly recall that it was about a heroic doctor fighting a plague. Our assignment was to imagine ourselves as the wife of this Dr. Arrowsmith. The wife had just learned that she had contracted the dread disease that her husband was away fighting, and she was about to die before he returned. We were to write a parting letter to our husband.

That night I sweated over that composition. I was utterly absorbed, really into it. I discovered then that if you put yourself in someone else's skin and really believed it, you can write as if you are that person, and it comes out sounding true. It was then that I discovered that finding just the right word to express what I wanted to say was delicious. I mean, I was aware that the word tasted good in my mouth. That kind of delicious.

It took me hours to write that composition, and when I was done, it was merely a page long.

I see in retrospect that I haven't much changed from that struggling girl. I can still take hours to write just a little bit; I don't put down a word on the page unless I feel it's the best I can do. And if it is just the right one, it tastes good. Delicious.

I don't give much thought to creating dialogue. By the time I start a novel I have already written pages and pages of notes to myself about the characters. I try to know them as deeply as I can, so that I can be inside them when they speak. What they say and how they say it can then fall naturally from my fingers to the page. Thinking doesn't have much to do with it.

The rhythm, the flow, the pace, the syllables, and the words that make up the sentences are part of a kind of music that I listen for. There is a judgment that the inner ear makes as I go along. It says yes, that's good, or no, no good, and I don't question it. It comes from some place where (if it's a good day) the mind and heart and ear are in balance. I have learned to trust it.

I have heard tennis players or baseball players talk about "the sweet spot" in their sport. That's the exact place on the racket or bat where the ball lands just right for the return. They say it's a great feeling. Writing, too, has its sweet spot. The joy, the sweet spot, is in the way I say a thing, and when I know it's right, there's nothing like it. It's the greatest.

Intriguing Language: A Personal Point of View

Zilpha Keatley Snyder

My first reaction on hearing that I had been selected as a contributor to a book dedicated to "intriguing and interesting" uses of language in children's literature was—why me? It really was. The reason being that I have never considered myself a particularly gifted wordsmith. Not that I wouldn't like to be. I can spend hours reading and rereading passages in books by authors who do have such a gift, and I am consumed by admiration and yes, let's admit it, a bit of jealousy.

At such times I have consoled myself by saying my special gifts lay elsewhere. Perhaps in my rather chaotically fertile imagination. (I've always said I have never worried about running out of ideas. I just have trouble keeping the ones I have fed and watered and under some sort of control.) Or perhaps in my ability to get inside my characters—a skill I've been developing since earliest childhood, when I constantly went about pretending to be someone else, often a character from a favorite book.

But since my use of language is considered, at least in some circles, as "intriguing and interesting," I took a moment, feeling rather proud and important, to consider "how" I do it—and came to the conclusion that I haven't a clue. No theories, no rules, no special procedures, nothing the least bit instructive or edifying. I do, in fact, have personal rules and procedures for other aspects of writing. Rules pertaining to plot development, foreshadowing, the uses of fantasy, and so on. But as far as my use of language is concerned, the only methodology I can identify is: write it—read it over—if it doesn't sound right, write it again.

But if I don't know the "how" of my use of language, I am absolutely certain about "how" I came to be a writer. I know with great certainty "how" I developed not only my ability to use the written word but also my rather freewheeling imagination. I did it by *reading*.

Starting at an early age, I have read both prose and poetry constantly, indiscriminately, and joyfully. All my life I have read because books were wonder, excitement, challenge, and escape. But while I was wondering and escaping, I was unconsciously absorbing not only reams of information about people, places, and events, but also a feeling for the rhythm and flow of language, an ear for various kinds of dialogue, and a delight in the intricate, complicated play of words and ideas.

So I do have a slightly oblique answer to the question, "How do you use language?" The answer is—I read.

The Simple Simile

Jerry Spinelli

Figurative language is sometimes viewed as fancy, grandstanding, "purple." Too often that's just what it is. But written well, figurative language is just the opposite. It clarifies. It simplifies.

In chapter 27 of *Maniac Magee*, Maniac is teaching old Grayson, the illiterate groundskeeper, how to read. My problem as writer: how to briefly and effectively show someone learning to read.

To begin with, I narrowed down the focus to consonants and vowels. Of these, it seemed to me, vowels would be the more difficult for Grayson to grasp. Vowels are fluid, elusive, hard to hit squarely. How could I help the reader to "see" Grayson's struggle with vowels?

Should I write of hard and soft sounds, long and short? of full and partial diphthongs? of voiced correlatives? Hardly.

I needed a simile. Since I was writing from Grayson's point of view, the place to go simile shopping was Grayson himself. What in Grayson's experience might be compared to his struggle with vowels?

Grayson was once a baseball pitcher. Pitchers pitch knuckleballs. Knuckleballs flutter all over the place. They are fluid, maddeningly elusive, all but impossible to hit squarely.

Bingo:

> To the old pitcher, they were like his own best knuckleball come back to haunt him. In, out, up, down—not even the pitcher, much less the batter, knew which way it would break. He kept swinging and missing. (P. 101)

Nothing fancy. Clear and simple.

Reference   Spinelli, Jerry. 1990. *Maniac Magee*. Boston: Little, Brown.

Making Words Come Alive

Ann Turner

Asking me to write about language is like asking a gourmand to write about food. It is so much a part of me, that I eat, breathe, and think language most hours of the day. I write down the wonderful words of my children (three and six), listen to the cadences of speech in the general store, and hear fragments of songs in my mind. How does all this internal business, this ferocious activity, get translated into written words? I will try and describe it for you.

To begin with, *Dakota Dugout* was written as a poem for adults, then changed to a story/poem for children. It came out in one long rush of words, with seemingly no conscious thought. In retrospect I can see why I made the choices I did. I chose a language of plain song, an unvarnished speech that would fit a woman living on the prairie. I wanted to give the loneliness of the prairie through her eyes:

> a heron flapped by with wings like sails
> and a sparrow jabbered the day long
> on a gray fence post.
> I jabbered back. (P. 15)

She is an unconscious poet, using internal rhymes like the plow "that sliced the long earth strips. / Matt cut them into bricks . . ." (pp. 8–9). In all you read about the Dakotas, you see, feel, and smell the presence of the wind; it never, ever stops. I knew that inside, though I had never felt the wind on my cheek until years after I wrote *Dakota Dugout*. So the wind became a song that wove throughout the text: blowing a dry winter wind, "*whish*-hush"; a wet spring wind, "*shoosh*-hush"; and "*Ssst-ssst*," the deadly wind of summer that baked their corn dry and dead. When they finally achieve what they think are their dreams—money and a house—the broom makes the "*whisp*-hush" sound and the clock tocks like "a busy heart." She tells us, almost without her knowing it, how much she has lost by moving out of her "cave in the earth" into a house with the "empty sound of too many rooms."

In *Nettie's Trip South,* the language Nettie uses is the language of pain and rage—the rage only a ten-year-old can feel at the injustice of an adult world. I used the device of a letter, of Nettie writing to her cousin Addy to tell "all I saw." And there really *was* a Netty, my great-grandmother, and she really did have a cousin Addy, who lived in Oneida, New York. I have Addy's letters, 2" by 1" sent to Albany, New York, in the 1830s. Nettie's speech must have the exciting jump of a child suddenly allowed into an adult world: "I admit I jumped / I admit I screamed—a little," at the train. Smell plays a part in Nettie's perceptions, when she sniffs the sweet cedar wind of the South, a scent that begins to cloy as she witnesses more of slavery. When she visits the slave quarters of a plantation, the boy who gives her water has a "face so black and round and fierce, / it could've been fired from a cannon in war." Her language and the image come from her horror and foretell what is to come. His face *is* his rage, and she sees and understands it. Then notice how suddenly her language shortens and sharpens at the slave auction:

> There was a platform.
> There was a fat man in a tight white suit.
> There was a black woman on the platform.
> "Jump, aunt, jump!" the man shouted." (Unpaged)

Her world and language are reduced to the immediate horror of what she sees. She is breathless with the horror, and that makes her language breathless. Nettie knows there is no real reprieve for what she has seen, "and I have bad dreams at night."

In a different vein, *Through Moon and Stars and Night Skies* uses the first-person narrator to tell the story of how a child came from South Korea to America and his new, adoptive family. When he is on the plane, the shortness of the sentences convey his fear:

> I was afraid.
> Of the night rushing by.
> Of the plane roaring.
> Of all the new things. (Unpaged)

Shortness can equal fear. But then the boy uses short, declarative sentences to describe the first view of his house:

> There was a white house with a green tree out front.
> Inside was a room waiting for me.
> And a bed just for me. (Unpaged)

All of the language circles back to this child, this little, frightened but intensely observing dot who can hardly believe what he sees. So much is new for him. I also use my memories of what it was like to be small and frightened when I describe his first sight of the room with its "dark corners." Then the language opens out and the sentences become somewhat longer as he relaxes into calm and warmth and begins to know his house, his new poppa, and his new momma.

Two short notes about two of my novels. In *Grasshopper Summer* I had to constantly rein myself in to keep to the authentic voice of a twelve-year-old boy in 1874. What would his experience let him see? What images might he use? When the locusts arrive at their farm and devour their first crop, this is how Sam describes the landscape: "The trees were black and spindly over the brown water. The prairie looked dead and squashed." Or, as his younger brother, Billy, says, "They ate up all the pretty things and left all the ugly things." I also wanted to give a sense of the rough saltiness of frontier language, without offending readers. When Sam and a friend want to write to someone in Washington for help after the locust invasion, the friend described politicians in this way: "What did those politicians, who Grandpa said were sewn up out of a pig's backside, care about us settlers . . . ?" Sticking to what Sam knew, I had him describe the locusts' departure with a familiar image: "The sky was brown with their bodies, brown like the bottom of a pot where something burned and smelled bad." For they did smell, awful and greasy and nauseating. His world and his perceptions always keep a rein on the language and the images.

In *Rosemary's Witch* I used the third-person narrator, mostly because I wanted to alternate points of view between Mathilda, the witch, and Rosemary, the nine-year-old heroine. I also had more leeway to be poetic that way. I wanted to give Mathilda's speech, which is that of a woman/witch who has barely spoken in over sixty years. When she does speak, the edges of her mouth crack and peel and her words come out in spurts: "Come—I—need—you." Mathilda is described in this way: "The witch stood in the corner, clothes still roiling about her with a sound like a far sea hissing." It is through Rosemary's confrontation with the witch that she learns how much she loves words, and how she has a facility for them. Her language mirrors that development throughout the book, from a child who has difficulty speaking (as does the witch at first) to a girl who is more fluent and can speak her mind (as does the witch, also).

In *Heron Street* the repetition of the grass's song weaves the story together. The plain, bald language in *Grass Songs* (a collection of poems about women going West in the nineteenth century) reflects how the characters I choose tell *me* what to say. I don't tell them—they tell me, and I write it down as if I were sitting in the front seat of a movie theater, observing a vivid and dramatic movie and taking notes on it.

References   Turner, Ann. 1985. *Dakota Dugout.* Illustrated by Ronald Himler. New York: Macmillan.

———. 1987. *Nettie's Trip South.* Illustrated by Ronald Himler. New York: Macmillan.

———. 1989. *Grasshopper Summer.* New York: Macmillan.

———. 1989. *Heron Street.* Illustrated by Lisa Desimini. New York: Harper and Row.

———. 1990. *Through Moon and Stars and Night Skies.* Illustrated by James Graham Hale. New York: Harper and Row.

———. 1991. *Rosemary's Witch.* New York: HarperCollins.

———. 1993. *Grass Songs.* Illustrated by Barry Moser. San Diego: Harcourt Brace Jovanovich.

How Possum Came a-Knockin'

Nancy Van Laan

Ideas are sly critters. Somehow they need to be coaxed out of the shadows and then pounced on before they have a chance to escape. Usually these critters come my way when my notebook is somewhere else. More times than I care to admit, my stories are first drafted in the margins of newspapers, across the backs of utility bills, or on paper tablecloths in restaurants.

The act of creating a work of fiction is a mysterious process. Why do ideas reveal themselves in the first place? What turns these initial concepts into rhythmic, poetic verse? The process I use probably evolved from my love of all kinds of music and from a former career in ballet. It seems that I have always begun to create books for children by feeling a particular rhythm—not words. I may spend months listening to a certain beat, allowing it to play inside my head, like a song rising up inside of me. Then an idea happens along—like the possum who came to my back door one night to discuss politics with my cat—and suddenly, there it is! I now have a real live creature to write about. At last, I can actually use words in conjunction with the noise that's been pounding inside my head for months on end! Just give this inspiration a little nudge in the right direction, and encourage it to develop a plot.

Before I undertook the task of writing *Possum Come A-Knockin'*, I thought about how possums are not generally admired for their good looks or friendly disposition. In fact, most people only know them as something dead lying alongside the road. In the backwoods of the South, however, possums are viewed as a delicacy, sometimes cooked in a delectable stew. I decided to draw on the memories of growing up with relatives from deep, down there, to write about a possum in a dialect I had no trouble recalling.

As I sat down, picked up a pencil, and wrote,

Possum come a-knockin'
at the door, at the door.
Possum come a-knockin'
at the door. (Unpaged, p. 5)

I visualized a large family sitting inside their hand-built home, each busy doing something and not paying a bit of attention to what the young narrator was saying. (Of course, this was me when I was little because nobody ever paid attention to what I had to say, partially due to the fact that I talked nonstop and made up whopper tales. On the rare occasion when they did listen, they never believed me.)

On the next page I wrote,

> Granny was a-sittin'
> and a-rockin' and a-knittin'
> when a possum come a-knockin'
> at the door. (P. 6)

(This was based on what my own Nannie would have done. Since she was hard of hearing, she wouldn't have realized that somebody was at the door.)

Quickly, one character followed the next, each given a logical reason to be preoccupied; then, naturally, a cat and dog had to be included to increase the suspense and add to the fun. Thus, the plot sort of developed itself as I went along, using dialect, keeping to the original rhythm, and building on the story's simple structure. Once the beat was established, finding words to rhyme with each other was not so difficult to do. If a particular word I wished to use didn't work in one spot, sometimes I changed the sequence, character, or plot so that I could incorporate it somewhere else.

Essentially, a picture book contains a simple plot which is short in length. Therefore, each word of every story has to convey a heavy load. This is why poetry lends itself so well to this particular genre, for an entire concept can be packed into a book by using a few choice words.

I rarely know how any story will end—it's as much of a surprise to me as it is to the reader. I do think last lines are very important. If the last line isn't written satisfactorily, whatever happens beforehand turns out to be a major disappointment. Since I knew how it felt to be shunned as a child, the ending of the possum story fell into place rather easily. None of the characters believes the narrator when she tells them a possum is at the door. When they finally look out, it hides: "That possum that was knockin' / made a fool of me!" But I didn't say that when the real possum came to my back door—I gave it a huge welcome and said, "Come right on in!"

Reference   Van Laan, Nancy. 1990. *Possum Come a-Knockin'*. Illustrated by George Booth. New York: Alfred A. Knopf.

Voices and Choices; or, How Bosh's Wife and Three Angels Dropped by for a Visit and Decided to Stay

Nancy Willard

When I'm asked the question, "Why did you choose to write this book in this particular way?" I'm tempted to say, "Don't ask me. Ask the story. Ask the poem," because the answer is different for each book.

The inspiration for *The High Rise Glorious Skittle Skat Roarious Sky Pie Angel Food Cake* came from a story my mother told me. When she and her two sisters were small, they decided to bake their mother a birthday cake. They planned to creep into the kitchen at night, bake the cake, and leave it on the kitchen table with a note crediting it to three enchanted bakers. The children did indeed creep into the kitchen, but none of them had ever baked a cake before, and the energetic clatter of pots and pans soon woke their mother, who sent them back to bed and spent the next hour cleaning up the kitchen.

Such is real life.

But in my version of the story, what should have happened does happen. Angels arrive, and with a little help from these heavenly visitors, the cake gets baked. I dropped the two sisters from the tale; one main character seemed simpler to manage. Since the original story was told (on request, over and over) and not written, what mattered most when I set out to write it was the voice of the teller. Once I heard her voice in my head, I let my character tell the story, and I wrote it as I heard it. To give the illustrator some freedom, I avoided specifying the gender and appearance of the angels.

The text of *Pish, Posh, Said Hieronymus Bosch* is a poem, and it's meant to be read aloud. One of the pleasures of reading poetry for me is memorizing it, something I was required to do in college. If children enjoy *Pish, Posh* enough to reread it, the rhyme and meter will make it easy for them to remember the words. Because the story unfolds in scenes of increasing chaos, I wanted the meter to skip and jig along, and I chose to write mostly in dactyls and anapests.

And Bosch's creatures—where do they come from? When I'm working on a book, I often make sculptures and toys of the characters in my head. Indeed, there are days when our dining room looks a little like a room in Bosch's house. Working with my hands seems to free my mind to mull over characters and ideas. I hope teachers who share *Pish, Posh* with children will encourage them to make their own "creatures"—and stories to go with them.

References   Willard, Nancy. 1990. *The High Rise Glorious Skittle Skat Roarious Sky Pie Angel Food Cake.* Illustrated by Richard Jesse Watson. San Diego: Harcourt Brace Jovanovich.

———. 1991. *Pish, Posh, Said Hieronymus Bosch.* Illustrated by the Dillons. San Deigo: Harcourt Brace Jovanovich.

Language in Books with a Multicultural and International Focus: In Praise of the Language Gods

Karen Lynn Williams

Which comes first? The concept or the feeling or the language or the story? Philosophers and developmental specialists have explored the question for years. As a writer, I'd have to say it depends. It depends on which book I'm discussing and what mood I'm in. Is it a picture book, a story book, or a chapter book? Am I feeling analytical or emotive or reflective?

In each of my three multicultural picture books the language was derived from a different starting point. *Galimoto* began as a concept. I wanted to share the idea of *galimotos* with my readers, *galimotos* in all their forms and possibilities. The first draft of *Galimoto* was really a few paragraphs in an article for a children's magazine about the things children in Africa like to do. The language was direct, easy to read, informative. Luckily, the article didn't sell, but the idea of *galimotos* stayed with me. *Galimotos* caught my imagination and became a passion. I wanted to sing praises and write sonnets to the *galimoto*. *Galimoto* also became a symbol for me of a certain quality of childhood that I observed in a rural African setting.

When Africa Was Home began as a feeling that I wanted to convey—what it felt like to live in Africa (the space, the color, the freedom)—and to make the story, I built the feelings around the concept of home and what makes home, home. I think for this reason, the language in *When Africa Was Home* is more evocative than in *Galimoto* or *Tap-Tap*. As I was writing that book at home in my study in Pittsburgh, I felt bathed in memories of Africa. Each time I got up from a writing session at my typewriter it was as though I had come back from the very distant place I was writing about, having been transported home to Africa by the language I was using. The return was wrenching.

The manuscript for *Tap-Tap*, a story about Haiti, came about in yet another way and was, I think, most directly inspired by the use of language. Two things about tap-taps captured my interest in them as a possible subject for a picture book. One was the name *tap-tap* itself. It is a great repetitive, play word. And also it is an example of what often happens in more primitive languages, the name of the object is derived from an innate quality of the object. In this case, tap-tap is what you do to make tap-taps stop. The story for me is already fun! The second and very closely related possibility that tap-tap offered was the possibility for repetition and roundness in the story. Simply, one by one all these people and things get on the brightly colored vehicle and then one by one they get off. Here the visual possibilities for a picture book also came into play and inspired the language, the brightly painted designs, and the humorous image of a vehicle packed with goats, chickens, tables, chairs, food, and people with yet still another ladened passenger to board.

Many people have remarked on the quality of the language in my picture books, and I am always surprised anew when I hear these comments because as the writer, I am so close to the material I will have to admit that I am not as aware of the language as it stands alone. I am intent on developing a story that is both satisfying and evocative. It is the story that I am aware of. The language comes from deep within. But as I read my books over, I have to admit that, yes, there is a certain quality of language in my multicultural books that adds to the stories. I approach picture books as if they were poetry, although I am not a poet. I am constantly aware of the need for spareness and the fact that each word must count. The language in a picture book must strike the reader quick and deep. Beyond that? How do I put the words together? choose the sentence length? dialogue? I am aware of the standard rules. New paragraph for a new idea, sentence length depends on the age of the audience, variety in sentence type makes the writing more interesting, and so on. But that is only a small part. The rest I owe to the Gods of Language Usage and to the unequalled experience of living in, learning the language of, and writing about cultures other than my own.

I found living in both Africa and Haiti intense and inspiring. Was it the rural existence, the simplicity of life and the proximity to a people on the edge of survival, a more primitive existence? I'm not sure, but I think all those things are reflected in the language I use in the books based on these experiences. Living in a new culture and learning the language make one very aware of elements of the language that one might take for granted in one's own culture or not even recognize.

In all three books I tried to use words and language that sounded and felt the way those places sounded and felt to me. For example, *Galimoto* begins,

> Kondi opened an old shoe box and looked inside. These were his things. They belonged to him. (Unpaged, p. 7)

While I don't know how a child in Malawi would have thought about that shoe box, it seemed to me that things were often simply stated and taken for granted, and I hoped to catch the flavor of both the language and life of a Malawian child. The sentence also says a lot more. Everything Kondi owned could fit in a shoe box. He doesn't have much, but perhaps he isn't even aware of how little he has—these things in the shoe box are treasures.

Because the language and relationships in both countries I was writing about seemed more formal to me than in our American culture, I used words and phrases that I hoped would evoke that flavor of life in those cultures, even though they weren't direct translations. I'm not sure that Kondi's uncle would have greeted him as, "the second son of my brother," or that Mayi, in *When Africa Was Home,* would have said exactly, "Such a child with golden hair should not play in the sun," but it is the way it *felt* to me. "When Africa was home, Peter played from the time the sun was still cool until his shadow danced in the moonlight." It is unlikely any Malawian would have expressed the idea this way, but it is the way time is thought of in rural Africa, in relation to the sun and the moon.

Some of the words I used were direct translations. "Go well." "Stay well." They were particularly apt, and I liked the sound. I used words from the language of the country I was writing about to give a feel for the language and the place because I think it is great fun for children to learn a word or phrase from another language. Too many such words would have been confusing and would have taken away from the writing. I chose the words I used, carefully, either for the importance of the sound or for their meaning. In *Tap-Tap* I used *au revoir* and *merci* because they are so well known as to be almost universal, and yet they give a feeling for the French Creole spoken in Haiti. *Bep-bep* instead of *beep-beep* is how Haitians describe the honking of a car horn, and I included it, at the risk of having it mistaken as a typing error, because I think it is the type of difference a child can appreciate and have fun with. Also, I was with an American friend one day, bicycling. She used the phrase to warn some children who were in our path. The children giggled with delight. "The *Blanc* knows *bep-bep*. Ha! *Bep-bep*. She says, '*Bep-bep*.'" It is a phrase Haitian children know well and enjoy.

In Malawi, *eeeee* is a common expression of delight or dismay, and so I used it also as an interesting fun sound near the end of *Galimoto*. *Kwatu* (home), *Mayi* (Peter's nanny), *Achimwewe* (the name the African children gave Peter)—all words important to the story of *When Africa Was Home*—are also fun to say. *Ndizabweronso* (I will come back) and *akubwera* (to come back) are words with the same root that sound to me like what they mean.

Much of the way I used language in my multicultural books was not conscious. The language I used grew out of the subjects and places and experiences that I was writing about—subjects, places, and experiences that touched my soul. Writing about beautiful places where the language spoken is lyrical and the people live eloquent lives, one can not help but use language that is evocative and meaningful.

> When Peter grew older, he and his friends slid down anthills and shimmied up paw-paw trees. They chased the cows from the maize fields and made toys from the smooth white stalks. They made dolls with wet earth from the river bed. (Unpaged)

I think the language derives much from the images it creates. For the rest, I am forever in debt to the Language Gods.

References   Williams, Karen Lynn. *Galimoto*. Illustrated by Catherine Stock. New York: Lothrop, Lee and Shepard Books.

———. 1991. *When Africa Was Home*. Illustrated by Floyd Cooper. New York: Orchard Books.

———. 1994. *Tap-Tap*. Boston: Houghton Mifflin.

Capturing Objects in Words

Valerie Worth

When I was a child, I had many favorite poems. Some had been written specifically for children: Edward Lear's nonsense rhymes, Rachel Field's "General Store" and "The Playhouse Key," and poems by Walter de la Mare, especially his "Silver." But there were also poems written primarily for adults: Tennyson's "The Owl," Amy Lowell's "Lilacs," and many of Carl Sandburg's. Then there was Rupert Brooke's "The Great Lover."

This last poem was for many years the one that meant the most to me. Some of its lines were hard for me to understand, but the greater part of it consisted of a long sequence of images—actually a list of things that the poet loved best in the world. I recognized among them much to which I myself had responded with affection and delight:

> White plates and cups, clean-gleaming,
> Ringed with blue lines; and feathery, faery dust;
> Wet roofs, beneath the lamp-light; the strong crust
> Of friendly bread; and many-tasting food; . . . the cold
> Graveness of iron; moist black earthen mould;
> Sleep; and high places; footprints in the dew;
> And oaks, and brown horse-chestnuts, glossy-new;
> And new-peeled sticks; and shining pools on grass.

Through being named and celebrated in poetry, the objects of the poet's love are given a kind of immortality, beyond the effects of time or change. And this idea appealed to me also—that poetry could have such power, that it could be used to reveal, extol, and even preserve the many beauties of the world. I realized that I often felt the same creative impulse: the desire to put the things I loved into words, so they could be held onto, and kept safe, and admired again and again—almost with the satisfaction of a miser poring over his treasures.

Reprinted from *The Horn Book Magazine* (September/October 1992: 568–69) by permission of The Horn Book, Inc.

I found it irresistible, then, to try using words in the same way. Just to write anything down, even a single noun—*moon*, or *rabbit*, or *flowerpot*—had a kind of magic about it. There something was, out in the world; but at the same time, it was here, caught hold of and set down on paper. The trick, of course, was to capture it whole and alive—to make its word self as true to its actual self as possible—which required the help of other words, too. And that's where the language of poetry came into play, creating a unique, complex reality out of a wide array of adjectives and verbs. Of course, they would have to be the right verbs, the right adjectives, or the precious image would fade away and be gone—and the magic as well.

I've been trying ever since to catch hold of things and put them into poems; poems that would somehow express an object's essential qualities, so that somebody else could read what I'd written and think, Yes, that's right—I've seen that myself. Rupert Brooke and many subsequent poets have done this for me, and I've tried to do the same for others—especially for children, who are encountering so much for the first time and responding to what they see so directly and intensely. Of course, such poems can offer much to adults, too: most people enjoy remembering their childhood perceptions, and poetry is certainly one of the best ways in which those first, freshest experiences can be recaptured and relived.

Returning to that poem of Rupert Brooke's—the fact that I found some part of it hard to understand didn't mean that I liked the poem any less for it. On the contrary, lines that seemed somewhat enigmatic, such as

> Shall I not crown them with immortal praise
> Whom I have loved, who have given me, dared with me
> High secrets, and in darkness knelt to see
> The inenarrable godhead of delight?

gave me a sense of being offered something new and momentous that went beyond my own experience—some world I did not yet know but which the poem hinted at and made me long to explore for myself. It wasn't just its embodiment of the familiar that made poetry so appealing to me, but also, very often, its overtones of strangeness, of mystery. This sense of mystery has allowed me to feel less restricted when I've wanted to introduce a word or a concept that might be new or strange to a child. Because in evoking the unknown, while also affirming the known, poetry can often reveal something quite unexpected in the midst of the familiar and ordinary.

Reference   Brooke, Rupert. 1933. "The Great Lover," in Franklyn Bliss Snyder and
Robert Grant Martin, eds., *A Book of English Literature,* 3d ed. New
York: Macmillan.

Literary Karaoke; or, Falling out of Love

Jane Yolen

Lately I have been in the middle of a number of discussions about the technology of writing and how—with the advent of computers and desktop publishing—we have the ability, each of us, to write and print and bind and distribute our own books. And while the old liberal in me welcomes this outpouring of expression, this turning to creativity, the conservative, elitist Luddite editor lurking inside me has a different label for such a thing. I call it "Literary Karaoke."

A writer without an editor, a second eye, an accomplished kibitzer, a naysayer, a remarker-upon, a redactor, is a writer who has fallen in love with the sound of his or her own voice. It is the literary equivalent of singing in the shower. And who of us would take the shower and all its accoutrements on stage? Well, Madonna, perhaps.

The single thing that used to take the breath away from all the elementary school children I visited—back in the days when I did school visits—was the fact that I often did as many as thirty revisions of a single story. I would show the children draft after draft of *The Seeing Stick,* for example, pages of manuscript with markings in blue and red and black and green, in pen and pencil. Some of those revisions were occasioned by my own misgivings about my words, sentences, paragraphs; some of them were pushed on me by my writer's group; some by my perspicacious husband; some by my editor, the copy editor, and then my own later reading of the galleys.

"You mean . . . ," the children would gasp, "that you had to do it again? A second time? It wasn't perfect the first time?" And the underlying subject was "If you, a successful, famous author"—or "famous otter" as one kindergartner called me—"have to rewrite, what does that mean we children are going to be asked to do?"

But I am reminded of something John Ciardi (I think) said about the writing of a poem. It is never finished, he said. Only abandoned.

Falling out of love with one's own words, one's own work, is as honest a reaction to the fact of writing as writing the stuff down in the first place. Edith Wharton said, "I dream of an eagle, I give birth to a hummingbird." It is the complaint of all writers. Of all artists, really. You grow *through* the writing of a piece, and you are not the same person at the end of it as you were at the start. Is it any wonder that when you end it you are ready to rewrite it? Even if you are heartily sick of the whole thing.

Bill Martin has said both in private and in public that he thinks my *Owl Moon* is a perfect poem, with not a word wrong. I have smiled and accepted the compliment for what it is. But he and I both know, being poets, that words are only—at best—an approximation of what one wants to say. They are slippery as fish. They peel off the page. I often think of the process of writing as "scripting in water." It is *that* elusive. If I were rewriting *Owl Moon* today, I might add something about Mama waiting at home, or something about the child walking in her father's footprints (which my children often did out in the woods after owls with their father), or I might even use a different owl altogether than the Great Horned Owl, which is not that easy to call in. Also, I wrestled a long time with the naming of Pa, since my children called their father *Daddy* and I called my own father *Dad*. If I were writing *Owl Moon* today, I might do it differently. Or I might not.

The time line in publishing is something that authors and editors are aware of and that the audience is not. What you read today is the author's past, even if it was just published. Reading is therefore akin to archeology; the shards you examine with such passion now are only bits and pieces of a long-dead activity.

References

Yolen, Jane. 1977. *The Seeing Stick.* Illustrated by Remy Charlip and Demetra Maraslis. New York: Thomas Y. Crowell.

———. 1987. *Owl Moon.* Illustrated by John Schoenherr. New York: Philomel Books.

Bibliography of Notable Books

Adkins, Jan. 1985. *Workboats.* New York: Charles Scribner's Sons. ISBN 0-684-18228-9.

Adler, David. 1983. *Bunny Rabbit Rebus.* Illustrated by Madelaine Gill Linden. New York: Thomas Y. Crowell. ISBN 0-690-04196-9.

Adoff, Arnold. 1991. *In for Winter, Out for Spring.* Illustrated by Jerry Pinkney. San Diego: Harcourt Brace Jovanovich. ISBN 0-15-238637-8.

Ahlberg, Janet, and Allan Ahlberg. 1986. *The Jolly Postman; or, Other People's Letters.* Boston: Little, Brown. ISBN 0-316-02036-2.

Aliki. 1986. *How a Book Is Made.* New York: Thomas Y. Crowell. ISBN 0-690-04496-8.

———. 1989. *The King's Day: Louis XIV of France.* New York: Thomas Y. Crowell. ISBN 0-690-04590-5.

Anderson, Joan. 1985. *Christmas on the Prairie.* Photographs by George Ancona. New York: Clarion Books. ISBN 0-89919-307-2.

Andrews, Jan. 1986. *Very Last First Time.* Illustrated by Ian Wallace. New York: Atheneum. ISBN 0-689-50388-1.

Anno, Mitsumasa. 1983. *Anno's U.S.A.* New York: Philomel Books. ISBN 0-399-20974-3.

———. 1989. *Anno's Aesop: A Book of Fables by Aesop and Mr. Fox.* New York: Orchard Books. ISBN 0-531-05774-7.

Arnosky, Jim. 1992. *Otters under Water.* New York: G. P. Putnam's Sons. ISBN 0-399-22339-8.

Avi. 1989. *The Man Who Was Poe.* New York: Orchard Books. ISBN 0-531-05833-6.

———. 1990. *The True Confessions of Charlotte Doyle.* New York: Orchard Books. ISBN 0-531-05893-X.

———. 1991. *Nothing but the Truth.* New York: Orchard Books. ISBN 0-531-05959-6.

Aylesworth, Jim. 1992. *Old Black Fly.* Illustrated by Stephen Grammell. New York: Henry Holt. ISBN 0-8050-1401-2.

Babbitt, Natalie. 1987. *The Devil's Other Storybook: Stories and Pictures.* New York: Farrar, Straus and Giroux. ISBN 0-374-31767-4.

Baker, Keith. 1988. *The Dove's Letter.* San Diego: Harcourt Brace Jovanovich. ISBN 0-15-224133-7.

Barrett, Judi. 1983. *A Snake Is Totally Tail.* Illustrated by L. S. Johnson. New York: Atheneum. ISBN 0-689-30979-1.

Base, Graeme. 1987. *Animalia.* New York: Henry N. Abrams. ISBN 0-8109-1868-4.

———. 1989. *The Eleventh Hour: A Curious Mystery.* New York: Henry N. Abrams. ISBN 0-8109-0851-4.

Baylor, Byrd. 1983. *The Best Town in the World.* Illustrated by Ronald Himler. New York: Charles Scribner's Sons. ISBN 0-684-18035-9.

———. 1986. *I'm in Charge of Celebrations.* Illustrated by Peter Parnall. New York: Charles Scribner's Sons. ISBN 0-684-18579-2.

Bedard, Michael. 1992. *Emily.* Illustrated by Barbara Cooney. New York: Doubleday. ISBN 0-385-30697-0.

Beisner, Monika. 1983. *Monika Beisner's Book of Riddles.* New York: Farrar, Straus and Giroux. ISBN 0-374-30866-7.

Benjamin, Carol Lea. 1985. *Writing for Kids.* New York: Thomas Y. Crowell. ISBN 0-690-04490-9.

Bial, Raymond. 1991. *Corn Belt Harvest.* Boston: Houghton Mifflin. ISBN 0-395-56234-1.

Bierhorst, John. 1986. *The Monkey's Haircut, and Other Stories Told by the Maya.* Illustrated by Robert Andrew Parker. New York: William Morrow. ISBN 0-688-04269-4.

———. 1987. *Doctor Coyote: A Native American Aesop's Fables.* Illustrated by Wendy Watson. New York: Macmillan. ISBN 0-02-709780-3.

Birdseye, Tom. 1988. *Airmail to the Moon.* Illustrated by Stephen Gammell. New York: Holiday House. ISBN 0-8234-0683-0.

Brittain, Bill. 1983. *The Wish Giver: Three Tales of Coven Tree.* New York: Harper and Row. ISBN 0-06-020686-1.

———. 1987. *Dr. Dredd's Wagon of Wonders.* Illustrated by Andrew Glass. New York: Harper and Row. ISBN 0-06-020713-2.

Brooks, Bruce. 1991. *Nature by Design.* New York: Farrar, Straus and Giroux. ISBN 0-374-30334-7.

Bruhac, Joseph, and Jonathon London. 1992. *Thirteen Moons on a Turtle's Back: A Native American Year of Moons.* Illustrated by Thomas Locker. New York: Philomel Books. ISBN 0-399-22141-7.

Bryan, Ashley. 1985. *The Cat's Purr.* New York: Atheneum. ISBN 0-689-31086-2.

Bunting, Eve. 1989. *The Wednesday Surprise.* Illustrated by Donald Carrick. New York: Clarion Books. ISBN 0-89919-721-3.

———. 1990. *The Wall.* Illustrated by Ronald Himler. New York: Clarion Books. ISBN 0-395-51588-2.

Burkert, Nancy Ekholm. 1989. *Valentine and Orson.* New York: Farrar, Straus and Giroux. ISBN 0-374-38078-3.

Byars, Betsy. 1988. *Burning Questions of Bingo Brown.* New York: Viking. ISBN 0-670-81932-8.

Cameron, Ann. 1988. *The Most Beautiful Place in the World.* Illustrated by Thomas B. Allen. New York: Alfred A. Knopf. ISBN 0-394-89463-4.

Cameron, Eleanor. 1988. *The Private Worlds of Julia Redfern.* New York: E. P. Dutton. ISBN 0-525-44394-0.

Carlstrom, Nancy White. 1987. *Wild Wild Sunflower Child Anna.* Illustrated by Jerry Pinkney. New York: Macmillan. ISBN 0-02-717360-7.

————. 1991. *Goodbye Geese.* Illustrated by Ed Young. Philomel Books. ISBN 0-399-21832-7.

Chandra, Deborah. 1990. *Balloons, and Other Poems.* Illustrated by Leslie W. Bowman. New York: Farrar, Straus and Giroux. ISBN 0-374-30509-9.

Cleary, Beverly. 1983. *Dear Mr. Henshaw.* Illustrated by Paul O. Zelinsky. New York: William Morrow. ISBN 0-688-02405-X.

Clifford, Eth. 1985. *The Remembering Box.* Illustrated by Donna Diamond. Boston: Houghton Mifflin. ISBN 0-395-38476-1.

Cole, Brock. 1989. *Celine.* New York: Farrar, Straus and Giroux. ISBN 0-374-31234-6.

Cole, Joanna. 1990. *The Magic School Bus Lost in the Solar System.* Illustrated by Bruce Degen. New York: Scholastic. ISBN 0-590-41428-3.

Coltman, Paul. 1985. *Tog the Ribber; or, Granny's Tale.* Illustrated by Gillian McClure. New York: Farrar, Straus and Giroux. ISBN 0-374-37630-1.

Conrad, Pam. 1990. *Stonewords: A Ghost Story.* New York: Harper and Row. ISBN 0-06-021316-7.

Craven, Carolyn. 1987. *What the Mailman Brought.* Illustrated by Tomie dePaola. New York: G. P. Putnam's Sons. ISBN 0-399-21290-6.

Day, Alexandra. 1988. *Frank and Ernest.* New York: Scholastic. ISBN 0-590-41557-3.

————. 1990. *Frank and Ernest Play Ball.* New York: Scholastic. ISBN 0-590-42548-X.

DeFelice, Cynthia. 1988. *The Strange Night Writing of Jessica Coulter.* New York: Macmillan. ISBN 0-02-726451-3.

Deming, Alhambra G. 1988. *Who Is Tapping at My Window?* Illustrated by Monica Wellington. New York: E. P. Dutton. ISBN 0-525-44383-5.

dePaola, Tomie. 1983. *Sing, Pierrot, Sing: A Picture Book in Mime.* San Diego: Harcourt Brace Jovanovich. ISBN 0-15-274988-8.

de Regniers, Beatrice Schenk. 1985. *So Many Cats!* Illustrated by Ellen Weiss. New York: Clarion Books. ISBN 0-89919-322-6.

Detz, Joan. 1986. *You Mean I Have to Stand Up and Say Something?* Illustrated by David Marshall. New York: Atheneum. ISBN 0-689-31221-0.

Dewey, Jennifer Owings. 1986. *Clem: The Story of a Raven.* New York: Dodd, Mead. ISBN 0-396-08728-0.

Domanska, Janina. 1985. *Busy Monday Morning.* New York: Greenwillow Books. ISBN 0-688-03833-6.

Dorris, Michael. 1992. *Morning Girl.* New York: Hyperion Books. ISBN 1-56282-284-5.

Dorsett, Lyle W., and Marjorie Lamp Mead, eds. 1985. *C. S. Lewis Letters to Children.* New York: Macmillan. ISBN 0-02-570830-9.

Dragonwagon, Crescent. 1987. *Alligator Arrived with Apples: A Potluck Alphabet Feast.* Illustrated by Jose Aruego and Ariane Dewey. New York: Macmillan. ISBN 0-02-733090-7.

———. 1990. *Home Place.* Illustrated by Jerry Pinkney. New York: Macmillan. ISBN 0-02-733190-3.

Duncan, Lois. 1985. *Horses of Dreamland.* Illustrated by Donna Diamond. Boston: Little, Brown. ISBN 0-316-19554-5.

Edwards, Patricia Kier. 1987. *Chester and Uncle Willoughby.* Illustrated by Diane Worfolk Allison. Boston: Little, Brown. ISBN 0-316-21173-7.

Ehlert, Lois. 1989. *Eating the Alphabet: Fruits and Vegetables from A to Z.* San Diego: Harcourt Brace Jovanovich. ISBN 0-15-224435-2.

———. 1990. *Feathers for Lunch.* San Diego: Harcourt Brace Jovanovich. ISBN 0-15-230550-5.

———. 1991. *Red Leaf, Yellow Leaf.* San Diego: Harcourt Brace Jovanovich. ISBN 0-15-266197-2.

Ekoomiak, Normee. 1990. *Artic Memories.* New York: Henry Holt. ISBN 0-8050-1254-0.

Esbensen, Barbara. 1992. *Who Shrank My Grandmother's House? Poems of Discovery.* Illustrated by Eric Beddows. New York: HarperCollins. ISBN 0-06-021827-4.

Fields, Julia. 1988. *The Green Lion of Zion Street.* Illustrated by Jerry Pinkney. New York: Margaret K. McElderry Books. ISBN 0-689-50414-4.

Fisher, Leonard Everett. 1985. *Symbol Art: Thirteen Squares, Circles, Triangles from Around the World.* New York: Four Winds Press. ISBN 0-387-15203-2.

Fleischman, Paul. 1985. *Coming-and-Going Men: Four Tales.* Illustrated by Randy Gaul. New York: Harper and Row. ISBN 0-06-021883-5.

———. 1985. *I Am Phoenix: Poems for Two Voices.* Illustrated by Ken Nutt. New York: Harper and Row. ISBN 0-06-021881-9.

———. 1988. *Joyful Noise: Poems for Two Voices.* Illustrated by Eric Beddows. New York: Harper and Row. ISBN 0-06-021852-6.

———. 1990. *Saturnalia.* New York: Harper and Row. ISBN 0-06-021913-0.

———. 1991. *The Borning Room.* New York: HarperCollins. ISBN 0-06-023762-7.

———. 1992. *Townsend's Warbler.* New York: HarperCollins. ISBN 0-06-021874-6.

Fleming, Denise. 1991. *In the Tall, Tall Grass.* New York: Henry Holt. ISBN 0-8050-1635-X.

Fox, Mem. 1987. *Hattie and the Fox.* Illustrated by Patricia Mullins. New York: Bradbury Press. ISBN 0-02-735470-9.

———. 1989. *Night Noises.* Illustrated by Terry Denton. San Diego: Harcourt Brace Jovanovich. ISBN 0-15-200543-9.

Fox, Paula. 1984. *One-Eyed Cat.* Scarsdale, NY: Bradbury Press. ISBN 0-02-735540-3.

Frasier, Debra. 1991. *On the Day You Were Born.* San Diego: Harcourt Brace Jovanovich. ISBN 0-15-257995-8.

Furlong, Monica. 1991. *Juniper.* New York: Alfred A. Knopf. ISBN 0-394-83220-5.

Gallaz, Christophe. 1985. *Rose Blanche.* Illustrated by Roberto Innocenti. Mankato, MN: Creative Education. ISBN 0-87191-994-X.

Gardner, Beau. 1984. *The Look Again, and Again, and Again, and Again Book.* New York: Lothrop, Lee and Shepard Books. ISBN 0-688-03805-0.

Gay, Marie-Louise. 1989. *Rainy Day Magic.* Morton Grove, IL: Albert Whitman. ISBN 0-8075-6767-1.

Geisert, Arthur. 1986. *Pigs from A to Z.* Boston: Houghton Mifflin. ISBN 0-395-38509-1.

George, Jean Craighead. 1984. *One Day in the Alpine Tundra.* Illustrated by Walter Gaffney-Kessell. New York: Thomas Y. Crowell. ISBN 0-690-04325-2.

Geras, Adèle. 1990. *My Grandmother's Stories: A Collection of Jewish Folk Tales.* Illustrated by Jael Jordan. New York: Alfred A. Knopf. ISBN 0-679-80910-4.

Gherman, Beverly. 1986. *Georgia O'Keeffe: The Wideness and Wonder of Her World.* New York: Atheneum. ISBN 0-689-31164-8.

———. 1992. *E. B. White: Some Writer!* New York: Atheneum. ISBN 0-689-31672-0.

Gibbons, Gail. 1984. *Fire! Fire!* New York: Thomas Y. Crowell. ISBN 0-690-04417-8.

Goble, Paul. 1988. *Her Seven Brothers.* New York: Bradbury Press. ISBN 0-02-737960-4.

———. 1991. *Iktomi and the Buffalo Skull: A Plains Indian Story.* New York: Orchard Books. ISBN 0-531-05911-1.

Goffstein, M. B. 1986. *Our Snowman.* New York: Harper and Row. ISBN 0-06-022152-6.

———. 1986. *School of Names.* New York: Harper and Row. ISBN 0-06-021984-X.

Goodall, John S. 1983. *Above and below the Stairs.* New York: Atheneum. ISBN 0-689-50238-9.

Goor, Ron, and Nancy Goor. 1983. *Signs.* New York: Thomas Y. Crowell. ISBN 0-690-04354-6.

———. 1986. *Pompeii: Exploring a Roman Ghost Town.* New York: Thomas Y. Crowell. ISBN 0-690-04515-8.

Greenfield, Eloise. 1991. *Night on Neighborhood Street.* Illustrated by Jan Gilchrist. New York: Dial Books. ISBN 0-8037-0777-0.

Grifalconi, Ann. 1987. *Darkness and the Butterfly.* Boston: Little, Brown. ISBN 0-316-32863-4.

Guiberson, Brenda. 1991. *Cactus Hotel.* Illustrated by Megan Lloyd. New York: Henry Holt. ISBN 0-8050-1333-4.

Hamilton, Virginia. 1983. *The Magical Adventures of Pretty Pearl.* New York: Harper and Row. ISBN 0-06-022186-0.

———. 1985. *The People Could Fly: American Black Folktales.* Illustrated by Leo and Diane Dillon. New York: Alfred A. Knopf. ISBN 0-394-86925-7.

———. 1988. *Anthony Burns: The Defeat and Triumph of a Fugitive Slave.* New York: Alfred A. Knopf. ISBN 0-394-98185-5.

Harvey, Brett. 1986. *My Prairie Year: Based on the Diary of Elenore Plaisted.* Illustrated by Deborah Kogan Ray. New York: Holiday House. ISBN 0-8234-0604-0.

———. 1987. *Immigrant Girl: Becky of Eldridge Street.* Illustrated by Deborah Kogan Ray. New York: Holiday House. ISBN 0-8234-0638-5.

He Liyi, trans. 1986. *The Spring of Butterflies, and Other Folktales of China's Minority Peoples.* Edited by Neil Philip. Illustrated by Pan Aiqing and Li Zhao. New York: Lothrop, Lee and Shepard Books. ISBN 0-688-06192-3.

Heide, Florence Parry, and Judith Heide Gilliland. 1990. *The Day of Ahmed's Secret.* Illustrated by Ted Lewin. New York: Lothrop, Lee and Shepard Books. ISBN 0-688-08894-5.

Henkes, Kevin. 1991. *Chrysanthemum.* New York: Greenwillow Books. ISBN 0-688-09700-6.

Hepworth, Catherine. 1992. <u>*Antics!*</u> *An Alphabet of Ants.* New York: G. P. Putnam's Sons. ISBN 0-399-21862-9.

Highwater, Jamake. 1984. *Legend Days.* New York: Harper and Row. ISBN 0-06-022303-0.

Hirst, Robin, and Sally Hirst. 1990. *My Place in Space.* Illustrated by Roland Harvey and Joe Levine. New York: Orchard Books. ISBN 0-531-05859-X.

Ho, Minfong. 1991. *The Clay Marble.* New York: Farrar, Straus and Giroux. ISBN 0-374-31340-7.

Hoffman, Mary. 1991. *Amazing Grace.* Illustrated by Caroline Binch. New York: Dial Books. ISBN 0-8037-1040-8.

Hogrogian, Nonny. 1988. *The Cat Who Loved to Sing.* New York: Alfred A. Knopf. ISBN 0-394-99004-8.

Hoguet, Susan Ramsay. 1983. *I Unpacked My Grandmother's Trunk: A Picture Book Game.* New York: E. P. Dutton. ISBN 0-525-44069-0.

———. 1986. *Solomon Grundy.* New York: E. P. Dutton. ISBN 0-525-44239-1.

Hooks, William H. 1987. *Moss Gown.* Illustrated by Donald Carrick. New York: Clarion Books. ISBN 0-89919-460-5.

———. 1990. *The Ballad of Belle Dorcas.* Illustrated by Brian Pinkney. New York: Alfred A. Knopf. ISBN 0-394-8464-5.

Hopkins, Lee Bennett. 1983. *A Song in Stone: City Poems.* Photographs by Anna Held Audette. New York: Thomas Y. Crowell. ISBN 0-690-04269-8.

Houston, Gloria. 1992. *My Great-Aunt Arizona.* Illustrated by Susan Condie Lamb. New York: HarperCollins. ISBN 0-06-022606-4.

Howe, James. 1983. *The Celery Stalks at Midnight.* Illustrated by Leslie Morrill. New York: Atheneum. ISBN 0-689-30987-2.

Hudson, Jan. 1989. *Sweetgrass.* New York: Philomel Books. ISBN 0-399-21721-5.

Hughes, Shirley. 1985. *Noisy.* New York: Lothrop, Lee and Shepard Books. ISBN 0-688-04203-1.

———. 1988. *Out and About.* New York: Lothrop, Lee and Shepard Books. ISBN 0-688-07691-2.

Hunt, Irene. 1985. *The Everlasting Hills.* New York: Charles Scribner's Sons. ISBN 0-684-18340-4.

Hutchins, Pat. 1986. *The Doorbell Rang.* New York: Greenwillow Books. ISBN 0-688-05251-7.

Ivimey, John W. 1987. *The Complete Story of the Three Blind Mice.* Illustrated by Paul Galdone. New York: Clarion Books. ISBN 0-89919-481-8.

Janeczko, Paul B., comp. 1990. *The Place My Words Are Looking For: What Poets Say about and through Their Work.* New York: Bradbury Press. ISBN 0-02-747671-5.

Johnston, Tony. 1987. *Whale Song: A Celebration of Counting.* Illustrated by Ed Young. New York: G. P. Putnam's Sons. ISBN 0-399-21402-X.

Kaye, Cathryn Berger. 1985. *Word Works: Why the Alphabet Is a Kid's Best Friend.* Illustrated by Martha Weston. Boston: Little, Brown. ISBN 0-316-48376-1.

Kennedy, X. J. 1985. *The Forgetful Wishing Well: Poems for Young People.* New York: Atheneum. ISBN 0-689-50317-2.

———. 1986. *Brats.* New York: Atheneum. ISBN 0-689-50392-X.

Kesey, Ken. 1990. *Little Tricker the Squirrel Meets Big Double the Bear.* Illustrated by Barry Moser. New York: Viking. ISBN 0-670-81136-X.

Khalsa, Dayal Kaur. 1986. *Tales of a Gambling Grandma*. New York: Crown. ISBN 0-51756-137-9.

Kimmel, Eric A. 1989. *Hershel and the Hanukkah Goblins*. Illustrated by Trina Schart Hyman. New York: Holiday House. ISBN 0-8234-0769-1.

Konigsburg, E. L. 1986. *Up from Jericho Tel*. New York: Atheneum. ISBN 0-689-31194-X.

Koontz, Robin Michal. 1988. *This Old Man: The Counting Song*. New York: Dodd, Mead. ISBN 0-396-09120-2.

Korty, Carol. 1986. *Writing Your Own Plays: Creating, Adapting, Improvising*. New York: Charles Scribner's Sons. ISBN 0-684-18470-2.

Kroll, Steven. 1988. *Happy Father's Day*. Illustrated by Marylin Hafner. New York: Holiday House. ISBN 0-8234-067-7.

Lankford, Mary D. 1992. *Hopscotch around the World*. Illustrated by Karen Milone-Dugan. New York: William Morrow. ISBN 0-688-08419-2.

Lasky, Kathryn. 1983. *Sugaring Time*. Photographs by Christopher G. Knight. New York: Macmillan. ISBN 0-02-751680-6.

———. 1992. *Surtsey: The Newest Place on Earth*. Photographs by Christopher G. Knight. New York: Hyperion Books. ISBN 1-56282-300.

Lattimore, Deborah Nourse. 1987. *The Flame of Peace: A Tale of the Aztecs*. New York: Harper and Row. ISBN 0-06-023708-2.

Lauber, Patricia. 1985. *Tales Mummies Tell*. New York: Thomas Y. Crowell. ISBN 0-690-04388-0.

———. 1989. *The News about Dinosaurs*. New York: Bradbury Press. ISBN 0-02-754520-2.

Leaf, Margaret. 1987. *Eyes of the Dragon*. Illustrated by Ed Young. New York: Lothrop, Lee, and Shepard Books. ISBN 0-688-06155-9.

Legum, Margaret Ronay. 1985. *Mailbox, Quailbox*. Illustrated by Robert Shetterly. New York: Atheneum. ISBN 0-689-31136-2.

Lewis, Claudia Louise. 1987. *Long Ago in Oregon*. Illustrated by Joel Fontaine. New York: Harper and Row. ISBN 0-06-023839-9.

Lewis, Richard. 1988. *In the Night, Still Dark*. Illustrated by Ed Young. New York: Atheneum. ISBN 0-689-31310-1.

Livingston, Myra Cohn. 1984. *Sky Songs*. Illustrated by Leonard Everett Fisher. Holiday House. ISBN 0-8234-0502-8.

———. 1985. *A Learical Lexicon: From the Works of Edward Lear*. Illustrated by Joseph Low. New York: Atheneum. ISBN 0-689-50318-0.

———. 1986. *Earth Songs*. Illustrated by Leonard Everett Fisher. New York: Holiday House. ISBN 0-8234-0615-6.

———. 1988. *There Was a Place, and Other Poems*. New York: Margaret K. McElderry Books. ISBN 0-689-50464-0.

Lobel, Anita. 1990. *Alison's Zinnia*. New York: Greenwillow Books. ISBN 0-688-08866-X.

Lobel, Arnold. 1983. *The Book of Pigericks.* New York: Harper and Row. ISBN 0-06-023982-4.

———. 1984. *The Rose in My Garden.* New York: Greenwillow Books. ISBN 0-688-02586-2.

———. 1985. *Whiskers and Rhymes.* New York: Greenwillow Books. ISBN 0-688-03835-2.

Lord, Betty Boa. 1984. *In the Year of the Boar and Jackie Robinson.* Illustrated by Marc Simont. New York: Harper and Row. ISBN 0-06-024003-2.

MacDonald, Suse. 1986. *Alphabatics.* New York: Bradbury Press. ISBN 0-06-024003-2.

MacLachlan, Patricia. 1985. *Sarah, Plain and Tall.* New York: Harper and Row. ISBN 0-06-024101-2.

———. 1991. *Journey.* New York: Delacorte Press. ISBN 0-385-30427-7.

Magnus, Erica. 1984. *Old Lars.* Minneapolis: Carolrhoda Books. ISBN 0-87614-253-6.

Mahy, Margaret. 1987. *Seventeen Kings and Forty-Two Elephants.* Illustrated by Patricia MacCarthy. New York: Dial Books. ISBN 0-8037-0458-5.

———. 1989. *The Blood-and-Thunder Adventure on Hurricane Peak.* Illustrated by Wendy Smith. New York: Margaret K. McElderry Books. ISBN 0-689-50488-8.

Martin, Bill, Jr. 1991. *Polar Bear, Polar Bear, What Do You Hear?* Illustrated by Eric Carle. New York: Henry Holt. ISBN 0-8050-1759-3.

Martin, Bill, Jr., and John Archambault. 1985. *The Ghost-Eye Tree.* Illustrated by Ted Rand. New York: Henry Holt. ISBN 0-8050-0208-1.

———. 1987. *Knots on a Counting Rope.* Illustrated by Ted Rand. New York: Henry Holt. ISBN 0-8050-0571-4.

———. 1988. *Listen to the Rain.* Illustrated by James R. Endicott. New York: Henry Holt. ISBN 0-8050-0682-6.

———. 1989. *Chicka Chicka Boom Boom.* Illustrated by Lois Ehlert. New York: Simon and Schuster. ISBN 0-671-67949-X.

Martin, Rafe. 1985. *Foolish Rabbit's Big Mistake.* Illustrated by Ed Young. New York: G. P. Putnam's Sons. ISBN 0-399-21178-0.

McCully, Emily Arnold. 1984. *Picnic.* New York: Harper and Row. ISBN 0-06-024099-7.

McDonald, Megan. 1990. *Is This a House for Hermit Crab?* Illustrated by S. D. Schindler. New York: Orchard Books. ISBN 0-531-05855-7.

McKay, Hilary. 1992. *The Exiles.* New York: Margaret K. McElderry Books. ISBN 0-689-50555-8.

McKissack, Patricia C. 1986. *Flossie and the Fox.* Illustrated by Rachel Isadora. New York: Dial Books. ISBN 0-8037-0250-7.

———. 1991. *A Million Fish—More or Less.* Illustrated by Dena Schutzer. New York: Alfred A. Knopf. ISBN 0-679-80692-X.

McMillan, Bruce. 1992. *The Baby Zoo.* New York: Scholastic. ISBN 0-590-44634-7.

McPhail, David M. 1985. *The Dream Child.* New York: E. P. Dutton. ISBN 0-525-44366-5.

————. 1985. *Farm Morning.* San Diego: Harcourt Brace Jovanovich. ISBN 0-15-227299-2.

Meddaugh, Susan. 1992. *Martha Speaks.* Boston: Houghton Mifflin. ISBN 0-395-63313-3.

Meltzer, Milton. 1985. *Dorothea Lange: Life through the Camera.* Illustrated by Donna Diamond and Dorothea Lange. New York: Viking. ISBN 0-670-28047-X.

Merriam, Eve. 1986. *Fresh Paint: New Poems.* Illustrated by David Frampton. New York: Macmillan. ISBN 0-02-766860-6.

————. 1987. *Halloween ABC.* Illustrated by Lane Smith. New York: Macmillan. ISBN 0-02-766870-3.

————. 1992. *Fighting Words.* Illustrated by David Small. New York: William Morrow. ISBN 0-688-09677-8.

Mollel, Tololwa M. 1990. *The Orphan Boy: A Maasai Story.* Illustrated by Paul Morin. New York: Clarion Books. ISBN 0-89919-985-2.

Moore, Inga. 1991. *Six-Dinner Sid.* New York: Simon and Schuster. ISBN 0-671-73199-8.

Moore, Lilian. 1988. *I'll Meet You at the Cucumbers.* Illustrated by Sharon Wooding. New York: Atheneum. ISBN 0-689-31243-1.

Morrison, Lillian. 1985. *The Break Dance Kids: Poems of Sport, Motion, and Locomotion.* New York: Lothrop, Lee and Shepard Books. ISBN 0-688-04553-7.

Moscovitch, Rosalie. 1985. *What's in a Word? A Dictionary of Daffy Definitions.* Boston: Houghton Mifflin. ISBN 0-395-038922-4.

Munro, Roxie. 1985. *The Inside-Outside Book of New York City.* New York: Dodd, Mead. ISBN 0-396-08513-X.

Nelson, Drew. 1991. *Wild Voices.* Illustrated by John Schoenherr. New York: Philomel Books. ISBN 0-399-21798-3.

Nelson, Vaunda Micheaux. 1988. *Always Gramma.* Illustrated by Kimanne Uhler. New York: G. P. Putnam's Sons. ISBN 0-399-21542-5.

Neumeier, Marty, and Byron Glaser. 1985. *Action Alphabet.* New York: Greenwillow Books. ISBN 0-688-05703-9.

Nixon, Joan Lowery. 1988. *If You Were a Writer.* Illustrated by Bruce Degen. New York: Four Winds Press. ISBN 0-02-768210-2.

O'Keefe, Susan Heyboer. 1989. *One Hungry Monster: A Counting Book in Rhyme.* Illustrated by Lynn Munsinger. Boston: Little, Brown. ISBN 0-316-63385-2.

O'Neill, Catharine. 1989. *Mrs. Dunphy's Dog.* New York: Viking/Kestrel. ISBN 0-14-050622-5.

Ormerod, Jan. 1985. *Reading.* New York: Lothrop, Lee and Shepard Books. ISBN 0-688-04127-2.

Orr, Katherine. 1990. *My Grandpa and the Sea.* Minneapolis: Carolrhoda Books. ISBN 0-87614-409-1.

Parnall, Peter. 1989. *Quiet.* New York: William Morrow. ISBN 0-688-08204-1.

Paterson, Katherine. 1991. *Lyddie.* New York: E. P. Dutton. ISBN 0-525-67338-5.

Paulsen, Gary. 1983. *Dancing Carl.* Scarsdale, NY: Bradbury Press. ISBN 0-02-770210-3.

————. 1987. *Hatchet.* New York: Bradbury Press. ISBN 0-02-770130-1.

————. 1988. *The Island.* New York: Orchard Books. ISBN 0-531-05749-6.

————. 1989. *The Winter Room.* New York: Orchard Books. ISBN 0-531-05839-5.

————. 1990. *Woodsong.* Illustrated by Ruth Wright Paulsen. New York: Bradbury Press. ISBN 0-02-770221-9.

Polacco, Patricia. 1990. *Thunder Cake.* New York: Philomel Books. ISBN 0-399-22231-6.

Purviance, Susan, and Marcia O'Shell. 1988. *Alphabet Annie Announces an All-American Album.* Illustrated by Ruth Brunner-Strosser. Boston: Houghton Mifflin. ISBN 0-395-48070-1.

Rankin, Laura. 1991. *The Handmade Alphabet.* New York: Dial Books. ISBN 0-8037-0974-9.

Reeder, Carolyn. 1989. *Shades of Gray.* New York: Macmillan. ISBN 0-02-775810-9.

Ringgold, Faith. 1991. *Tar Beach.* New York: Crown. ISBN 0-517-58030-6.

Robertson, Joanne. 1991. *Sea Witches.* New York: Dial Books. ISBN 0-8037-1070-4.

Roop, Peter, and Connie Roop. 1985. *Keep the Lights Burning, Abbie.* Illustrated by Peter E. Hanson. Minneapolis: Carolrhoda Books. ISBN 0-87614-275-7.

Root, Phyllis. 1992. *The Listening Silence.* Illustrated by Dennis McDermott. New York: HarperCollins. ISBN 0-06-025092-5.

Rosen, Michael. 1989. *We're Going on a Bear Hunt.* Illustrated by Helen Oxenbury. New York: Margaret K. McElderry Books. ISBN 0-689-50476-4.

Roth, Susan L., and Ruth Phang. 1984. *Patchwork Tales.* New York: Atheneum. ISBN 0-689-31053-6.

Ryder, Joanne. 1985. *Inside Turtle's Shell, and Other Poems of the Field.* Illustrated by Susan Bonners. New York: Macmillan. ISBN 0-02-778010-4.

————. 1992. *Dancers in the Garden.* Illustrated by Judith Lopez. San Francisco: Sierra Club Books. ISBN 0-87156-578-1.

Rylant, Cynthia. 1984. *This Year's Garden.* Illustrated by Mary Szilagyi. Scarsdale, NY: Bradbury Press. ISBN 0-02-777970-X.

————. 1984. *Waiting to Waltz: A Childhood.* Illustrated by Stephen Gammell. Scarsdale, NY: Bradbury Press. ISBN 0-02-778000-7.

————. 1985. *Every Living Thing: Stories.* Illustrated by S. D. Schindler. New York: Bradbury Press. ISBN 0-02-777200-4.

————. 1986. *A Fine White Dust.* New York: Bradbury Press. ISBN 0-02-777240-3.

————. 1986. *Night in the Country.* Illustrated by Mary Szilagyi. New York: Bradbury Press. ISBN 0-02-777210-1.

————. 1987. *Children of Christmas: Stories for the Season.* Illustrated by S. D. Schindler. New York: Orchard Books. ISBN 0-531-05706-2.

————. 1991. *Appalachia: The Voices of Sleeping Birds.* Illustrated by Barry Moser. San Diego: Harcourt Brace Jovanovich. ISBN 0-15-201605-8.

————. 1992. *Missing May.* New York: Orchard Books. ISBN 0-531-05996-0.

Salisbury, Graham. 1992. *Blue Skin of the Sea.* New York: Delacorte Press. ISBN 0-385-30596-6.

Sanders, Scott R. 1985. *Hear the Wind Blow: American Folk Songs Retold.* Illustrated by Ponder Goembel. New York: Bradbury Press. ISBN 0-02-778140-2.

San Souci, Robert D. 1989. *The Talking Eggs: A Folktale from the American South.* Illustrated by Jerry Pinkney. New York: Dial Books. ISBN 0-8037-0619-7.

Schwartz, Alvin. 1983. *Unriddling: All Sorts of Riddles to Puzzle Your Guessery.* Illustrated by Sue Truesdell. New York: Harper and Row. ISBN 0-06-446057-6.

————. 1992. *And the Green Grass Grew All Around: Folk Poetry from Everyone.* Illustrated by Sue Truesdell. New York: HarperCollins. ISBN 0-06-022757-5.

Selden, Bernice. 1983. *The Mill Girls: Lucy Larcom, Harriet Hanson Robinson, Sarah G. Bagley.* New York: Atheneum. ISBN 0-689-31005-6.

Sender, Ruth Minsky. 1988. *To Life.* New York: Macmillan. ISBN 0-02-781831-4.

Shannon, George. 1985. *Stories to Share: Folktales from Around the World.* Illustrated by Peter Sis. New York: Greenwillow Books. ISBN 0-688-04303-8.

Siebert, Diane. 1989. *Heartland.* Paintings by Wendell Minor. New York: Thomas Y. Crowell. ISBN 0-690-04730-4.

Singer, Marilyn. 1989. *Turtle in July.* Illustrated by Jerry Pinkney. New York: Macmillan. ISBN 0-02-782881-6.

Slepian, Jan. 1988. *The Broccoli Tapes*. New York: Philomel Books. ISBN 0-399-21712-6.

Smith, Doris Buchanan. 1986. *Return to Bitter Creek*. New York: Viking. ISBN 0-670-80783-4.

——. 1989. *Voyages*. New York: Viking. ISBN 0-670-80739-7.

Snyder, Zilpha Keatley. 1985. *The Changing Maze*. Illustrated by Charles Mikolaycak. New York: Macmillan. ISBN 0-02-785900-2.

——. 1990. *Libby on Wednesday*. New York: Delacorte Press. ISBN 0-385-29979-6.

Sperling, Susan Kelz. 1985. *Murfles and Wink-a-Peeps: Funny Old Words for Kids*. Illustrated by Tom Bloom. New York: C. N. Potter. ISBN 0-517-55659-6.

Spier, Peter. 1986. *Dreams*. New York: Doubleday. ISBN 0-385-19336-X.

Spinelli, Jerry. 1990. *Maniac Magee*. Boston: Little, Brown. ISBN 0-316-80722-2.

Springer, Nancy. 1992. *The Friendship Song*. New York: Atheneum. ISBN 0-689-31727-1.

Staines, Bill. 1989. *All God's Critters Got a Place in the Choir*. Illustrated by Margot Zemach. New York: E. P. Dutton. ISBN 0-525-44469-6.

Stanley, Diane. 1983. *The Conversation Club*. New York: Macmillan. ISBN 0-02-786740-4.

Stanley, Diane, and Peter Vennema. 1992. *Bard of Avon: The Story of William Shakespeare*. Illustrated by Diane Stanley. New York: William Morrow. ISBN 0-688-09108-3.

Steig, William. 1986. *Brave Irene*. New York: Farrar, Straus and Giroux. ISBN 0-374-30947-7.

Stevens, Janet. 1987. *The Town Mouse and the Country Mouse: An Aesop Fable*. New York: Holiday House. ISBN 0-8234-0633-4.

Stevenson, James. 1984. *Yuck!* New York: Greenwillow Books. ISBN 0-688-03829-8.

Summerfield, Geoffrey. 1983. *Welcome, and Other Poems*. Illustrated by Karen Usborne. London: Andre Deutsch. ISBN 0-233-97528-4.

Tchudi, Susan, and Stephen Tchudi. 1984. *The Young Writer's Handbook*. New York: Charles Scribner's Sons. ISBN 0-684-18090-1.

Temple, Frances. 1992. *Taste of Salt: A Story of Modern Haiti*. New York: Orchard Books. ISBN 0-531-05459-4.

Terban, Marvin. 1985. *Too Hot to Hoot: Funny Palindrome Riddles*. Illustrated by Giulio Maestro. New York: Clarion Books. ISBN 0-89919-319-6.

Testa, Fulvio. 1983. *If You Look around You*. New York: Dial Books. ISBN 0-8037-0003-2.

Tompert, Ann. 1990. *Grandfather Tang's Story*. Illustrated by Robert Andrew Parker. New York: Crown. ISBN 0-517-57487-X.

Turner, Ann. 1985. *Dakota Dugout*. Illustrated by Ronald Himler. New York: Macmillan. ISBN 0-02-789700-1.

———. 1986. *Street Talk*. Illustrated by Catherine Stock. Boston: Houghton Mifflin. ISBN 0-395-39971-8.

———. 1987. *Nettie's Trip South*. Illustrated by Ronald Himler. New York: Macmillan. ISBN 0-02-789240-2.

———. 1991. *Rosemary's Witch*. New York: HarperCollins. ISBN 0-06-026127-7.

Van Allsburg, Chris. 1984. *The Mysteries of Harris Burdick*. Boston: Houghton Mifflin. ISBN 0-395-35393-9.

———. 1986. *The Stranger*. Boston: Houghton Mifflin. ISBN 0-395-42331-7.

———. 1987. *The Z Was Zapped: A Play in Twenty-Six Acts*. Boston: Houghton Mifflin. ISBN 0-395-44612-0.

Vande Velde, Vivian. 1985. *A Hidden Magic*. Illustrated by Trina Schart Hyman. New York: Crown. ISBN 0-517-55534-4.

Van Laan, Nancy. 1987. *The Big Fat Worm*. Illustrated by Marisabina Russo. New York: Alfred A. Knopf. ISBN 0-394-98763-2.

———. 1990. *Possum Come a-Knockin'*. Illustrated by George Booth. New York: Alfred A. Knopf. ISBN 0-394-82206-4.

Ventura, Piero. 1984. *Great Painters*. New York: G. P. Putnam's Sons. ISBN 0-399-21115-2.

Waddell, Martin. 1992. *Farmer Duck*. Illustrated by Helen Oxenbury. Cambridge, MA: Candlewick Press. ISBN 1-56402-009-6.

Wallace, Ian. 1987. *Morgan the Magnificent*. New York: Margaret K. McElderry Books. ISBN 0-689-50441-1.

Wallace-Brodeur, Ruth. 1989. *Stories from the Big Chair*. Illustrated by Diane de Groat. New York: Margaret K. McElderry Books. ISBN 0-689-50481-0.

Wiesner, David. 1991. *Tuesday*. New York: Clarion Books. ISBN 0-395-55113-7.

Willard, Nancy. 1990. *The High Rise Glorious Skittle Skat Roarious Sky Pie Angel Food Cake*. Illustrated by Richard Jesse Watson. San Diego: Harcourt Brace Jovanovich. ISBN 0-15-234332-6.

———. 1991. *Pish, Posh, Said Hieronymus Bosch*. Illustrated by the Dillons. San Diego: Harcourt Brace Jovanovich. ISBN 0-15-262210-1.

Williams, Karen Lynn. 1990. *Galimoto*. Illustrated by Catherine Stock. New York: Lothrop, Lee and Shepard Books. ISBN 0-688-08789-2.

Williams, Linda. 1986. *The Little Old Lady Who Was Not Afraid of Anything*. Illustrated by Megan Lloyd. New York: Thomas Y. Crowell. ISBN 0-690-04584-0.

Williams, Terry Tempest. 1985. *Between Cattails*. Illustrated by Peter Parnall. New York: Charles Scribner's Sons. ISBN 0-684-18309-9.

Williams, Terry Tempest, and Ted Major. 1984. *The Secret Language of Snow.* Illustrated by Jennifer Dewey. San Francisco: Sierra Club/Pantheon Books. ISBN 0-394-96574-X.

Williams, Vera B., and Jennifer Williams. 1987. *Stringbean's Trip to the Shining Sea.* New York: Greenwillow Books. ISBN 0-688-07162-7.

Williamson, Duncan. 1983. *Fireside Tales of the Traveller Children: Twelve Scottish Stories.* Illustrated by Alan B. Herriot. New York: Harmony Books. ISBN 0-517-55852-1.

Wilson, Budge. 1992. *The Leaving, and Other Stories.* New York: Philomel Books. ISBN 0-399-21878-5.

Winter, Jeanette. 1988. *Follow the Drinking Gourd.* New York: Alfred A. Knopf. ISBN 0-394-99694-1.

Wolff, Ashley. 1985. *Only the Cat Saw.* New York: Dodd, Mead. ISBN 0-396-08727-2.

Wood, Audrey. 1987. *Heckedy Peg.* Illustrated by Don Wood. San Diego: Harcourt Brace Jovanovich. ISBN 0-15-233678-8.

———. 1988. *Elbert's Bad Word.* Illustrated by Audrey and Don Wood. San Diego: Harcourt Brace Jovanovich. ISBN 0-15-225320-3.

Worth, Valerie. 1986. *Small Poems Again.* Illustrated by Natalie Babbitt. New York: Farrar, Straus and Giroux. ISBN 0-374-37074-5.

Wrightson, Patricia. 1985. *Night Outside.* Illustrated by Beth Peck. New York: Atheneum. ISBN 0-689-50363-6.

Yolen, Jane. 1984. *Children of the Wolf: A Novel.* New York: Viking. ISBN 0-670-21763-8.

———. 1986. *Ring of Earth: A Child's Book of Seasons.* Illustrated by John Wallner. San Diego: Harcourt Brace Jovanovich. ISBN 0-15-267140-4.

———. 1987. *Piggins.* Illustrated by Jane Dyer. San Diego: Harcourt Brace Jovanovich. ISBN 0-15-261685-3.

———. 1988. *Best Witches: Poems for Halloween.* Illustrated by Elise Primavera. New York: G. P. Putnam's Sons. ISBN 0-399-21539-5.

———. 1989. *Dove Isabeau.* Illustrated by Dennis Nolan. San Diego: Harcourt Brace Jovanovich. ISBN 0-15-224131-0.

———. 1990. *Bird Watch: A Book of Poetry.* Illustrated by Ted Lewin. New York: Philomel Books. 0-399-21612-X.

Zeifert, Harriet. 1986. *Sarah's Questions.* Illustrated by Susan Bonners. New York: Lothrop, Lee and Shepard Books. ISBN 0-688-05614-8.

Editors

Amy A. McClure is professor of education at Ohio Wesleyan University, where she teaches courses in reading, language arts, and children's literature and directs the university honors program. She is a former chair of the Notable Children's Trade Books in the Language Arts Committee and president-elect of the Children's Literature Assembly of NCTE. She is author of *Sunrises and Songs: Reading and Writing Poetry in an Elementary Classroom*, co-editor (with Janice Kristo) of *Inviting Children's Responses to Literature* (NCTE), and author of book chapters and articles on children's response to literature, using poetry with children, whole language teaching strategies, and other related topics. McClure was named NCTE Promising Young Researcher in 1985.

Janice V. Kristo is professor of literacy education at the University of Maine, where she teaches courses in reading, language arts, and children's literature. She is a former chair of the Notable Children's Trade Books in the Language Arts Committee. With Amy McClure she co-edited the NCTE publication *Inviting Children's Responses to Literature.* She has written articles on children's response to literature, evaluation of whole language teaching, integration of the language arts, and classroom-based research. She is also co-author of a forthcoming text on teaching the language arts.

Contributors

Aliki was born in Philadelphia and graduated from the Philadelphia College of Art. She has written and illustrated over fifty children's books—both fiction and nonfiction—which have been translated into fifteen languages and have won numerous awards. She divides her time unequally between the United States, Switzerland, Greece, and London, where she currently lives.

Avi, a recipient of many state and national honors, has published some thirty-three books, including two Newbery Honor Books, *True Confessions of Charlotte Doyle* and *Nothing but the Truth*. His most recent book is a two-volume Victorian adventure, *Beyond the Western Sea*. He lives in Boulder, Colorado.

Natalie Babbitt is the author and illustrator of thirteen books for children, among them *Tuck Everlasting, Kneeknock Rise* (a Newbery Honor Book), and, most recently, *Bub—or The Very Best Thing*. She lives in Providence, Rhode Island.

Tom Birdseye, the author of four novels and seven picture books, lives in Corvallis, Oregon, with his wife (also a writer) and two daughters. When not writing or in schools talking with children and teachers about writing, he enjoys hiking, skiing, canoeing, camping, biking, climbing, and, of course, reading.

Bill Brittain began writing while teaching in junior high school. In addition to thirteen books for young people, he has had more than seventy-five short mystery stories published. His book *The Wish Giver* was a Newbery Honor Book.

Ashley Bryan's books—from his first book, *Moon, For What You Wait*, to his most recent—have been loved by critics as well as children. His *Beat the Story Drum, Pum Pum* received the Coretta Scott King Award for Illustration and the Parents' Choice Award. He was also honored with the Coretta Scott King Award for *I'm Going to Sing, The Lion and the Ostrich Chicks, What a Morning!* and *All Night, All Day*. He is the first recipient of the Lee Bennett Hopkins Award and was chosen as an Arbuthnot Lecturer.

Eve Bunting has written nearly 150 books for children. Her honors include the Golden Kite, the Edgar Allan Poe mystery award, and, most important, awards from children in thirty-two different states. She is the author of the recent Caldecott book *Smoky Night* and lives in California.

Ann Cameron is the author of the Julian series of chapter books for young readers. *The Stories Julian Tells* was a Notable Children's Trade Book in the Field of Social Studies; *More Stories Julian Tells* was cited as an ALA Notable Children's Book and received a Parents' Choice Award. *The Most Beautiful Place in the World* takes place in Guatemala, where the author now resides and volunteers time as the supervisor of the Panajachel public library.

Eleanor Cameron has written seventeen novels for youth and two essay collections of appreciation, *The Green and Burning Tree* and *The Seed and the Vision*. *The Court of the Stone Children* won the National Book Award; *A Room Made of Windows* won the Boston Globe–Horn Book Award; and, for a body of work, she was awarded the Kerlan Award and the Hope Dean Memorial Award.

Nancy White Carlstrom is the author of over forty books for children, including *Jesse Bear, What Will You Wear?*, *Northern Lullaby*, *Baby–O*, and *Does God Know How to Tie Shoes?* She has been a first- and second-grade teacher, has owned a children's bookshop, and currently lives in Fairbanks, Alaska, with her husband and two sons.

Deborah Chandra is a recent recipient of the IRA Lee Bennett Hopkins Promising Poet Award. Her two books of poetry—*Balloons* and *Rich Lizard*—were chosen as Notable Children's Trade Books in the Language Arts. Her latest book, *Who Comes?*, tells in verse the tale of survival at a moonlit waterhole.

Barbara Chatton is professor of curriculum and instruction at the University of Wyoming, where she teaches courses in children's and young adult literature and humanities education. She is the author of *Using Poetry across the Curriculum: A Whole Language Approach*.

Eth Clifford has been writing award-winning books for young children and young adults since the 1960s. Her publications include *The Year of the Three-Legged Deer* (a Newbery nominee), *The Remembering Box* (a Children's Choices book and Notable Children's Trade Book in the Field of Social Studies), and *The Rocking Chair Rebellion* and *Help! I'm a Prisoner in the Library* (both nominated for the Mark Twain Award).

Paula Fox is the author of twenty-two books for children, the most recent of which is *The Eagle Kite*. She has written six other novels, including *A Servant's Tale*; *The Slave Dancer*, which won the Newbery Medal; and *One-Eyed Cat*, which was named a Newbery Honor Book. She has also received the Hans Christian Andersen Medal, the Brandeis University Fiction Citation, and the Empire State Award.

Christine Doyle Francis teaches children's literature, storytelling, and American literature at Central Connecticut State University. She has edited the journal *Children's Literature*, published in *Children's Literature in Education* and *The Lion and the Unicorn*, and published curriculum guides on the work of E. L. Konigsburg and Gerald McDermott.

Susan Hepler is a children's literature specialist and consultant to schools and other groups that wish to include more literature in the curriculum. She is co-author, with Charlotte Huck and Janet Hickman, of *Children's Literature in the Elementary School* (sixth edition, forthcoming).

Mary Hoffman has been writing children's books for twenty-five years and has notched up over fifty titles. Her best known, apart from *Amazing Grace,* are *Boundless Grace; Earth, Fire, Water, Air;* and *Henry's Baby.* She is also a consultant and lecturer on literacy issues.

William H. Hooks is the author of forty-three books for children. Notable book awards include those from NCTE, NCSS, ABA, and ALA and a Parents' Choice Award. He has also received a medal for Lifetime Achievement in Children's Literature from the Irma and James Black Award. Many of his books carry a "southern accent," reflecting a childhood spent on a tobacco plantation in the South.

James Howe is best known for his popular and award-winning Bunnicula series for middle-grade readers. Among his other books are the Sebastian Barth mysteries, the Pinky and Rex series for beginning readers, and numerous picture books and nonfiction titles, including the highly acclaimed *The Hospital Book.*

Shirley Hughes trained at art school in Liverpool and at Oxford and then began freelancing as an illustrator. She started to write picture books when she had a young family of her own. She has won several major awards, including the Kate Greenaway Medal and the Eleanor Farjeon Award for services to children's literature.

Tony Johnston is a product of the West, of a childhood steeped in country and the mysteries of nature. From this, *Whale Song, Yonder,* and *Once in the Country* grew. Fifteen years in Mexico led to *Iguana Brothers* and *My Mexico.* Book honors include awards from Parents' Choice, Library Guild, and the Southern California Council on Literature for Children and Young People, and an Aesop Accolade.

X. J. Kennedy, formerly professor of English at Tufts, has written *Literature* and other textbooks; *Dark Horses: New Poems;* ten books of verse for children; and (with Dorothy M. Kennedy) *Knock at a Star: A Child's Introduction to Poetry,* an NCTE Teachers' Choice in 1983 and still in print.

Inga Kromann-Kelly is professor of literacy education at Washington State University, Pullman, where she teaches children's and adolescent literature courses and directs graduate student research. She has taught grades K–8, is past president of the Children's Literature Assembly of NCTE, is past U.S. editor of the IBBY journal *Bookbird,* and has been consulting editor of *Child Study Journal.*

Linda Leonard Lamme is professor of education at the University of Florida, where she teaches courses in children's literature and language arts methods. She is the author of numerous articles in professional journals and several books, including *Growing Up Reading, Learning to Love Literature,* and *Literature-Based Moral Education.*

Patricia Lauber is the author of some ninety books for young people. Her *Volcano* was a Newbery Honor Book. Her work has also been honored by, among others, the New York Academy of Sciences, the American Nature Society, and the *Washington Post*/Children's Book Guild. Two recent books are *Who Eats What?* and *How Dinosaurs Came to Be.*

Susan Lehr is professor of education at Skidmore College, where she is chair of the Department of Education. She is president of the Children's Literature Assembly and author of *The Child's Developing Sense of Theme.*

Myra Cohn Livingston, author of eighty-one books of her own poetry, anthologies for young people, and books concerning poetry, has received many awards, including the NCTE Excellence in Poetry Award, the Texas Institute of Letters Award (twice), and the Kerlan Award at the University of Minnesota. She is senior instructor in the UCLA Writers' Program.

Anita Lobel was born in Poland and emigrated to the United States as a young adult. She is the illustrator or author-illustrator of numerous books, including several collaborations with her late husband, Arnold. Credits include one Caldecott Honor Book, two Boston Globe–Horn Book Honor Books, and several other books named notable by the ALA, American Booksellers, and *The New York Times.*

Anthony L. Manna teaches children's literature, young adult literature, and drama at Kent State University.

Joan Lowery Nixon has won four Mystery Writers of America's "Edgars," two Western Writers of America's "Spurs," and fifteen Children's Choices awards. But her greatest rewards are letters like this one: "I never liked reading until I read your book, *The Stalker.* Now I'm reading all your mysteries. Thank you for the gift of reading."

Katherine Paterson is best known for her works of contemporary realistic fiction and historical fiction. Born in China, she became an elementary school teacher and later a missionary in Japan. She is the recipient of numerous book awards, including the Newbery Medal for *Bridge to Terabithia* and *Jacob Have I Loved,* the Newbery Honor for *The Great Gilly Hopkins,* and recommendations from the ALA, the *School Library Journal,* and IRA Children's Choices.

Gary Paulsen has had many careers besides that of a writer: soldier, engineer, teacher, farmer, trapper, and sailor, among others. He is best known for writing exciting adventure stories, such as the Newbery Honor Book *Hatchet.* His other Newbery Honor Books include *Dogsong,* coming from his experiences in the Iditarod dogsled race, and *The Winter Room.* He has also been recognized by the ALA for such titles as *Dancing Carl, Tracker,* and *The Island.*

Peter Roop, a Wisconsin State Teacher of the Year, and **Connie Roop,** an AAUW Outstanding Wisconsin Educator, have written twenty-five children's books together. Seven of their books are *Reading Rainbow* books, including *Keep the Lights Burning, Abbie,* which was a feature book on the program. Their books have received recognition from NCTE, NCSS, NSTA, and the Children's Book Council. He currently teaches first and second grades, and she teaches middle school science.

Diane Siebert is the author of *Truck Song,* an ALA Notable Children's Book and a *Reading Rainbow* selection; *Mojave,* on the ALA Booklist and Teachers' Choices list; *Heartland,* a Notable Children's Trade Book in the Language Arts and in the Field of Social Studies; *Train Song,* an ALA Notable Children's Book and a *School Library Journal* Best Book; *Sierra,* a Notable Children's Trade Book in the Field of Social Studies and an Outstanding Science Trade Book for Children; and *Plane Song,* on the Teachers' Choices list.

Marilyn Singer, a former high school English teacher, has written nearly fifty children's and young adult books. Her poetry book *Turtle in July* was named a Notable Children's Trade Book in the Language Arts. Her latest collection of poems is called *The Morgans Dream.* For a complete bibliography on the Internet, go to: **http://users.aol.com/writerbabe/marilyn.htm.**

Yvonne Siu-Runyan, associate professor at the University of Northern Colorado and former classroom teacher, teaches graduate and undergraduate courses on literacy development and coordinates the graduate programs in elementary education. She serves on editorial review boards for *The Reading Teacher, Language Arts, The New Advocate,* and the IRA Publications Committee, and is on the Elementary Section Committee for NCTE. She is the author of articles, chapters, and books on literacy and integrative learning.

Jan Slepian is the author of the widely acclaimed *The Alfred Summer,* the sequel *Lester's Turn, The Night of the Bozos, Getting On with It,* and *Something beyond Paradise,* as well as several books for young children. She lives and writes in Summit, New Jersey, and is a popular lecturer in schools and universities.

Zilpha Keatley Snyder's thirty-third book for young people, *The Trespassers,* was published in 1995. Over the years she has received many awards, including three Newbery Honors, two Christopher Medals, and a William Allen White Award. Her recent book *Cat Running* was given the Beatty Award by the California Library Association.

Jerry Spinelli once broke the record for strikeouts in a game as a Little League pitcher in Norristown, Pennsylvania. His best pitch was a curve ball. He's still working on the knuckler. His novel *Maniac Magee* won a Newbery Medal.

Jon C. Stott is professor of English at the University of Alberta and the author of several books on children's literature, including (most recently) *Native Americans in Children's Literature.* The first president of the Children's Literature Association, he has been working for over two decades in elementary and junior high school classrooms, developing children's literature programs.

Deborah Thompson is assistant professor of education at American University in Washington, D.C. She teaches, writes, and researches in the area of multicultural children's literature and literacy development of at-risk students.

Carl Tomlinson teaches courses in language arts and children's literature in the Department of Curriculum and Instruction at Northern Illinois University. He is co-author of *Essentials of Children's Literature* and author of the forthcoming book *Children's Books from Other Countries.*

Ann Turner is the popular author of such diverse books as *Grass Songs, Rosemary's Witch, Dakota Dugout, Nettie's Trip South,* and *Grasshopper Summer.* She is a poet, novelist, and picture book author, as well as a much-sought-after lecturer. She lives with her husband and two children in Williamsburg, Massachusetts.

Nancy Van Laan is the author of many wonderful books, including *This Is the Hat; Buffalo Dance; Sleep, Sleep, Sleep;* and *Possum Come a-Knockin'.* She and her youngest child live in New Hope, Pennsylvania.

Sylvia M. Vardell is currently associate professor at the University of Texas at Arlington, where she teaches graduate and undergraduate courses in children's literature and literacy. She served on the committee that established the NCTE Orbis Pictus Award for Outstanding Nonfiction for Children and publishes widely on literature-based teaching in such publications as *The Reading Teacher, Language Arts, The New Advocate*, and *Horn Book.*

Nancy Willard's books include *Telling Time,* a collection of essays on writing; *Sister Water,* a novel; and *Among Angels,* poems co-authored with Jane Yolen. Her *Visit to William Blake's Inn* won a Newbery Medal. She teaches at Vassar College.

Karen Lynn Williams has lived in Malawi, Africa, and in Haiti. Her publications include *Galimoto,* a *Reading Rainbow* feature; *Tap-Tap,* a Hungry Mind Review Book of Distinction; *When Africa Was Home; Baseball and Butterflies; First Grade King; Applebaum's Garage;* and *A Real Christmas This Year.*

Valerie Worth was the author of many books for children, including *Small Poems, More Small Poems, Still More Small Poems,* and *Small Poems Again.* She has been hailed by the *New York Times Book Review* as a writer who "brilliantly employs all aspects of the poet's craft."

Jane Yolen, author of over 150 books (including the Caldecott Medal winner *Owl Moon*), has often been called the Hans Christian Andersen of America for her many fairy tales. She is also editor-in-chief of the Jane Yolen Books imprint for a major publishing house, a line of fantasy and science fiction novels for children and young adults.

Credits